Routine Activity and Rational Choice

Routine Activity and Rational Choice

Advances in Criminological Theory
Volume 5

Ronald V. Clarke and Marcus Felson, editors

Transaction Publishers
New Brunswick (U.S.A.) and London (U.K.)

ISSN: 0894-2366
ISBN: 1-56000-087-2 (cloth); 0-7658-0831-5 (paper)
Printed in the United States of America

In Memoriam

Franco Ferracuti
1927–1992

Contents

    Violence
    Max Taylor   159

8. Ransom Kidnapping in Sardinia, Subcultural Theory
    and Rational Choice
    Pietro Marongiu and Ronald V. Clarke   179

9. "Successful" Criminal Careers: Toward an
    Ethnography within the Rational Choice Perspective
    Bruce D. Johnson, Mangai Natarajan,
    and Harry Sanabria   201

Part Two: Bridging the Gaps

10. The Rational Choice/Opportunity Perspectives as a
    Vehicle for Integrating Criminological and
    Victimological Theories
    Ezzat A. Fattah   225

11. Environment, Routine, and Situation: Toward a
    Pattern Theory of Crime
    Patricia L. Brantingham and Paul J. Brantingham   259

12. A Strategic Analysis of Crime: Criminal Tactics as
    Responses to Precriminal Situations
    Maurice Cusson   295

13. Conscience, Opportunity, Rational Choice, and Crime
    Gordon Trasler   305

14. Crime Prevention through Environmental Design,
    Opportunity Theory, and Rational Choice Models
    C. Ray Jeffery and Diane L. Zahm   323

15. Theories of Action in Criminology: Learning Theory
    and Rational Choice Approaches
    Derek Cornish   351

    Contributors   383

    Author Index   389

    Subject Index   401

Acknowledgments

When the essays for this collection were being commissioned, one of the contributors, Pietro Marongiu, offered to convene a conference that would give contributors the opportunity to debate some of the broader issues surrounding the routine activity and rational choice approaches. These issues, such as the relationship between these new approaches and existing criminological theory, would not be directly addressed in many of the essays, but were still of considerable importance to all contributors. The meeting would also provide the occasion for the valuable, informal discussions that always take place when academics with similar interests meet together.

The conference was held in June 1992 in Chia Laguna, Sardinia, in conjunction with the Second National Congress of the Italian Society of Forensic Psychiatry. It proved to be a most pleasant occasion, more than amply fulfilling its original goals, and enriched by the contributions of the psychiatrists attending the sessions. The conference also helped the production of this volume in some tangible ways: It set a natural deadline for the completion of essays and assisted us, as editors, in identifying topics needing to be addressed in our Introduction.

We are therefore most grateful to Professor Marongiu for arranging the meeting, to Professor Nereide Rudas, President of the Italian Society of Forensic Psychiatry, who facilitated the conference by consenting for it to be held in tandem with the Society's own meeting, and to The Honorable Giorgio Oppi, Assessore all'Igiene e Sanità della Regione Autonoma della Sardegna, without whose support and encouragement the meeting would not have been possible.

It had always seemed appropriate that a meeting on "Advances in Criminological Theory" should be held in Italy, the cradle of criminology. We therefore had no hesitation in agreeing when Freda Adler, the series editor, suggested that this volume be dedicated to the memory of Franco Ferracuti who died in March 1992. Franco Ferracuti was not only the author (with Marvin Wolfgang) of *The Subculture of Violence,* a theoretical treatise known to every academic criminologist, but was also the most distinguished Italian criminologist of his generation.

R.V.C
M.F.

Introduction:
Criminology, Routine Activity,
and Rational Choice

Ronald V. Clarke and Marcus Felson

It might seem strange that proponents of two distinct theoretical approaches should join forces in a single volume less than fifteen years after the appearance of what might be considered competing paradigms. This theoretical cooperation may be all the more surprising when both proponents feel confident in the viability and vitality of their respective approaches. In fact, the routine activity and rational choice approaches, though differing in scope and purpose, are compatible and, indeed, mutually supportive. This volume provides the opportunity to acknowledge this compatibility and to give shape to the informal collaboration that has existed for some years among the contributors and editors. It has also provided an opportunity to consider the relationship between routine activity and rational choice and some other related theoretical and preventive approaches. Lastly, it has encouraged a fuller treatment of the relationship between these new approaches to crime and the traditional theories that currently dominate the textbooks. These topics are discussed below, but first we turn to brief descriptions of the routine activity and rational choice approaches.

The Routine Activity Approach

The routine activity approach (Cohen and Felson 1979) began by considering only direct-contact predatory violations. These required that at

1

least one offender take or damage the property of at least one other person. This excluded any interest in such criminal violations as fights between equally "guilty" parties or illegal drug sales between consenting persons. Note also the use of the word *violations* rather than the word *crime*. The latter word is ambiguous about whether it refers to any single event or a general category, whereas the word *violation* directly refers to an event. To emphasize this point, the original paper continuously repeated the words *incident* and *event,* also using the modifier *direct-contact* to under-line the concern for direct physical contact between offender and target of crime. Similarly, the word *victim* was avoided, since this person need not be immediately present, whereas the routine activity approach insisted upon discussing who and what was present during a criminal incident. Persons were treated virtually as objects and their motivations were scru-pulously avoided as a topic of discussion, in stark contrast to the heavy motivational emphasis of virtually all contemporary criminology at that time. Even the word *motivation* was avoided, and the word *inclination* substituted so as to avoid reminding the reader that motivations might exist. Thus, at the outset the approach distinguished clearly between criminal inclinations and criminal events and made that distinction a cen-terpiece rather than a footnote. Moreover, it cast its lot unquestionably with events rather than inclinations. It did not deny the existence of crimi-nal inclinations, but took these as given, virtually dismissing what was central to most contemporary criminology of the 1960s and 1970s.

The routine activity approach stated three minimal elements for direct-contact predatory crime: a likely offender, a suitable target, and the absence of a capable guardian against crime. A likely offender was anybody who for any reason might commit a crime. How this likelihood might vary was avoided since that would bring up the forbidden issue of criminal motiva-tion. A suitable target of crime was any person or object likely to be taken or attacked by the offender. The word *target* was selected to avoid the moral implications of the word *victim* and to treat persons and property exactly the same — as objects with a position in space and time. Each victim of personal attack was treated as a body in the physical world, thus ignoring all issues of socioeconomic or racial motivation for attacking someone, all issues of personal hatred, indeed, anything going on inside the head of offender or victim. Any such concern would have redirected the minds of the readers back to conventional criminology and distracted them from the point that criminal incidents are physical acts. In addition, the routine activity approach offered a thought experiment: to see how far one could go in explaining crime trends without ever discussing any of the various theories about criminal motivations. This same goal was best served by avoiding any psychology or social psychology, giving no entreé to distracting information. The routine activity approach was not to be relegated to a footnote. Criminal events were moved onto center stage and motivations pushed aside.

The third minimal element of direct-contact predatory crime, the capable guardian, was not seen to be a policeman or security guard in most cases. This was the result of a conscious effort to distance routine activity theory from the rest of criminology, which is far too wedded to the criminal justice system as central to crime explanation. This perverse tendency is an unfortunate artifact of (1) the location of many criminologists in criminal justice programs with the task of training people to work in the criminal justice system, (2) the linkage of research money to criminal justice policy, and (3) the widespread media linkage of the police and courts to crime, when in fact most crime involves neither agency. Indeed, the most likely persons to prevent a crime are not policemen (who seldom are around to discover crimes in the act) but rather neighbors, friends, relatives, bystanders, or the owner of the property targeted. Note that the *absence* of a suitable guardian is crucial. Defining a key element as an absence rather than a presence is surely the ultimate in depersonalizing and depsychologizing the study of crime. Certain kinds of people are no doubt more likely to be absent than others, but the fact that absence is emphasized is another reminder that the movement of physical entities in space and time is central to the approach. An offender must find a target in the absence of guardians. The moment that happens a crime may occur.

The routine activity approach is fundamentally different from almost all other criminology in its intellectual roots, namely, the human ecology theory of Amos Hawley (1950). While Shaw and McKay were human ecologists in the Chicago school and well-known in criminological literature, they worked mainly in the spatial dimension, plotting neighborhood structure and linking it to crime distributions. They also included a strong motivational component in their analysis, which the routine activity approach did not. Amos Hawley, on the other hand, recognized that the spatial aspect of human behavior was but one aspect. The temporal aspect was another, making the timing of different activities by hour of day and day of week important for the understanding of human society. These points were central also to the routine activity approach. No matter at what level data were measured or analyzed, that approach kept returning at least intellectually to specific points in time and space, jointly considered, and to changes from moment to moment and hour to hour in where people are, what they are doing, and what happens to them as a result.

Hawley's work has two other important intellectual characteristics that carry over to the routine activity approach. First, it includes *macro* analysis of human populations, often ignoring individuals. Second, it offers *systemic thinking,* not merely describing the ebb and flow of human activities and their interrelationships, but also offering intellectual tools and empirical examples of how these activities change over time. The organizing feature of the system is a population's drive to gain sustenance from the environment, including other populations. The essential point is that each group, as well as the whole population, must carve out its niche in a larger system of activities.

The Rational Choice Perspective

The rational choice perspective, as discussed in this volume, had its beginnings in work on "situational" crime prevention, which seeks to block opportunities for crime by environmental change (Clarke 1980). Although supported by evidence of the role of opportunity in crime (Mayhew et al. 1976), situational prevention flew in the face of most contemporary theorizing of the time. Whether sociological, psychological, or biological in its premises, this theorizing regarded situational variables as playing a relatively minor part in crime compared with the powerful, driving force of criminal dispositions (see Gordon Trasler's chapter in this volume). Situational variables might determine the timing and location of offending, but reducing opportunities at a particular time and place would result simply in displacement of offending to other times, places, or crimes, with no net reduction in crime. In other words, situational prevention would be wasted effort for society as a whole.

The experience of situational prevention was quite contrary to this theoretical prediction. In many cases, perhaps most, crime was prevented with little displacement (Barr and Pease 1990; Gabor 1990; Clarke 1992). Offenders seemed much more responsive to changes in the risks and effort of crime than predicted by contemporary crime theories. This finding led to an interest in offender decision making, not just in relation to specific crime opportunities, but also in relation to crime as a way of life. Work on criminal decision making was being undertaken in four separate disciplines: (1) Within the sociology of deviance, ethnographic studies were revealing the purposive, rational, and mundane nature of much crime; (2) within environmental criminology, crime pattern analyses were being illuminated by interviews with offenders about their target selection strategies; and (3) within economics and (4) cognitive psychology, models of information processing and decision making were being applied to the analysis of criminal choices. A synthesis of these different strands of work resulted in the rational choice perspective discussed here, which was intended to assist thinking about displacement (Clarke and Cornish, 1985).

Before describing the perspective, we should explain why the formulations of rational choice theory by economists such as Becker (1968), which gave a central role in explanation to offender perceptions of risk, effort, and reward, could not be adopted wholesale. These theories represented an attempt to express utilitarian philosophy in mathematical terms, with individuals maximizing satisfaction by choosing one of a finite set of alternatives, each with its particular costs and benefits. Crime was discussed using such classic economic terms as *supply and demand,* a translation that involved treating "being a criminal" as an "occupational option," fundamentally similar to legal occupations in society. Each individual makes a "rational choice" of one among these options in order to maximize satisfaction. "Being a criminal" is more likely to be selected when legal options are less rewarding for the individual or when crime is less punishing.

While consistent with the opportunity-reducing objectives of situational prevention, the economic model was seriously limited in a number of respects. First, the rewards of crime were treated mainly in material terms (e.g., how much money can an offender make), while mostly ignoring rewards that could not easily be translated into cash equivalents. This reflects a second limitation, that economists have not been sensitive to the great variety of behaviors falling under the general label of crime, with their variety of costs and benefits, and instead have tended to lump them together as a single variable in their equations. Third, economists rarely seemed to appreciate how difficult it is for a modern society to deliver punishment, that is, how easy it is for offenders to avoid detection. Fourth, economists have overlooked the fact that a good deal of crime is committed at work. Indeed, most retailers find that losses from employee theft exceed losses from shoplifting. How can crime be a unique occupational choice when some occupations help people commit more crime? Fifth, economists ignored the fact that many offenders (indeed most for some occupations) are too young to be in the labor force anyway, so the "occupational choice" model is largely beside the point for juvenile delinquency. Sixth, the market model did not fit most ordinary crime; although there is a supply of victims, there is no demand by victims to be victimized. While economists have made important contributions in analyzing illegal markets for drugs or prostitution (Reuter and Haaga 1989), their terminology is confusing when applied to most other crime. Seventh, the formal mathematical modeling of criminal choices by economists often demanded data that was unavailable or could not be pressed into service without making unrealistic assumptions about what they represented. Finally, the economist's image of the self-maximizing decision maker, carefully calculating his or her advantage, did not fit the opportunistic, ill-considered, and even reckless nature of much crime.

Thus, the normative economic theories of crime as defined by Becker could not serve the needs of situational prevention for a general theory of criminal decision making without very substantial modification. This led to the development of the informal version of rational choice theory discussed in this volume (Clarke and Cornish 1985; Cornish and Clarke 1986), in which relationships between concepts are expressed not in mathematical terms but in the form of "decision" diagrams. Concepts were adapted from the other disciplines involved in the analysis of criminal decision making, as well as economics, to give greater weight to noninstrumental motives for crime and the "limited" nature of the rational processes involved. It is assumed, in other words, that crime is purposive behavior designed to meet the offender's commonplace needs for such things as money, status, sex, and excitement, and that meeting these needs involves the making of (sometimes quite rudimentary) decisions and choices, constrained as these are by limits of time and ability and the availability of relevant information.

A second important premise is that any attempt to explain criminal choices requires a crime-specific focus, not only because different crimes may serve different purposes, but also because the situational context of decision making and the information being handled will vary greatly among offenses. A third premise is that a decision-making approach to crime requires a fundamental distinction to be made between criminal involvement (or criminality) and criminal events (or crime). Criminal involvement refers to the processes through which individuals choose to become initially involved in particular forms of crime, to continue, and to desist. The decision processes at these three stages of involvement are influenced in each case by a different set of factors and needs to be separately modeled. In the same way, the decision processes involved in the commission of a particular crime (i.e., the criminal event) are dependant upon their own special categories of information. Involvement decisions are characteristically multistage and extend over substantial periods of time. Event decisions, on the other hand, are frequently shorter processes, utilizing more circumscribed information largely relating to immediate circumstances and situations.

Most criminological theories seek to provide general explanations of crime by reference to motivational concepts such as delinquency, deviance, or rule breaking. Little importance is attached to the specific forms of crime committed, which are seen to be largely a matter of chance. The rational choice perspective, on the other hand, sees the nature of the crime committed as crucial to explanation, since the decisions leading to one type of crime are different from those leading to another. In addition, decisions leading to crime early on in one's life are not the same as when one has more experience. Each behavior and each stage deserves its own explanatory model. It is these principles that permit the rational choice perspective to serve as a general explanatory framework for all forms of crime, without imposing a rigid conceptual unity upon divergent criminal behaviors.)

Some other features of the rational choice perspective are important. First, the authors used the term *perspective* advisedly to indicate that they were providing not a substantive theory of crime, but rather an organizing perspective or "blueprint" from which theories for specific crimes could be developed or within which existing ones could be usefully located (Clarke and Cornish 1985: 163). Second, they declined to take a position on the issue of free will, preferring to see the focus on choices and decisions as a heuristic device permitting large quantities of information to be organized into a coherent framework. Third, while acknowledging that their formulation of the rational choice approach had developed from the need to assist situational prevention, they by no means saw themselves as confined to that goal. Had they been, it would not have been necessary to have given detailed consideration to the three stages of criminal involvement, which are irrelevant to most situational measures. Instead, the authors regarded their efforts as being directed to the more complete understanding and, ultimately, more efficient control of crime — an objective requiring a wider range of methods than simply the reduction of opportunities.

In pursuing this goal, they believed that their decision models could encompass any of the existing theories of crime that could help to account for the particular direction taken by an offender's decisions. However, there were two respects in which they limited the reach of their models. The first was through the heuristic criterion that a decision model need never be "complete," but only had to be "good enough" to serve the immediate explanatory task in hand. The second was through an explicit policy orientation that stipulated that models should be assessed principally in terms of their utility to assist thought about crime control.

Much of the subsequent discussion about the rational choice perspective has focused on the meaning of *rational* and the extent to which the perspective is able to handle violent and sexual crimes, as well as predatory property crimes (e.g. Trasler 1986; Heal and Laycock 1986). These issues were never seen as particularly problematic to the authors (though it is surprising how difficult others have found the concept of "limited" rationality), but they acknowledged the need for rational choice analyses of "expressive" and violent crimes (Cornish and Clarke 1986); this need is addressed by a number of the chapters in Part One of this volume.

Comparing and Contrasting the Two Approaches

Despite their different histories and disciplinary origins, the many features that the routine activity and rational choice approaches have in common and that set them apart from most other criminological theories will be apparent from these brief descriptions. Both approaches put far more weight on the situational determinants of crime. Both recognize the crucial distinction between criminality and crime (Gottfredson and Hirschi 1990) and the need for crime-specific explanation. And both provide organizing perspectives within which to analyze crime — routine activity through the concept of minimal elements and the rational choice perspective through its four decision models.

But these similarities mask some important points of difference. The explanatory focus of the routine activity approach is exclusively on crime, while the rational choice perspective, by attempting to model both involvement and event decisions, constitutes a "theory" of both crime and criminality. Second, while both recognize the need for crime-specific explanation, the rational choice perspective regards the making of increasingly fine distinctions within broad offense categories (such as burglary) as essential to the development of models with preventive implications. The routine activity approach, on the other hand, recognizes that different crimes might inhabit the same ecological niche (a purse snatched and a car stolen in a parking garage) and might profitably be handled together (Felson in press). It also attempts to develop models that will encompass broader categories of offense, such as "direct-contact predatory violations" or "dispute-related violence" (see Richard Felson's chapter in this volume). Third, while both provide organizing perspectives, routine activity is also a causal theory in the sense that it links changes in routine activities to changes in crime rates; thus in the original paper (Cohen and Felson 1979) increasing rates of residential burglary in the United States after 1960 were explained by reference to the increasing proportion of empty homes in the day (due to more single person households and greater female participation in the labor force) and the increased availability of lightweight portable electronic goods. Fourth, when it functions as a causal theory, routine activity is oriented to the macro, population level, while the decision models of rational choice are firmly located at the micro, individual level . (It is as though the rational choice theorist has entered the box labeled "motivated offender" and has surveyed the world from that vantage point.) Fifth, while the relevance for policy of routine activity theory has only recently been developed (Felson 1987, 1992), policy relevance was a fundamental objective of the rational choice perspective from its beginnings. Finally, the concept of rationality so explicit in the

TABLE I.1
Routine Activity and Rational Choice; Comparing and Contrasting the Approaches

	Routine Activity	Rational Choice
Organizing perspective	Yes	Yes
Explanatory focus:		
a. Criminal events	Yes	Yes
b. Criminal dispositions	No	Yes
Level of explanation	Macro	Micro
Causal theory	Yes	No
Situational focus	Yes	Yes
Crime specific	Yes	Yes
Rational offender	Implicit	Explicit
Policy orientation	Implicit	Explicit
Disciplinary parentage	Geography, demography, human ecology	Psychology, economics, sociology of deviance, environmental criminology

one perspective was only implicit in the other. These similarities and differences are summarized in table I.1.

A further difference between the two approaches, mentioned in the brief descriptions but not included in the table, concerns the question of theoretical integration with the remainder of criminology. This topic is addressed in the concluding section, but first we consider some developments in criminology directly related to the approaches under discussion.

Other Related Approaches

Cusson (1986) and Felson (in press) have noted a "startling convergence" of routine activity and rational approaches and some other recent developments in criminology, many of which are represented in the contributions to this volume. These include a variety of theoretical approaches, such as "environmental criminology" (Brantingham and Brantingham 1981), "strategic thinking" (Cusson 1986), the "geography of crime" (e.g., Harries 1990; Evans and Herbert 1989), "hot spot" analysis (Spring and Block 1988; Sherman et al. 1989), and "life-style" theories of victimization (Hindelang et al. 1978), all of which interpret crime patterns in terms of the location of targets and the movement of offenders and victims in time and space. Also included are some preventive approaches, such as "defensible space" (Newman 1972), "crime prevention through environmental design" (or CPTED) (Jeffery 1971), "situational prevention" (Mayhew et al. 1976; Clarke 1980, 1992) and "problem-oriented policing" (Goldstein 1979, 1990) all of which attempt to manipulate environment to reduce opportunities for crime.

Despite their varying emphasis on explanation and control, and despite the fact that these developments have arisen out of different disciplines and subdisciplines, they share some important features that facilitate communication among their adherents. In particular, all seem to have accepted a similar image of the criminal in which temptation and opportunity are central to the explanation of crime. Without denying that some people are more likely to commit crimes than others, they believe that there is a substantial variability due to situational influences. All persons have some probability of committing crime and can be criminal one moment and noncriminal the next. Legal behavior is malleable and displacement of illegal to legal behavior may be complete.

Equally important, all these approaches, whether implicitly or explicitly, assume that offenders are purposive or goal-oriented. In pursuit of their goals, humans are neither so reckless that they evade attempts to limit their behaviors, nor so careful that they can completely defeat such attempts. Rather, their decisions are "satisficing" (Simon 1983), not calculated to maximize success, but rather to meet their needs with the minimum of effort. The idea is that men and women are middling in morality, in self-control, in careful effort, in pursuing advantage, and that all of these are to some extent a function of contingent circumstance. It is a great irony that this view of criminality, so different from the view permeating the rest of criminology, in which criminal behavior is the expression of relatively fixed "criminal" traits, allows for dramatic shifts in behavior and hence vast potential for mischief.

A shared concept of criminality is not the only common element of these various perspectives. They have a common concern for the modus operandi of offenders, not merely as interesting material for undergraduate classes, but rather as central information for professional criminologists. They share methodologies, in particular the plotting of specific categories of crimes in time and space and the relation of these patterns to objective features of the environment and to offenders' accounts of the factors influencing their decisions. Finally, and most important, they recognize in common that explaining criminal acts is a quite different activity from explaining criminal inclinations. The more traditional criminological work of the past half century has made short shrift of this distinction, assuming that criminal acts must imply criminal inclination, and vice versa. Treating crime opportunity as an intervening variable makes criminal acts the subject of inquiry in their own right. A concern for criminal acts as distinct from criminality directs attention to situational factors. The interest in situational factors is consistent with the image of the reasoning criminal. This is why the same people who consider how to reduce opportunities for crime would be interested in how offenders pick their targets or what practical goals and means of doing crime are in their heads. It is also why those interested in crime situations would be interested in environments, geographic patterns, and routine activities feeding such situations and making certain spots more dangerous. And it explains the mutual interest of all of these investigators in variations in the opportunities to carry out illegal acts.

In criminology, as in other fields, different points of departure and different perspectives can converge at nearly the same place, despite differences of detail and nomenclature. This reminds us of some of the branches of mathematics that often deal with exactly the same phenomena, while looking at different aspects using different terms. Thus matrix algebra looks as the same equations as regular algebra in different form. Geometry can give its representation of those same equations, adding its own insights. Calculus has its formulation and supplement to the same substance. We would not throw one out and subsume it in the other. Some of us like one better than the other and thus can more readily participate in mathematics.

This analogy may help to explain why we do not as yet favor formal integration of the different approaches discussed here, despite their common features. Adherents of the various approaches routinely attend one another's meetings and have little trouble accepting one another's ideas. They cite one another explicitly in many written papers and unwritten talks. They have a sense of a common position, even if nobody has attempted to cement the approaches together in a single theory. Given the differences mentioned in this section, that cementing would be no easy task. Even resolving some of the apparent inconsistencies in the contributions to this volume would have required a much longer introduction than we felt was appropriate. Information and research is uneven and many gaps remain to be filled. More important, integration may require suppression. A common vocabulary (Maurice Cusson's "conceptual toolbox") would be helpful, but only if this developed naturally as a result of living together for a while, rather than through a forced marriage. The effort at integration might take what are now mutually supportive groups and render them unnecessary enemies. The energy that might otherwise be devoted to extending the reach of the various approaches (see Part One of this volume) and to bridging the gaps (Part Two) might be uselessly dissipated on petty squabbles and one-upmanship.

Relationship to Traditional Criminology

This spirit of cooperation and goodwill does not necessarily extend to the remainder of criminology. The question here is to what extent the approaches represented in this volume should seek to coexist with traditional theory, or should seek to subsume or replace it. This question begs the more fundamental one of whether a single unifying theory is possible for criminology or whether its subject matter is so broad and diverse that it is destined to remain in a preparadigmatic state, locked forever in internecine "theory wars." Here a final difference between the routine activity and rational choice approach is evident. One of us (MF) agrees with Gottfredson and Hirschi (1990), who argue the futility of trying to merge theories whose basic image of the criminal and other fundamental components are completely at odds. Indeed, as explained earlier, an early objective of the routine activity approach was to provide a means for explaining crime trends without reference to the concept of criminal motivation, the staple of traditional theories. (Felson [1986] was quite willing to link routine activity theory with Hirschi's [1969] social control theory, but only because he felt that their concepts of the offender were completely consistent.)

The other of us (RVC) believes that the rational choice perspective provides an organizing framework or, in Derek Cornish's terms (see his chapter in the volume), a "metatheory" within which existing theories can all find a place as influences on decision making in respect to different explanatory tasks. Whether this is a more or less ambitious objective than the attempt to explain crime without reference to the rest of criminology remains to be seen, but some success in incorporating traditional theories is evident in the analyses of kidnapping, terrorism, and firearm use reported in Part One of this volume. A theoretical formulation that deals with the three stages of criminal involvement as well as the occurrence of criminal events, and which provides a more flexible and dynamic view of criminal action than most contemporary criminology, ought certainly to be capable of handling a much wider range of criminological phenomena than other theories.

In conclusion, we should not forget that theory is a human device for a human purpose. A theorist is trying to make sense of complex phenomena for human minds, including the theorist's own. This means keeping terms simple enough to be used and understood, yet broad enough to represent adequately the phenomena in question. Building theory is a human process, too, taken in steps and presented according to the theorist's interests, knowledge, and abilities, as these develop over time. Admitting these human aspects of theorizing may open the door to cooperation in building better theory. We have also tried to keep constantly in mind the ultimate purpose of criminological theory, not "understanding" in the abstract, but rather understanding to help control a variety of mostly selfish acts injuring society and often, in time, the perpetrators themselves.

References

Barr, R. and Pease, K. 1990. Crime placement, displacement and deflection. In M. Tonry and N. Morris (Eds.), *Crime and justice: A review of research* (12). Chicago: University of Chicago Press.

Becker, G.S. 1968. "Crime and punishment: An economic approach." *Journal of Political Economy*, 76:169–217.

Brantingham, P.J. and Brantingham, P.L. 1981. *Environmental Criminology*. Beverly Hills, CA: Sage.

Clarke, R.V. 1980. Situational crime prevention: Theory and practice. *British Journal of Criminology*, 20:136–147.

Clarke, R.V. (Ed.). 1992. *Situational crime prevention: Successful case studies*. Albany, NY: Harrow and Heston.

Clarke, R.V. and Cornish, D.B. 1985. Modeling offenders' decisions: A framework for policy and research. In M. Tonry and N. Morris (Eds.), *Crime and justice: An annual review of research* (Vol. 6). Chicago: University of Chicago Press.

Cohen, L.E. and Felson, M. 1979. Social change and crime rate trends: A routine activity approach. *American Sociological Review*, 44:588–608.

Cornish, D.B. and Clarke, R.V. (Eds.). 1986. *The reasoning criminal: Rational choice perspectives on offending*. New York: Springer-Verlag.

Cusson, M. 1986. L'analyse stratégique et quelques développements récents en criminologie. *Criminologie*, 19:53–72.

Evans, D.J. and Herbert, D.J. (Eds.). 1989. *The geography of crime*. London: Routledge.

Felson, M. 1986. Linking criminal choices, routine activities, informal control, and criminal outcomes. In D.B. Cornish and R.V. Clarke (Eds.), *The reasoning criminal: Rational choice perspectives on offending*. New York: Springer-Verlag.

Felson, M. 1987. Routine activities and crime prevention in the developing metropolis. *Criminology*, 25:911–931.

Felson, M. 1992. Routine activities and crime prevention: Armchair concepts and practical action. *Studies on Crime and Crime Prevention*, 1:31–34.

Felson, M. in press. Integrative crime prevention. In G. Saville and D. Morley (Eds.), *Crime problems and community solutions: Environmental criminology as a developing prevention strategy*. Toronto: ABL, York University.

Gabor, T. 1990. Crime displacement and situational prevention: Toward the development of some principles. *Canadian Journal of Criminology*, 32:41–74.

Goldstein, H. 1979. Improving policing: A problem-oriented approach. *Crime and Delinquency* (April):234–258.

Goldstein, H. 1990. *Problem-oriented policing*. New York: McGraw Hill.

Gottfredson, M.R. and Hirschi, T. 1990. *A general theory of crime*. Stanford, CA: Stanford University Press.

Harries, K.D. 1990. *Serious violence: Patterns of homicide and assault in America*. Springfield, IL: Charles C. Thomas.

Hawley, A. 1950. *Human ecology: A theory of community structure.* New York: Ronald.

Heal, K. and Laycock, G. (Eds.). 1986. *Situational crime prevention: From theory into practice.* London: HMSO.

Hindelang, M.J., Gottfredson, M.R., and Garofalo, J. 1978. *Victims of personal crime.* Cambridge, MA: Ballinger.

Hirschi, T. 1969. *Causes of delinquency.* Berkeley and Los Angeles: University of California Press.

Jeffery, C.R. 1971. *Crime prevention through environmental design.* Beverly Hills, CA: Sage.

Mayhew, P., Clarke, R.V., Sturman, A., and Hough, J.M. 1976. *Crime as opportunity.* London: HMSO.

Newman, O. 1972. *Defensible space: Crime prevention through urban design.* New York: MacMillan. (Published by Architectural Press, London, in 1973).

Reuter, P. and Haaga J. 1989. *The organization of high-level drug markets.* Santa Monica, CA: Rand Corporation.

Sherman, L.W., Gartin, P., and Buerger, M.E. 1989. Hot spots of predatory crime: Routine activities and the criminology of place. *Criminology,* 27:27–55.

Simon, H.A. 1983. *Reasoning in human affairs.* Oxford: Blackwell.

Spring, J.V. and Block, C.R. 1988, March 25. *Finding crime hot spots: Experiments in the identification of high crime areas.* Paper presented at the Midwest Sociological Association.

Trasler, G. 1986. Situational crime control and rational choice: A critique. In K. Heal and G. Laycock (Eds.), *Situational crime prevention: From theory into practice.* London: HMSO.

Part One

Extending the Reach

1

Searching for Suitable Co-offenders

Pierre Tremblay

In a variety of situations, the probability that a given violation will occur will partly depend on motivated offenders' ability to find "suitable" co-offenders. Instead of considering individual or group offending as a basis for characterizing or classifying offenders, an alternative view might be to conceptualize the frequency and intensity of interactions between offenders as the intelligible outcome of a pattern of individually reasoned choices and constraints that vary across settings, across crimes, and over a given offender's life cycle. The question raised in this chapter is whether or not (and if so, to what extent) should this search for suitable co-offenders be incorporated as a distinct or additional component of the basic crime function specified by the routine activities theory provided by Cohen and Felson (1979).

Brantingham and Brantingham (1981a; 1981b) have shown the useful-ness of uncovering the dynamics involved in the search of criminal tar-gets. Although related in various ways to the search for crime opportunities, the search for suitable co-offenders raises a number of distinctive issues. Part One offers a brief overview of criminal sociology and argues that most students of crime have assumed the search for co-offenders to be unproblematic either because offenders are conceived as isolates or be-cause they are defined as engulfed in criminal subcultures. In both cases the search for co-offenders becomes theoretically irrelevant (either be-cause the search is costless or because offenders have no motivation to undertake such a search). We are assuming in this chapter that searching for co-offenders is inherently problematical and does not, in fact, yield constant outcomes (whether successful or not). Part Two examines various conditions that increase or decrease the availability of other offenders, keeping in mind that the search depends partly on their social and geographical proximity. All potential co-offenders are not, however, equally suitable, and the search involves more perhaps than "bodily convergences." Part Three specifies some of the suitability criteria governing this search and some of the not-so-easy choices and trade-offs that shape the duration and the crime mix of criminal careers. Part Four, finally, provides a preliminary overview of various social conditions that may increase or decrease the number of suitable co-offenders available.

Searching for Co-offenders.

One major focal concern of offenders is to "know" people, to have "contacts" and "connections." Sam Goodman, the subject of Darrell Steffensmeier's biography of a "fence," is quoted as saying, "The hardest thing is getting connections, 'cause you have to have the contacts with all different kinds of people" (Steffensmeier 1986:156). Notice that Goodman is not simply saying that maintaining crime-relevant contacts is less than obvious; he is also arguing that even more problematic is developing a sufficiently wide range of very "different" kinds of such ties. Similarly, Akerstrom's survey of Swedish male prison inmates concludes that "contacts are essential to the criminal in several ways, both for his criminal pursuits and for his overall living pattern" (1985: 22) and provides a detailed analysis of the various social skills required. Both Steffensmeier and Akerstrom's descriptions illustrate the fact that "finding" a suitable pool of partners, intermediates, and contacts constitutes in fact a crucial, focal, problematic, "choice-structuring" (Cornish and Clarke 1987) concern for a wide range of motivated potential offenders.

Unfortunately, most students of crime have chosen to move back and forth from an undersocialized to an oversocialized view of offenders. Although cohort and crime career analyses have been very informative, one of their drawbacks is that each individual crime sequence observed is methodologically and theoretically extracted from its setting and that crime careers are conceptualized as the aggregate outcome of independent trajectories. "The artificial divorce of the cohort from a changing environment and its reduction to a population of individuals unrelated in time and space restrict considerably what can be learned about individual crime careers" (Reiss 1988: 166). The possibility that a given offender's crime career depends on the way it intersects or consciously parallels the crime sequences of various co-offenders is left undiscussed. For example the criteria for assessing whether offenders may be labeled professionals or specialists (Peterson et al. 1980) is based solely on the basis of repeat occurrences of similar and (rather vague) crime activities. A very different definition could be provided, however, based on the ability of a given offender to build a viable or complex network of crime-relevant contacts and co-offenders (obviously an option that Sam Goodman, for one, would prefer).

Similarly, Cohen and Felson (1979) have argued that the probability that a violation will occur at any specific time and place can be taken as a function of the convergence of motivated offenders and suitable targets in the absence of capable guardians. However, many targets become suitable only in the presence of a loose network of co-offenders. Routine credit card and cheque frauds often require either a market of stolen or counterfeited company cheques and credit cards or a market for defrauded goods. As a result, crime rates may depend on two separate search processes: the search for co-offenders and the search for targets. If so, any variations in crime rates will depend not only on the convergence of motivated offenders and suitable targets, but also on the ability of such offenders to interact among themselves.

Although the literature on networks of offenders and criminal subcultures is extensive, it views offenders as already tightly embedded in cliques of mutually suitable co-offenders. Just as the random sampling procedure used in crime career and cohort studies extracts offenders from their environment, the snowball sampling procedure used in field investigations tends to emphasize closed and tight networks. The analysis of the constraints and choice patterns involved in the search for co-offenders is therefore bypassed. Even in those studies that have emphasized the short duration of juvenile gangs, their limited cohesiveness, and their intrinsic instability, (Yablonsky 1963; Klein and Crawford 1967), it remains unclear whether this instability should be attributed to the inherent impulsivity of members (a possibility strongly emphasized by Hirschi 1969), the intrinsic instability of crime opportunities and constraints of crime life itself (a theoretical option emphasized by Cornish and Clarke 1989), or the fact that such groups were only partly designed in the first place to provide their members illicit opportunities.

Curiously enough, those students who have analyzed the work and social niches of offenders provide only a limited understanding of the choices and constraints involved in the search for co-offenders. Prus and Irini (1980), for example, provide a fascinating analysis of how the working routines of prostitutes are structured by the interactions of a variety of supporting and complementary actors who are part of what they call the "hotel community" (the world of strippers, bartenders, bouncers, desk clerks, bar patrons, and rounders). One can also find in Miller's (1978) descriptions of the various roles and relationships that structure the work niches of thieves, con men, and other deviant workers, crucial insights (for example Miller's argument that such interactions do not develop under or aside from other spheres of social life and that there is no "underworld" as such). In both cases however, the main emphasis is on specifying a cast of various complementary and supportive "roles" and the analysis of the social niche of a career thief limits itself to a brief and undetailed description of the functional categories of individuals with whom a thief interacts on a regular basis: the victims themselves, those individuals who inform him of a given opportunity, those who buy the stolen property, and those who pay his bail following arrest or who represent him in court. A lack of comparative analysis across thieves, across settings, or over time, as well as the absence of any attempt to link qualitative or quantitative changes in crime levels to changes in the interaction patterns that shape the social and work "niches" of the offenders interviewed, limit, at least for the purposes in this chapter, the theoretical usefulness of such studies.

Reiss's (1988) seminal study of the changing prevalence of co-offending patterns (as revealed by victimization surveys) across crimes and age groups of offenders as well as his discussion of the impact of such patterns on various crime-control strategies, provide instead a basic conceptual framework for analyzing the search, the selection, and the maintenance of suitable accomplices. Reiss's analysis however limits itself to a given offender's set of actual accomplices and these, of course, constitute only a subset of the actual pool of potential co-offenders. Many offenses may be committed on a solo basis but nevertheless depend on the availability of other offenders. The term *co-offenders,* in this chapter, is given, therefore, a larger definitional scope and refers not only to the subset of an offender's pool of accomplices but rather to all those other offenders he must rely on before, during, and after the crime event in order to make the contemplated crime possible or worthwhile.

Patterns in the Availability of Co-offenders

Any concentration of offenders increases the likelihood that a given offender will find available co-offenders suitable for joint or supportive criminal activities. In this section, I will examine three mechanisms by which the availability of co-offenders may vary over time and across settings: unemployment, residential allocation, and incarceration.

1. The pervasiveness of nonsignificant and weak positive relationships between unemployment and crime levels, as well as the presence of surprising negative effects, have led Cantor and Land (1985) to suggest that these null findings may be the result of two processes that ultimately cancel themselves out. On the one hand, an upward swing in unemploy-

ment levels may increase the prevalence of motivated potential offenders (hence an expected positive impact of unemployment on crime levels). On the other hand, increased unemployment levels may amplify the concentration of sustenance and leisure activities within primary group locations. This in turn may reduce crime levels because individuals as well as their property benefit from increased guardianship. Since unemployment is often coincident with a general slowdown in social activities, it may also trigger (as suggested initially by Cohen and Felson 1979 and Felson and Cohen 1981) a slowdown in crime opportunities (fewer clients for hookers, fewer interesting marks for pickpockets, etc). Moreover, Cantor and Land show that whereas the negative impact of an upswing in unemployment levels on crime opportunity should be relatively instantaneous, the positive impact it may have on criminal motivation is more likely to lag in time since economic hardship in contemporary developed societies is cushioned by institutional welfare agencies and social support networks. Both their analyses and those by Allen and Steffensmeier (1989) offer some encouraging empirical support (see however, Chiricos 1987).

This clever analysis does not explicitly delineate the potential impact of changing levels in unemployment on the search for co-offenders. But it could. For example, an increase in the concentration of sustenance and leisure activities within primary group locations may affect the search for co-offenders. Inasmuch as this search requires time, one may assume that an increase in unemployment levels also increases the amount of time potential offenders can devote to it. If so, we should expect the prevalence of joint-offending to increase with higher unemployment levels.

Moreover, to the extent that a slowdown in economic activities reduces the scope or quality of crime opportunities, offenders may adapt and increase their willingness to invest time and energy in joint-offending or to engage in crime activities that require more elaborate weak ties (fencing arrangements). They may even settle for lower individual monetary returns. It is therefore not simply that potential offenders have more time to interact; they may be more willing to interact. In short we should expect not only a parallel change in the proportion of solo or co-offending, but also an increase in the proportion of property thefts supplying the fencing markets (for example the proportion of unrecovered stolen vehicles). Moreover, once networks of suitable co-offenders have developed, they may develop a life of their own. Increased interactions among potential offenders, if sufficiently innovative and efficient, may maintain themselves despite changing conditions (a decrease in unemployment levels). If so, we should expect crime levels to be more responsive to upward than downward changes in unemployment levels. Finally, we should expect all these patterns to be more pronounced in areas where the pool of actual or potential unemployed individuals live close to each other than in neighborhoods where they are scattered.

2. Housing arrangements may also shape the search for co-offenders. High-crime areas take a variety of forms. Offenders may be concentrated in an area that experiences low to moderate crime levels ("racketville" neighborhoods as described by Spergel 1964). In other areas, one finds both high levels of victimization and high residential concentration of offenders. And there are crime areas that experience high levels of crime events even though residential concentration of known or arrested offenders is limited.

Brantingham and Brantingham (1984; 1990) suggested that differential impunity across urban neighborhoods (unequal policing) and limited mobility of offenders (targets had to be in walking distance) explain, at least partly, the substantial residential concentration of offenders in most large nineteenth-century cities. Bureaucratization of law enforcement agencies, increased individual mobility of individuals (cars, public transport) as well as the related urban dispersion of work, school, shopping, and entertainment destinations, have all contributed to the residential dispersion of offenders. As a result, the correlation between offender and offense areas has weakened. Indeed, Baldwin and Bottoms (1976) obtained a negative correlation in Sheffield, England, between areas of offender residence and areas of crime occurrences.

There has been no attempt to assess the impact of these urban patterns on the search for co-offenders. But a preliminary outline can be provided. For example, it may be that as a result of their increasing mobility, offenders have access to a wider range of crime opportunities and that therefore the need to search for suitable co-offenders has become less attractive. Conversely, it may be that the increase in residential dispersion of potential offenders has made the search for co-offenders more costly and that offenders settle instead for a solo search of suitable targets. If the latter hypothesis is more powerful, we should expect the average loss experienced by high-crime, low-offender neighborhoods to be lower, all else being equal, than in other crime areas.

Physical proximity of multiple offenders does not itself resolve the search for co-offenders. Indeed it may complicate it. Cooperation among offenders requires some level of trust, and trust itself takes time to develop. Disorganized crime areas tend to be characterized by a substantial residential instability of both offenders and nonoffenders. Potential offenders living in such areas may either choose a solo offending strategy (because of the cost involved in developing stable ties with other offenders) or may seek strong ties with a closed network of co-offenders (because individuals are more vulnerable). In short, the various patterns in the residential distribution of offenders structure (at least partly) their search for co-offenders, and the constraints under which this search is undertaken, in turn, determine how offenders choose to commit their crimes and the kinds of crime activities they may select to practice. And this should hold not only across urban neighborhoods, but also across cities, countries, and over time.

3. Prison is a crucial life event in most crime careers. Prisons are theoretically interesting for our purposes because they constitute the ultimate experience in full-time residential concentration of offenders. Indeed, it is precisely on this ground that prisons have always been damned as perverse institutions, even though alternatives have yet to be found. Murray and Cox (1979) have criticized "the popular belief that institutions are "schools of crime" — an assertion that has been repeated so often that it has attained the status of a truism." Their analyses of arrest velocity before and after incarceration have provided some evidence that incarcerated offenders do not in fact "get smarter" in crime as a result of this "schooling." It may be, as Murray and Cox suggest, that most juvenile offenders are not "attentive to crime as a craft" (hence no learning process), or that much of the crime learning process occurs in settings where crimes can in fact be committed (in the juvenile delinquents' neighborhoods and school yards).

There are perhaps four reasons why the metaphor of prisons as schools of crime has been so popular: first, the assumption that residential concentration of offenders in an institution is bound to increase the level of cooperation among inmates; second, the assumption that the age mix of offenders is conducive to the transmission of criminal skills from the more experienced to the less experienced offenders; third, the assumption that a key feature of the convict world is its cohesiveness and solidarity; fourth, the assumption that prisons offer to a significant subset of inmates a route for upward mobility in crime careers (the "queer ladder mobility" argument). A schooling or teaching process, however informal, requires a number of conditions: a pool of motivated students, a pool of motivated and recognized teachers, a set of applied skills and expertise that can be effectively transmitted and experimented with, and an overall environment that is conducive to the teaching process.

As suggested by Murray and Cox, many criminal skills are more difficult to learn in prisons than in civil society for lack of relevant, up-to-date "documentation" (credit card frauds) and opportunity for manipulation (auto theft and explosive skills). In the absence of any "skills" to teach, the school model falls down. It may be, however (an empirical issue to settle), that certain offense skills can be more easily experimented with within prisons than others and in this sense, one of the conditions for an effective "schooling process" could be satisfied on a limited basis. The second requirement is that the teaching process requires an environment conducive to cooperative interactions among offenders. However the common thread of all of the most recent descriptions of prison settings since Sykes's (1970) case study has been precisely to underline the limitations of Sykes's emphasis on inmate cooperation. They provide instead vivid descriptions and analyses of either anomic or conflict-ridden "communities" (Carroll 1974; Jacobs 1977; Marquart and Roebuck 1985; Marquart 1986). In fact, whereas Sykes assumed that prison environment attenuated outside social conflicts (racial segregation), contemporary descriptions suggest precisely the opposite (Jacobs 1977). A third requirement is that a pool of motivated "students of crime" meet a subset of motivated "teachers of crime." The motivation for an offender to teach less experienced offenders a set of relevant skills or to provide them with relevant contacts is quite unclear. Because of the constant mobility of inmates throughout the correctional agencies and the opportunities for betrayal, potential teachers of crime may in fact be induced to find some other settings to transmit their skills.

In short, although prisons provide offenders with a large pool of contacts and potential co-offenders, it remains to be seen whether such contacts can effectively shape a given offender's future sequence of offenses or his way of committing these crimes. Although prisons as a useful research setting for the study of crime careers has been (finally) recognized (Petersilia 1980; Peterson et al., 1980), we are currently unable to either revise, specify, or reformulate the "school of crime" model. It is clear, however, from Ianni's (1975) detailed investigation of adult co-offender networks that prisons have very different impact on various cohorts and kinds of offenders. "It was a major finding for us that prison courts (associational network based on past prison experiences) are far more important in the formation of . . . [co-offender] networks among blacks and Puerto Ricans than they ever were among Italian-Americans" (Ianni 1975: 291). The overall implication here is that the extent to which a given offender's network of co-offenders will rely on kinship, neighborhood, prison, work, and sentimental or love ties depends partly on their relative availability, partly on their suitability for the specific kinds of crime tasks contemplated, partly also on generalized social tastes. For example the stronger emphasis on prison ties found in black and Puerto Rican than Italian co-offender networks is interpreted by Ianni as a function of the differential size and instability of family ties across these ethnic groups.

Suitability of Co-offenders

Pure availability, then, does not by itself fully determine or exhaust the search for co-offenders. Finding or being exposed to a pool of available co-offenders is only part of the search process. What remains to be clarified, in general terms at least, is the selection routines by which a given offender finds a suitable subset of co-offenders. What are the criteria for suitable co-offenders and what are the social conditions that may increase or decrease their prevalence?

One criterion emphasized by most students of crime is trustworthiness. Steffensmeier and Terry (1982) interviewed a convenience sample of male thieves and reported that the most important perceived quality of a good criminal was his trustworthiness. Akerstrom (1985), similarly, argues that trust, for offenders, is "essential both in determining who of the others is reliable, and in establishing a reputation of being trustworthy" (p. 144). Indeed, because unjustified claims about one's worth or skills may have fatal consequences, ferreting out phony talk or behavior is a crucial concern and accounts for the surprising intensity of the inmates' moral indignation reported by Irwin (1972). "Since contacts and trustworthy relationships are so important for criminals, it is not surprising that they, more than others, react strongly to a 'bogus front' which to someone else might even be slightly amusing" (Akerstrom 1985:146).

Notice, however, that the above studies mainly point out the perceived "need" for trustworthy relationships between co-offenders and recognize that this demand for trust is not in fact easily satisfied; that suitable offenders are hard to come by; and that the preferred strategy for offenders is to maintain instead a stand of careful distrust. Indeed, if trustworthy co-offenders were easily available, the search itself would be pointless (as well as offender's complaints and yearnings over the issue). Comparing the views of inmates to a control group of nonoffenders, Akerstrom finds that the issue of trustworthiness is, as expected, more salient for offenders: whereas two thirds of the inmates interviewed agreed with the proposition that "one cannot be too careful in one's dealings with other people," less than a third of nonoffenders concurred.

There are very good reasons why offenders tend to prefer distrust in their dealings with other offenders. First, the argument of self-selection. Hirschi (1969) for example has argued that "the idea that delinquents have comparatively warm, intimate social relations with each other (or with anyone) is a romantic myth." In fact the more seriously delinquent juveniles are less likely to identify with or admire their best friends, including their best delinquent friends. If offenders are mainly people whose lack of self-control make them "impulsive, insensitive, short sighted and non-verbal" (Gottfredson and Hirschi 1990: 90), then offenders are quite right about being suspicious of establishing ties with co-offenders. Second, even if Gottfredson and Hirschi's typification of offenders is inappropriate, one can expect that the occupational hazards of doing crime are relatively well-established facts of life. A follow-up survey of a 1945 Philadelphia birth cohort has found that the best predictor of being an ongoing offender is to have been previously victimized: two thirds of the cohort's victims reported having committed a serious assault compared with 27% of the nonvictims (Singer 1981). Similarly the British Crime Survey showed that 42% of the subjects who reported having committed violent crimes were also victims of such crimes, compared with 6% of nonoffenders (Gottfredson 1984). More specifically, Sampson and Lauritsen (1990) have shown that serious or minor violent offense activity directly increases the risk of personal victimization, independently of life-style (e.g., nights out of home) and demographic variables. Similarly, Cordeau's (1989a) analysis of underworld killings (defined as all crime-related homicides involving offenders) shows that the odds of being killed is 10 to 20 times higher for serious or chronic offenders than for other comparable social groups. A subsequent reanalysis of the same data sets (Cordeau 1989b) suggests that most of these underworld killings could not be explained away as "normative sanctions" (the "law" of the underworld) or as the simple outcome of betrayals triggered by police informants or undercover agents.

Although a theory that holds that close interactions among offenders are intrinsically conflictual has much to be said for it, "the internecine image of delinquents's associations may be extreme to the point of violating sociological principles. Just as groups with no internal dissension are difficult or impossible to find, a minimal level of cooperation and loyalty is also found in all but the most narrow and predatory relationships" (Gills and Hagan 1990: 33). Bernard Barber (1983) has argued that "distrust is a functionally equivalent instrument for maintaining social order" and that we "tend in everyday discourse and even in social science to exaggerate both the need for full trust and the evils of imperfections in trust processes" (p. 166).

Even if the issue of trustworthiness is a crucial concern in the search for suitable co-offenders, it remains only one of its aspects. Just as the search for a suitable target involves the search for two properties (value of the target and its vulnerability), the search for suitable co-offenders involves the attempt to combine two goals: the search for the strongest ties possible with co-offenders so as to minimize the chances of betrayal and failure; and the search for weak but useful ties so as to increase the scope and value of crime opportunities. The search for weak but useful ties is just as crucial as the search for strong ties.

It should not therefore come as a surprise to find that existing models of the search for job opportunities appear to be highly relevant to our understanding of crime patterns. Granovetter's (1982) argument about the strength of weak ties (and the weakness of strong ties) is particularly enlightening here. Granovetter argues that in the matter of job opportunities, individuals with strong ties will be deprived of information from distant parts of the social system and will be confined to the provincial news and views of their close friends; this will insulate them from the latest ideas and fashions, and also put them in a disadvantaged position in the labor market, where advancement depends in part on knowing about appropriate job openings at just the right time. More generally, social systems lacking in weak ties will be fragmented and incoherent. New ideas will spread slowly, and subgroups who are separated by race, ethnicity, geography, and other characteristics will have difficulty reaching a modus vivendi. On the other hand, the most important generator of weak ties is the division of labor, since increasing specialization and interdependence result in a wide variety of specialized role relationships.

Similarly, we can assume that a variety of suitable crime opportunities are accessible to offenders only if mediated by a "very different kind" (as Sam Goodman would say) of other offenders and supportive contacts. The ability to establish a loose and open-ended network of weak and useful crime-relevant ties is here again anything but obvious and remains to be researched empirically. Reuter (1983; 1985) has emphasized, in an analytical rather than empirical fashion, the intrinsic fragility of such networks. Although crime markets are often considered as "just like any other legitimate market," the consequences of illegality are shown by Reuter to be very profound indeed. Given the much shorter planning time horizons of criminal market participants, potential employers have little incentive to invest in training so as to acquire and preserve needed skills. An additional disincentive is that monitoring of performance is much more difficult to organize in markets where transactions are covert. Second, criminal "firms" are more likely to be small and ephemeral because potential criminal entrepreneurs cannot benefit from the development of external credit markets (lack of auditing procedures, absence of easily-seized collateral) but are forced to operate instead on a personal loan basis. Third, whereas legal markets expand through publicity and brand loyalty marketing, such options are not present in criminal markets. Customers may be loyal to a particular vendor but not to the product itself. Moreover, both customers and other entrepreneurs represent a much more significant threat to illegal entrepreneurs than can ever be the case in legitimate markets. Fourth, whereas geographical distance is a minor impediment to the expansion of legal firms because of the development of low-cost means of rapid information transfer and communication, illegal markets are at a competitive disadvantage: the multiplication of law enforcement agencies increases with distance; means of communication can be covertly tapped; lack of publicity prevents the spread of national retailing and production enterprises; the need for intimidation and higher wages to neutralize negligence or cheating in the performance of employees also increases with distance. As a result, criminal markets should be populated by small, ephemeral, and local markets and firms. And this, of course, implies that job opportunities for motivated offenders will be intrinsically ephemeral, local, volatile, and unpredictable. Even commercial prostitution firms (massage parlors, escort agencies), an illicit market that is not perceived as very damaging to the social fabric and can rely therefore on an efficient advertising system (ads in the daily newspapers), have been found to have a life expectancy of less than 6 months on average (Leguerrier 1989).

Although a theory that underlines the inherent difficulty in building weak, instrumental, or pragmatic ties between offenders may account perhaps for the high levels of offenders dropping out of crime (the follow-up of a birth cohort of offenders undertaken by Tracey et al. 1990, finds that by age 30, 87% of offenders will have desisted from crime after their the fifth arrest), it remains clear nonetheless that crime markets do exist, that co-offending remains a favorite option for a large number of offenders and that students of crime should probably be intellectually more appreciative of the means by which offenders in general can, given the odds, still manage to neutralize or mitigate the constraints of crime life.

The search for co-offenders, then, involves developing two different kinds of networks. Whereas the concern for safety and trust involves the building of a network of strong ties (a community), the concern for wealth involves building a network of useful but less intimate ties (a market). Moreover, both concerns (trust and wealth, cooperation and social mobility) are difficult to reconcile. In fact, the search for suitable co-offenders is confronted with the same kind of dilemma as the search for suitable targets. Just as the value of targets tends to be inversely related to their vulnerability, income and trust concerns are difficult to balance. A heightened concern for trustworthy offenders tends to limit the number of suitable co-offenders, to reduce the amount of interaction with other offenders, and ultimately imposes sharp restrictions on the desired income one can obtain from crime activities. On the other hand, a heightened concern for illicit income accumulation requires expanding the number of interactions with other offenders in search of more competence and division of labor, all of which cannot be developed without simultaneously increasing the likelihood of betrayal, victimization, and arrest.

Hence the theoretical need to analyze more closely the various strategies used by offenders in order to overcome the intrinsic difficulties involved in the search for co-offenders. Strategy number 1 (the "exclusive" strategy) involves selecting one kind of co-offender network over the other, and limiting oneself to those kinds of crime most congenial or compatible with the kind of ties one has decided to rely on. If a given offender (for various reasons) lacks or wants to avoid strong ties, he can concentrate on those crimes in which strong ties are not crucial (solo thefts of merchandise) but in which weak ties are required. If on the other hand, a given offender lacks or wants to avoid dependency on weak ties, he may concentrate on those crimes in which weak ties are not crucial but strong ties are required (cash-oriented group offending).

Strategy number 2 (the "avoidance" strategy) involves the deliberate attempt to minimize weak as well as strong ties with co-offenders and committing offenses that satisfy this requirement (cash-oriented solo thefts or frauds). Strategy number 2, if pursued systematically over time, makes the offender a social isolate within the offender population. This strategy has been very well described in Edwin Lemert's (1967) analysis of check forgers. Most interesting, perhaps, is Lemert's clear understanding of the constraints such a strategy imposes (constraints of pseudonymity and mobility across cities for example). Although Lemert's analysis limits itself to a convenience sample of check forgers operating in a given time and setting, a fruitful theoretical exercise would be to compare various avoidance strategies across crimes, settings, and offender cohorts.

Strategy number 3 (the "mixed" strategy) involves the decision to develop simultaneously both weak and strong ties and to keep, at the same time, both networks at a distance. An offender may, for example, mobilize both kinds of networks on a rotating (or parallel) basis and engage serially in short sequences of those kinds of offenses most relevant for each kind of network. In short, such an offender would engage both in solo theft of merchandise and cash-oriented offenses, but alternatively. The crucial feature of this strategy is to keep both sets of co-offenders at arm's length so as to avoid expecting unrealistic income returns from strong ties and unrealistic loyalty from weak ties.

It may be tempting to classify offenders on the basis of their preferred strategy. One problem with this approach is that it assumes each strategy to be viable at all times, in all circumstances, and for all crimes. Lemert (1967) for example has described in detail how the avoidance strategy "contains the seeds of its own destruction or one which generates its own 'psychopathology'"(p. 132). It remains unclear whether the self-defeating outcomes of this particular strategy could not, in the long run, apply to all other available strategies. If this is true, one should expect most offenders to be highly cautious in their commitment to a given strategy and induced instead to change strategies over time, across crimes, and across settings.

The Social Fabric and the Search for Suitable Co-offenders

Cullen (1984) has argued that social conditions that motivate or predispose people to become offenders are quite distinct from those conditions that account for their specific crime choices. Conventional motivational theories generally do not account for the particular form a given criminal career (whether short or long) takes. Indeed they do not even account for the particular form of deviance selected as the most suitable. The more indeterminate the motivational variables, the more useful becomes the task of specifying the relevant structuring variables. I suggest that the search for suitable co-offenders be considered a significant component of the structuring process and that social conditions that increase or decrease co-offender transaction costs be added to the existing provisional list of "structuring variables" already provided by Cullen (technological innovations, cultural stereotypes, location in the social structure, societal reaction). In this section I will attempt to show how current or past discussions on a variety of issues — age patterns among offenders, the impact of war conditions on crime levels, the cumulative deterrence debate — can benefit from a more determined attempt to include the search for co-offenders as a distinctive intervening process.

1. Consider first the treatment of the age and crime relationship offered by David Greenberg (1977). Greenberg has argued that the preponderance of juvenile delinquents in the overall composition of street offender population in contemporary societies is the joint outcome of three factors: the exclusion of juveniles from the labor market, the increasing reliance on peers as a source of self-validation, and overall prosperity (consumerism and increasing crime opportunities). The idea of an overrepresentation of juvenile delinquents in contemporary Western societies has received strong empirical support (Farrington 1986; but see, Hirschi and Gottfredson 1983).

This analysis could, however, be pursued along different lines. For example, the fact of being excluded from the labor market has probably shielded an increasing number of motivated juvenile offenders from the hazards of economic self-sustenance. We should therefore expect them to invest less time and energy in their search for crime opportunities, to commit less serious crimes (Rand 1987) and to be satisfied with low-yield theft targets (Allen and Steffensmeier 1989). Thus, we should anticipate a weaker emphasis on the search for useful co-offenders (weak ties) among juveniles than among adult offenders. This does not fit very well with Greenberg's argument of higher motivational disposition to offend among contemporary youths. However, if self-validation among peers as a focal concern is as crucial as Greenberg's assumes it to be, we should expect juvenile offenders to invest more time and energy in searching for strong and intimate ties (with other co-offenders of the same age category) than adult offenders. Hence the higher proportion of group offending among juveniles than among adults (Reiss 1988). This in turn, may account, in part, for the intense social visibility that characterizes juvenile delinquency in our societies. In short, the changing status of juveniles in the social fabric can be seen both as a motivational background variable and as a generator of structuring processes.

2. War is perhaps the ultimate quasi-experiment in social upheaval and its complicated impact on crime patterns has probably not received as much theoretical attention as it should have. One popular (and purely motivational) explanation of war crime patterns (in Austria during World War I) was formulated by Franz Exner (cited by Sutherland 1973). Exner argued that thefts increased during wartime because of the pressure of unsatisfied needs and the restrictions on legitimate methods of securing commodities; sex offenses and assaults, on the other hand, decreased during wartime because of the scarcity of alcohol and the fact that under-nourished people had little surplus energy for sex offenses and assaults (Sutherland 1973: 122). Sutherland severely criticized this explanation because it did not account for a number of important facts: thefts increased in England as well as in Austria, even though economic distress was much less serious in England; thefts increased in Canada, although economic distress in fact decreased during World War I; finally, Exner's distress theory did not explain why thefts committed by juveniles increased more than thefts by adults.

Sutherland's reanalysis is particularly interesting. Instead of analyzing wartime conditions as simply a factor of increased strain or crime opportunity levels, he conceptualized it as a change in social interaction patterns between offenders and nonoffenders and among offenders themselves. His argument, briefly, is to show how a wartime context entails typically a decrease in guardianship (owners of property spent a larger amount of time away of home) and supervision (concern for supervision in industrial and commercial establishments may decline); an increase in the scope of accessible crime opportunities and in the number of weak ties available (scarcity in the labor market allows a larger number of persons not selected on the basis of trustworthiness—e.g., railroad employees—to be placed in positions of trust and responsibility); an increase in the incidence of interactions among potential offenders (because of the increase in the geographic mobility of individuals, and because of the passage of large numbers of children and women away from the sheltered environment of the home and the school to the heterogeneous environment of the factory, shop, and store); and in an increase in interaction levels among crime market participants as the result of the increasing variety, complexity, and connectedness of illicit markets (illicit markets now include black markets of rationed goods as well). In short, wartime conditions affect the search for crime opportunities as well as the search for suitable co-offenders. These intervening processes in turn shape the specific configuration of crime choices available to motivated offenders.

3. Students of deterrence have been particularly sensitive to the social conditions that regulate the communication and diffusion of legal and informal threats. Cook (1980) has analyzed the channels by which information on the certainty and severity of penalties is communicated to potential offenders and has observed that although each arrest and conviction will go unnoticed by the public at large, it will affect the arrestee's friends and associates. The larger the size of an offender's network of weak and strong ties with other offenders, the more "knowledgeable" about penalties he will become. Ekland-Olson et al. (1984) have argued that sanctions are perceived as more severe the more they threaten to disrupt the subject's interpersonal relationships ("persons rich in associations will fear sanctions more than loners") and have shown how the sanctioning process has an important structuring impact on co-offender networks because they tend to increase "network density and closure" on the one hand, but to restrict simultaneously the scope of suitable crime opportunities.

The notion of cumulative or delayed deterrence especially requires some fusion of network and rational choice theories. Williams and Hawkins (1986) have indicated how current perceptual studies of deterrence have avoided tackling the notion of cumulative deterrence, a common enough experience however for all offenders who in the process of their crime involvement develop the "rough notion that their luck is running out." Cusson and Pinsonneault (1986; see also Cusson 1983) have shown how the combined impact of specific shocks or jolts (resulting from some aversive experience when committing an offense) and delayed deterrence (rising estimates of the likelihood and expected severity of punishment, increasing difficulty of doing time, and an overall increase in the anxiety connected with crime life) accounts for many of the patterns observed in desistance from crime.

Obviously, delayed deterrence involves more than the "law of averages" and the simple fact that the more crimes one commits, the greater the cumulative probability of arrest. Delayed deterrence (increasing levels of anxiety, exhaustion, fear) is experienced when hazards (shocks) witnessed by a given offender increase around him, and when the sociometric distance between self and damaged others decreases over time. This process may occur in a variety of ways. It may occur as a result of his own doing or of his increasing visibility for law enforcement officials. Or it may occur as a result of the behavior of his interactions with other co-offenders.

The larger the size of an offender's crime-relevant ties, the more likely the chances of experiencing hazards of various sorts (offender is betrayed, burned, injured, or killed, or gets arrested as a result of the arrests of his co-offenders). Cumulative deterrence can also be experienced in a variety of ways depending on the mix of strong and weak ties a given offender has managed to develop. It may be experienced as a sense of loss: "so i went back to Omaha\to live with my folks\but everyone i used to know\was either dead or in prison" (Tom Waits, "Christmas Card from a Hooker in Minneapolis"). This feeling of personal loss, grief, and estrangement is most likely to be experienced by offenders relying on a network of strong ties with co-offenders. But cumulative deterrence can also be experienced as falling into a whirl of increasing complexity, uncertainty, unreliability, and mistrust. Rather than loss and grief, cumulative deterrence takes here the form of paranoia, uncontrolled double-guessing and confusion and should be experienced mainly by offenders who rely on networks of weak ties with co-offenders. In short, interaction patterns among offenders should therefore be considered as crucial structuring variables for both deterrence and delayed deterrence processes.

Conclusion

Our basic idea, then, is that the probability that a given violation will occur depends partly on the ability of motivated offenders to find suitable co-offenders. If so, then any changes in social conditions that increase the availability of co-offenders or levels of chance encounters among motivated offenders (unemployment, housing policies, incarceration, for example) should in principle shape the nature and the mix of crime opportunities available. The search for co-offenders, however, does not appear to be simply a matter of bodily convergences but involves complicated mating processes by which potential co-offenders select themselves as mutually suitable or unsuitable for crime purposes. Cornish and Clarke (1987, 1989) have shown the usefulness of understanding the choice-structuring properties of deviant behaviors (crimes, suicide, gambling) that make them attractive to particular individuals and subgroups. In this chapter paper we have examined some of the choice-structuring attributes of offenders that make them suitable as co-offenders, some of the constraints and transaction costs that are built into this searching process, and some of the various strategies by which efficient crime networks can nonetheless develop. A comprehensive understanding of the various suitability criteria that regulate the search for co-offenders and of the specific social conditions and settings that facilitate or inhibit the likelihood that such suitable co-offenders can be found may also provide the empirical basis upon which one could perhaps integrate, within an overall rational choice perspective, the routine activity crime opportunity theory, social network research, and the Sutherland's cultural transmission tradition.

References

Akerstrom, Malin. 1985. *Crooks and squares: Lifestyles of thieves and addicts in comparison to conventional people.* New Brunswick, NJ: Transaction Publishers.

Allen, Emilie A., & Steffensmeier, Darrell J. 1989. "Youth, underemployment, and property crime: Differential effects of job availability and job quality on juvenile and young adult arrest rates." *American Sociological Review* 54: 107–23.

Baldwin, John, & Bottoms, Anthony E. 1976. *The urban criminal: A study in Sheffield.* London: Tavistock.

Barber, Bernard. 1983. *The logic and limits of trust.* New Brunswick, NJ: Rutgers University Press.

Brantingham, Patricia L., & Brantingham, Paul J.1981a. "Notes on the geometry of crime." In P.L. Brantingham & P.J. Brantingham (Eds.), *Environmental Criminology* (27–54). Beverly Hills, CA: Sage.

Brantingham, Patricia L., & Brantingham, Paul J. 1981b. "Mobility, notoriety, and crime: A study in the crime patterns of urban nodal points." *Journal of Environmental Systems* 11(1): 89–99.

Brantingham, Paul J., & Brantingham, Patricia L. 1984. *Patterns in crime.* New York: Macmillan.

Brantingham, Patricia L., & Brantingham, Paul J. 1990. "Malls and crime." *Security Journal* 1(3): 175–82.

Cantor, David, & Land, Kenneth. 1985. "Unemployment and crime rates in the post-world war II United States: A theoretical and empirical analysis." *American Sociological Review* 50 (June): 317–24.

Carroll, Leo. 1974. *Hacks, blacks and cons.* Lexington, MA: Lexington Books.

Chiricos, Theodore G. 1987. "Rates of crime and unemployment: An analysis of aggregate research evidence." *Social Problems* 34(2): 187–212.

Cohen, Lawrence E., & Felson, Marcus. 1979. "Social change and crime rate trends: A routine activity approach." *American Sociological Review* 44: 588–608.

Cook, Philip J. 1980. "Research in criminal deterrence: Laying the groundwork for the second decade." In N. Morris & M. Tonry (Eds.), *Crime and justice: An annual review of research* (211–68). Chicago: Chicago University Press.

Cordeau, Gilbert. 1989a. "Les règlements de comptes au Québec et les mécanismes de la dissuasion endogène." *Canadian Journal of Criminology* 2: 253–79.

Cordeau, Gilbert. 1989b. "Les homicides entre délinquants: une analyse des conflits qui provoquent des règlements de compte." *Criminologie* 22(2): 13–34.

Cornish, Derek B., & Clarke, Ronald V. 1987. "Understanding crime displacement: An application of rational choice theory." Criminology 25(4): 933–47.

Cornish, Derek B., & Clarke, Ronald V. 1989. "Crime specialisation, crime displacement and rational choice theory." In H. Wegener, F. Losel, & J. Haisch (Eds.), *Criminal behaviour and the justice system: Psychological perspectives* (103–117). New York: Springer-Verlag, 1989.

Cullen, Francis T. 1984. *Rethinking crime and deviance theory.* Totowa, NJ: Rowman & Allanheld.

Cusson, Maurice. 1983. *Le contrôle social du crime.* Paris: Presses Universitaires de France.

Cusson, Maurice, & Pinsonneault, Pierre. 1986. "The decision to give up crime." In Derek B. Cornish & Ronald V. Clarke (Eds.), *The reasoning criminal* (72–82). New York: Springer Verlay.

Ekland-Olson, Sheldon, Lieb, John, & Zurcher, Louis. 1984. "The paradoxical impact of criminal sanctions: Some microstructural findings." *Law and Society Review* 18 (2): 160–78.

Farrington, David P. 1986. "Age and crime." In M. Tonry & N. Morris (Eds.), *Crime and justice: An annual review of research* (189–250). Chicago: University of Chicago Press.

Felson, Marcus, & Cohen, Lawrence E. 1981. "Modeling crime rate trends — a criminal opportunity perspective." *Journal of Research in Crime and Delinquency* 18: 138–64 (corrected 1982, 19:1).

Gills, A.R., & Hagan, John. 1990. "Delinquent Samaritans: Network structure, social conflict and the willingness to intervene." *Journal of Research in Crime and Delinquency* 27(1): 30–51.

Gottfredson, Michael R. 1984. *Victims of crime: The dimensions of risk* (Home Office Research Study No. 81). London: HMSO.

———. 1986. *Victims of crime: The dimensions of risk* (Home Office Research Study No. 81). London: Her Majesty's Stationery Office.

Gottfredson, Michael R., & Hirschi, Travis. 1990. *A general theory of crime.* Stanford, CA: Stanford University Press.

Granovetter, Mark. 1982. "The strength of weak ties: A network theory revisited." In Peter V. Marsden & Nan Lin (Eds.), *Social structure and network analysis* (105–30). Beverly Hills, CA: Sage.

Greenberg, David. 1977. "Delinquency and the age structure of society." *Contemporary Crises* 1: 189–223.

Hirschi, Travis. 1969. *Causes of delinquency.* Berkeley, CA: University of California Press.

Hirschi, Travis, & Gottfredson, Michael. 1983. "Age and the explanation of crime." *American Journal of Sociology* 89(3): 552–84.

Ianni, Francis. 1975. *Black mafia: Ethnic succession in organized crime.* New York: Pocket Books.

Irwin, John. 1972. "Participant observations of criminals." In Jack Douglas (Ed.), *Research in deviance* (117–38). New York: Random House.

Jacobs, James B. 1977. *Stateville: The penitentiary in mass society.* Chicago: University of Chicago Press.

Leguerrier, Yves. 1989. "Les entreprises de prostitution commerciale: les commerces éphémères des marchés illicites." *Criminologie* 22 (2): 35–64.

Lemert, Edwin M. 1967. *Human deviance, social problems and social control.* Englewood Cliffs, NJ: Prentice Hall.

Klein, William, & Crawford, L.Y. 1967. "Groups, gangs and cohesiveness." *Journal of Research in Crime and Delinquency* 14 (4): 142–65.

Marquart, James W. "Prison guards and the use of physical coercion as a mechanism of prisoner control." 1986. *Criminology* 24 (2): 347–66.

Marquart, James W., & Roebuck, Julian B. 1985. "Prison guards and snitches." *British Journal of Criminology* 25: 217–37.

Miller, Gale. 1978. *Odd jobs: The world of deviant work.* Englewood Cliffs, NJ: Prentice-Hall.

Murray, Charles, & Cox, Louis A. 1979. *Beyond probation: Juvenile corrections and the chronic delinquent.* Beverly Hills, CA: Sage.

Petersilia, Joan. 1980. "Criminal career research: A review of recent evidence." In N. Morris & M. Tonry (Eds.), *Crime and justice: An annual review of research* (321–380). Chicago: University of Chicago Press.

Peterson, Mark A., Braiker, Harriet B., & Polich, Suzanne M. 1980. *Doing crime: A survey of California prison inmates.* Santa Monica, CA: Rand Corporation.

Prus, Robert, & Irini, S. 1980. *Hookers, rounders and desk clerks: The social organization of the hotel community.* Toronto: Gage.

Rand, Alicia. 1987. "Transitional life events and desistance from delinquency and crime." In M.E. Wolfgang, T.P. Thornberry, & R.M. Figlio (Eds.), *From boy to man: From delinquency to crime* (134–62). Chicago: University of Chicago Press.

Reiss, Albert. 1988. Co-offending and criminal careers. In M. Tonry and N. Morris (Eds.), *Crime and justice: An annual review of research.* Chicago: University of Chicago Press.

Reuter, Peter. 1985. *The organization of illegal markets: An economic analysis.* Washington: National Institute of Justice.

Reuter, Peter. 1983. *Disorganized crime: The economics of the visible hand.* Cambridge, MA.: MIT Press.

Sampson, Robert J., & Lauritsen, Janet L. 1990. "Deviant lifestyles, proximity to crime, and the offender-victim link in personal violence." *Journal of Research in Crime and Delinquency* 27 (2): 110–39.

Singer, Simon I. 1981. "Homogeneous victim-offender populations: A review and some research implications." *Journal of Criminal Law and Criminology* 72 (2): 779–88.

Spergel, Irving. 1964. *Racketville, slumtown and haulburg: An exploratory study of delinquent subcultures.* Chicago: University of Chicago Press.

Steffensmeier. Darrell J., & Terry, Robert M. 1982. "Institutional sexism in the underworld: A view from the inside." Paper presented at the annual meeting of Midwest Sociological Association.

Steffensmeier, Darrell J. 1986. *The fence: In the shadow of two worlds.* Tioga, NJ: Rowman and Littlefield.

Sutherland, Edwin. 1973. *On analyzing crime.* Chicago: University of Chicago Press.

Sykes, Gresham M. 1970. *Society of Captives: A Study of a Maximum Security Prison.* New York: Atheneum. (original work published 1958.)

Tracey, P.E., Wolfgang, M.E., & Figlio, R.M. 1990. *Delinquency careers in two birth cohorts.* New York: Plenum Press.

Williams, Kirk R., & Hawkins, Richard. 1986. "Perceptual research on general deterrence: A critical review." *Law and Society Review* 20 (4): 545–72.

Yablonsky, Lewis. 1963. *The violent gang.* New York: Macmillan.

2

A Rational Choice Theory
of Corporate Crime

Raymond Paternoster and Sally Simpson

Currently, the problem of corporate crime is the subject of much conjecture and debate. Case after case of corporate wrongdoing has reinforced American cynicism about business ethics (Rickleffs 1983) and our ability to control the illegal activities of powerful corporations. In this context much attention is centered on the issue of deterrence and the effectiveness of formal legal sanctions in curbing corporate wrongdoing (Braithwaite and Geis 1982; Coffee 1980; Cullen and Dubeck 1985; Schlegel 1990; U.S. Sentencing Commission 1991).

Corporate crime consists of illegal acts by corporations or their representatives that are undertaken to further the goals of the organization. These acts violate civil, administrative, or criminal statutes (Clinard and Yeager 1980; Sutherland 1949) and as such encompass a variety of behaviors. For instance, corporate crime includes acts of fraud, bribery, price-fixing, toxic dumping, insider trading; crimes against employees, consumers, suppliers, buyers, and competitors (among others).

The traditional deterrence model[1] as applied to corporate crime specifies that: (1) the greater the certainty of punishment, the less the likelihood of corporate crime and (2) the greater the severity of punishment, the less the likelihood of corporate crime.[2] Among those who share this point of view, it is thought that current sanctions are neither certain nor severe enough to affect the behavior of corporate entities (or, more specifically, the individuals who manage them). Thus, recommendations have been made to change corporate sanctions at the federal level in order to achieve deterrent, among other, goals (U.S. Sentencing Commission 1991).

Our goals in this chapter are threefold: First, we examine a traditional deterrence framework as it applies to corporate offenders. We lay out the assumptions of the model, evaluate the empirical evidence, and weigh the strengths and weaknesses of this approach. Second, we expand formal deterrence by drawing on the rational choice perspective. Corporate offenders and their criminal acts have unique characteristics (motivations, behavioral requirements, and circumstances) that require a more broadly conceived theoretical model of decision making than that offered by a strictly deterrence framework, and that are, at the same time, offender or crime specific (Clarke and Cornish 1985:165). Third, we suggest a general strategy to empirically test our proposed theoretical model.

Formal Deterrence and Corporate Crime

Justifications for a Formal Deterrence Model

There are many reasons to believe that a traditional model of deterrence should be helpful in understanding corporate crime. It has been argued that white-collar (and especially corporate)[3] offenders are less committed to offending than conventional criminals (Chambliss 1967). Further, in their business and personal lives, managers are risk-averse, "unwilling to engage in activity that poses even minimal threats to the future of the corporation or their own position in it" (Schlegel 1990:16). Therefore, formal sanctions such as fines or incarceration provide a meaningful threat to potential corporate offenders.

Another argument for the deterrability of corporate crime is the nature of the offense. Corporate crimes are instrumental and strategic. Typical crimes are described as "calculated and deliberative and directed to economic gain" (Kadish 1977:305). They are "almost never crimes of passion; they are not spontaneous or emotional, but calculated risks taken by rational actors" (Braithwaite and Geis 1982:302). Accordingly, these offenses are presumed to be more amenable to a cost-benefit calculus on the part of the perpetrator (Chambliss 1967; Braithwaite and Geis 1982). The utilitarian calculus assumed by the deterrence model, in which threats are weighed against potential gains, seems particularly ideal for these offenders and circumstances.

Finally, public opinion plays an important role in the justification for corporate deterrence. The general public is generally supportive of harsher sanctions for white-collar offenders, particularly in cases of corporate violent offenses (Cullen and Dubeck 1985). The public believes that "stiff jail sentences will stop most white-collar criminals from breaking the law" (Cullen, Mathers, Clark, and Cullen 1983:485). However, they discriminate between organizations (where harsh sanctions are generally favored) and business executives (where support depends on the degree of harm and individual culpability; see Frank, Cullen, Travis, and Borntrager 1989).

These justifications for corporate deterrence are more philosophical and ideological than scientific (Schlegel 1990; Simpson and Koper 1992). The general public, regardless of any evidence to the contrary, believes that deterrence works (Gibbs 1975). Yet, among conventional offenders, data show that informal sanctions are a more effective means of social control than the threat of formal sanctions.[4] There is only one study, to our knowledge, that explicitly tests a perceptual deterrence model for corporate executives (Braithwaite and Makkai 1991).[5] It is to this study that we turn for empirical tests of a deterrence model.

Formal Deterrence and Corporate Crime: Empirical Evidence

Braithwaite and Makkai (1991:11) posit a simple expected utility model of organizational compliance that assumes compliance to be a function of (1) the probability that noncompliance will be discovered; (2) the probability of punishment given discovery; and (3) the cost of punishment. The focus of their research was a sample of 410 Australian nursing home executives (essentially CEOs) who were asked to estimate the chances that discovery and sanctioning would occur under a condition of continual violation of six "standards" and "regulations." Sanction source was allowed to vary, tapping both state and commonwealth regulatory efforts. Executives were asked to gauge the costs to their organization of several sanction types in the event that they were caught and disciplined.

Using cross-sectional self-report and official measures of compliance, the authors estimated both individual and multiplicative deterrent effects, controlling for a variety of demographic, regional, and organizational factors. Zero-order correlations revealed only one variable — probability of state detection — to have a significant relationship with either self-reported or official indicators of rule compliance. In their fully specified models (including controls, additive and multiplicative deterrence factors), the formal deterrence model was revealed as a "stark failure" (1991:29). The authors concluded that formal deterrence

fails under a variety of ways of specifying additive and multiplicative models. It fails even after an attempt to excise from consideration actors who do not give much thought to sanctions, actors who are high in emotionality, actors who believe strongly in the standards, and actors who are not proprietors of the nursing home as well as directors of nursing. (p. 35)

Why Formal Deterrence Fails

The lack of a discernable deterrent effect in Braithwaite and Makkai's (1991) study may be due to research design flaws or to more general limitations of the deterrence doctrine. First, the researchers employed a cross-sectional rather than a panel design. Consequently, perceptions may be the consequence of past experience with sanctions (Saltzman et al. 1982), instead of tapping true deterrent effects (Paternoster 1987). Second, a key assumption of a subjective utility model is that risks and consequences will be weighed against the perceived benefits of illegality. The benefits of crime are not modeled in this or other traditional deterrence studies. Third, respondents were queried about perceived organizational risks absent questions about their personal sanction risks. Since both can be sanction targets, a true test of corporate deterrence must incorporate threats to the individual as well as to the corporation.

Finally, Braithwaite and Makkai's simple utility model failed to measure nonpenal consequences, that is, threats to self-esteem, future opportunities, respect of significant others, and so forth. These informal factors may inhibit corporate criminality independently or in conjunction with legal sanctions. For instance, moral imperatives may keep most managers from violating the law regardless of legal sanction risk or consequence. For others, however, threats to self-respect or job mobility may be activated by the threat of formal processing (see, e.g., Benson 1984).

A Rational Choice Model of Corporate Crime

The preceding section has suggested that a strictly deterrence model, one that only includes formal sanction threats, is likely to be inadequate to explain corporate crime. This, of course, does not mean that those seeking explanations for corporate offending must abandon all utility-based models. In this section, we will offer a competing, and much more general, model of corporate crime. This model is based on a more inclusive understanding of social control than deterrence alone — rational choice theory. Our rational choice model of corporate crime will include, but will not be restricted to, formal sanction threats.

The Elements of a Rational Choice Theory of Crime

As suggested in the paragraph above, the rational choice perspective is a utility-based theory of criminal offending that is more inclusive than a strictly deterrence-based model. Although there are variations of rational choice theory, there are a few common elements. First, the decision by would-be offenders to commit a crime is a rational decision that is affected by the perceived costs and benefits of the action.[6] The costs of offending include, but are not restricted to, the possibility and severity of formal legal sanctions. Other costs include the certainty and severity of informal sanctions, lost legitimate alternatives to action, moral costs, and self-imposed costs such as a loss of self-respect. Also included in most rational choice models of offending, but not most deterrence models, are the perceived benefits of offending. Second, rational choice models of offending should be crime-specific since the kind of information both needed and employed by offenders varies considerably across crimes. The third common element is that decisions to offend in a specific instance (the "criminal event") are affected by the immediate contextual characteristics of the crime (Clarke and Cornish 1985; Cornish and Clarke 1986). For street crimes, the decision to offend is influenced by such situational considerations as how accessible a crime target is, the ease with which an escape may be made, the existence of security devices or the perceived likelihood of an armed or resisting victim. For corporate crimes, offending decisions are probably affected by such considerations as the profitability of the firm and the size of the corporation.

Rational Choice Theory and Corporate Crime

Given the discussion above concerning the elements of a rational choice theory of crime, we can now outline the structure of a rational choice theory of *corporate* crime.

Our rational choice theory of corporate crime presumes that the decision of a corporate employee to commit a crime is influenced by the perceived costs and benefits of the offense. This simple proposition includes several additional assumptions. First, we are constructing a *subjective utility theory* of corporate offending. That is, we hypothesize that what is important are not the objective costs and benefits of corporate offending, but the subjectively perceived costs and benefits, that is, what persons believe they stand to gain or lose by committing offenses. This, of course, implies that tests of our theory (to be discussed below) must be conducted at the individual level (persons as decision makers) rather than at the organizational level (corporations) of analysis.

This focus can seem contradictory when corporate crimes are considered; yet, many personal costs and benefits may accrue to the individual though the act ostensibly serves organizational ends. For instance, Gandossy (1985) describes an extensive fraud perpetrated by top executives and middle managers at OPM (Other Peoples' Money), a computer leasing company that grew to be one of the largest in the world. The company was insolvent from its inception and was kept afloat through bribery, laundered money, and extensive bank frauds. Not only did the firm "benefit" from the illegal activities, but the original partners amassed extensive personal fortunes, business perks such as chauffeur-driven limousines and officers' loan accounts, and the status that comes from "rubbing shoulders with giants." The personal costs for the OPM executives were equally high. Criminal charges were brought against five officers; four served prison terms.

It is important to note that the subjective utility of corporate crime will vary by crime type and organizational position. For instance, corporate personnel who violate environmental protection standards are less apt to receive the extensive financial and status rewards that the fraud garnered top executives at OPM, but may feel rewarded by the peer admiration and the attention of the boss for "pulling one over on the EPA." We are offering, then, a social-psychological model of corporate rule compliance.

The fact that we are focusing on the individual decision maker, however, does not restrict the scope of our model, or any empirical tests of this model, solely to corporate executives. Rather, we believe that since decisions related to corporate rule compliance occur at many levels in a business organization, any rational choice model of corporate crime must focus on decision makers at those different levels. Empirical tests of our model would therefore be directed to upper level executives, plant managers, accountants, quality control experts, scientists, and others whose decisions are related to rule compliance.

Second, our discussion assumes that a general model of corporate social control should include *both* the benefits and costs of offending. In the past, deterrence models have considered only the costs of offending, and only a select few of those possible costs (formal legal sanctions). A more general and fully specified rational choice model of corporate crime should incorporate the benefits of offending and the costs corporations must absorb when they comply with rules and regulations.

Costs and Benefits of Corporate Crime

There are several different kinds of costs that are included in our rational choice model of corporate crime. One type of cost is the *perceived certainty and severity of formal sanctions*. These are the "typical" deterrence variables. The perceived certainty of formal punishment reflects would-be offenders' estimation of the likelihood of different legal sanctions should they commit a proscribed behavior. Since previous deterrence research has shown that self-referenced measures of formal sanction threats (what is the chance that *you* would be caught/arrested/punished) are a more potent source of deterrence than a generalized measure (Jensen et al. 1978; Paternoster 1987), the most appropriate indicator of the perceived certainty of sanction threat would come from the individual decision maker involved.

This underscores our belief that any rational choice model of corporate crime should focus on the individual rather than the organization. We contend that decision makers are influenced more by what they believe to be the risk and benefits of noncompliance to themselves than to the organization. That is, both risks and benefits are more salient when the individual decision maker is *personally at risk.*

The perceived severity of punishment would reflect the estimated cost (to the individual) should the pertinent sanction be imposed. In the past, this concept has been operationalized in terms of "how much of a problem would it be if you (were arrested)?" (Grasmick and Bryjak 1980). Comparable operationalizations could be employed for the possible sanctions that may be imposed on corporate decision makers (fines, arrest, and prison).[7]

In addition to perceived formal sanction threats, our rational choice model of corporate crime includes a measure of *perceived informal sanctions.* Previous deterrence research with "street crimes" has consistently demonstrated that the possibility of informal costs is far more effective in inhibiting offending that formal sanction threats (Paternoster 1987). Ethnographic and survey research of corporate offending has also suggested the potency of informal sanctions (Fisse and Braithwaite 1983; Benson 1984; Kagan and Scholz 1984; Simpson 1992). Informal sanctions would include such things as negative publicity for the corporation; a perceived loss of the company's "good name" and reputation; the possibility that colleagues, close friends, or family would devalue and disapprove of the individual. Collectively, these informal sanctions constitute a kind of social censure for would-be offenders, and are included in what Braithwaite (1989) has recently referred to as "shame." Separate measures of the perceived certainty and severity of different types of informal sanctions could be constructed. These measures would refer to the perception of informal costs that may accrue to the individual as a result of noncompliance to the rules and regulations binding on the corporation. The important point is that previous constructions of corporate crime deterrence models have neglected to consider the possibility of perceived informal costs. To the extent that these costs are effective in inhibiting corporate crime, such models are misspecified.

A consideration of formal and informal sanctions does not, however, exhaust the kinds of costs that may accrue to corporate offenders. Another potent inhibition for would-be offenders is the imposition of sanctions by oneself. Persons may refrain from offending not because they fear the social reaction to their behavior, but because they wish to avoid losing self-respect in their own eyes. Braithwaite (1989) has suggested that such self-imposed sanctions may be a potent source of social control, a suggestion given some credence by the recent deterrence research of Williams and Hawkins (1989) and Grasmick and Bursik (1990). Another element in our rational choice model of corporate crime, then, would include the perceived certainty and severity of a *loss of self-respect* for breaking rules.

Our rational choice model of corporate offending also includes the *perceived costs of rule compliance* and the *perceived benefits of rule violation*. These factors are included because would-be offenders' decisions are doubtlessly affected by their estimate of the expense of not violating the law and the perceived advantages they would reap from noncompliance. The corporate crime literature has repeatedly suggested that many corporate crimes are committed not in direct anticipation of gain but to avoid what is perceived to be an avoidable expense of compliance. Some regulations may be perceived as simply too costly for some corporations to abide by, and they are subsequently violated. In addition, offenders consider the direct benefits of violating the law. This is an important instrumental consideration that has unfortunately been absent from most deterrence models (for exceptions, see Piliavin et al. 1986 and Klepper and Nagin 1989a,b). Some of the perceived benefits of corporate noncompliance include market control, higher prices, greater worker productivity, lower cost per commodity unit, and reduced safety expenses.

Moral Beliefs and Perceived Legitimacy as Inhibitions on Crime

Supplementing the formal and informal costs of punishment in our rational choice model of corporate crime are considerations of moral belief and the perceived legitimacy of the law. *Moral beliefs* refer to the extent to which persons perceive a particular criminal act to be morally offensive. It is presumed that those who view an act with opprobrium will be less likely to commit the offense than those who are more morally tolerant. In criminological research with ordinary street crimes, moral inhibitions have consistently been found to be strong correlates of offending (Paternoster 1987; Grasmick and Green 1980, 1981), and there is no reason not to hypothesize that would-be corporate offenders are also inhibited by their moral evaluations of possibly criminal actions.

Two things should be emphasized here. First, moral beliefs constitute a noninstrumental consideration for a would-be offender's decision to commit a crime. Those with strong moral inhibitions are predicted to refrain from committing a particular offense no matter what the formal or informal costs or the perceived benefits of offending. Second, our reference to moral beliefs in the context of corporate crime does not necessarily refer to an organized and fully developed ethical system that corporate employees develop and import into their working environment. Rather, we suggest that those who work in corporations develop moral rules about the acceptability of *particular* conduct within a *particular* context. These moral rules will change somewhat depending upon the specific situation. Our notion of contextually anchored moral rules is comparable to Jackall's (1988:6) notion of the "rules-in-use" employed by corporate managers:

> What matters on a day-to-day basis are the moral rules-in-use fashioned within the personal and structural constraints of one's organization. As it happens, these rules may vary sharply depending on various factors, such as proximity to the market, line or staff responsibilities, or one's position in a hierarchy. Actual organizational moralities are thus contextual, situational, highly specific, and, most often, unarticulated.

To capture or measure a decision maker's rules-in-use, then, would require the stipulation of a contextually specific and relevant situation in which an offense is contemplated.

Moral beliefs or moral rules-in-use, are related to but conceptually distinct from the notion of a *perceived sense of the legitimacy of the rules and rule enforcers.* We argue that corporate decision makers will be less inclined to comply with rules and regulations that they perceive as unreasonable or capricious (Kagan and Scholz 1984:75). Kagan and Scholz have also suggested that an important consideration for businesspersons is the degree to which they are treated with respect and dignity by those who would regulate them. Furthermore, in an extensive empirical study of the etiology of rule compliance, Tyler (1990) found that people comply with rules because in large measure they believe them to be proper, independent of any instrumental concerns. He also noted that rules are more likely to be obeyed when people perceive them to be fairly administered and when they feel that they have been treated with respect and dignity. This would suggest that an important variable in any rational choice model of corporate offending would be the degree to which decision makers perceived the rules to be rational, reasonable, and perceive themselves to be fairly treated.

Characteristics of the Criminal Event

The preceding paragraphs have suggested that would-be corporate offenders are influenced by the costs and benefits of rule compliance (both formal and informal), the moral implications of their behavior, and perceptions of legitimacy and respect. In addition to these concerns, the decision not to comply with a law or business regulation is doubtlessly also affected by various situational and contextual factors.

One of the things that makes corporate crime distinct from other crimes is the context of the criminal event. Offenders are situated within formal organizations that are characterized by distinct cultures and structural features — *the internal organization of the firm*. The organizations themselves operate within and attempt to influence *external environments* comprising political, economic, and cultural forces (Fligstein 1987). Both can affect corporate offender motivations and crime opportunities (Coleman 1987).

Empirical research has identified a number of factors that are correlated with corporate offending (see Yeager 1986; Finney and Lesieur 1982 for summaries of this literature). However, these factors vary by organizational context considerably in their respective influences on the decision to commit corporate crime. For instance, unanticipated or costly changes in legal regulations, coupled with managerial cost-reduction policies, may produce greater pressure to offend in marginally profitable companies than in firms that can more easily absorb the increased costs of compliance. Larger firms may be more able to control their environments (say, through lobbying efforts or aggressive competitive practices) than smaller firms, thus reducing compliance costs and pressures to offend. On the other hand, the greater autonomy and invisibility that accompanies firm size and diversification may offer criminals greater protection from discovery and sanction. Thus, threats to profitability alone are not sufficient to cause managers across firms, or even the majority of managers within a firm, to violate the law (Simpson 1986). Nor are factors like business type (Sonnenfeld and Lawrence 1978), the degree of firm delegation (Braithwaite 1978), division strength (Ross 1980), scarce economic environments (Staw and Szwajkowski 1975), or "criminogenic cultures" (Sutherland 1949; Geis 1967; Zey-Ferrell and Ferrell, Weaver, and Ferrell 1979) satisfactory as causal mechanisms. Instead, the crime process is best understood as developmental and contingent in nature.

> Not only does [criminal] . . . action involve a temporal sequence, but as commonly put, one thing leads to another; events in the sequence are causally associated or interlinked. Viewed retrospectively, such links involve numerous situational contingencies. Strategically important steps in the process won't be taken *unless* prior pressures exist or potential controls are inoperative; illegal solutions to problems won't be perceived as feasible *unless* the problem cannot be solved in other ways or only in significantly less profitable ways. (Finney and Lesieur 1982:260, emphasis in original)

Managers located in different structural positions within the firm (hierarchial or task-specific) will sift through a set of distinct contingencies, progressively narrowing the decision choice of crime or noncrime. Thus, situational and contextual factors may be specified in general and manager-specific terms.

Finally, since criminological research has consistently shown that the best predictor of future offending is past offending, we include the latter in our model. Some persons within business organizations, because of personal attributes that are consistent over time or the unique pressures and opportunities of their position, may be generally inclined to noncompliance with rules and regulations. We expect some stability and consistency in offending, therefore, above and beyond what is explained by the other exogenous variables in the model.

In sum, we are offering a rational choice model of corporate crime that includes the following as possible explanatory variables:

1. Perceived certainty/severity of formal legal sanctions
2. Perceived certainty/severity of informal sanctions
3. Perceived certainty/severity of loss of self-respect
4. Perceived cost of rule compliance
5. Perceived benefits of noncompliance
6. Moral inhibitions
7. Perceived sense of legitimacy/fairness
8. Characteristics of the criminal event
9. Prior offending by the person

We schematically show these possible explanatory factors in figure 2.1. It can be seen that we are suggesting a more general model of the social control of corporate crime than has previously been described and empirically tested.

Specifying the Relationships among the Explanatory Variables

Our discussion to this point has suggested that the decision to commit corporate crime is affected by numerous considerations — the formal and informal costs and benefits of offending, moral considerations and perceptions of legitimacy, and the context within which the organization operates. The question to address now is the process through which these explanatory variables affect would-be offenders' decision to commit a corporate crime. There are two competing hypotheses, both of which are a priori plausible.

The first of these hypotheses states that the effect of formal sanctions, informal sanctions, and moral considerations are additive and independent. Blake and Davis (1964:477–81) for example, describe five sources

FIGURE 2.1
A General Rational Choice Model of Corporate Crime

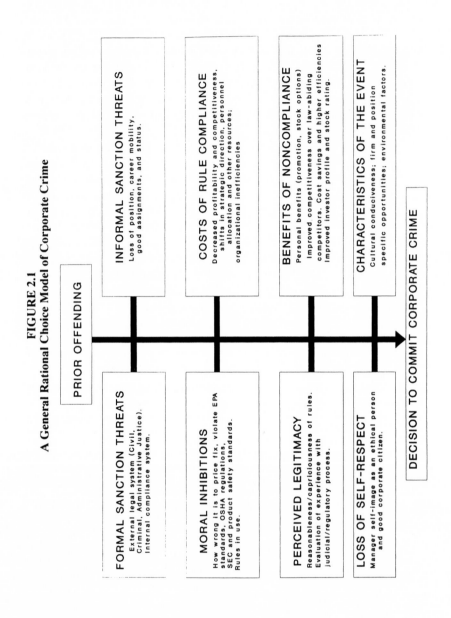

of social control: (1) internalization of norms (moral beliefs), (2) desire for social approval (informal sanctions), (3) anticipation of formal punishment (legal sanctions), (4) anticipation of nonreward (failure to achieve the benefits of deviance, and (5) lack of opportunity. Blake and Davis's position is that each of these has a distinct effect on the inclination to commit a deviant act, that is, the effect of one source of social control does not depend upon the level of any other. This theoretical position hypothesizes an additive effect for each explanatory variable. For example, the effect of perceived formal sanction threats is presumed to produce the same amount of social control regardless of the level of moral beliefs or informal sanctions.

An alterative, second hypothesis about the effect of different sources of social control would predict that the effect of one source of the inclination to commit an offense is related to the level of another source. Contrary to the above, then, this alternative hypothesis suggests a multiplicative or interactive effect. A specific example of one derivation of this hypothesis can be found in the work of Talcott Parsons. In *The Structure of Social Action* (1937:402–3), Parsons suggests that the "principal basis" of social control is an internalization of the norms. In this hypothesis, those who have strong moral inhibitions are thought to conform to the requirements of rules no matter what the costs or consequences. For such morally inhibited persons, there is no cost-benefit analysis in the contemplation of conformity, and instrumental considerations are irrelevant. For those unbound by moral inhibitions, however, instrumental factors are highly salient and may be the only source of conformity. Parsons's hypothesis would predict, then, that formal sanction threats are irrelevant for those with strong moral beliefs but highly significant for those with weak moral beliefs.

A related, but slightly different, interactive effect has recently been suggested by Williams and Hawkins (1986). They argue that formal legal sanctions deter best when they are complemented by informal costs, such as social censure and a loss of material opportunities. Where such possible informal costs are absent, they contend, the law cannot effectively control behavior. Their hypothesis, then, is that there is an interaction between formal and informal sanctions; formal sanctions deter only at high levels of informal sanctions.

The empirical literature with respect to these two competing hypotheses is inconsistent, with some studies indicating an interactive effect between different sources of social control (Silberman 1976; Teevan 1976) and others revealing an independent, additive effect (Grasmick and McLaughlin 1978; Grasmick and Green 1981; Nagin and Paternoster 1991).

It is also conceivable that both hypotheses may be correct. For example, it may be that instrumental concerns are irrelevant within the subgroup effectively restrained by moral inhibitions. For those with weaker moral inhibitions, however, the effect of formal and informal sanction costs may be additive. We offer no judgment as to whether or not the rational choice model of corporate crime sketched out here presumes additive or interactive effects. We simply note the alternative specifications and suggest that the exploration and resolution of these issues must await empirical research conducted on the theoretical model we are suggesting here.

Testing the Rational Choice Model of Corporate Crime

At this point we would like to suggest one way to empirically test our proposed rational choice model of corporate crime. In conducting the empirical test, two features must be kept in mind: (1) we contend that our model is relevant to decision makers at all levels in the corporate organizational hierarchy (executives, marketing managers, quality control experts, factory and plant managers, scientists), (2) we contend that, at the outset at least, offense-specific models of corporate crime must be constructed and tested. This means that researchers should first conduct empirical tests of different variants of corporate crime such as price fixing, toxic dumping, noncompliance with safety regulations, and so forth. Given the breadth of offending possibilities, it may make sense to test the model within particular categories of crime (e.g., financial, environmental, antitrust, manufacturing, labor, and administrative).[8] If it is empirically determined that the significant explanatory variables are invariant over offense types, a more general rational choice model of corporate crime could begin to be constructed. With the understanding that empirical research should be conducted with different kinds of corporate decision makers within the context of particular corporate crimes, we can now more specifically detail a research methodology.

In the past, researchers testing both deterrence and rational choice theories of crime have used survey methodologies. In this survey research, respondents were asked to estimate (among other things) the certainty and severity of formal punishment if they committed (or were arrested for) a particular offense. An example of such a query is as follows: "How likely is it that you would be arrested if you committed 'crime x'?" These questions were asked within the structure of a cross-sectional or panel research design. For the past few years, however, panel survey designs have been recommended by those conducting such research because it was believed that only with longitudinal data could researchers hope to control for the temporal order of sanction and criminal offending variables. It was thought that with panel designs, deterrent and other effects could be estimated by the relationship between explanatory variables measured at one time (T_1) and subsequent self-reported offending (T_{t-1}).

Recent critics of panel designs in social control research have made two critical observations, however. First, it was observed that general perceptual questions about the costs and benefits of crime fail to specify the precise context of the offense (Klepper and Nagin 1989b). That is, respondents have been asked very general questions that require them to imagine the specific circumstances they would confront when contemplating the commission of an offense. If the imagined circumstances under which the responses are given are different from those existing at the time that the decision to offend is actually made, however, these perceptions are likely to be measured with substantial error and any estimated structural effects will be attenuated. It has been argued (Klepper and Nagin 1989b), therefore, that deterrence researchers should supply respondents with contextually specific situations for them to consider before querying them about the perceived costs and benefits of offending.

Second, critics have contended that longitudinal data offer no better a solution to the problem of temporal order than the cross-sectional designs they replaced (Klepper and Nagin 1989b; Grasmick and Bursik 1990). It was observed that if people are affected by perceptions of the costs and benefits of offending, what is pertinent for them is the perception of those costs and benefits *at the time* that they are contemplating offending. This means that the perceptions ⟶ behavior relationship should be measured as an *instantaneous* one rather than the lagged relationship implicit in either cross-sectional or panel research (Grasmick and Bursik 1990).

In reviewing these criticisms of past social control and deterrence research, it is clear that future studies should measure the instantaneous perceptions ⟶ behavior relationship, and the measurement of perceptions should specify important features of the context within which an offense may occur. We suggest that empirical tests of our rational choice model of corporate crime should include hypothetical offending scenarios. These scenarios would describe for our subject-decision makers hypothetical, but contextually specific, situations involving the possible commission of a corporate crime. Important dimensions of the situation would be experimentally manipulated in order to estimate the effect that such situational factors have on inclinations to offend. The following is one example of the kind of hypothetical offending scenario we have in mind.

John Jones is emissions control supervisor at Steelcorp—net income in 1990 was 400 million (down 100 million from the prior year). The firm, like others in its product market, is losing ground to foreign competitors. The EPA has recently announced new emission standards for the industry that will go into effect at the start of the new fiscal year — estimated yearly cost to Steelcorp is 40 million dollars. John Jones orders his managers to reduce emissions to one-fourth of the EPA requirements by the new fiscal year.

This scenario depicts several factors that can influence corporate offense decisions: manager position and responsibility; law type (EPA); economic constraints both internal and external to the firm; and the cost of compliance. We also allow the compliance decision to vary by degree.[9]

As noted earlier, these scenarios should be crime- and manager-specific in order to allow for different exogenous variables to influence offense decisions. We also believe that exogenous variables may be interactive at one level but not at others. For instance, middle managers may be more vulnerable to the formal costs of both legal and organizational sanctions because they are required to implement rather than determine policy. However, top managers may perceive greater informal threats if legally processed than middle managers, as they have much more at stake (reputation, job rewards, and so on).

In our proposed methodology, respondents would review this scenario and respond to queries regarding their estimate of the perceived costs and benefits of offending and their beliefs about legitimacy and felt moral condemnation of the hypothetical act under the specific conditions described in the scenario. In this way, we would have contextually specific measures of key exogenous variables.

Importantly, respondents would also be asked to estimate the probability that they would do the same thing as the person described in the scenario under the same set of conditions. The outcome or dependent variable would, then, not be self-reported actual behavior, but self-reported *intentions* to offend.[10] The collected data would reflect each respondent's estimate of the costs and benefits and moral beliefs for the described act and the likelihood that they would commit the act under the described conditions. These data would both capture the instantaneous nature of the perceptions → behavior relationship and would ensure the measurement of contextually specific estimates of independent variables. In addition, we will be able to estimate the effect of experimentally manipulated scenario conditions on self-reported intentions to offend.

A scenario approach comparable to the one suggested here has been employed in recent deterrence research with much success. Klepper and Nagin (1989a,b) and Thurman (1989) both employed hypothetical scenarios in their research on deterrence and tax compliance. Grasmick and Bursik (1990) persuasively argued for and employed behavioral intentions in their recent study of adult offending. Although this approach has not been employed in studies of corporate crime control to date, we believe that the use of hypothetical offending scenarios will offer a very useful strategy in testing both the rational choice model of corporate crime proposed here, and other substantively interesting questions that pertain to the social control of corporate criminals.

Conclusion

It has often been presumed that, due to the risk-aversive nature of businesspersons and the instrumental nature of the types of crimes that they have the opportunity to commit in their business roles, corporate crime would be the quintessential deterrable offense. Perceptions of the certainty and severity of formal legal sanctions should, therefore, inhibit corporate employees from committing business crimes. In the most rigorous empirical test of this hypothesis to date, however, formal sanction threats were found to be unrelated to the frequency of rule violations. In fact, the authors of this study concluded that a formal deterrence model was a "stark failure" (Braithwaite and Makkai 1991:29).

In trying to understand this seeming anomaly, we have suggested in this chapter that a strictly deterrence model of corporate crime, that is, one that includes only formal sanction variables, is incomplete. We have suggested that corporate offending could best be understood with a more general model of social control and have suggested the contours of just such a model.

In constructing this preliminary model of corporate crime, we have drawn upon the rational choice perspective. Our proposed rational choice model of corporate crime includes a broad range of both utilitarian (instrumental) and nonutilitarian (moral) sources of social control. More specifically, our model contains perceived formal sanction threats, perceptions of diverse forms of informal sanctions such as social censure, loss of professional status and reputation, a perceived loss of self-respect, the perceived benefits of both rule compliance and noncompliance, moral inhibitions, and characteristics of the criminal event itself. In describing the conceptualization of our model, we have stressed the idea that it is a social-psychological model of corporate crime control. That is, it is premised on the perceptions that decision makers have about the personal costs and benefits of their behavior and its possible moral implications.

We also indicate that the specific elements of the model may vary for different decision makers within the corporate structure and, therefore, for different types of corporate crimes. We believe that this preliminary model is more fully specified, and therefore more theoretically accurate, than previous models of corporate crime.[11]

In addition, we have offered one possible research strategy for empirically testing our proposed theoretical model. We have emphasized the fact that tests of our model must be conducted at the individual level of analysis since it is predicated upon subjective, that is perceptual, under-standings of utilities, disutilities, and moral positions. Influenced by re-cent critiques of traditional cross-sectional and panel research designs we have proposed a hybrid approach that includes the use of hypothetical offending scenarios supplemented with survey-type questions. Important contextual dimensions of the criminal event would be deliberately ma-nipulated in these scenarios, and would provide a specific referent for queries regarding the certainty and severity of sanctions. With these sce-narios, researchers would be able to examine the instantaneous relation-ship between key theoretical variables and self-reported intentions to commit a corporate offense.

Recent research within the deterrence tradition has indicated that hypo-thetical scenarios may be an effective research strategy. We believe that both our proposed theoretical model and research design will enable re-searchers to address substantively interesting and pragmatically important issues regarding the social control of corporate crime. To the extent that scenarios demonstrate that corporate personnel, like their conventional offending counterparts, are constrained more by informal than formal sanctions, control strategies that promote internal systems of compliance and self-regulation make sense—particularly if crime benefits are per-ceived as organizationally bestowed, that is, promotions, status, and perks. Yet, until the model is fully tested, policy recommendations are premature.

Notes

1. A traditional deterrence model assumes that formal sanction risk and consequence will inhibit involvement in illegal activity. Specifically, fear of legal sanctions is thought to deter individuals from criminal/delinquent participation.
2. Celerity of punishment, although discussed in the deterrence literature, is not considered here. Its effects are ambiguous theoretically and unsupported empiri-cally (Gibbs 1975; Simpson and Koper 1991).
3. White-collar crime is defined by Sutherland (1949:9) as "crime committed by a person of respectability and high social status in the course of his occupation." Corporate crime, as a subtype of white-collar crime, is "any act committed by corporations that is punished by the state, regardless of whether it is punished under administrative, civil, or criminal law" (Clinard and Yeager 1980:16). In the latter, criminal actors include individual decision makers (typically corporate man-agers) and organizations that violate the law in the pursuit of corporate objectives.
4. See Paternoster (1987) for a review of these findings.
5. We wish to be clear about this claim. There are a number of deterrence studies that might be deemed white-collar or corporate in accordance with Sutherland or Clinard and Yeager's definitions (see, e.g., Hollinger and Clark 1983; Jesilow, Geis, and O'Brien 1986; Lewis-Beck and Alford 1980; Block, Nold, and Sidak 1981; Simpson and Koper 1991; Stotland, Britnall, L'heureux, and Ashmore 1980). However, none of these studies exclusively focus on the *perceptions* of sanction threat by

managers/executives whose primary responsibility is to pursue organizational objectives. In some cases, objective sanction risk is assessed; in others, the organization rather than the individual is examined for deterrent effects.

6. The belief that the commission of a crime involves a rational decision does not, however, imply the notion that would-be offenders are strictly rational calculators, that is, that they are utility maximizers. Rational choice theorists recognize that humans are limited in the amount and kind of information they are able to process, the amount of information they are able to store, and in how the information gets processed and interpreted. This is the notion of bounded or minimal rationality (Simon 1957; Cherniak 1986).

7. We recognize that organizations may be sanctioned for the action of their agents, but argue that even this aggregate level punishment is salient to individuals primarily in terms of how they are personally affected by it.

8. Simpson (1986), however, cautions against the construction of premature crime typologies. Her analysis of corporate antitrust offending demonstrates significant within-group variation in the underlying factors associated with price-fixing, price discrimination, advertising violations, and illegal tying arrangements.

9. Partial compliance with regulations is possible with certain types of crime, for example, EPA standards, OSHA standards, but not others (price-fixing or stock fraud). Such differences underlie our rationale for constructing crime-specific rational choice models of corporate crime.

10. An objection may be raised here that intentions to offend may be a poor dependent variable because it does not measure actual behavior. The use of behavioral intentions, however, has a long and successful history in social psychology (see Fishbein and Ajzen 1975), by cognitive psychologists interested in judgments under uncertainty (Kahneman et al. 1982; Nisbett and Ross 1980), and recent deterrence research (Klepper and Nagin 1989a,b; Grasmick and Bursik 1990).

11. We acknowledge that our model may be overly reductionist. For instance, it is difficult to assess how individuals evaluate and respond to organizational costs and benefits that do not directly affect them, but matter nonetheless (e.g., organizational loyalty). Rational choice theory, as currently developed, offers little direction for sorting out and calibrating such factors.

Bibliography

Benson, Michael L. 1984. "The fall from grace." *Criminology* 22:573–93.

Blake, Judith, & Davis, Kenneth. 1964. "Norms, values and sanctions." In R. Faris (Ed.), *Handbook of modern sociology* (456–84). Chicago: Rand McNally.

Block, Michael K., Nold, Frederick C., & Sidak, Joseph G. 1981. "The deterrent effect of antitrust enforcement." *Journal of Political Economy* 89:429–45.

Braithwaite, John. 1978. "Corporate crime and the internalization of capital." Unpublished manuscript, Australia Institute of Criminology, Canberra.

———. 1989. *Crime, shame and reintegration.* Cambridge: Oxford University Press.

Braithwaite, John, & Geis, Gilbert. 1982. "On theory and action for corporate crime control. *Crime and Delinquency* 28:292–314.

Braithwaite, John, & Makkai, Toni. 1991. "Testing an expected utility model of corporate deterrence." *Law and Society Review* 25:7–39.

Chambliss, William J. 1967. "Types of deviance and the effectiveness of legal sanctions." *Wisconsin Law Review* (Summer) :705–19.

Cherniak, Christopher. 1986. *Minimal rationality.* Cambridge, MA: MIT Press.

Clarke, Ronald V., & Cornish, Derek B. "Modeling offenders' decisions." In M. Tonry & N. Morris (Eds.), *Crime and justice* (Vol. 6, 147–85). Chicago: University of Chicago Press 1985 .

Clinard, Marshall B., & Yeager, Peter C. 1980. *Corporate crime.* New York: The Free Press.

Coffee, John C. 1980. "A nonChicago view of the economics of criminal sanctions." *American Criminal Law Review* 17:419–76.

Coleman, James William. 1987. "Toward an integrated theory of white-collar crime." *American Journal of Sociology* 93:406–39.

Cornish, Derek B., & Clarke, Ronald V. 1986. *The reasoning criminal.* New York: Springer-Verlag.

Cullen, Francis T., & Dubeck, Paula J. 1985. "The myth of corporate immunity to deterrence." *Federal Probation* 49:3–9.

Cullen, Francis T., Mathers, R., Clark, G., & Cullen, J.B. 1983. "Public support for punishing white-collar crime." *Journal of Criminal Justice* 2:481–93.

Finney, Henry C., & Lesieur, Henry P. 1982. "A contingency theory of organizational crime." In S.B. Bacharach (Ed.), *Research in the Sociology of Organizations* (Vol. 1, 255–99). Greenwich, CT: JAI Press.

Fishbein, Martin, & Ajzen, Icek. 1975. *Belief, attitudes, intention and behavior.* New York: Addison-Wesley.

Fisse, Brent, & Braithwaite, John. 1983. *The impact of publicity on corporate offenders.* Albany, NY: State University of New York Press.

Fligstein, Neil. 1987. "The intraorganizational power struggle." *American Sociological Review* 52:44–58.

Frank, James, Cullen, Francis T., Travis, Lawrence F., III, & Borntrager, John L. 1989. "Sanctioning corporate crime." *American Journal of Criminal Justice* 13:139–69.

Gandossy, Robert P. 1985. *Bad business: The OPM scandal and the seduction of the establishment.* New York: Basic Books.

Geis, Gilbert. 1967. "White collar crime: The heavy electrical equipment antitrust cases of 1961." In M.B. Clinard & R. Quinney (Eds.), *Criminal behavior systems: A typology* (140–51). New York: Holt, Rinehart, & Winston.

Gibbs, Jack P. 1975. *Crime, punishment and deterrence.* New York: Elsevier.

Grasmick, Harold G., & Bryjak, George J. 1980. "The deterrent effect of perceived severity of punishment." *Social Forces* 59:471–91.

Grasmick, Harold G., & Bursik, Robert J. 1990. "Conscience, significant others, and rational choice: Extending the deterrence model." *Law and Society Review* 24:837–61.

Grasmick, Harold G., & Green, Donald. 1980. "Legal punishment, social disapproval and internalization as inhibitors of illegal behavior." *Journal of Criminal Law and Criminology* 71:325–35.

———. 1981. "Deterrence and the morally committed." *Sociological Quarterly* 22:1–14.

Grasmick, Harold G., & McLaughlin, Steven D. 1978. "Deterrence and social control: Comment on Silberman." *American Sociological Review* 43:272–77.

Hollinger, Richard C., & Clark, John P. 1983. "Deterrence in the workplace." *Social Forces* 62:388–418.

Jackall, Robert. 1988. *Moral mazes: The world of corporate managers.* New York: Oxford University Press.

Jensen, Gary F., Erickson, Maynard L., & Gibbs, Jack P. 1978. "Perceived risk of punishment and self-reported delinquency." *Social Forces* 57:57–78.

Jesilow, Paul, Geis, Gilbert, & O'Brien, Mary Jane. 1986. "Experimental evidence that publicity has no effect in suppressing auto repair fraud." *Sociology and Social Research* 70:222–23.

Kadish, Sanford H. 1977. "The use of criminal sanctions in the enforcement of economic regulations." In G. Geis & R.F. Meier, (Eds.), *White-collar crime* (296–317). New York: The Free Press.

Kagan, Robert A., & Scholz, John T. 1984. "The 'criminology of the corporation' and regulatory enforcement strategies." In K. Hawkins & J.M. Thomas (Eds.), *Enforcing Regulation* (67–95). Boston: Kluwer-Nijhoff.

Kahneman, Daniel, Slovic, Paul, & Tversky, Amos. 1982. *Judgment under uncertainty: Hueristics and biases.* Cambridge: Cambridge University Press.

Klepper, Steven, & Nagin, Daniel. 1989a. "Tax compliance and perceptions of the risks of detection and criminal prosecution." *Law and Society Review* 23:209–40.

———. 1989b. "The deterrent effect of perceived certainty and severity of punishment revisited." *Criminology* 27:721–46.

Lewis-Beck, Michael S., & Alford, John R. "Can government regulate safety?" *American Political Science Review* (1980):746.

Nagin, Daniel S., & Paternoster, Raymond. 1991. "The preventive effects of the perceived risk of arrest: Testing an expanded conception of deterrence." *Criminology* 29:561–87.

Nisbett, Richard, & Ross, Lee. 1980. *Human inference: Strategies and shortcomings of social judgment.* Englewood Cliffs, NJ: Prentice-Hall.

Parsons, Talcott. 1937. *The structure of social action.* New York: McGraw-Hill.

Paternoster, Raymond. 1987. "The deterrent effect of the perceived certainty and severity of punishment." *Justice Quarterly* 4:173–217.

Piliavin, Irving, Gartner, Rosemary, Thorton, Craig, & Matsueda, Ross. 1986. "Crime, deterrence and rational choice." *American Sociological Review* 51:101–19.

Rickleffs, R. 1983. "Public gives executives low marks for honesty and ethical standards." *Wall Street Journal* (November):31.

Ross, Irwin. 1980. "Illegal corporate behavior: Big companies?" *Fortune* (December):57–61.

Saltzman, Linda, Paternoster, Raymond, Waldo, Gordon P., & Chiricos, Theodore G. 1982. "Deterrent and experimental effects." *Journal of Research in Crime and Delinquency* 19:172–89.

Schlegel, Kip. 1990. *Just deserts for corporate criminals.* Boston: Northeastern University Press.

Silberman, Matthew. 1976. "Toward a theory of criminal deterrence." *American Sociological Review* 41:442–61.

Simon, Herbert. 1957. *Models of man.* New York: John Wiley.

Simpson, Sally S. 1986. "The decomposition of antitrust." *American Sociological Review* 51:859–75.

———. (1992). "Corporate crime deterrence and corporate control policies." In K. Schlegel & D. Weisburd (Eds.), *White-Collar Crime Reconsidered* (289–308). Boston: Northeastern University Press.

Simpson, Sally S., & Koper, Christopher C. 1992, "Deterring corporate crime." *Criminology* 30:347–75.

Sonnenfeld, Jeffrey, & Lawrence, Paul R. 1978. "Why do companies succumb to price-fixing?" *Harvard Business Review* 56:145–57.

Staw, Barry N., & Szawajkowski, Eugene. 1975. "The scarcity-munificence component of organizational acts." *Administrative Science Quarterly* 20:245–354.

Stotland, Ezra, Britnall, Michael, L'heureux, Andre, & Ashmore, Eva. 1980. "Do convictions deter home repair fraud?" In G. Geis & E. Stotland (Eds.), *White-collar crime: Theory and research* (252–65). Beverly Hills, CA: Sage.

Sutherland, Edwin. 1949. *White-collar crime.* New York: The Dryden Press.

Teeven, James J. 1976. "Subjective perception of deterrence (cont'd)." *Journal of Research in Crime and Delinquency* 13:155–60.

Thurman, Quint C. 1989. "General prevention of tax evasion: A factorial survey approach." *Journal of Quantitative Criminology* 5:127–46.

Tittle, Charles R. 1980. *Sanctions and social deviance.* New York: Praeger Press.

Tyler, Tom R. 1990. *Why people obey the law.* New Haven: Yale University Press.

United States Sentencing Commission. 1991, November. *Guidelines manual* (Chap. 8).

Williams, Kirk R.., & Hawkins, Richard. 1989. "The meaning of arrest for wife assault." *Criminology* 27:163–81.

———. 1986. "Perceptual research on general deterrence: A critical overview." *Law and Society Review* 20:545–72.

Yeager, Peter C. 1986. "Analyzing corporate offenses." In J.E. Post (Ed.), *Research in Corporate Social Performance and Policy* (Vol. 8, 93–120). Greenwich, CT: JAI Press.

Zey-Ferrell, Mary K., Weaver, Mark, & Ferrell, O.C. 1982. "Predicting unethical behavior among marketing practitioners." *Human Relations* 32:557–69.

3

Drivers Who Drink and Rational Choice: Random Breath Testing and the Process of Deterrence

Ross Homel

On 17 December 1982, random breath testing (RBT) was introduced in New South Wales (NSW). Under RBT, large numbers of motorists are pulled over at random by police and required to take a preliminary breath test, even if they are in no way suspected of having committed an offense or been involved in an accident. Thus RBT should be sharply distinguished from the American use of sobriety checkpoints, in which police must have evidence of alcohol consumption before they can require a test (Voas 1988). The RBT law was very extensively advertised and vigorously enforced, with about a million tests being given in the first year to a licensed driving population of 3 million. In later years, police improved on this ratio of 1:3. Indeed, RBT in NSW must rank as one of the best enforced and most widely publicized laws ever enacted (Homel 1990a). It is properly understood not as a "police crackdown" or "blitz," which would generally imply a "backoff" after a period of intense police activity generating many arrests (Sherman 1990), but as an entirely new form of ongoing law enforcement.

RBT was a radical departure from previous drink-driving enforcement campaigns in NSW, since it embodies a preventive, general deterrent philosophy, in contrast to the traditional approach emphasizing the detection and punishment of offenders. Very few of those tested using RBT are arrested for drinking and driving (the arrest rate is typically about 0.4%), but this is not regarded as a problem, since the aim is to influence the behavior of *potential* offenders, not to arrest offenders after the event. RBT as a drink-driving countermeasure also stands in sharp contrast to the approach based on treatment of apprehended offenders, which was seen as a progressive countermeasure in Australia and other countries in the late 1960s and early 1970s. The problem of alcohol-related road crashes is laid not at the door of the problem drinker, the "juvenile delinquent of traffic," but at the door of Everyman, "rational, socially responsible, given to occasional and human lapses of conduct but basically law-abiding, controllable and controlling, and responsive to norms of social cooperation and control" (Gusfield 1981a: 99–100).

The results of the new approach were, on the face of it, dramatic. There was an instantaneous 22% decline in total fatal crashes, and a drop of about 36% in alcohol-related fatal crashes, relative to the previous 3 years (Homel, Carseldine, and Kearns 1988). Although these are large declines in terms of what would be expected from experience with drink-driving laws around the world (Ross 1982), what really distinguishes RBT in NSW from new laws or police crackdowns elsewhere is that the effects appear to have been sustained for nearly 10 years, with only occasional signs of a diminution in effectiveness.[1] This can be clearly seen from figure 3.1, which shows trends in all fatal crashes in NSW for each day from 1 July 1975 to 30 June 1991.

A CUSUM is a series of numbers that are the cumulative sum of the differences between an observed series and a corresponding expected series (in this case the mean number of daily fatal crashes for the 7.5 years prior to the law). Thus the key to interpreting figure 3.1 is to regard the number below the zero (pre-RBT) line as the "accumulated benefit" due to RBT at any time after its introduction. For example, by mid-1991 there were more than 2000 fatal crashes fewer than would have been expected if the pre-RBT trend had been maintained. If the CUSUM graph maintains a downward slope (which it does in the figure), a benefit is still being derived from RBT, in comparison with the average crash level that would have prevailed if RBT had not been introduced.

Further evidence is required before one can accept the proposition that RBT actually *caused* all or some of the observed decline in crashes, despite the use of the term *benefit* in the interpretation of figure 3.1. Time series and other statistical analyses of crash data (e.g., Barnes 1988; Homel 1992; Homel, Carseldine & Kearns 1988; Kearns & Goldsmith 1984; Thomson & Mavroleftou 1984) do tend to confirm that RBT did indeed have a substantial causal impact, although the precise size of the effect might be disputed. However, for present purposes, it is sufficient to know that RBT changed behaviors to a marked extent in the target population.

Given this causal impact, and given that RBT is based explicitly on the

FIGURE 3.1

Cumulative sum graph showing daily fatal crashes in NSW from 1 July 1975 to 30 June 1991 (based on data provided by the Road Safety Bureau, Roads and Traffic Authority of NSW).

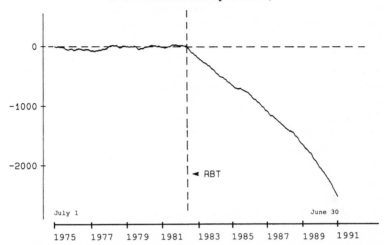

principles of general deterrence and has been vigorously implemented and publicized for nearly 10 years, it is reasonable to assume that a large and sustained deterrent effect has been achieved, even if nondeterrent factors such as economic conditions are also important over time. What this means, in crude terms, is that we expect that the target population (drivers who drink) will have become aware of the law and have been exposed to its operation in some ways; that as a result they will have increased their perceptions of the chances of apprehension for drinking and driving; and that as rational actors they will have changed their driving or drinking practices to avoid committing the offense, or at least to avoid detection and the consequent loss of licence.

The purpose of this chapter is to present a model of the deterrence process that I began to develop in the early days of RBT in NSW. This model, derived both from the deterrence literature (especially the work of Gibbs 1975) and from hunches about how RBT would affect behavior, is essentially a more sophisticated version of the simple causal chain outlined in the last paragraph, incorporating nonlegal as well as legal sanctions. It has been modified in view of the results of empirical research in NSW and other states and in the light of experience with the implementation of RBT across Australia.

A major advantage of theorizing about deterrence processes in the context of a specific legal intervention that is known to have had an impact on the target behavior is that there is a real phenomenon of consid-

erable magnitude to be explained. In much survey research that attempts
to test propositions derived from deterrence theory, the correlations between perceptions of legal sanctions and reported offending are weak or
nonexistent (Braithwaite 1989). This may be because the theory is wrong
or misspecified, but it may also be because the situations and laws discussed are hypothetical and remote from the present experiences of the
respondents, even if they have in the past committed the offenses in
question. Alternatively, it may be because perceptions of (say) the chances
of arrest are below a threshold level required for deterrence to operate.
These problems are less likely to occur if one studies the effects of a
powerful deterrent that affects nearly the whole population, although the
technical problems of developing valid and reliable measure of key concepts, such as the perceived chances of arrest, remain.

To clarify my research design, and to counter the charge of circularity
in logic (assuming a deterrent effect and then finding one), it may be
helpful to summarize my strategy. First, I take RBT as a very pure expression of the doctrine of general deterrence, with its emphasis on influencing the behaviors of large numbers of motorists by increasing their
fear of the legal consequences of violating the law. Second, I accept as
historical fact that the intensity of the enforcement and advertising of
RBT in NSW is virtually without parallel. Third, it is a reasonably well-
established research finding that RBT has had a causal impact on fatal
crashes. While it does not necessarily follow from these three premises
that RBT acted as a deterrent, the argument is that it is very *plausible* that
deterrence was part of the explanation for its substantial impact. In this
situation it makes sense to develop and test a model of the deterrence
process. A fit between the model and data would strengthen the argument
that deterrence as I define it (behavior change due to fear of the legal
consequences) was indeed operating through RBT. More important, the
collection of other kinds of data (socio-demographic information, perceptions of nonlegal sanctions, etc.) facilitates the development and testing of
a more sophisticated model of how legal interventions may affect behavior.[2]

Previous versions of the model discussed in this paper (see Homel
1986; 1988) have been discussed by social scientists with a specific interest in drinking and driving (e.g., Ross 1988; Snortum 1988; Vingilis
1990), and have influenced drink-driving policy in Australia (Homel, in
press). This work appears less well known to criminologists, especially
those outside Australia, although the model incorporates many features
that have been recognized as important in the deterrence literature since
the publication of my research (e.g., Paternoster 1989; Grasmick and
Bursik 1990; Williams and Hawkins 1986). For example, I recognized
from the outset that informal sanctions, particularly those operating among

groups of drinkers, would play a crucial role and would interact in complex ways with legal sanctions. Other aspects of the model that anticipated some current concerns include the incorporation of influences on risk perception, especially the impact of police activity; the recognition that deterrence is a dynamic process, with offenders repeatedly making new decisions; the distinction between perceptions and evaluations of arrest risk and punishment severity; and recognition of the crucial need to be offense-specific if strong models of the deterrence process are to be constructed. In addition, following the pioneering work of Gibbs (1975) the model incorporates all elements of the deterrence process, from the enforcement of the law through to rates of offending, and so has policy relevance and can be used to generate fresh predictions that can be tested.

There are many obvious points of similarity between the deterrence process as I formulate it and the rational choice perspective on offending as formulated by Cornish and Clarke (1986), although our work was carried out quite independently. Their view of offending as "the result of broadly rational choices based on analyses of anticipated costs and benefits" (p. vi) is of course central to any understanding of deterrence, and we are also agreed on the need for offense-specific models and on the dynamic nature of criminal decision making. However, one fundamental feature of their perspective, the sharp distinction between criminal involvement and criminal events, does not have an immediate counterpart in the model proposed in this chapter. This may point to a deficiency in the model; it may also suggest that the distinction is not as useful or meaningful for drinking and driving as it is for predatory offenses such as burglary.

The Model

Deterrence as an Unstable Process: Perceptions and Evaluations

Some elements of the model are represented in diagrammatic form in figure 3.2. This figure is a development of figure 2.1 in Homel (1988) (see also Homel 1986) in that it explicitly allows for variation in the key elements over time, something that was only implicit in the earlier formulation. A key finding of the analysis of panel data collected soon after the introduction of RBT in NSW was that deterrence should be seen as

a dynamic and unstable situation, with a constantly changing mix of those deterred through personal exposure to RBT and those "undeterred" through a successful drink-driving episode or through nonexposure to the operation of RBT. . . . RBT is always in the process of losing its effectiveness among drivers who, because they feel under pressure to drink or because they have not

FIGURE 3.2
Model of the Deterrence Process

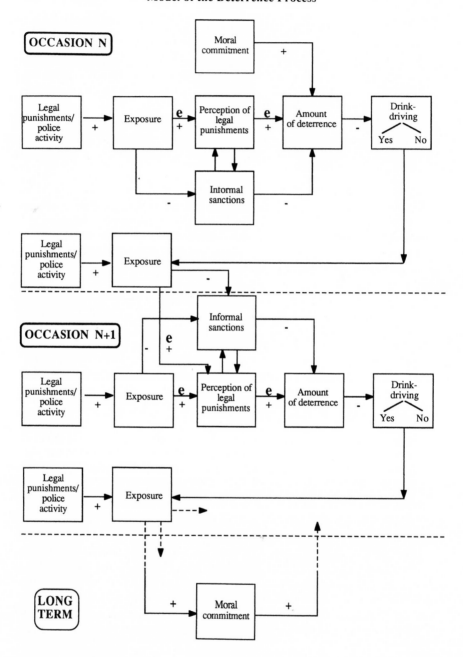

seen RBT in operation for some time, take the risk of driving after drinking. (Homel 1988: 244–45) emphasis in original

Four key propositions undergird the model, and are explained in further detail below. First of all, individuals must be exposed personally to law enforcement, or must receive information about law enforcement (perhaps through media publicity), before they can be deterred (these are the exposure boxes in figure 3.2). Second, neither exposure to law enforcement nor perceptions of legal sanctions have any influence on behavior apart from a process of evaluation whereby these experiences or cognitions are given a meaning (the "e" symbols over some of the arrows). Third, the extent to which an individual is deterred can, in principle, be measured by questioning him or her about behavior change caused by exposure to law enforcement (the deterrence boxes). Finally, there must be an investigation of the effects of official legal activity on nonlegal sanctions that inhibit or encourage drinking and driving, so that the deterrent effects of legal activity can be clearly distinguished from the probably substantial effects of other kinds of sanctions. In the diagram, these are the "informal sanctions" and "moral commitment" boxes.

Since informal sanctions are included, the behavior of all types of persons is described in the model, even the behavior of persons who might have highly developed consciences concerning drinking and driving and the behavior of "high risk" people such as those labeled problem drinkers or alcoholics. Following figure 3.2, it is proposed that drink-driving and official legal activities such as RBT are linked through exposure to law enforcement, leading to perceptions of severe and/or certain sanctions and hence to attempts to avoid committing the offense when there is a risk of driving while impaired. The more strategies are adopted to avoid drinking and driving (through fear of legal sanctions or through the operation of nonlegal sanctions), the less likely it is that an individual will drive over the legal limit on a given occasion. The "drink-driving" box refers to the decision to comply with the law or to drive with a blood alcohol concentration that is likely to be over the legal limit.

The model assumes the influence of a range of social and demographic variables, such as alcohol consumption, age, and sex. All components of the model could be affected, including rates of exposure to police enforcement or publicity, evaluations of the meaning of this exposure, perceptions and evaluations of legal sanctions, strategies to avoid drinking and driving, drink-driving decisions, and the intensity with which nonlegal sanctions apply. However, as Tittle (1980) points out, little can be said about the nature of "differential deterrability"—the extent to which different individuals or groups such as heavy drinkers or young drivers perceive and respond to legal sanctions—without augmenting deterrence theory with insights from other theoretical traditions. For this reason, figure 3.2 does not include any predictions about the effects of socio-demographic variables (but see figure 2.2 and discussion in Homel 1988).

At the heart of the model are the perceptions of legal sanctions. However, these perceptions on their own are not sufficient to explain behavior; a process of evaluation takes place during which the individual weighs the personally determined costs of the threatened consequences of his behavior. Thus two individuals might have exactly the same perception of the penalties that would be applied to them for drinking and driving, but one might be much less worried than the other at the prospect of actually experiencing those penalties. The interaction of perceptions and evaluations is a major reason why decisions based on fear of legal threats are constantly being reassessed by potential offenders. While in principle objective sanctions and police enforcement can be maintained at a given level, subjective assessments of these official activities are likely to be much more unstable.

The distinction between perceptions and evaluations of sanction severity is usually drawn in formulations of deterrence based on utility theory, via the concept of the "utility" to the potential offender of the consequences of an action (Carr-Hill & Stern 1979; Homel 1988). It is also an integral part of formulations based on prospect theory, a more modern decision theory, via the "value function" (Homel 1988; Lattimore & Witte 1986; Tversky & Kahneman 1981). However, prospect theory has the additional advantage that it distinguishes between the subjective probability of an event (say, getting caught), and the "decision weight" attached to that perception. The decision weight is conceived as a monotonic function of the perceived probability of arrest, but not itself as a probability. While the need to distinguish between perceptions of sanction severity and evaluations of those perceptions appears generally recognized in the literature (Tittle 1980), the vital importance of the distinction between perceptions and evaluations of the perceptions of arrest likelihood seems less commonly recognized despite the increasing interest in prospect theory. In the context of RBT the distinction makes a lot of intuitive sense. For example, two potential offenders may agree that the chance of being randomly tested in the next month is quite high, but differ markedly in the weight they accord this perception in their drinking and driving decisions.

In order to be a sociological model and to have policy relevance, perceptions must be linked in some way with the objective legal actions. It is proposed that official legal activity is relevant to the individual only inasmuch as it enters the world of his everyday experience. In the model, exposure to the legal actions is the variable linking official activity with perceptions and evaluations of sanctions. The more intensive or frequent the official activity, the more intense or frequent will be the exposure of the threatened or punished population. Exposure might occur through observing or experiencing police breath testing, or through knowing others exposed in this way. In addition, the experience of punishment through a conviction is a form of exposure. The model predicts that those exposed to legal sanctions in any of these ways will be fearful of the consequences of drinking and driving and will modify their behaviors accordingly. On the other hand, individuals who have broken the law with impunity, particularly those who have successfully driven over the legal limit, will not fear legal sanctions as much as those without this experience of law breaking (the "experiential effect": Minor & Harry 1982). Thus successful drink-drive episodes are also a form of exposure to objective legal activity.

However, the relationship between exposure and fear of sanctions is not automatic: once again it is proposed that an individualized process of evaluation takes place. One way of illustrating this is to consider how an individual's decision to drive after drinking or not to drive after drinking on a particular occasion affects his behavior on subsequent occasions. This involves tracing the paths in figure 3.2 that link Occasion N with Occasion N+1. Whatever his decision, the motorist will be exposed to police enforcement or will notice the *absence* of police activity on the way home, or on an occasion soon after (see the exposure box at the bottom of the "Occasion N" section of figure 3.2). If he complies with the law, at some cost in terms of pleasure, time, or money, he may be annoyed that police are nowhere to be seen on the way home or in the month before the next party, and re-evaluate the risks involved in driving after drinking. On the other hand, he may find his virtuous behavior rewarded when he passes a random breath test. Such an experience will affect people in different ways; for some, the experience of a single random breath test will leave an indelible impression, while for others many tests or observations of police activity will be required to convince them that compliance with the law is the least costly option.

If a motorist decides to drive after drinking he may get a real scare if he drives past an RBT operation, even if he gets home without being pulled over for a test. Although he has successfully driven when he may be over the legal limit, because he has seen police conducting RBT he may not reduce his perceptions of the chances of detection as predicted by the experiential effect. Alteratively, he may decide that not being pulled over had something to do with his ability to drive brilliantly when drunk, and thereafter dismiss RBT as a "paper tiger" (fulfilling the experiential prediction).

Driving after drinking may of course lead to detection and arrest, whether through RBT or through some other means. This is another form of exposure to law enforcement included in the exposure boxes in figure 3.2. While the experience of arrest and conviction (in Australia more than 98% of those arrested are convicted) may make people more *sensitive* to the legal threat, in other words increase their subjective assessment of the chances of getting caught again, it may also (or instead) make them more *responsive* (Tittle 1980). What this means is that a motorist with a previous conviction for drinking and driving may perceive the chances of apprehension for drunk-driving at exactly the same level as a motorist without a conviction, but may because of his earlier encounter with the law respond more strongly to the legal threat by adopting more strategies to avoid drinking and driving. This effect would be expected to be particularly strong if the experience of arrest was recent, and underlines the potential importance of the distinction between perceptions and evaluations of those perceptions. The concepts of sensitivity and responsiveness also illustrate aspects of what could be meant by "differential deterrability."

These scenarios clarify the dynamic nature of the deterrence process, with potential offenders constantly reassessing the legal threat and modifying their behaviors accordingly. They also illustrate that different forms of exposure to legal activity, or differing constructions of the meaning of similar experiences, will lead to differing evaluations of threatened or actual legal sanctions even if there are no differences in perceptions of what the legal threat actually is.

Nonlegal Sanctions

The incorporation of nonlegal sanctions in the model highlights the importance of the physical and social environment. (A further development of the model to account for the broad impact of RBT on the social environment is presented by Homel [1990a].) The individual is assumed to be subject to three and only three types of social control mechanisms: guilt feelings resulting from the internalization of norms, the threat of social stigma or a sense of shame resulting from informal sanctions, and the threat of physical and/or material deprivation (Grasmick & Green 1980; Grasmick & Bursik 1990). One source of material deprivation is formal, legal punishments (loss of licence, and so on), but other sources include the costs and inconveniences involved in *not* driving after drinking (e.g., paying for a taxi home after a party and then again the next morning to pick the car up), as well as the nonlegal material costs entailed in committing the offense. Probably the major material cost that can result from drink-driving is having a crash. Fear of crashing has presumably restrained many a driver from foolhardy and illegal driving behaviors even when the direct legal threat has had negligible impact.

Braithwaite (1989) has recently reminded criminologists of the central importance of shaming as a powerful mechanism of social control. Mostly shaming operates to reduce crime: "... the key to crime control is cultural commitments to shaming in ways that I call reintegrative" (p. 1). However, historically in most Western societies, especially Australia, there has been very little shame attached to the offense of drinking and driving (Homel 1988; Gusfield 1981a). The relative weakness of informal sanctions directed at the drinking driver is one reason why the offense has attracted the attention of social scientists interested in assessing the deterrent potential of legal interventions (e.g., Ross 1982). It has been assumed that in the absence of nonlegal norms, changes in behavior caused by a legal intervention must be due to the operation of deterrence.

While the usual assumptions about the lack of stigma surrounding drinking and driving are largely correct, at least in Australia and the United States, if not in Scandinavia (Berger et al. 1990), a sense of shame nevertheless plays a vital role in the model. Based on ethnographic work in bars, Gusfield (1981b) argues that to understand risk-taking behavior such as drinking and driving, it is less important to know how much drinkers consume than whether they are portrayed in their own eyes and in those of their peers as competent or incompetent drinkers. There is an implicit assumption that in the barroom environment, adequate drinkers (especially men) do not get caught and do not have an accident when they drive after drinking.

For Gusfield what needs to be explained is why people *don't* drive after drinking, and it is here that exculpatory defenses, legitimate excuses, come into play. One exculpatory defense is the responsibility to work; another is past arrests for drink-driving. These circumstances make the avoidance of driving understandable and reasonable and allow the image of competence of the drinker to be preserved. In view of this, it is quite reasonable to argue that RBT has achieved its impact in NSW by allowing many drinkers to maintain their image of competence while reducing their level of drinking. In effect, the presence of police carrying out RBT provides a powerful exculpatory defense, since there are in principle few steps the drinker can take to avoid being pulled over. Since it could happen to anyone, there is no disgrace in not drinking or in not driving.

Thus while for many offenses the threat of social stigma operates to discourage offending, for drinking and driving the reverse frequently occurs, with the peer group imposing informal punishments if an individual does *not* drive after drinking. However, RBT affects this process, with police activity reducing group pressure to drive after drinking by providing an exculpatory defense or legitimate excuse for actions taken to avoid the offense. Just as threatening to shame people is a powerful tool for inducing compliance with the law, creating the circumstances in which people *cease to be shamed for not committing an offense* can be an equally powerful strategy for promoting law-abiding behavior. The inverse nature of these relationships is the reason for the minus signs on the arrows linking exposure with informal sanctions and informal sanctions with the deterrence boxes in figure 3.2.

The other kind of nonlegal sanction is moral commitment: individuals who believe that drinking and driving is an immoral or antisocial act may experience strong feelings of guilt if they do drink and drive (Norström 1981). Zimring and Hawkins (1968) have argued for the existence of a law-abiding group in the community who have received strong moral training in their early years and who cannot commit crimes because their self-concepts will not permit them to do so. However, the model proposed in this study corresponds to a parallelogram of forces rather than to a division of the population into those to whom deterrence applies and those to whom it does not. A person's conscience is only one force influencing behavior, competing with peer pressure and fear of punishment, although in some cases the force of conscience may be the major influence.

In contrast to informal group sanctions, it is not clear that RBT would have an immediate impact on the sense of moral commitment. However, theorists such as Andenaes (1974) have argued that in the long term, law may have an educative or habit-forming effect, operating as a "moral eye-opener" (Andenaes 1983:2). Although people may change their behaviors in the short term because of fear or peer processes, in the longer term they internalize the legal standards and start to police their own behaviors. Given the strong evidence that beliefs about the rightness or wrongness of drinking and driving have a big influence on behavior (Loxley & Smith 1991), moral commitment is included as an influence on behavior in figure 3.2. However, a link is shown between exposure and moral commitment only at the bottom of the diagram, which represents long-term effects. It is proposed that repeated exposure to RBT and to publicity about RBT, perhaps over a period of years, will begin to mold beliefs and induce law-abiding habits in the manner predicted by Andenaes.

The Framing of Decisions

Prospect theory has begun to be applied widely in analyses of criminal decision making (e.g., Lattimore & Witte 1986; Robben et al. 1990). One of the key concepts of prospect theory is that of the "decision frame." In a series of experiments, Tversky and Kahneman (1981) showed that in situations of decision making under uncertainty, decisions are influenced by whether the alternatives are framed as a choice between gains or as a choice between losses. For example, in hypothetical situations where 600 lives are at risk, when the alternatives are presented as an actuarially equivalent choice between a certain saving of (say) 200 lives and a 1/3 chance of saving 600 lives and a 2/3 chance that no people will be saved, decisions tend to be *risk averse*: people opt for the certain saving of lives. On the other hand, if the alternatives are presented as being between certain and possible losses, rather than between certain and possible gains, decisions tend to be *risk seeking*: people reject the alternative that involves a certain loss.

Having clarified the nature of the potential gains and losses for the prospective drinking driver, the concept of decision frame can be applied to the driving decision. Imagine that a man has traveled by car to a party and knows that he has drunk enough alcohol to put him over the legal limit; this is his current situation or "wealth" position. Depending on his circumstances, he has a number of choices. He could simply drive home and run the risk of a crash and the risk of apprehension and punishment for driving with the proscribed amount of alcohol, or perhaps he could leave his car, take a bus or taxi home and return to pick up his car the next day, or perhaps he could persuade a sober companion to drive him home, either in his or his companion's car. The precise options are not as important as the general question: How is he likely to frame the decision problem? In general, it seems highly likely that the problem will be construed as a choice between *losses,* a sure loss if he doesn't drive home, and a possible loss if he does. According to prospect theory, he will probably act in a risk-seeking manner; in other words, commit the offense. Prospect theorists would not deny that offenders might be influenced by calculations concerning possible losses if apprehended, but would argue that given the framing of the problem as a choice between certain and possible losses, there is in most cases a bias toward avoiding the certain loss. Moreover, as Carroll and Weaver (1986) observed for shoplifters, few offenders consider the *distal* consequences of offending, which in the case of drinking and driving are also the merely possible consequences: arrest and conviction or having an accident. The demands of the immediate situation are paramount.

In summary, the decision whether or not to drink and drive seems best framed as a choice between losses. There are two kinds of certain losses associated with not drinking and driving: the costs and inconveniences entailed in finding alternative transport, and one's portrayal as incompetent in one's own eyes and in the eyes of one's peers. On the other side of the coin, feelings of guilt, to the extent to which they occur, may be viewed as a sure loss entailed in the decision to drink and drive. In addition, some possible losses flowing from arrest and conviction or having an accident are entailed in the commission of the offense. Prospect theorists would predict that unless guilt feelings are very strong, people will generally behave in a risk-seeking manner and avoid the certain losses inherent in finding another way home.

Evidence for the Model

Theoretical Problems in the Measurement of Deterrence

Perceptual research on deterrence always seems to involve as dependent variables self reports of past offending or statements concerning peoples' intentions to violate the law in the future (e.g., Grasmick & Bursik 1990; Paternoster 1989). Although there is much controversy in this literature about the exact form questions should take and whether longitudinal designs are essential for distinguishing deterrent from experiential effects (e.g., Paternoster & Iovanni 1986), the focus is always on measures of offending. This is of course logical, since deterrence is ultimately concerned with influencing crime rates, but analysis of the direct links between perceptions of sanctions and offending overlooks an important link in the chain: the deterrence box in figure 3.2.

Strictly speaking, deterrence occurs when an individual contemplates but refrains from offending because of the perceived risk of punishment. Ideally, therefore, to develop and test the model a direct measure of deterrence is required. However, as Gibbs (1975) recognized, such a measure would involve questioning a potential offender about the reasons for his behavior, a procedure that is anathema to those working in the positivist tradition, with its emphasis on direct observation and its rejection of "subjectivity." Gibbs simply says, ". . . it would be naive to base a purported measure of deterrence on reasons given by individuals for refraining from criminal acts (not to mention practical problems entailed in attempting to gather such data)" (p. 15). Thus he objects to a direct measure on the grounds of methodological difficulty as well as on philosophical and theoretical grounds.

A full discussion of this issue can be found in Homel (1988). For present purposes, it will be sufficient to observe that if an individual is not to commit an offense, he must *do* something else instead. This is obvious when one considers the various scenarios that could lead to drinking and driving, but in the general deterrence literature seems only to have been recognized by Beyleveld (1979). The act of drinking away from home necessarily confronts the motorist with a variety of choices of the kind discussed earlier. He may plan in advance to leave the car at home, and travel with friends or use public transport. If he takes his car, he must count drinks, drink low-alcohol beverages or soft drinks, or leave his car at the party and get home some other way. There are perhaps 10 or 15 major behavioral strategies that can be adopted to avoid driving over the legal limit, and there seems to be no reason why potential offenders could not be questioned about their use of these strategies, something I did in my research on the impact of RBT (Homel 1988).

The evidential problems arise with the attempt to attribute the adoption of these strategies to RBT, and not to some other influence. Thus the questions must involve direct reference to RBT as the cause of the behavior change, but following Nisbett and Wilson (1977) and other psychologists interested in the relationship between verbal reports and their relationship to cognitive processes, it is necessary to establish that legal sanctions are a plausible and salient cause of the relevant behaviors. In the case of RBT in NSW, the case would seem to be assured, given that nearly the whole target population was aware of RBT soon after it was introduced (Homel 1990a). This is not to say that the act of enforcement and publicity proves the effectiveness of RBT, but that the conditions required for people to be able to report accurately on RBT as a possible cause of their actions are fulfilled.

The development of measures of strategies adopted by potential offenders to avoid offending opens up many new possibilities for deterrence research. While reports of past or intended future offending should of course still be included, direct measures of deterrence increase the usefulness of cross-sectional surveys, since in principle perceptions of legal sanctions can be regarded as being synchronic with behaviors adopted to avoid offending, although longitudinal studies are still essential to measure instability in deterrent effects. Direct measures also allow stronger tests of hypotheses derived from the deterrence model by throwing light on the processes linking perceptions with offense rates. For example, the well-known research of Sherman and Berk (1984) on the effects of police intervention in domestic violence cases would have been even more enlightening if it had been possible to probe behavior change due to fear of legal punishments. How many men gave up drinking, sought professional counseling for their temper, or simply spent more time away from home as a response to the legal intervention?

Perceptual Research on RBT in NSW

The model outlined in this chapter was developed in the context of an intensive and sustained legal intervention. One would therefore expect that the model would provide a good explanation for the effects of that intervention. Perceptual data collected by myself and by NSW government agencies has been generally consistent with this expectation (Cashmore 1985; Carseldine 1985; Cairney & Carseldine 1989; Homel 1986, 1988; Homel, Carseldine & Kearns 1988; Loxley et al. 1992).

In a survey of NSW residents conducted 10 weeks after the introduction of RBT in NSW, I found that 58% of motorists who drank had modified their drinking or travel habits as a result of RBT. The survey procedures confirmed the feasibility of probing behavior change caused by exposure to police activity, a technique I refined in later work.[3] As expected, the intensity of police random testing in an area was a major determinant of an individual's chances of being randomly tested, and was therefore a determinant of other aspects of exposure, such as the number of friends tested. The number of one's friends tested, more than other aspects of exposure, was in turn a strong predictor of the perceived chances of being tested and arrested. Thus objective levels of enforcement were linked with perceptions of sanctions through aspects of exposure. Following the causal chain hypothesized in figure 3.2, perceptions of the chances of arrest predicted the number of ways in which respondents were modifying their drinking and their driving practices.

Analysis of 185 repeat interviews conducted 6 weeks later strongly supported the concept of deterrence as an unstable process, since reported behavior change was heavily dependent on exposure to enforcement and peer pressure. The experiential effect was clearly in sight. Unfortunately, the short time between interviews produced too few reported drink-driving violations to verify that this variable correlated negatively with the number of strategies adopted to avoid drink-driving (the final link in the causal chain).

The analysis also produced evidence that drivers with a previous drink-driving conviction were more responsive, but not more sensitive, to the threat posed by RBT. These results are consistent with the impact of RBT on convicted offenders in South Australia (Homel 1990a). Other pertinent findings include: perceptions of arrest certainty had a much bigger influence on behavior than perceptions of penalty severity, although the effect of the latter could be significant in the short term for offenders with a previous conviction and for those who believe the chances of getting caught are high; media publicity was not as important as direct exposure to police activity; and heavy drinkers changed their behaviors more than light drinkers. This last result is consistent with the image of the drinking driver as a rational decision maker rather than a hopeless alcoholic beset by an addiction he finds impossible to moderate.

Perhaps my major finding was that the effect of RBT on group drinking pressures was at least equally as important as perceptions of legal sanctions as influences on behavior. In fact, in terms of variance explained, this "indirect path" was more important than the direct path via the measure of arrest certainty. This is an extremely important result, since it suggests that even when law enforcement could be expected to have a major deterrent effect and when nonlegal sanctions may not be as influential as for more clearly criminal offenses, the direct deterrent effect is not as important as the way the law affects nonlegal sanctions. More than this, drivers who felt the greatest pressure to drink tended to report more fear of RBT, but they also often reported that RBT had made it harder, not easier, to refuse another drink (contrary to the main trend in the data). Among this group, the longitudinal data revealed that despite an increase in the perceived chances of being tested, attempts to avoid drinking and driving *declined* between surveys. This is consistent with the effects of framing the drink-driving decision as a choice between losses, since the sure loss (of being seen as incompetent by one's drinking companions) outweighed the merely possible losses entailed in breaking the law.

A major deficiency of my initial research on RBT was the failure to investigate fully the role of moral commitment. This defect has to some extent been remedied by other researchers and by my more recent work. Using nonlongitudinal government survey data collected in several waves over some years, Homel, Carseldine, and Kearns (1988) and Cairney and Carseldine (1989) present evidence that public beliefs in NSW about the morality of drink-driving have begun to change. Although, as Ross (1982) comments, it is extremely hard to demonstrate the origins of nonlegal norms in the historical exposure of a population to a specific legal threat, it is certainly plausible that RBT has been part of the cause, especially since moral condemnation tends to be greater in NSW, where RBT has been enforced most intensively, than in other states of Australia (Loxley et al. 1992).

In summary, many of the major predictions of the model were supported by the data analyses. However, other aspects of the model, such as the distinction between perceptions and evaluations, were not properly tested. Moreover, many of the measures of exposure and perceptions posed problems of reliability, with the statistical models explaining at best modest proportions of the variance. Perhaps the scientifically safest conclusion to draw is that none of the major predictions of the model have been clearly contradicted by the perceptual research, while other predictions have received statistically significant support that is modest in terms of variance explained.

*RBT in Other States in Australia: Testing Predictions
of the Deterrence Model*

Braithwaite (1989) observes that "a theory must not only explain the facts we know; it must also generate fresh predictions, of which policy predictions are the most useful sort. . . ." (p. 152). Based on the model and on the survey research, it is possible to produce a "recipe" for effective police enforcement and effective publicity of RBT (see Homel 1990a,b). The prediction is that adherence to the recipe (which allows for local implementation consistent with the general principles) will produce results comparable with those achieved in NSW. Some key elements: RBT operations must not only be visible and obviously RBT (rather than some other police activity), the visibility should be "threatening," so that drivers should not believe that RBT operations can be easily evaded once they are in sight; all drivers pulled over should be tested, regardless of evidence of alcohol use; media publicity should reinforce police enforcement, rather than being focused on the moral culpability or stupidity of the drunken driver, and mobile RBT (pulling over individual drivers at random in back streets) should be restricted to support of visible stationary RBT operations (by, for example, patrolling obvious escape routes).

All these rules flow from the model and from existing research, and all have been broken at one time or another by state police departments. For example, in Western Australia (WA), which introduced RBT in October 1988 after a long period of enforcement based on a roadblock or sobriety checkpoint approach, only about half of all drivers pulled over are tested. In addition, RBT sites are frequently not easily visible to passing motorists, and there has been little media publicity. Not surprisingly, evaluation suggests no impact on crashes (Henstridge 1990). The effectiveness of the roadblock approach used previously in WA was tested by Loxley and Smith (1991) by fitting my deterrence model (Homel 1988) to survey data using LISREL. None of the major deterrence paths could be identified in the data, although the measurement model fitted well. The authors conclude not that the model is wrong but that deterrence was not operating at that time in WA. The analysis did confirm the importance of moral commitment as an influence on drinking and driving behaviors (and on the strength of informal sanctions).

The state of Victoria represents a happier situation than WA. After a long period when nonrandom testing had become the dominant enforcement mode and the alcohol-related death rate had risen steadily (I describe the problem in Homel 1990a), Victoria in late 1989 adopted key elements of my RBT recipe. The Traffic Accident Commission paid for extensive media publicity and also provided several million dollars to equip police with extremely visible "booze buses" so that the number of tests conducted through stationary RBT was vastly increased, on an ongoing basis. Low-visibility "preliminary breath test" procedures were de-emphasized. Preliminary evaluations of crash data indicate marked reductions in alcohol-related crashes, especially in Melbourne, where enforcement was most intense (Drummond, Sullivan & Vulcan 1991), and there is anecdotal evidence of savings so far of about $100 million in insurance claims.

The results of adhering or failing to adhere to the enforcement rules derived from the model constitute further tests of the model and facilitate its continuing modification and development, especially at the police activity/exposure end. As experience accumulates with the enforcement of RBT in a variety of ways in different states, it should become possible to specify the model more precisely. For example, it is now generally accepted that the enforcement threshold for effective RBT is to test one driver in three every year, since this was the level achieved in NSW in the first year. However, some small states such as South Australia have increased testing to NSW levels without experiencing a sustained drop in casualties (Homel 1990a). This raises important questions about the way police are organized and the precise components of enforcement that translate into effective exposure. It is a fascinating possibility that small police services may simply not be able to "pack the punch" required to achieve the NSW result no matter how hard they try, or that small states may not be able to fund adequate publicity. In this connection, Tasmania with a population of only 455,000 is a critical test case, since RBT in that state (introduced only one month after NSW) has been enforced even more vigorously than in NSW, but with largely unknown results.[4]

These examples illustrate the general principle that constant de facto experimentation across states should allow "operating constants" to be derived for the enforcement and exposure components of the model, although special surveys will be required to derive critical thresholds for variables such as the perceived chances of apprehension. The derivation of such parameters has obvious policy relevance, but more importantly, without detailed testing and numerical specification through cross-jurisdictional comparisons it is difficult to see how the explanatory power of the model, in both the statistical and theoretical senses, can be improved.

Conclusion: Deterrence and Rational Choice

The model outlined in this chapter has a number of features that, I believe, make it both accurate in the predictive sense and comprehensive as an explanation of how drunk-driving law enforcement might work. The main strength of the model is its specificity — it is grounded in a major and ongoing legal intervention that takes a variety of forms in different states but that is always directed at the single offense of drinking and driving. I am in hearty agreement with Cornish and Clarke (1986) when they affirm the need for a crime-specific focus on the grounds that the situational context of decision making and the information being handled will vary greatly among offenses. Because the model is offense-specific, it is possible to develop detailed and realistic concepts and measures that tend to be ignored or glossed over in more general theoretical formulations of deterrence. This can be seen at all stages of the assumed causal chain depicted in figure 3.2.

For example, one reason why studies of the determinants of perceived risk are so rare (Williams & Hawkins 1986) is the offense-specific nature of forms of exposure to legal punishments. Exposure to drink-driving law enforcement raises different (although related) theoretical and empirical problems from exposure to (say) taxation law enforcement. Indeed, the almost complete lack of attention to exposure in the perceptual deterrence literature probably arises from the difficulties entailed in developing measures of exposure (other than prior arrests or unpunished infractions) that would make sense across a variety of offenses. But in the absence of exposure as an integral part of the analysis, deterrence research tends to lose policy relevance and be unrelated to the theoretical and political issues that arise in debates about the nature and intensity of law enforcement.

The need for an offense-specific model is even more apparent when one considers the problems of measuring the amount of deterrence, the nature of informal sanctions, or decision processes. My finding that informal sanctions exceeded in importance the direct effects of fear of legal sanctions is consistent with the general literature on deterrence (Braithwaite 1989), but the additional finding that RBT had a marked effect on the operation of the informal sanctions would not have been possible without the ethnographic research on drinking that provided a basis for the specific measures used. Again, the use of prospect theory to understand deterrence decision processes is gaining in popularity, but it is becoming apparent that the exact nature of the processes involved depends on the precise offense being studied. For example, compliance with tax law appears to depend on whether the potential offender faces the prospect of a refund or a tax bill after withholding; in other words, whether the decision is framed as a choice between gains or losses (Robben et al. 1990).

A further strength of the model is its dynamic nature. Deterrence is an inherently unstable process since it depends on individuals' perceptions and evaluations of the legal punishments, and these will always be influenced by factors that vary over time, including fluctuations in police

enforcement and media publicity. Probably few individuals are permanently deterred, and the goal of police enforcement should therefore be to
re-deter as many people as become undeterred through lack of exposure,
peer processes, or experience in successfully driving after having drunk
more than the legal limit.

It is assumed in the model that any motorist who drinks might, at any
time, drive after drinking, even after a long period of compliance with the
law. Figure 3.2 and the supporting concepts (such as the framing of
decisions) most clearly reflect the "crime event" and the process of "con-
tinuance," to use Cornish and Clarke's (1986) terminology, with "desistance" being implied by changes in informal sanctions, such as a person's
growing belief, fed by a constant diet of media publicity and exposure to
police enforcement, that it is wrong to drink and drive. However, probably the main reason why people cease to drink and drive is not moral
commitment, but simply the fact that maturation and life-style changes
reduce or eliminate the situations in which the offense is likely to occur.
Drink-driving, more than most other offenses, is a response to social
circumstances — it can be regarded as normal and rational behavior in a
society that likes to drink and often forces people, particularly young
people, to drive to get to their place of entertainment. Any time a driver
who drinks has to drive to a party, he has to take some action to ensure
that he complies with the law, reinforcing Gusfield's (1981b) argument
that what needs to be explained is not why people do drink and drive but
why they don't.

The peculiar nature of drinking and driving as normal rather than deviant behavior accounts for the absence of an explicit "initial involvement"
component in the model as I developed it, although the incorporation of
informal sanctions captures some of the elements discussed by Cornish
and Clarke (1986). Their initial involvement model ends in a "readiness"
to commit the offense, but I just assumed that in principle any driver who
drinks is "ready" to drink and drive — the offense is inherent in social
arrangements. Further reflection in the light of their discussion suggests
to me that my model could be strengthened by developing a model not of
initial involvement, which seems to need no explanation not already part
of the deterrence model, but of *permanent noninvolvement,* emphasizing
opportunities to commit the offense, moral beliefs, and group drinking
practices. Why do some nonteetotal drivers, despite the fact that they are
frequently faced with the need to get home after a drinking event, never
drive after having drunk more than the legal limit? Why are some potential offenders exposed less often than others to situations in which they
are forced to make a choice? Such a model, together with the model of
the deterrence process already developed, would provide a strong expla-

nation of the social distribution of drinking and driving and would throw further light on the interactions between legal and nonlegal sanctions.

The need to invert one's perspective when studying drinking and driving is one reason why study of the offense can make a useful contribution to the development of the rational choice perspective. It could be argued that drinking and driving is one of a class of "less serious" offenses for which opportunities arise frequently as a natural part of social interaction rather than being sought out by the potential offender (Hirschi 1969). Other offenses in this class could include marijuana use and tax evasion. These kinds of offenses often require effort *not* to commit and attract little opprobrium among potential offenders' reference groups. A model of permanent noninvolvement rather than initial involvement seems most appropriate for this whole class of offenses, suggesting that the rational choice approach as formulated by Cornish and Clarke (1986) could be extended by operationalizing the criteria for identification of offenses in this class and by specifying the general features of a noninvolvement model.

Other aspects of drinking and driving enhance its value for deterrence research, and hence for the rational choice perspective. For example, it is an offense that is validly and reliably indexed by traffic crash statistics, and driving and drinking practices can also be reported reasonably accurately (and with less embarrassment than for many other offenses) by a wide cross section of the population. In addition, since drinking and driving is the object of great community concern, it attracts a great deal of law enforcement attention and experimentation. These features all facilitate the construction of a powerful model that through comparison with similar models for other offenses can make a significant contribution to the development of a general theory of deterrence.

Notes

1. An American reviewer of this chapter pointed out that in the United States, one state's action against alcohol is easily undermined by the actions of adjoining states, since there is a great deal of traffic across state borders. This is of course true to some extent in Australia as well, although the problem is not as great since the population is concentrated in capital cities far from state borders. Sydney contains about 60% of the population of NSW, and is sufficiently far from other states to be insulated from their practices.

2. The restriction of the term *deterrence* to the effects of legal punishments operating through fear of detection is consistent with my earlier usage (Homel 1988) and also with that of Gibbs (1975). However, the heavy emphasis on nonlegal sanctions in my model underlines the obvious fact that these also act as a "deterrent," using the term in its broader sense. My use of the restricted definition should in no way be taken to imply that I believe that nonlegal punishments do not have a major "deterrent" impact.

3. In the original surveys (Homel 1986), the question probing behavior change due to RBT was of the following form:

When they first brought in random breath testing just before Christmas, what effects did it have on you at the time? From this card (SHOWCARD 4) what if anything did you do at the time?

And what about now . . . what effects are random breath testing having on you now? What (SHOWCARD 4) if anything are you doing now?

Showcard 4 contained a list of 17 strategies, such as: "Not using the car as much," "Stopped driving to places where you will be drinking," and "Carefully limiting your drinking when driving."

In more recent work (summary results for the survey are in Berger et al. 1990) the following questions was used:

Over the past year or so, when you have been in a drinking situation away from home, how often have you taken steps to make sure you didn't drive over the legal limit—have you always, usually, sometimes or never taken steps so that you didn't drive over the legal limit?

ASK THOSE ALWAYS, USUALLY, SOMETIMES TAKE STEPS:
What steps have you taken? And what other steps?

ASK THOSE ALWAYS, USUALLY, SOMETIMES TAKE STEPS:
And can you tell me from this card again (SHOWCARD 4) how important the fear of being stopped by the police was when you decided to take these steps to avoid driving over the legal limit?

SHOWCARD 4: Not at all important; Slightly important; Quite important; Very important; Unsure.

4. These questions and others are the subject of research I am currently carrying out in four states: NSW, WA, SA, and Tasmania (*The Optimisation of Random Breath Testing,* funded by the Federal Office of Road Safety).

References

Andenaes, J. 1974. *Punishment and deterrence.* Ann Arbor, MI: The University of Michigan Press.

Andenaes, J. 1983. "Prevention and deterrence—general and special." Paper presented at the 9th International Conference on Alcohol, Drugs and Traffic Safety, San Juan, Puerto Rico.

Barnes, J.W. 1988, September. "The effect of the introduction of random breath testing in New South Wales on accident patterns." In Seminar Papers (Vol. 2: 453–65). Road Traffic Safety Seminar, Road Traffic Safety Research Council, Wellington, NZ.

Berger, D.E., Snortum, J.R., Homel, R.J., Hauge, R., & Loxley, W. 1990. "Deterrence and prevention of alcohol-impaired driving in Australia, the United States, and Norway." *Justice Quarterly* 7: 453–65.

Beyleveld, D. 1979. "Identifying, explaining and predicting deterrence." *The British Journal of Criminology* 19:205–24.

Braithwaite, J. 1989. *Crime, shame and reintegration.* Cambridge: Cambridge University Press.

Cairney, P.T., & Carseldine, D. 1989. *Drink-driving and random breath testing: A survey of knowledge, attitudes, beliefs and self-reported behaviour.* Sydney: Road Safety Bureau, Roads and Traffic Authority.

Carr-Hill, R.A., & Stern, N.H. 1979. *Crime, the police and criminal statistics: An analysis of official statistics for England and Wales using econometric methods.* London: Academic Press.

Carroll, J., & Weaver, F. 1986. "Shoplifters' perceptions of crime opportunities: A process tracing study." In D.B. Cornish & R.V. Clarke (Eds.), *The reasoning criminal: Rational choice perspectives on offending* (19–38). New York: Springer-Verlag.

Carseldine, D. 1985. *Surveys of knowledge, attitudes, beliefs and reported behaviours of drivers — on the topic of drunk-driving and random breath testing.* Sydney: Traffic Authority of New South Wales.

Cashmore, J. 1985. *The impact of random breath testing in New South Wales.* Sydney: NSW Bureau of Crime Statistics and Research.

Cornish, D.B., & Clarke, R.V. 1986. "Introduction." In D.B. Cornish & R.V. Clarke (Eds.), *The reasoning criminal: Rational choice perspectives on offending* (1–16). New York: Springer-Verlag.

Drummond, A.E., Sullivan, G., & Vulcan, P. 1991. *A descriptive analysis of the 1990 Victorian road toll.* Melbourne: Monash University Accident Research Centre.

Gibbs, J.P. 1975. *Crime, punishment and deterrence.* New York: Elsevier.

Grasmick, H.G., & Green, D.E. 1980. "Legal punishment, social disapproval and internalization as inhibitors of illegal behaviour." *Journal of Criminal Law and Criminology* 71:325–35.

Grasmick, H.G., & Bursik, R.J. 1990. "Conscience, significant others, and rational choice: Extending the deterrence model." *Law and Society Review* 24:837–59.

Gusfield, J.R. 1981a. *The culture of public problems: Drinking-driving and the symbolic order.* Chicago: The University of Chicago Press.

Gusfield, J.R. 1981b. "Managing competence: An ethnographic study of drinking-driving and the context of bars." In T.C. Harford & L.S. Gaines (Eds.), *Social drinking contexts. Research monograph no. 7* (155–172). Washington, DC: U.S. Government Printing Office.

Henstridge, J. 1990. *An analysis of the effect of random breathtesting in Western Australia.* Perth: Data Analysis Australia.

Hirschi, T. 1969. *Causes of delinquency.* Berkeley: University of California Press.

Homel, R. 1986. *Policing the drinking driver: Random breath testing and the process of deterrence.* Canberra: Federal Office of Road Safety.

Homel, R. 1988. *Policing and punishing the drinking driver: A study of general and specific deterrence.* New York: Springer-Verlag.

Homel, R. 1990a. "Random breath testing and random stopping programs in Australia." In R. Jean Wilson & Robert E. Mann (Eds.), *Drinking and driving: Advances in research and prevention* (159–202). New York: The Guilford Press.

Homel, R. 1990b. "Random breath testing the Australian way: A model for the United States?" *Alcohol Health and Research World* 14(1):70–75.

Homel, R. 1992. "Drink-driving law enforcement and the legal blood alcohol limit: An analysis of daily fatal crashes in New South Wales from July 1, 1975 to December 31, 1986." Unpublished manuscript.

Homel, R. (in press) "Random breath testing in Australia: getting it to work according to specifications." *Addiction* 88 (Suppl. 1).

Homel, R., Carseldine, D., & Kearns, I. 1988. "Drink-drive countermeasures in Australia." *Alcohol, Drugs, and Driving* 4(2):113–44.

Kearns, I., & Goldsmith, H. 1984. "The impact on traffic crashes of the introduction of random breath testing in New South Wales." *Australian Road Research Board Proceedings* 12:81–95.

Lattimore, P., & Witte, A. 1986. "Models of decision making under uncertainty: The criminal choice." In D.B. Cornish & R.V. Clarke (Eds.), *The reasoning criminal: Rational choice perspectives on offending* (129–155). New York: Springer-Verlag.

Loxley, W., & Smith, L. 1991. "Roadblock testing in Western Australia and the process of deterrence." *Australian Journal of Psychology* 43:101–6.

Loxley, W., Kai Lo, S., Homel, R., Berger, D., & Snortum, J. 1992. "Young people, alcohol and driving in two Australian states." *International Journal of Addiction,* 27(9): 1119–1129.

Minor, W., & Harry, J. 1982. "Deterrent and experiential effects in perceptual deterrence research: A replication and extension." *Journal of Research in Crime and Delinquency* 19:190–203.

Nisbett, R.E., & Wilson, T.D. 1977. "Telling more than we know: Verbal reports on mental processes." *Psychological Review* 84: 231–59.

Norström, T. 1981. *Studies in the causation and prevention of traffic crime.* Stockholm: Almqvist & Wiksell.

Paternoster, R. 1989. "Decisions to participate in and desist from four types of common delinquency: Deterrence and the rational choice perspective." *Law & Society Review* 23:7–40.

Paternoster, R., & Iovanni, L. 1986. "The deterrent effect of perceived severity: A reexamination." *Social Forces* 64:751–77.

Robben, H., Webley, P., Weigel, R., Wärneryd, K., Kinsey, K., Hessing, D., Alvira Martin, F., Elffers, H., Wahlund, R., Van Langenhove, L., Long, S., & Scholz, J. 1990. "Decision frame and opportunity as determinants of tax cheating." *Journal of Economic Psychology* 11:341–64.

Ross, H.L. 1982. *Deterring the drinking driver: Legal policy and social control.* Lexington, Mass.: Lexington Books.

Ross, H.L. 1988. "Deterrence-based policies in Britain, Canada, and Australia." In Michael D. Laurence, John R. Snortum, & Franklin E. Zimring (Eds.), *Social control of the drinking driver* (64–78). Chicago: The University of Chicago Press.

Sherman, L. 1990. "Police crackdowns: Initial and residual deterrence." In Michael Tonry & Norval Morris (Eds.), *Crime and justice: An annual review of research* (1–48). Chicago: University of Chicago Press.

Sherman, L., & Berk, R. 1984. "The specific deterrent effects of arrest for domestic assault." *American Sociological Review* 49:261–72.

Snortum, J.R. 1988. "Deterrence of alcohol-impaired driving: An effect in search of a cause." In Michael D. Laurence, John R. Snortum, & Franklin E. Zimring (Eds.), *Social control of the drinking driver* (189–226). Chicago: The University of Chicago Press.

Thomson, J., & Mavrolefterou, K. 1984. "Assessing the effectiveness of random breath testing." *Proceedings of the Conference of the Australian Road Research Board* 12:72–80.

Tittle, C.R. 1980. *Sanctions and social deviance: The question of deterrence.* New York: Praeger.

Tversky, A., & Kahneman, D. 1981. "The framing of decisions and the psychology of choice." *Science* 211:453–58.

Vingilis, E.R. 1990. "A new look at deterrence models." In R. Jean Wilson & Robert E. Mann (Eds.), *Drinking and driving: Advances in research and prevention* (99–115). New York: The Guilford Press.

Voas, R.B. 1988. "Emerging technologies for controlling the drunk driver." In Michael D. Laurence, John R. Snortum, & Franklin E. Zimring (Eds.), *Social Control of the Drinking Driver* (321–370). Chicago: The University of Chicago Press.

Williams, K., & Hawkins, R. 1986. "Perceptual research on general deterrence: A critical review." *Law & Society Review* 20:545–72.

Zimring, F., & Hawkins, G. 1968. "Deterrence and marginal groups." *Journal of Research in Crime and Delinquency* 5: 100–14.

4

Gun Use in Crime, Rational Choice, and Social Learning Theory

Richard W. Harding

Rational Choice and Social Learning: The Theoretical Context

While the idea of "crime as choice" is never too distant from criminological debate (Wilson and Herrnstein 1985:43–5), it was the publication of *The Reasoning Criminal* (Cornish and Clarke 1986:1–15) that gave it a contemporary slant. The editors of this seminal work on rational choice perspectives made no grandiose claims, but conscientiously tried to delineate the limitations of its approach. Thus, they emphasized that it was indeed a *perspective,* not a theory; as such, it sought to establish a framework for *policy-relevant research,* including research on situational crime prevention and sentencing strategies; its focus was *crime-specific* rather than general; and it sought to distinguish the dynamics of *criminal involvement in particular crime events* from supposed general crime proneness.

The authors also recognized that they might possibly have a tiger by the tail, referring to the "likely long-term consequences of thus 'depathologizing crime.' If most criminal behavior is portrayed as rational, normal and commonplace, what will be the effect upon everyday thinking and moralizing about crime?" they asked.[1]

Bottomley, reviewing the book (1988), was concerned about this aspect. He considered that the perspective had "been espoused by some of its main proponents for the purposes of achieving better leverage on the *crime control* front" — shorthand evidently for oppressive prophylactic and/ or penal measures — and considered that the terms of the "theory," as he now characterized it, were not necessarily clear enough to forestall this. The anxiety that Bottomley expressed is quite often encountered, less mildly expressed, in progressive criminological circles (Braithwaite 1987).

Akers (1990) also treats rational choice as purporting to be a full-blown theory. As such, it could be, he fears (p. 654), that it might develop an inexorable intellectual momentum. It "may be on the verge of becoming for the 1980s and 1990s what neo-Marxist perspectives were in the 1970s, as it spreads to virtually all social science disciplines and law."

His concerns, however, are of a quite different nature from Bottomley's, namely that far from "de-pathologizing" our understanding of crime it actually draws substantially, indeed almost wholly, upon conventional social learning theory without either acknowledging that fact nor seeking to tie together the two notions. Rational choice, in other words, is neither new nor intellectually cohesive. His arguments are sufficiently cogent to merit fuller exposition and analysis.

Having carefully reviewed the main rational choice literature, Akers states: "[R]ational choice theory does not assume that all or even most criminal acts result from well-informed calculated choices. The rational choice models in the literature leave room for all levels of rationality, except the most mindless, pathological and irrational" (1990:665). The counterpoint is the history of the development of social learning theory, in relation to which Akers concludes:

> By the time that rational choice models began to take hold in criminology, there already had developed a rich body of theory and research on crime and deviance within the social behaviorist tradition, a tradition which had already incorporated the central proposition of rational choice theory. Yet none of that tradition was consulted by proponents of rational choice theory. Rather, economic theory was imported and modified as rational choice models of crime. These models were then referred to in modifying the deterrence doctrine in criminology, as if none of the behavioral tradition existed. (1990:675–76)

Akers notes that the literature on rational choice is burgeoning, and thus that "there could be some analysis [I have missed] which explicitly tries to show the connection between rational choice and social learning" (p. 657, fn. 16). In previous research, published at about the same time as Akers's piece, I myself had indeed attempted to make this connection in the particular context of weapon choice in violent crime and strategies for gun control (Harding and Blake 1989; Harding 1990).

In this chapter, I shall attempt to show by reference to my own West Australian research, as well as data drawn from research carried out in the United States and in Switzerland and to a lesser extent in Japan, that rational choice theory may be enriched by its links with social learning theory generally, and differential association in particular. It will be seen that the notion of "bounded rationality,"[2] which is central to rational choice, is tied up with social learning experiences that precede the crime event; and that social learning, and thus the manner and extent of the "boundedness" of rationality for the purpose of rational choice theory, may be profoundly influenced by the cultural context and meaning of those learning experiences.

Both behaviorists and cognitive theorists accept that associations are a key dynamic in learning. Sutherland's differential association theory was formulated in terms that appear to be primarily cognitive but that in fact can accommodate the approaches of each of these main schools of learning theory. This is particularly so because it is concerned with both the substance of what is learned and the process by which this occurs. The theory finesses the need to identify exclusively with either school. Indeed, Sutherland did not purport to be contributing to learning theory in the strict sense at all, but rather to the theory of criminal behavior.

Social learning theory does not so much finesse these theories as positively draw upon each of them. It emphasizes that behaviors may be influenced or reinforced not only by actual rewards and punishments (behaviorist learning) but also by expectations or calculations derived vicariously by watching and learning from other people (cognitive learning). In this sense the links between differential association and social learning are close.

The aspect of differential association that should be particularly productive in linking the more modern social learning theory to rational choice arises within the fourth head of Sutherland's formulation (Sutherland and Cressey 1978:6–7). This is concerned with learning the particular modus operandi of the crime: "When criminal behavior is learned, the learning includes (a) techniques of committing the crime, which are sometimes very complicated, sometimes very simple. . . . "

Implicit in Sutherland's whole analysis is the point that the learning also includes the process by which one modus operandi may be rejected in favor of another—negative as well as positive learning. It is no part of social learning or differential association theory that everyone will inexorably react in an identical way to what seem to be virtually identical experiences. Personal or subjective responses are catered for, responses that in some sense constitute "choice."

Sutherland covered this by stressing that the process of learning has to be understood in the context of the *frequency, duration, priority,* and *intensity* of the relevant experiences, and that these concepts give substance to the notion of definitions favorable or unfavorable to the violation of law. However, critics have complained that such matters cannot be measured, that this renders the theory virtually untestable (de Fleur and Quinney 1966), and generally that the value of the theory as a predictive instrument is thereby crucially diminished.

These criticisms are certainly telling in relation to individual offending behavior. However, the obverse of this is that the theory is arguably enhanced as an explanatory tool. Furthermore, its value as a predictor of broad phenomena, and thus as a basis for policy-making, would not seem to be diminished.

Gun Use in Crime

The main issues of gun use in crime need to be briefly explored so that it can more readily be seen how research drawing upon both rational choice and social learning theory may shed light upon key areas.

First, regarding the technology of violence, it has been established that a firearm is the most dangerous weapon available to ordinary citizens in assault situations. Controlling for key variables such as motivation, commitment, sex, race, and crime situation, a firearm *once actually fired* is several times more likely to cause death than the next most dangerous weapon, a knife.[3] One can say, therefore, that the homicide rate "is a function of the dangerousness of the weapon used multiplied by the number of serious attacks" (Zimring 1967–68:724). As most murder situations are spontaneous, arising out of altercations, rather than planned, and as many are also domestic, it would seem that firearm availability in the form of house guns has a bearing upon murder rates. Gun control is thus an integral aspect of situational crime prevention (Clarke and Mayhew 1980:6,14; Harding 1983).

The counterargument is the "substitute weapon" theory. People who kill others using a gun will kill in some other way if a gun is not available, the argument goes. "Guns don't kill; people do," is the slogan epitomizing this argument. In criminological terms, it is being asserted that Felson's "likely offender" will always somehow or other create an opportunity or discover a means to achieve his homicidal purpose. On this view, situational crime prevention by way of restricted access to firearms is likely to be fruitless.[4]

A whole literature has sprung up around this theory. Perhaps the most cogent technical evidence against it is the finding that the *caliber* of a firearm is a key variable in whether its use will be lethal (Zimring 1972). It can hardly be seriously propounded that a person who grabs a house gun that happens to be of .22 caliber and only wounds his victim is more ambivalent about his intention to kill than someone who, in like circumstances, grabs a .38 caliber house gun and succeeds in actually killing his victim.

However, the terms of the substitute weapon theory do serve to focus the debate upon the pathology of offenders, thus facilitating a shift into a discussion of gun use in *planned* crime, such as robbery. Gun control can never, it is said, stop a professional criminal from obtaining such a weapon. Only honest citizens would be interdicted by such laws (Wright and Rossi 1986:238).

Be that as it may, the argument begs the question as to why some professional criminals choose to use guns and others do not. Have they been socialized differently? Is their appreciation of crime-scene risks more accurate or less? In any case, why are patterns of gun use in crime so different from country to country and from time to time? Clearly, the availability argument, without more, is too simplistic; while the single-minded offender argument fails to locate crime events and persons in relevant social contexts.

Research drawing upon both the rational choice perspective and social learning theory could thus enhance understanding of the phenomenon of gun use in crime, with consequential policy implications.

Weapon Choice by Violent Offenders

The West Australian research

The West Australian research focused upon the decision-making processes of 123 recent violent offenders confined in the prison system at the time of the survey. Particular attention will be given to the subsample of 37 robbers, of whom 15 were gun robbers.[5]

It has been well documented that "victim management" is a key aspect of robbery events (Lettkemann 1973:114; Skogan 1978:68; Wright and Rossi 1986:125–39; Katz 1988:178–81). Particularly in enclosed locations, gun use is, because of the volatile nature of the human situation, the most efficacious way of achieving victim management. In this context, "gun use" does not necessarily equate with firing a gun but rather with presenting one (Harding and Blake 1989:24–25; Harding 1990:433). In Western Australia, gun use in robbery is much more frequent than in other violent crimes, and the survey sample conformed with this observation.

The question arose, in deciding to use the weapon that is apparently the optimum tool for victim management, were gun robbers more "rational" than other robbers? In any case, how far was this rationality bounded, that is, reasoned within constraints so as to not necessarily maximize expected utility. And to the extent that rationality was bounded, was this because prior social learning experiences had in effect circumscribed the capacity of the actor to calculate and pursue expected utility, without more?

TABLE 4.1
Gun Use by Armed Robbers – Reasons.

	"Agree" – Number and % of Respondents		"Very Important" – Number and % of those in Agreement	
Enables offender to get the victim to do what you want.	15	(100.0%)	9	(60.0%)
Enables offender to control victim.	13	(86.7%)	9	(64.3%)
Prevents resistance by victim.	15	(100.0%)	10	(66.7%)
Enables several people to be controlled at the same time.	14	(93.3%)	9	(64.3%)
Enables robbery to be carried out quickly.	13	(86.7%)	11	(84.6%)
Reduced the chance of offender himself getting hurt.	14	(93.3%)	11	(78.0%)
Made offender feel more self-confident.	13	(86.7%)	8	(61.5%)
A gun is a tool of one's trade.	10	(71.4%)	7	(77.8%)

The answer will be seen to be both that the decision to use a gun did follow upon a significantly greater degree of risk assessment and planning than was made by other robbers, and that the choice of the modus operandi to deal with the exigencies of the crime event was significantly influenced by prior and ongoing social learning experiences. In a sense, gun robbers were both more and less rational than other robbers.

Turning, then, to planning and prior risk assessment, it was found that gun robbers were significantly more likely than other robbers to have planned their crime[6] and also to have made some check of crime-scene arrangements. Also, they were significantly more likely to have given thought to the implications of being caught – something that most other robbers hardly seemed to weigh in the balance at all (Harding and Blake 1989:25). Moreover, their sentence expectations were quite precise and were related to the fact that gun robbery was likely to attract a greater sentence than other forms of robbery (ibid.: 32). Interestingly, the majority nevertheless significantly underestimated the sentence that they in fact received.

Prior risk assessment was evidenced by responses to a series of questions relating to classic aspects of victim management (see table 4.1). The converse was a recognition of what they would *not* need guns for (see table 4.2).

Discounted factors are, of course, as much a component of rational decision making as are positive factors. The rationality of gun robbers is that of persons seeking insurance against the crime situation developing in a way that is beyond their power to control. In their own perception,

TABLE 4.2
Gun Use by Armed Robbers — False Suggested Reasons for Use.

Reason	Number and % of Gun Robbers Deeming it False	
The victim might have been armed.	7	(53.9%)
Offender knew victim would be armed.	13	(92.9%)
Security guards might be armed.	9	(60.0%)
Offender knew security guards would be present at scene.	13	(100.0%)
Gun needed as protection from security guards.	11	(84.6%)
Gun needed as protection from police.	9	(64.3%)
Gun needed as protection from other criminals.	11	(84.6%)

gun robbers were behaving rationally, optimizing their chances of committing their crimes successfully and of not getting caught at the crime scene. They were seeking to control their work environment by managing their victims.[7]

By contrast, other robbers (armed with knife, other arms, or strong-arm) tended to give less thought to such matters as crime-scene arrangements, the risks of being caught, and likely sentences. However, they seemed to have no less ready access to firearms than did gun robbers; though they were slightly, but not significantly, less familiar with them, both in the general sense of knowing how to use them and in terms of early exposure and use.[8] Why, then, did they not use a firearm, with its evident operational advantages?

The most compelling evidence came from robbers armed with a knife. One third of these had actively considered carrying a gun rather than a knife as a crime weapon but had then rejected the possibility. They considered that they would not trust themselves with a gun, or that someone might get hurt, or that they themselves were more likely to get hurt by the police if the crime situation got out of control. They also considered that they were likely to receive a harsher sentence if caught and that this in itself was a very important reason for not using a gun in committing their robberies.[9]

Thus, coming to a similar crime situation, these two groups made fundamentally different choices as to the modus operandi. Was this attributable to different levels of intellectual appreciation — a kind of desiccated, pseudo-Benthamite calculation of risks and benefits — or did socialization play a significant part? It was clear that socialization was the key variable. This emerged as follows.

First, although gun users and nonusers were first introduced to firearms at comparable ages, nonusers were significantly more likely to have been

TABLE 4.3
Categories of Persons Involved in Offenders' First Use and Early Experience with Firearms.[10]

	No Gun Use	Gun Use	Total
Authority figures	28	4	32
Peer-group members	21	11	32
Other	22	2	24
Total	71	17	88

$p = < 0.05$

introduced to them and to have received their first practical experience in the company of authority figures — grandfathers, fathers, and uncles. Gun users, by contrast, developed their practical experience much more in the company of peer-group figures — brothers, cousins, friends, and persons involved in criminal activities with firearms (see table 4.3).

An interesting subsidiary question concerned the motives of those authority figures themselves regarding gun ownership. In relation to criminal gun users, the motives of authority figures involved in their own process of familiarization with firearms were significantly likely to have been for defense purposes — either of themselves or of their property. In other words, those offenders had been socialized in an ethos where guns were a permissible means of structuring one's potential relationships with other people. As will be seen, this socialization experience is in sharp contrast to that of the least gun–prone category of violent offenders — traditional Aborigines.

Third, this socialization pattern seemed to flow through to behaviors in later life. Gun users were much more likely as adults to continue to mix with gun owners, including those who themselves used guns from time to time in crime. Thus the impact of earlier socialization experiences continued to be reinforced.

The United States Research

Findings from Wright and Rossi's U.S. study, derived from a much larger sample, lend striking support to the first and third propositions (they did not explore the second). They stated:

> [T]he average gun-owning criminal, like the average legitimate gunowner, was raised around guns and introduced early in life to their use. It may be that there are multiple gun-cultures, some of which strongly disapprove of the illegal . . . uses of guns and some of which do not. . . .
> When considering the more normal or legitimate aspects of firearms behav-

ior (whether the felon ever owned a gun, how many he has owned, how old he was when he first fired or acquired one, etc.) fathers appeared to be the predominant influence (reinforced to be sure by all the other agents of socialization as well). When considering the seamier or clearly criminal aspects of firearms behavior, however, the influence of father (and other family agents) paled considerably, and the effects of one's peer-group came to dominate. (1986:116, 122)

Wright and Rossi do not analyze their findings from the point of view of rational choice. But their data (chap. 5, passim), like the West Australian data, strongly suggest that the processes of social learning are at work in Sutherland's precise terms—the *frequency, duration, priority,* and *intensity* of the relevant experience reinforcing their attitudes, so that the gun robber comes to the point of choosing his modus operandi with circumscribed notions of effective behavior. As the gun user makes his choice, his rationality truly is bounded by his social learning experiences.

Socialization and Culture

The Case of Traditional Aborigines

Curtis (1975:17–19), in his important study of urban violence among American blacks, described culture as the key intervening variable between current social conditions and behavior. The culture that Curtis identified among urban blacks as a whole was exaggerated manliness, brittle defensiveness, poor verbal skills, and a corresponding tendency to settle disputes by violence. That observation is fortified by the West Australian results and by overall patterns of intragroup violence by traditional Aborigines.

Over the last twenty years, Australia's murder rate has been in the range of 1.8 to 2.3 per 100,000. Figures are not available nationally to identify the homicide rate of Aborigines, either as a total ethnic group or broken down into urban and traditional subgroups. Apart from anything else, there are complex definitional problems as to who falls into what category.

However, there is strong if imprecise evidence that the vulnerability of Aborigines generally and traditional Aborigines in particular far exceeds that of the general population. Thus, the overall Aboriginal murder victimization rate in New South Wales was found to be 11.9, and the 1981 rate on Queensland reserves (the residents of which were exclusively traditional Aborigines) was 39.6 per 100,000 (Chappell, Grabosky, and Strang 1991:35).

Although not written explicitly from the point of view of social learning theory, Wilson's classic account (1982) of traditional Aboriginal intragroup violence fits comfortably within the sort of model identified by Curtis — the impact of social conditions upon behavior being mediated by culture. Particularly interesting was the fact that the highest vulnerability was found where traditional culture appeared to be in the course of breaking down — a disintegrating culture being itself a "culture" for these purposes (Biles 1983:17).

Yet, when it came to the *modus operandi as opposed to the incidence of intraracial murder* and violence, the West Australian results confirmed the importance of culture as a mediating event or integral part of the socialization process. It was found that Aborigines still linked to the traditional indigenous life-style were significantly less likely to use guns in violent crime than any other segment of the offender population. Specifically, only one out of 15 violent offenders had used a gun in carrying out his offense. This was despite the fact that they possessed equal familiarity with firearms, and had been subjected to early exposure and use.

The key variables were as follows: higher gun ownership rates by fathers and other authority figures; higher rates of learning gun use with an authority figure; and the fact that these authority figures owned and used their firearms for some legitimate practical reason, notably hunting or destroying vermin. As one offender graphically put his attitude to gun use in crime, "Guns are for shooting tucker [food], not people" (Harding and Blake 1989:17).[11]

Recent data confirm not only the much higher vulnerability of Aborigines to death by homicide but also their much lower use, as offenders, of guns as murder weapons. Overwhelmingly, Aboriginal murders involve knives or arise out of assault situations.[12]

It has been well documented that socialization processes among traditional Aborigines are quite distinctive from those found in modern white societies. While these processes are in the course of evolution and while one cannot generalize with complete accuracy across all indigenous Aboriginal peoples, this general observation nevertheless retains validity.

Berndt and Berndt (1978:131), leading scholars in this area, point out that "under the apparent softness of early socialization practices was a core of firm and almost unyielding rules. On the larger scene, the same blend was reflected in the broader field of social control. Behind the routine of every day, with its co-operation and conflicts, lay the shadow of 'higher authority,' the aura of the sacred." However (ibid.: 125), "children are not passive figures. Adults expect them to participate actively in the progression from childhood to maturity, with all that that entails."

In this regard, "girls continue to go out with the women, learning how to copy what they do, because this is the pattern they are expected to follow. But boys cannot use the same model: there is no place, traditionally speaking, for men who might try to imitate the food-collecting activities of women and pay no attention to hunting. After a few years, therefore, they spend much more time with adult men" (Berndt and Berndt 1985:163). Once their stamina is sufficient, they join in hunting expeditions. It is on such expeditions, of course, that the model of the firearm as an essential tool required for a pro-social purpose becomes paramount. "Guns are," indeed, "for shooting tucker, not people."

The Swiss Experience

Pursuing further the point that culture is the key intervening variable between social conditions and behavior, Clinard (1978:114–15) has identified for Switzerland both a high gun ownership rate and a low homicide rate. He observed that "homicide is due to the tendency to use extreme violence to settle disputes, and not always because firearms are readily available. It appears that the Swiss do not have this tendency to use violence, in terms of a full 'sub-culture of violence,' which often involves using weapons to settle serious disputes."

This attempted explanation is perhaps a little disingenuous in that it both fails to acknowledge the "substitute weapon" debate with all its ideological implications and also ignores what social learning theory may tell us about this phenomenon. In fact, Clinard fails to trip over the clue that he has laid in his own path, namely that the bulk of gun ownership arises out of the arrangements relating to membership in the citizen army of that nation.

I myself have previously suggested (Harding 1983:4–5) that the historically low gun homicide rates in Switzerland, and also those in Israel, against a background of high private availability of firearms, may arise out of the fact that in those countries the citizen predominantly owns firearms as an aspect of his obligation to the state rather than as a means of expressing his own desires and values. *The social meaning of gun ownership is anchored in civic responsibility.* Different socialization processes may thus help to explain the completely different gun homicide rates from those found, say, in the United States, where personal gratification is the overwhelming motive for private gun ownership (Zimring and Hawkins 1987: chaps. 4, 7, and 8). This supposition has not yet been researched by an appropriate methodology; but it is quite capable in principle of being tested empirically by way of survey methodology in relation both to offenders and nonoffenders.

Killias (1990) has recently sought to question what he characterizes as the "criminological myth" of low gun homicide risks in Switzerland. However, in practice, his figures lend some support to the socialization theory. What they show is that, in comparison to other countries with medium-level household gun ownership rates (Belgium, France, Australia, Finland, Canada, Norway, and Switzerland) (van Dijk, Mayhew, and Killias, 1991), Switzerland has significantly the lowest gun homicide rate. The point is that in each of these other countries the social meaning of gun ownership is not anchored in civic responsibilities so much as in personal gratification. Moreover, whereas the Swiss gun ownership rate by household is two-thirds that of the United States, its gun homicide rate is only one-tenth.

One can certainly say, therefore, that the comparative Swiss and international figures are not inconsistent with the view that culture (civic responsibility) is a key component of the socialization process that in turn mediates social phenomena (gun ownership) and behaviors (gun homicides).[13]

Rational Choice, Social Learning Theory, and Criminal Justice Policies

Crime Prevention

Rational choice theory is particularly concerned with crime analysis from the point of view of crime prevention. The data described above begin to tell us that availability per se, while a primary determinant, is not the only factor bearing on gun use in homicide and other violent offenses, so that a more sophisticated approach than merely reducing the gun inventory is likely to be required. It also tells us that the substitute weapon theory is deficient; gun robbers select a firearm precisely because of its instrumental advantages in their work. These insights in turn move us on quite a distance in the gun control debate. It requires us to identify the multiple gun cultures not only across societies but within particular societies, and to develop refined strategies to take account of them.

This can best be done by melding social learning theory research techniques with the rational choice approach. The authors of *The Reasoning Criminal* seemed to recognize this, without perhaps spelling it out explicitly.[14] Akers's criticisms have pushed the natural links to the forefront. In the case of gun control strategies, for example, it can be seen that two quite minor limitations on ownership might have disproportionately productive impact. One would be to screen out persons for whom protection or defense is a primary motive for ownership; the other would be to require in any case training as a prerequisite to gun ownership.

The first strategy would hinge on properly drafted licence application questionnaires plus, if necessary, a follow-up interview. If fathers who set high store by the defense gun are screened out, we have seen that a key component of the socialization experience of gun using violent criminals may likewise be screened out a generation later. The second strategy revolves around the fact that properly trained shooters — that is, shooters trained in the safe handling and storage of firearms and thus acutely aware of their antisocial propensities — not only have lower accident rates but as a by-product may be somewhat less likely to use firearms as a first resort in crime (Harding 1981:98–111).

It is not, of course, suggested that such strategies, standing in isolation, would reverse long-evolving social attitudes toward and cultural meaning of firearms, particularly in the United States. But they do exemplify the sort of crime prevention methods that could take hold, because of their strong theoretical base. Previous gun control approaches seem to have depended predominantly on a classicist approach to the ordering of social behaviors.

Sentencing

The research outlined above is not only of some interest in itself but also may suggest a workable methodology for exploring other issues of current policy concern. One such matter relates to sentencing. This may be the means whereby, in relation to carefully identified offenders, socialization inputs may be re-arranged or differently balanced so as to engineer a changed response to a crime situation among a proportion at least of that group.

The West Australian research, described earlier, identified what I called a "deterrence hiatus" — a rationality gap between the expectations and the consequences of chosen behaviors and between past experience and future intentions. To reiterate: gun robbers gave far more attention to the consequences of being caught, thought they could anticipate the sentence they were likely to receive, but almost invariably underestimated it. In addition, despite what one would have thought would be the shattering of their illusions, they overwhelmingly asserted that *they would continue to use firearms as the crime weapon when committing their next robbery offense* (Harding and Blake 1989:33).

This dynamics of this gap seemed to arise as follows. First, at the time of the crime decision their supposed sentencing savvy was derived principally from other gun using criminals; second, the sentencing rules were themselves unclear, permitting a fudged understanding of them; third, at the time of committing the offense, many of the offenders were under the influence of drugs (other than alcohol); fourth, their experience of prison did not seem to break down their subcultural identity as gun using offenders.

It has been argued that a mandatory minimum additional sentence for the gun use element of the principal offense, irreducible by whatever are the prevailing rules as to parole, could operate so as to alter the deterrence calculus (ibid.: 33–39). More important, the vicarious social learning emphasized by Bandura (1969:118) would mean that the peer group that may graduate to gun crime may be socialized differently.

There are Canadian data to lend broad support to such a supposition (Solicitor-General Canada 1983; Harding and Blake 1989:34–36). Of course, any such proposal if implemented should not be taken on faith, but would need to be evaluated both at a macrolevel and as to the individual dynamics of particular offenders. In other words, decision-making processes and social learning theory could be meshed into a research methodology and the outcomes evaluated.

Conclusion

A marriage between social learning theory and rational choice is natural, useful, and robust. An analysis of factors relevant to weapon choice in crime predicated simply on the rational choice perspective might fail to identify important differences between offending groups based on prior socialization. Conversely, a similar analysis from a social learning point of view might tend to underestimate the extent to which choice does in fact play a part in crime decisions.

However, an approach that melds rational choice with social learning opens the way to differentiated crime prevention strategies. These may, for example, relate to the circumstances of early exposure to firearms or to the impact of training, or to future crime prevention by way of targeted sentencing, or to efforts to minimize knife use in assault in Aboriginal communities rather than concentrating on firearms reduction.

The same theoretical approach may cross crime categories. For example, is there a deterrence hiatus in relation to some kinds of convicted sex offenders and, if so, how could it be filled? Or could we discover more about, say, arsonists who set the bush on fire (a fairly frequent event and a terrible hazard in Australia) so as to enhance crime prevention? The answers to these questions are uncertain. But what is relatively certain is that a mono-theoretical approach would not be productive, while a multitheoretical approach may be.

Finally, perhaps the greatest benefit of melding the two approaches is to ensure that rational choice theory cannot be hijacked by ideological zealots of whatever complexion. This is because a theoretical approach of this kind compels one to go where the data leads one. Far from de-pathologizing crime and criminals, as some critics have feared, it would re-pathologize them in terms that are testable and fairly precise.

Notes

1. Ibid., 15. Hirschi echoes this concern in his contribution to *The Reasoning Criminal:* "In the current counterrevolt [against positivist sociological explanations for crime] there is a reverse tendency to see the offender as thoughtful and intellectually sophisticated. I think this tendency should be resisted" (p. 115).
2. *Bounded rationality* is the term used to express the notion that human information-processing limitations put constraints upon or bring about distortions in decision processes. The bounded rationality hypothesis states that behavior is reasoned within constraints, but is not necessarily fully rational in the strict sense of maximizing expected utility.
3. The literature is immense. Key contributions include the following: Franklin E. Zimring (1967–68) Philip J. Cook (1983) and Philip J. Cook (1991).
4. Once more, the literature is immense. However, a good feel for it is found in James D. Wright and Peter H. Rossi (1986:209–38). See also James D. Wright, Peter H. Rossi, and Kathleen Daly (1983) where they state:
   > Even the most ardent proponents of stricter gun laws no longer expect such laws to solve the hard-core crime problem, or even to make much of a dent in it. There is also reason to doubt whether the 'soft-core' violence, the so-called crimes of passion, would decline by very much. Stated simply, these crimes occur because some people have come to hate others, and they will continue to occur in one form or another as long as hatred persists. . . . If we could solve the problem of interpersonal hatred, it may not matter much what we do about guns, and *unless* we solve the problem of interpersonal hatred, it may not matter very much what we do about guns. There are simply too many other objects in the world that can serve the purpose of inflicting harm on another human being. . . . [The crimes] would be committed with other weapons. Quoted in Franklin E. Zimring and Gordon Hawkins [1987:14–15]).
5. Tables 4.1 and 4.2, below, relate to the subsample of 15 gun robbers; at various points in the text reference is made to the other robbers (n = 22) in the robber sample. Table 4.3 (n = 105), relates to the sample of 123 violent offenders less the traditional Aboriginal subsample though there are 17 missing values; and at various points in the text reference is made to the subsample of traditional Aborigines (n = 18).
6. "Planning" did not mean the kind of thought processes that might go into a complex business arrangement, and could be quite cursory. However, the key thing was that the robbers thought of themselves as having planned it, rather than having acted merely impulsively.
7. This reasoning process of gun robbers finds support in the work of Wright and Rossi (1986). However, these authors do not link their research to rational choice, and although much of their data is given extra meaning by social learning theory, they nevertheless insist that their study is atheoretical (ibid.: ix, x).
8. With regard to access, the response rate was too low to be statistically significant, but what responses there were flowed strongly in the direction suggested. With regard to early exposure and use, 83% of gun robbers and 75% of other robbers

were shown how to use guns before they were 16; with regard to first use, 93% of gun robbers and 82% of other robbers first used a gun on their own account before that age.

9. Once more, the numbers were too low for statistical significance. However, they flowed strongly in the directions indicated. These results are remarkably similar to Wright and Rossi's (1986) findings.

> The armed-not-with-a-gun criminals were also asked why they had opted not to carry firearms; the unarmed criminals were asked why they had opted not to carry any weapons. Remarkably, there was virtually perfect agreement between the two groups. . . . In both cases, the most important reason for not carrying was that "the guy who carries [a gun or weapon] is just asking for trouble," . . . followed by "you get a stiffer sentence if you get caught with [a gun or a weapon]." . . . The other top four finishers in both groups were: "I never needed [a gun or a weapon] for the kinds of crime I did"; . . . and "if you carry [a gun or a weapon] somebody is going to get hurt"; . . . "I just wouldn't feel right [carrying a gun or a weapon]"; . . . and "I just never thought about carrying a [gun or weapon]."

10. Note that this table refers to the whole sample of 123 violent offenders less the traditional Aboriginal sample (n = 18). There are 17 missing values. The traditional Aboriginal sample was much more likely to have been socialized to gun use by authority figures. It is for this reason that this group has been removed from the sample considered in table 4.3, so as to leave the socialization point unpolluted by the inclusion of a distinctive subsample. See further, note 5, above.

11. See also William R. Tonso, (1982:26–27):

> The practical function of firearms in people's lives must be considered as part of a response to objective conditions as these conditions have been filtered through a subjective frame of reference, rather than as an automatic response to a world that can be shown to exist . . . in some objective sense. Such little research as has been done on the firearms phenomenon has failed to take this point into consideration. . . . *When firearms function practically in people's lives, they function as tools; and tools are created or selected by their users according to the tasks the users feel they must accomplish with them.* . . . Prospective tool users consider conditions "out there" in the "real world" as these conditions have been socially defined and subjectively experienced. (Emphasis added)

12. See Heather Strang (1991:20). The information published there is not quite comprehensive. However, at my request the data was recomputed and confirms the pattern referred to in the text. Specifically, 2/51 (4%) of murder victims where an Aborigine was the offender were killed by use of firearms, whereas 74/255 (29%) of the victims of non-Aboriginal offenders were killed by use of firearms.

13. Tonso (1982) has traced the evolution of gun ownership patterns in Japan and reached a comparable conclusion as to the importance of culture in imparting social meaning to gun ownership: "When the peasant was reintroduced to firearms in the third quarter of the nineteenth century, this reintroduction was accomplished within a military rather than a civilian context, and the gun still had no place in village life. While formal regulations against firearm ownership by ordinary citizens still existed, they do not seem to have been needed" (ibid.: 94).

14. See Cornish and Clarke (1986: 10, 13, and in particular 217–18):

> Our own view would be, first, that a concept of human reasoning as "situated" is not only compatible with but given explicit recognition in a rational choice approach. . . . Each event . . . is linked to a previous (new, standing or revised) involvement decision sequence, and it is there, *where wider social forces and*

personal histories have most impact upon decision making, that the situated
nature of practical reasoning is most clearly to be appreciated and structural
explanations of offending sought. (Emphasis added)

References

Akers, Ronald L. 1990. "Rational choice, deterrence and social learning theory in
criminology: The path not taken." *Journal of Criminal Law and Criminology*
81:653–76.

Bandura, Albert. 1969. *Principles of behavior modification.* New York: Holt,
Rinehart and Winston.

Berndt, Catherine H., & Berndt, Ronald M. 1978. "Aborigines." In Frederick J.
Hunt (Ed.), *Socialization in Australia.* Sydney: Angus and Robertson.

Berndt, Ronald M., & Berndt, Catherine H. 1985. *The world of the first Austra-
lians.* Adelaide: Rigby.

Biles, David. 1983. *Groote Eylandt prisoners.* Canberra: Australian Institute of
Criminology.

Bottomley, Keith. 1988. [Review of D.B. Cornish and R.V. Clarke (Eds.), "The
reasoning criminal"]. *British Journal of Criminology* 28:536.

Braithwaite, John B. 1987. "Review essay: The mesomorphs strike back." *A.N.Z.
Journal of Criminology* 20:45–53.

Chappell, Duncan, Grabosky, Peter N., & Strang, Heather, 1991. *Australian violence: Contemporary perspectives.* Canberra: Australian Institute of Criminology.

Clarke, Ronald V., & Mayhew, Pat. 1980. *Designing out crime.* London: Home
Office Research Publication.

Clinard, Marshall B. 1978. *Cities with little crime: The case of Switzerland.*
Cambridge: Cambridge University Press.

Cook, Philip J. 1983. "The influence of gun availability on violent crime patterns." *Crime and justice: An Annual Review of Research* 4:49–89.

———. 1991. "The technology of personal violence." *Crime and Justice: A Review of Research* 14:1–71.

Cornish, Derek B., & Clarke, Ronald V. 1986. *The reasoning criminal: Rational
choice perspectives on offending.* New York: Springer–Verlag.

Curtis, Lynn A. 1975. *Violence, race and culture.* Lexington, MA: Heath.

de Fleur, Melvin L., & Quinney, Richard. 1966. "A reformulation of Sutherland's
differential association theory and a strategy of empirical verification." *Journal
of Research in Crime and Delinquency* 3:1–22.

Harding, Richard W. 1981. *Firearms and violence in Australian life.* Perth: University of Western Australia Press.

———. 1983. "An ounce of prevention . . . : Gun control and public health in
Australia." *A.N.Z. Journal of Criminology* 16:3–19.

———. 1990. "Rational choice gun use in armed robbery: The likely deterrent
effect on gun use of mandatory additional imprisonment." *Criminal Law Fo-
rum* 1:427–50.

Harding, Richard W., & Blake, Ann. 1989. Weapon choice by violent offenders
in Western Australia: A pilot study. *Research Report No. 1.* Perth: Crime Research Centre, The University of Western Australia.

Katz, Jack. 1988. *Seductions of crime: Moral and sensual attractions of doing
evil.* New York: Basic Books.

Killias, Martin. 1990. "Gun ownership and violent crime: The Swiss experience in international perspective." *Security Journal* 1:169–74.

Letkemann, Peter. 1973. *Crime as work.* New Jersey: Spectrum Books.

Skogan, Wesley G. 1978. "Weapon choice in robbery." In James A. Inciardi (Ed.), *Violent crime: Historical and contemporary issues.* Newbury Park, CA.: Sage Publications.

Solicitor-General Canada. 1983. *Firearms control in Canada: An evaluation.* Ottawa: Ministry of Solicitor-General.

Strang, Heather. 1991. *Homicides in Australia, 1989–90.* Canberra: Australian Institute of Criminology.

Sutherland, Edwin H., & Cressey, Donald R. 1978. *Criminology* (10th ed.). Philadelphia: Lippincott.

Tonso, William R. 1982. *Gun and society.* Washington, DC: University Press of America.

van Dijk, Jan, Mayhew, Pat, & Killias, Martin. 1991. *Experiences of crime across the world: Key findings of the 1989 international crime survey.* Boston: Kluwer.

Wilson, James Q., & Herrnstein, Richard J. 1985. *Crime and human nature: The definitive study of the causes of crime.* New York: Simon and Schuster.

Wilson, Paul. 1982. *Black death, white hands.* Sydney: Allen and Unwin.

Wright, James D., & Rossi, Peter H. 1986. *Armed and considered dangerous: A survey of felons and their firearms.* New York: Aldine de Gruyter.

Wright, James D., Rossi, Peter H., & Daly, Kathleen. 1983. *Under the gun: Weapons, crime and violence in America.* New York: Aldine de Gruyter.

Zimring, Franklin E. 1967–68. "Is gun control likely to reduce violent killing?" *University of Chicago Law Review* 35:721–37.

———. 1972. "The medium is the message: Firearm caliber as a determinant of death." *Journal of Legal Studies* 1:97–123.

Zimring, Franklin E., & Hawkins, Gordon. 1987. *The citizen's guide to gun control.* New York: Macmillan.

5

Predatory and Dispute-related Violence: A Social Interactionist Approach

Richard B. Felson

Harm doing is studied under different guises. Social psychologists interested in aggression study shock delivery in laboratory settings. Other social psychologists study competitive choices and contentious tactics in experimental games, but identify their subject as social conflict. Criminologists study physical violence under the rubric of crime, sociologists study family violence, and anthropologists study the sometimes violent expression of grievances in societies with rudimentary legal systems. All of these scholars are interested in why people purposefully harm each other.

Two theories proposed by social psychologists have been particularly influential in the study of physical violence. The frustration-aggression hypothesis suggests that individuals are likely to engage in aggression when their goals have been blocked (Dollard et al. 1939) or — in the most recent version of the theory — when faced with aversive stimuli (Berkowitz 1989). This approach has been influential in studies of the effect of stress on criminal and family violence, and in the study of the effects of poverty and social inequality on homicide rates (e.g., Messner 1988; Straus 1980).

Another influential approach — social learning theory — stresses the importance of modeling and rewards in the socialization of violent behavior (Bandura 1973). Social learning theory provides the rationale for extensive research on the effects of media violence, and on the intergenerational

I wish to thank Steve Messner for his comments on an earlier draft of this manuscript.

transmission of violence (Widom 1989). The claim is made that people engage in violence because they've observed their parents and their TV heros engaging in violence.

These theories parallel the distinction that is generally made between angry aggression and instrumental aggression (Buss 1961). Angry aggression refers to involuntary acts that are compelled by aggressive drive or energy — forces inside the person. Harm to the target is an end in itself. In contrast, in instrumental aggression, harm doing is a means to an end. Individuals harm others because it brings them some benefit or reward.

A relatively new approach to aggression and violence challenges this distinction. What might be called a "social interactionist" perspective emphasizes the role of social interaction — as opposed to conditions inside the person — in aggressive behavior (Averill 1982, 1983; Black 1983; Felson 1978, 1984; Goode 1971; Kennedy 1990; Luckenbill 1977; Tedeschi 1970; Tedeschi, Gaes, and Rivera 1977; Tedeschi, Smith, and Brown 1974).[1] It interprets all aggressive behavior as goal-oriented or instrumental, that is, as an attempt to achieve what people value. Aggressive actions seek to compel and deter others, to achieve a favorable social identity, and to obtain justice, as defined by the actor. While much aggression is done "in anger," anger and aggression reflect a social control reaction to perceived misdeeds rather than involuntary responses to frustration. In contrast to the frustration-aggression hypothesis, people only get angry when they *blame* someone for frustrating or aversive events. While they may behave impulsively in the sense that they fail to consider long-range consequences (Gottfredson and Hirschi 1990), their behavior is still the consequence of a decision-making process.

Note that a social interactionist approach is concerned with an actor's point of view, not the truth of any allegations. While the target does play at least some causal role in most incidents of dispute-related violence, I do not use the term *victim precipitation*. This value-laden term confuses cause and blame (Felson 1991). Assigning a causal role to targets does not necessarily imply that they were blameworthy. For example, whether an individual kills someone in self-defense or in response to mild criticism, the target's behavior has an effect. Whether the target is blameworthy may be relevant to the legal system but it is irrelevant to a scientific analysis of violence.[2]

In this chapter, I apply a social interactionist approach to criminal violence. Two general types of violence are distinguished: predatory and dispute-related. Predatory violence — physical aggression committed without provocation — is discussed in the first part of the chapter. In this section, I focus on violence oriented toward gaining compliance and bullying. The rest of the paper focuses on dispute-related violence, that is,

TABLE 5.1
Motives in Predatory and Dispute-Related Violence

	Type of Violence	
Actor's Concern	Predatory	Dispute-Related
Compliance	"Compellence"	Deterrence
Justice	Redistribution	Retribution
Social Identities	Assertive self-presentation	Defensive self-presentation

violence that involves a reaction to some alleged wrong. I describe factors that produce conflict, including stress, as well as factors that inhibit it. I also discuss violence as an informal means of social control, including its use by parents and police. The escalation of these disputes is discussed, emphasizing the role of social identities and third parties. I then apply the routine activity approach — which has mainly been applied to predatory crime — to dispute-related violence. I conclude with a description of incidents that involve both predation and disputes.

Predatory Violence

Three general concerns of actors in violent incidents are presented in table 5.1: generating compliance; pursuing justice; and the achievement of desired social identities. These concerns are relevant to both types of violence. Thus, the table suggests three reasons why individuals might engage in predatory or unprovoked violence. First, they may use coercion to compel the target to engage in some desired behavior. In these incidents, contingent threats or bodily force are used to compel a person to do something they would not otherwise do. For example, threats may be used in order to obtain money or sex. A second form of predatory violence involves an attempt to establish or assert some identity, using what Arkin (1980) has described as an assertive form of self-presentation. The person is commonly referred to as a "bully" — someone who preys on a vulnerable target in order to demonstrate his power. The bully's domination of the target demonstrates power and may increase his or her status for some audiences.

A third form of predatory violence involves equity restoration (see Tedeschi and Norman 1985; Donnerstein and Hatfield 1982). When individuals decide that the distribution of rewards and costs is unfair, they may attempt to restore equity by harming the person perceived as privileged, even when that person is not held responsible for the injustice. By increasing the costs or reducing the rewards of the overbenefited party they can produce equity or distributive justice. The redistribution can be described as predatory rather than dispute-related because the action does not have a dispute with the target. Such a process helps explain why jealousy might lead to violence.

The redistribution process has been demonstrated in an experiment in which subjects had to wait for another subject who did not show up for a research appointment (Nacci and Tedeschi 1977). Subjects then participated in a learning task in which they were given the opportunity to deliver shocks to someone who was allegedly recruited to take the place of the missing partner. Subjects who had to wait delivered more shocks to their partner, but not if the partner had experienced a similar delay. That subjects only delivered greater shocks to partners who had not experienced the delay suggests that they were attempting to restore equity rather than engaging in displaced aggression.[3]

The following discussion focuses on predatory violence oriented toward either compliance or self-presentation. We shall not discuss equity restoration further for two reasons. First, there has not been much research done on the topic. Second, this type of violence is probably infrequent. When people feel they have been unjustly treated, they usually attack the person they blame for the injustice, not the person who has benefited from the inequity. Retribution against the person responsible for the injustice will be discussed as a form of dispute-related violence.

Gaining Compliance

In these incidents contingent threats or bodily force are used to compel a person to comply with some directive. For example, in the typical blackmail, the offender threatens to reveal information to legal authorities for punishment unless the victim complies. In the typical robbery, the offender threatens to deliver harm themselves unless the victim complies. The offender is usually motivated to obtain money or property and is using the threat of violence as a means of social influence. He usually selects targets who are likely to comply and to provide a good "take" (Cook 1976).

Most robbery offenders use violence strategically, that is, in order to successfully complete the crime . They make their threat, and if the victim complies, they do not engage in any further violence (Luckenbill 1980). Armed offenders rarely attack the victim while unarmed offenders sometimes engage in preemptive strikes designed to give their threats credibility (Cook 1982; Luckenbill 1980). The minimal, strategic use of force suggests that the purpose of most robbers is to gain compliance and not to harm their victim. It also demonstrates that an actual attack is sometimes a sign of weakness: it is used when the threat of violence fails to influence a target (Goode 1971).

Rape involves the use of contingent threats or bodily force to compel a person to engage in sexual intercourse. The three major outcomes in a completed rape are sexual activity, harm to the victim, and domination of the victim. The question of motive involves determining which of these outcomes is the goal of the offender and which are incidental. For a sexually motivated offender, domination and harm to the victim are incidental outcomes; his interest is in influencing the victim to have sexual activity.

In contrast to popular thinking, there is considerable evidence that many rapes are sexually motivated.[4] First, like robbers, rapists generally use violence in a strategic fashion—using only enough force to obtain compliance (Felson and Krohn 1990). They attempt to establish a credible threat but they are unlikely to carry out the threat if the victim complies. Second, there is evidence that men tend to use sexual coercion as a last resort in incidents involving people they know (Kanin 1967, 1985). In other words, they use coercion after other methods of influence have failed. Third, the use of sexual coercion is related to high "sexual aspirations" (Kanin 1965, 1967, 1985). College men who are dissatisfied with the frequency of their sexual activity, or who indicate that a higher frequency of orgasms was necessary for them to be sexually satisfied, are more likely to engage in coercive sexual behavior. Fourth, "date rapes" usually occur when a male is sexually aroused. In all 71 incidents of date rape studied by Kanin (1985), the rape occurred during an intensive consensual sexual encounter, most commonly involving oral-genital sex. Finally, the targets of rape are almost always young women (Shields and Shields 1983; Thornhill and Thornhill 1983). There is obviously a strong relationship between age and sexual attractiveness. Felson and Krohn (1990) find evidence that the age pattern reflects a *preference* for young women and not just differential opportunity. This is indicated by evidence that a young woman is more likely to be raped during a robbery than an older woman.

Evidence for a sexual motive comes also comes from a study of sexual violence in a New York State prison facility (Lockwood 1980). The study finds that inmates who use sexual coercion target young attractive men who most resemble females. In addition, offenders use both noncoercive and coercive techniques to influence targets to engage in sexual activity.

Rape in prison in part reflects the fact that prisons are filled with young men who lack inhibitions about using violence. It probably also reflects sexual deprivation and the reluctance of many heterosexual men to take the "passive role" in homosexual sex. In other words, there are many inmates willing to play the active role and relatively few willing to play the passive role. As a result, it is probably difficult to find partners to engage in consensual sexual activity. Powerful inmates who seek sexual satisfaction are likely to force weaker men to play the passive role. This is similar to the situation outside prison where there is a surplus of males interested in casual sex and a scarcity of females with this interest.

Bullying: Assertive Self-presentation

Bullying involves the unprovoked use of aggression against targets to assert some identity rather than produce a material gain. For the bully, dominating the victim is an accomplishment, a way of demonstrating power to himself and others. The bully's general strategy appears to be to dominate a vulnerable low-status target using coercive means (Besag 1989). Research on young bullies shows that they tend to be 1–2 years older than their victims and physically stronger (Olweus 1978). Typically, they victimize children who are unpopular, physically unattractive, and physically uncoordinated. The role of self-presentation is suggested by evidence that bullies tend to seek out situations in which their behavior can be witnessed by their peers (Besag 1989). That bullies sometimes operate in groups also suggests that the attack can confer status on those who use it. Adults, even when they are aware of bullying, are apparently reluctant to intervene, fearing that they might make things worse (Besag 1989). Apparently, they expect the victim to stand up to the bully.

Some incidents of rape could reflect the offender's desire to bully the victim and demonstrate power. A male who uses sexual coercion for this purpose may view his ability to control the target as an accomplishment. This explanation is similar to a feminist approach, which suggests that men use sexual coercion because it gives them a feeling of power, control, or dominance over female victims (Deming and Eppy 1981). An offender with this motive wants to coerce the victim to do something she would not do otherwise in order to demonstrate his power. In contrast to a sexually motivated offender, he would prefer coercive sex to consensual sex; he would prefer that victims initially resist him; and he would use coercive techniques as a first rather than as a last resort. Evidence on date rape suggests that this is not the typical scenario: offenders usually use coercion as a last resort when woman resist intercourse during consensual sexual encounters (Kanin 1985). However, there could be some rapists who are motivated to demonstrate their power.

Dispute-Related Violence

Dispute-related violence occurs as a result of social control reactions to perceived wrongdoing (Black 1983). Individuals feel aggrieved when they believe that they have been wronged, and they are motivated to punish the miscreant. Unlike individuals engaged in predatory violence, antagonists are likely to feel angry in dispute-related violence (Averill 1982). Like the criminal justice system, they use punishment either to deter the target and others from repeating the offense, or because of their beliefs about justice. They view their behavior as retribution, that is, as a legitimate and justifiable response to the misdeeds of others. The initial attack is usually verbal, but it can lead to retaliation in the form of physical violence. One of the goals of retaliation is to "save face" (or defend "honor"), and thus it is a defensive form of self-presentation (Arkin 1980). As indicated in table 5.1, deterrence, retribution, and defensive self-presentation are central to dispute-related violence.

Studies of the sequence of events in violent incidents provide evidence for this approach (Felson and Steadman 1983; Luckenbill 1977). For example, Felson (1984) finds that most violent incidents begin with a social control process in which one party admonishes the other for violating a rule or not complying with an order. After the aggrieved party challenges the alleged transgressor, the transgressor may give an account to explain his or her behavior. When the transgressor fails to give an account, verbal attacks are more likely. The aggrieved party is usually the first to attack. This act of punishment—usually a verbal attack—often leads to retaliation and escalation.

Some rapes could also reflect the expression of grievances. An man who feels aggrieved against a woman may use rape as a form of punishment. In these cases, one would expect some prior conflict between them. The social interaction is likely to be similar to homicides and assaults where verbal conflict escalates, culminating in physical attacks. Since grievances are less likely between strangers, this explanation should primarily apply to people who know each other.

If grievances are involved in sexual coercion, then one might expect offenders to mistreat victims in a variety of ways during the incident. They might insult and humiliate the victim or they might physically attack the victim even when they have a credible threat and the victim is complying. Evidence that rapes involving estranged couples are likely to be particularly violent suggests that grievances play a role in these incidents (Felson and Krohn 1990).

Transgressions as Sources of Conflict

If violence results from attempts at informal social control, then it should be associated with the occurrence of transgressions. When transgressions are serious, one is likely to observe severe forms of punishment in response — the punishment is likely to "fit the crime." Those who are harmed by transgressions are the most likely to feel angry and aggrieved and to attack. However, anyone who observes the misdeed may punish the offender, whether or not they were harmed or whether or not anyone was harmed. Justice demands that a wrongdoer be punished.

Evidence that individuals who engage in frequent transgressions are more likely to be targeted for violence comes from the literature on child abuse. That literature suggests that children with behavior problems are more likely to be the targets of abuse (for reviews of the evidence, see Burgess 1979; Parke and Collmer 1975; Wolfe 1985). Also important is the response of children to other forms of control. Children who are more easily influenced, because they are more fearful, or more susceptible to reasoning, are less likely to elicit coercive behavior from parents (Parke and Collmer 1975).

A parent's interpretation of a child's behavior may be a more important factor than the child's actual behavior. There is likely to be greater conflict when parents have unrealistically high standards and expectations for their children (Parke and Collmer 1975). In addition, parents who view their child's misbehavior as intentional, blameworthy, and as representative of stable internal states are more likely to use violence (e.g., Frodi and Lamb 1980; Larrance and Twentyman 1983).

One would expect violence to occur more frequently in social contexts in which rules are frequently violated. In general, the greater the level of conflict and the less clear the rules for resolving conflict, the more likely grievances will develop. For example, Felson (1983) suggests that one reason siblings fight so frequently is that siblings share material goods and participate in a household division of labor, and the rules for the use of goods and the division of labor are unclear. This argument suggests that these attacks reflect realistic conflict not rivalry over status or parental attention.

The theory suggests an additional explanation of the effect of alcohol intoxication on violent behavior. The typical explanations are that alcohol leads to violence because it reduces inhibitions, lowers self-control, or provides an individual with an excuse to use violence (see, e.g., Wilson and Herrnstein 1985). It is also possible that alcohol leads people to engage in behaviors that others find offensive. The social control responses of others may then lead to violent exchanges. This is consistent with evidence that alcohol is common in homicide victims as well as offenders (Wolfgang 1958).

The tendency for transgressions to lead to violence may be a factor in the explanation of the versatility of people who commit crime. Evidence suggests that those who commit violent offenses are likely to commit a variety of offenses. Gottfredson and Hirschi (1990) suggest that low self-control leads to this versatility. However, it may also be that those persons who commit transgressions are more likely to become involved in conflicts with others. Others may be offended by their stealing, drinking, and drug use, or their drinking or drug use may lead them to engage in other offensive behavior. This is likely to lead to attempts to control them and sometimes violent encounters.

Inhibition of Grievance Expression

It is also important to examine factors that inhibit aggression and violence. Moral inhibitions, self-control, and external controls probably play a role, as they do in other forms of criminal behavior (Gottfredson and Hirschi 1990; Hirschi 1969). Also important may be those factors that inhibit the expression of grievances. Averill's (1982, 1983) research shows that disputes are infrequent relative to the frequency of anger and grievances and the level of underlying conflict in social relations. Thus, Averill finds that in most instances people who are angry do not express their grievances. Felson (1984) also found that many rule violations are ignored: respondents indicated that they were angry at someone but did nothing. Such a response was particularly likely when the target of the grievance was someone they worked with or a relative outside the immediate family. On the other hand, grievances are readily expressed in the immediate family (unpublished data).

The reason that people do not express their grievances is primarily because of the costs involved. The aggrieved may keep silent because they fear retaliation or because they do not want to destroy their relationship with the target of their grievance. They may also wish to avoid an embarrassing scene. The rules of conversation require politeness and deference (Goffman 1959). People usually go to considerable effort to hide any critical opinions they may have; they "bend over backwards" to avoid any slights. As a result of these rules, many grievances go unexpressed and many coercive encounters are "nipped in the bud." One would expect that people who are easily embarrassed are less likely to express their grievances and therefore less likely to become involved in coercive interactions.

Stress and Conflict

Many studies have shown a positive correlation between physical violence and stress (e.g., Mueller 1983; Straus 1980). The effects of stress, like the effects of aversive stimuli in the laboratory, are generally assumed to be due to some sort of frustration-aggression mechanism. The social interactionist approach, on the other hand, suggests that stress may be one source of the types of behavior that lead to grievances. There is considerable evidence that stress negatively affects performance in school and work (see, e.g., Cohen 1980; Holmes and Masuda 1974; Motowidlo, Packard, and Manning 1986). In addition, one would expect that people who are stressed are less likely to perform the interaction ritual competently (Felson 1978). Because of their mood, they are less likely to be polite and friendly, to feign positive emotions, or to show ritualized support for others. If distressed persons are likely to perform less competently, violate expectations, or annoy others, they are likely to become the object of grievances. This is likely to lead to their involvement in aggressive interactions, often, initially, as targets. As indicated above, evidence suggests that the aggrieved party is more often the first to engage in an aggressive act (Felson 1984).

Support for this argument comes from research that shows that stressful life events are a better predictor of being the target of violence than engaging in violence (Felson 1991). Further, the correlation between stressful life events and violence disappears when being the target of aggression is controlled. This suggests that distressed persons engage in more violence because they are targeted by others. One assumes that their behavior must have played a role in eliciting this response.

Legal Recourse as an Alternative to Violence

A grievant may seek the aid of third parties to mediate a dispute or to punish the offender and help restore justice. Black (1983) emphasizes this alternative in his discussion of "crime as social control." He suggests that some people use the police and the courts to satisfy their grievances, while others engage in "self-help", and punish the violator themselves. Thus, many acts of criminal violence reflect decisions of offenders to settle grievances themselves when they the perceive that police are unavailable or ineffective.

Black suggests that many crimes involving people who know each other result from grievances, including burglaries, robberies, vandalism, and arson. However, crimes between people who know each other are not necessarily grievance-oriented. People may covet their neighbors' possessions and steal them, for example. On the other hand, people sometimes have grievances against strangers after a brief encounter.

Some forms of vandalism can be interpreted as an attempt by youth to punish adults generally. In this case punishment is directed at targets with whom the offender has no personal grievance. The target is punished because they share some social category with someone with whom the offender does have a grievance. Here there is some notion of collective liability, or guilt by association, where an aggrieved party blames the entire group for the misbehavior of one member (Tedeschi and Norman 1985).

Black (1983) focuses on barriers to the use of legal resources in handling one's grievances. He argues that legal recourse is often not as available to persons with lower status, particularly when their status is lower than the status of the person with whom they have a grievance. Low status grievants may avoid the criminal justice system because they feel that their charges will not be believed or that the police cannot be trusted. Black's theory would predict that low status victims are less likely to report crimes to the police than victims of higher status. The evidence from victimization studies is generally not supportive regarding the effects of race. Minorities who are victims of household burglary and motor vehicle theft are just as likely as whites to report the crime to the police (Bureau of Justice Statistics 1983). Further, black crime victims are more likely than white crime victims to demand that police make an arrest when they are the victim of a crime (Black and Reiss 1970). On the other hand, there is some supporting evidence in regard to the social class of victims. Victims of household burglary and motor vehicle theft are more likely to report the crime to the police if they have higher income (Bureau of Justice Statistics 1983).

Since the antagonists in disputes are usually of similar race and class, one suspects that the role of status in seeking police assistance is likely to be limited. However, there may be other factors that affect the tendency to use self-help. First, an absence of formal authority produces high levels of violence (Black 1983). Where legal systems are absent, undeveloped, or ineffective, or when third-party mediators are unavailable, self-help should be common. Second, self-help is more likely when the grievance is against a family member because legal authorities are less likely to intervene in such cases. Thus, Black's theory of self-help provides one explanation for the high frequency of domestic violence. Third, when a young male is attacked, he may have difficulty convincing the police that he is the victim and not a co-offender. Finally, persons involved in other forms of criminal activity, such as drug sales, are more likely to use self-help because the law is not available to them when grievances develop over matters of business. Obviously, a drug customer who is shortchanged cannot protest to the police or the Better Business Bureau.

Access to third-party mediators does not necessarily discourage aggression between two antagonists. In some instances, it may encourage a weaker antagonist to become aggressive. This is suggested by evidence that parental intervention increases the incidence of aggression between siblings (Felson 1983; Felson and Russo 1988). When parents intervene, they usually act in behalf of the younger sibling. Knowing that they enjoy parental protection, younger siblings are more willing to fight.

Parents and Police as Agents of Social Control

One would expect dispute-related violence to be particularly likely to occur in incidents involving individuals acting in the role of a social control agent. The best examples are parents and police.[5]

Much of the extralegal use of violence by police can be described as dispute-related. Toch (1969), for example, finds that in the most common sequence of events, the officer gives orders or instructions, the suspect expresses his contempt, which leads the officer to use bodily force. The officer frequently feels that the suspect's behavior challenges his reputation, and after he makes the opening move, he feels that he must persevere. The suspect, on the other hand, perceives police action as arbitrary and unfair and an attack on his identity (see also Westley 1970).

In regard to parents, Goode (1971) argues that there is always an element of coercion in parent-child relations, even when parents use other forms of influence. Thus, children may comply when parents reason with them because they are aware that they will be punished otherwise. One can interpret reasoning as the justification parents use when they coerce their children.

The basic coercive tool for parents is the contingent threat. When threats are ineffective then punishment is likely. As indicated earlier, the actual use of punishment suggests that threats have been ineffective. Because of their authority over children, parents have a wide range of punishments available to them. Physical punishment is an available resource because its use is supported (legally and normatively) by the larger society (Goode 1971) and because, for younger children at least, parents have superior size and strength. Deprivation of resources is also a common punishment strategy since parents control goods desired by the child. When parental acts of coercion are viewed as inappropriately severe relative to the child's behavior, they are labeled "child abuse."

When the perceived probability of success using noncoercive forms of influence is low, coercion is more likely to be used. This assertion is supported by evidence that parents who lack verbal skill's for persuasion are more likely to use violence (Parke and Collmer 1975). There is also evidence that stress may affect the use of coercion because it impairs parental competence, which includes the ability to control children using noncoercive means (Wolfe 1985).

Retaliation and Escalation

When people think that another person has intentionally harmed them, they are likely to retaliate. Experimental research shows that perceived intentional attack is the most reliable elicitor of aggressive behavior. In fact, subjects tend to retaliate for intended shocks even when they do not actually receive the shock (Shuck and Pisor 1974). Note that this is directly counter to the frustration-aggression hypothesis, which, in the most recent version (Berkowitz 1989), suggests that aversive stimuli, not "bad intentions," leads to aggression.

There are at least three reasons why people retaliate. First, an attack is likely to be perceived as wrongdoing by the target and thus creates a grievance. Second, by retaliating, the target of an attack deters his or her tormentor and others from future attacks. Finally, an initial attack casts the target into a negative identity by making the target appear weak and ineffectual. The target can nullify that image, i.e., can "save face," by a counterattack.

I view these as complementary explanations of retaliatory behavior. It may be that in some instances, the behavior is motivated by identity concerns but that a belief in justice acts as a disinhibitor. The person counterattacks in order to save face and is able to legitimate the counterattack by claiming that the target deserved it. This is a case of "justice in the service of revenge."

Concerns for justice and self-image do not always have the same effects, however. Aggrieved individuals are interested in seeing that the wrongdoer receives a punishment that is proportional to the offense, while individuals concerned with their identities want to win the battle and make a good show of themselves. They prefer to dominate antagonists, which means harming them more than they, the aggrieved individuals, have been harmed.[6] In these instances, justice concerns might inhibit the strength of retaliation.

The two motives imply different responses to unsuccessful attacks. Antagonists who engage in unsuccessful attacks have misbehaved but they have spoiled their own image more than the target's. They deserve to be punished but they have not threatened the target's identity. Therefore, a target concerned with saving face does not feel compelled to retaliate when an attack has failed. For the same reasons, misdeeds directed at third parties are more likely to produce a concern for justice than a concern for identity, unless the person is closely identified with the third party.

Since a counterattack casts its target into a negative identity, it often motivates a counter-counterattack, creating a "conflict spiral." These attacks can become more serious as the incident progresses, sometimes resulting in physical assaults or homicides (Felson 1984; Felson and Steadman 1983; Luckenbill 1977). In some instances an individual may impulsively make a threat in order to elicit compliance, with no intention of actually carrying it out. When the target fails to comply, the threatener may feel committed to carry out the threat or lose face. In this way actors may inadvertently become committed to violence. Finally, actors losing a verbal conflict may turn to physical violence if they feel they have a greater chance at success. They may shift the competition to one in which success is more likely.

Whether third parties mediate, instigate, or simply observe a conflict can play an important role in whether escalation occurs. There is evidence of third-party effects from both experimental and natural settings (e.g., Borden 1975; Felson 1978). For example, conflicts involving antagonists of the same sex are more likely to escalate to physical violence if third parties are present (Felson 1982). On the other hand, the presence of third parties inhibits escalation in incidents involving antagonists of the opposite sex. During homicides and assaults, there is medical evidence that offenders deliver more blows when third parties also use violence and fewer blows when they mediate (Felson, Ribner, and Siegel 1984).

The effects of third parties are also suggested in a study of the effect of attitudes toward retaliation on violence among high school boys (Felson, Liska, South, and McNulty n.d.). Boys whose own attitudes were statistically controlled, were more likely to engage in physical violence when their schoolmates valued retaliation. That the frequency of a boy's physical violence reflects the values of his schoolmates suggests that impression management is involved.

Routine Activities and Dispute-related Violence

The routine activity approach was originally designed as a theory of predatory crime (Cohen and Felson 1979). It suggests that there are three elements necessary to produce a predatory crime: a motivated offender, a suitable target, and the absence of capable guardians. Miethe, Stafford, and Long (1987) suggest that the routine activity approach has limited relevance for violent crime because most violent crimes are spontaneous and irrational. Since a social interactionist approach treats violence as goal-oriented, it would reject this argument.[7]

Evidence that the routine activity approach is relevant for dispute-related violence comes from studies of assault victimization. For example, research based on the National Crime Survey indicates that the risk of victimization for assault is greater if people are unemployed and unmarried, and if they live near the central city and low income neighborhoods (Cohen et al. 1981). Those who frequently go out for nighttime entertainment are also more likely to be the victim of violent crimes (Clarke, Ekblom, Hough, and Mayhew 1985; Miethe, Stafford, and Long 1987). Evidence from the Canadian Urban Victim Survey shows that residents who patronize bars, who work or go to class, or who go out for a walk or drive at night, are more likely to be victims of assault than those who do not engage in these activities (Kennedy and Forde 1990).

The three-element scheme developed for predatory violence is not quite suitable for dispute-related violence, however. In dispute-related violence, the distinction between offender and victim is not necessarily clear. In some instances it is more accurate to describe the offender and victim as two antagonists and then examine the routine activities that are likely to bring them together. If one, and particularly if both, have a proclivity to use violence, then one expects that violent incidents are more likely. For example, any activity that causes intoxicated young males to congregate in one location will also increase the likelihood of violence, since young males are the segment of the population most likely to engage in violence, and since alcohol is strongly associated with violence. Thus, the frequency of violence in some bars may be due to the fact that bars result in the congregation of young intoxicated males in a single location. The key predictor of the frequency of violence in bars is the age of the clientele (R. Felson, Baccaglini, and Gmelch 1986).

The routine activity approach to predatory crime treats offender motivations as a constant. In dispute-related violence, however, the motivation of an offender (or antagonist) is formed in interaction with the target (or adversary). There must be a grievance (or a history of grievances) as well as contact between the two parties. Contact is likely to have an effect on the probability of dispute-related violence, but the strength of the effect is likely to be weaker, since a grievance is also required. As a result, one would expect that nighttime activity and other factors that expose people to strangers create a greater risk of predatory violence for the victim than dispute-related violence; for the latter victims must not only be available but they must aggravate potential offenders.[8]

Routine activities that lead to grievances are likely to result in violence. Thus, activities in which there is likely to be conflict, such as competitive sports contests, are likely to produce occasions for violence, for fans as well as players. Also, the routine activities of families — the dependence of family members on each other and the necessity for joint decisions — creates opportunities for grievances. Thus, siblings fight over ownership and use of tangible goods in the home, and over the division of labor (Felson 1983). When siblings get older and their interdependence and contact decreases, the frequency of violence dramatically decreases. Husbands and wives argue over sex and money (Buss 1989). Violence may also result from extramarital affairs, divorce settlements, and conflicts over child custody.

Dispute-related violence feeds on routine nonviolent forms of social control, since it is an alternative when routine social control fails, and since it generates grievances from the target. This helps explain dispute-related violence involving agents of social control, for example, between parents and children, police and suspects, prison guards and inmates, teachers and students, debt collectors and debtors, and bartenders and patrons.

The actions of targets are likely to be important in dispute-related violence. In predatory violence, targets are substitutable: if the situation is not opportune, the offender can choose another target.[9] In a dispute-related crime, the offender is only interested in one target — the person with whom he is aggrieved. The routine activities of targets that lead them to become the object of grievances are therefore important. For example, the behavior of persons who are stressed or intoxicated are likely to elicit social control reactions, as indicated earlier. Many nighttime and weekend activities away from home involve alcohol, which may help explain why violence is most frequent during these time periods (Felson 1986).

Third parties are less likely to serve as guardians in dispute-related violence than in predatory violence.[10] Dispute-related violence is more likely to be perceived as legitimate, and in some circumstances third parties may encourage the antagonists or take sides. Evidence cited earlier suggests that their presence alone during the incident can affect behavior. For example, the presence of third parties increases face-saving concerns, and tends to increase the probability of retaliation in conflicts involving antagonists of the same sex (Felson 1982).

The influence of third parties is likely to enhance any social-demographic differences in violence that already exist. This increase is due to third-party influence and to the fact that individuals tend to associate with people similar to themselves. If individuals with a proclivity for violence are likely to associate with individuals with similar proclivities, there is likely to be an increase in likelihood of violence due to mutual influence. For example, age differences in violence are likely to be stronger because of the tendency for people who are similar in age to associate with each other and because young people are more likely than older people to encourage each other to use violence. Thus, Felson et al.(1984) found that third parties engaged in fewer mediating actions and more violent actions during homicides and assaults involving young offenders. Recall that these third-party actions affected the number of blows given by the offender.

Concern for the response of legal authorities is likely to be less for dispute-related violence. Legal authorities are less likely to intervene in dispute-related violence and when they do the response is less likely to be severe. Thus, the police are reluctant to intervene in domestic disputes. Also, antagonists in dispute-related violence are less likely to be vulnerable to legal charges because it is often difficult to establish who is the victim. Therefore, the presence of third parties is more likely to deter predatory violence than dispute-related violence.

The dispersion of kinship and friendship over a wider metropolitan space increases predatory crime because it decreases the level of informal control (Felson 1986). For dispute-related crime, the effect of dispersion is less clear-cut. On the one hand, the dispersion of activities away from the home may give violent individuals exposure to more people, with no friends available to act as peacemakers. On the other hand, dispersion may also produce fewer contacts between people most likely to be antagonistic to each other. Most acts of dispute-related violence involve family members and other people who know each other and if such people are spread out over large distances, then avoidance is possible. Thus, Baumgartner (1988) argues that one reason why violent behavior is infrequent in suburban settings is the relative ease with which suburbanites can avoid each other.[11] In addition, dispersion makes it easier for people to choose their company and avoid interaction with people they do not like. Finally, there is evidence that domestic violence occurs more frequently if the nuclear family is isolated from the extended family (Parke and Collmer 1975). Extended family may serve as guardians in preventing violence directed against spouses and children.

These complications may explain why *daytime* activities, such as working outside the home, predicts victimization for property crimes but not violent crimes (Miethe, Stafford, and Long 1987). Similarly, participation of females in the labor force predicts a nation's property crime rate but not its personal crime rate (Bennett 1991).

The routine activity approach and a social interactionist approach are compatible because both emphasize the importance of situational variables and opportunities for violent behavior. Both theories give particular emphasis to the role of targets and third parties. Further, both theories assume that offenders consider the rewards and costs of their actions and are therefore compatible with rational choice models.

The discussion above suggests that the routine activity approach is applicable to dispute-related violence, although alterations in the theory are necessary. Dispute-related violence can be seen as a response to routine rule-breaking and as an alternative to routine forms of social control. For dispute-related violence to occur one might expect the following elements to be present: (1) at least one person with a proclivity toward violence; (2) a provocation; (3) supportive third parties.

Mixed Cases

The distinction between predatory and dispute-related violence is not as clear as the above discussion implies; some instances of violence may involve both. First, grievances may develop during predatory violence. Targets of predatory incidents are certainly likely to feel aggrieved, and if they retaliate their actions are dispute-related. Alternatively, predators may feel aggrieved when targets resist. For example, a robber or rapist may become aggrieved during the crime if the victim resists or does not fully comply. Thus, incidents that start out as predatory may develop into disputes.

Second, grievances may act as disinhibitors if they are used as justifications for predatory behavior. For example, an individual may desire some good and justify his stealing it by citing some grievance with the owner. This may explain why predatory attacks are more likely against devalued targets. For example, recall the evidence that bullies attack unpopular children. Also, police who engage in violence in order to obtain information may feel justified because they believe the target is a criminal (Westley 1970). There is also evidence that males are more likely to use sexual coercion against women they consider deviant (Amir 1971; Kanin 1985). Evidently, some men believe that rape is justifiable against women who violate certain standards, and they tend to select these women as targets.

Finally, some incidents of bullying are difficult to classify as either assertive or defensive self-presentation. These involve instances in which individuals believe they have been assigned some unwanted identity, but not from a personal attack. These people find themselves in a predicament and they may use violence to attain a more favorable identity. For example, if individuals are losing a competition, they may shift the contest to one in which they think they can do better. Thus, a poor student with good fighting skills may challenge a superior student, or someone else, to physical combat, and try to compete in this domain. One would expect people to use violence during competitions in which they are losing, and to target their competitors.[12] If necessary, one can shift the competition by changing competitors. An individual who is unable to compete against a powerful opponent may seek weaker competition. Some incidents that appear to be displaced aggression may involve attempts to tackle someone with whom one is more likely to be successful. "If you can't beat 'em, beat someone else." Melburg and Tedeschi have demonstrated the process in the laboratory (1989).

In conclusion, whether dispute-related or predatory, violence can be interpreted as goal-oriented behavior. The goals of violence are similar to the goals of many other social behaviors – social influence, justice, and favorable social identities. A social interactionist approach emphasizes relative simple processes that are well established in the social psychological literature and helps make sense of a wide variety of violent behaviors.

Notes

1. This approach should not be confused with a symbolic interactionist approach.
2. Confusion of cause and blame is particularly likely when the victim is a member of a protected group (Felson 1991).
3. Displaced aggression is usually interpreted in terms of the frustration-aggression hypothesis (e.g., Dollard et al. 1939; Berkowitz 1989). Tedeschi and Norman (1985) suggest alternative explanations of experimental studies showing displaced aggression using a social interactionist approach.
4. For discussions, see Ellis 1989; Palmer 1988; Shields and Shields 1983; Symons 1979; Thornhill and Thornhill 1983).
5. Many instances of barroom violence begin when the bartender refuses to serve a customer, either because the customer is too intoxicated or underage. Violence sometimes occurs when the customer takes the refusal as an offense (Felson, Baccaglini, and Gmelch 1986). Ironically, laws instituted to regulate alcohol consumption have the unintended consequence of leading to interpersonal violence.
6. If winning is impossible, standing up to the antagonist maintains some level of honor and provides a measure of satisfaction. Also, someone concerned with identity is likely to attempt to hide injuries, whereas someone interested in justice is more interested in displaying injuries.
7. However, dispute-related violence may be more likely to be impulsive than predatory violence because it involves greater emotion.
8. Contact between the two parties may increase the likelihood that grievances will be expressed for another reason. If the grievant expects further contact, he is more likely to find it necessary to attempt to deter the target's behavior. On the other hand, if avoidance is possible, then a social control response is unnecessary as a deterrent.
9. However, the choice is affected by the vulnerability and attractiveness of the target.
10. This may explain why participation of females in the labor force predicts a nation's property crime rate but not its personal crime rate (Bennett 1991).
11. She also suggests that suburbanites tend to be too busy to tend to their grievances.

12. In contrast, the frustration-aggression hypothesis suggests that members of the losing team engage in aggression because they feel frustrated.

References

Amir, Menachem. 1971. *Patterns in forcible rape.* Chicago. University of Chicago Press.

Arkin, R.M. 1980. "Self-presentation." In D.M. Wegner & R.R. Vallacher (Eds.), *The self in social psychology.* New York: Oxford University Press.

Averill, James R. 1982. *Anger and aggression: An essay on emotion.* New York: Springer-Verlag.

———. 1983. "Studies on anger and aggression: Implications for theories of emotion." *American Psychologist* 38:1145–60.

Bandura, A. 1973. *Aggression: A social learning analysis.* Englewood Cliffs, NJ: Prentice-Hall.

Baumgartner, M.P. 1988. *The moral order of a suburb.* New York: Oxford University Press.

Bennett, Richard R. 1991. "Routine activities: A cross-national assessment of a criminological perspective." *Social Forces* 70:147–63.

Berkowitz, Leonard. 1989. "The Frustration-aggression hypothesis: An examination and reformulation." *Psychological Bulletin* 106:59–73.

Besag, Valerie. 1989. *Bullies and victims in school.* Philadelphia: Open University Press.

Black, Donald. 1983. "Crime as social control." *American Sociological Review* 48:34–35.

Black, D.J., & Reiss, A.J. 1970. "Police control of juveniles." *American Sociological Review* 35:63–77.

Borden, R.J. 1975. "Witnessed aggression: Influence of an observer's sex and values on aggressive responding." *Journal of Personality and Social Psychology* 31:567–73.

Bureau of Justice Statistics. 1983. "Report to the National on Crime and Justice: The Data." Washington DC: U.S. Department of Justice.

Burgess, Robert L. 1979. "Child abuse: A social interactional analysis." In Benjamin D. Lahey & Alan E. Kazdin (Eds.), *Advances in clinical child psychology* (Vol. 2). New York: Plenum.

Buss, A.H. 1961. *The psychology of aggression.* New York: Wiley.

Buss, David. 1989. "Conflict between the Sexes: Strategic interference and the evocation of anger and upset." *Journal of Personality and Social Psychology* 56:735–47.

Clarke, Ronald, Ekblom, Paul, Hough, Mike, & Mayhew, Pat. 1985. "Elderly victims of crime and exposure to risk." *The Howard Journal* 24:1-9.

Cohen, Lawrence E., & Felson, Marcus. 1979. "Social change and crime rate trends: A routine activity approach." *American Sociological Review* 44:588–608.

Cohen, Lawrence, Kluegel, James, & Land, Kenneth C. 1981. "Social inequality and predatory criminal victimization: An exposition and a test of a formal theory." *American Sociological Review* 46:505–24.

Cohen, S. 1980. "After-effects of stress on human performance and social behavior: A review of research and theory." *Psychological Bulletin* 88:82–108.

Cook, Philip J. 1976. "A strategic-choice analysis of robbery." In Wesley G.

Skogan (Ed.), *Sample Surveys of the Victims of Crime* (Pp. 173–87). Cambridge, MA: Ballinger.

———. 1982. "The role of firearms in violent crime: An interpretive review of the literature." In Marvin E. Wolfgang & Neil A. Weiner (Eds.), *Criminal violence.* Beverly Hills, CA: Sage.

Deming, Mary Beard, & Eppy, Ali. 1981. "The sociology of rape." *Sociology and Social Research* 64:357–80.

Dollard, J., Doob, L. W., Miller, N. E., Mowrer, O., & Sears, R. R. 1939. *Frustration and aggression.* New Haven: Yale University Press.

Donnerstein, Edward, & Hatfield, Elaine. 1982. "Aggression and inequity." In Jerald Greenberg & Ronald Cohen (Eds.), *Equity and justice in social behavior* (Pp. 309–36). New York: Academic Press.

Ellis, Lee. 1989. *Theories of rape: Inquires into the causes of sexual aggression.* New York: Hemisphere Publishing.

Felson, Marcus. 1986. "Linking criminal choices, routine activities, informal control, and criminal outcomes." In Derek B. Cornish & Ronald V. Clarke (Eds.), *The reasoning criminal: Rational choice perspectives in offending* (Pp. 119–28). Berlin: Springer-Verlag.

———. 1982. "Impression management and the escalation of aggression and violence." *Social Psychology Quarterly* 45:245–54.

———. 1983. "Aggression and violence between siblings." *Social Psychology Quarterly* 46:271–85.

———. 1984. "Patterns of aggressive interaction." In Amelie Mummendy (Ed.), *Social psychology of aggression: From individual behavior to social interaction* (Pp. 107–126). Berlin: Springer-Verlag.

Felson, Richard. 1978. "Aggression as impression management." *Social Psychology* 41:205–13.

———. 1991. "Blame analysis: Accounting for the behavior of protected groups." *American Sociologist* 22:5–23.

Felson, Richard B., Baccaglini, William, & Gmelch, George. 1986. "Bar-room brawls: Aggression and violence in Irish and American bars." In Anne Campbell & John J. Gibbs (Eds.), *Violent transactions* (Pp. 153–66). Oxford: Basil Blackwell.

Felson, Richard B., & Krohn, Marvin. 1990. "Motives for rape." *Journal of Research in Crime and Delinquency* 27:222–42.

Felson, Richard B., Liska, Allen E., South, Scott J., & McNulty, Tom L. "The subculture of violence: Individual vs. school context effects." Unpublished manuscript.

Felson, Richard B., Ribner, Steve, & Siegel, Merril. 1984. "Age and the effect of third parties during criminal violence." *Sociology and Social Research* 68:452–62.

Felson, Richard B., & Russo, Natalie. 1988. "Parental punishment and sibling aggression." *Social Psychology Quarterly* 51:11–18.

Felson, Richard B., & Steadman, Henry J. 1983. "Situations and processes leading to criminal violence." *Criminology* 21:59–74.

Frodi, A.M., & Lamb, M.E. 1980. "Child abusers' responses to infant smiles and cries." *Child Development* 51:238–41.

Goffman, E. 1959. *The presentation of self in everyday life.* New York: Doubleday Anchor.

Goode, William J. 1971. "Force and violence in the family." *Journal of Marriage and the Family* 33:624–35.

Gottfredson, Michael, & Hirschi, Travis. 1990. *A general theory of crime*. Stanford: Stanford University Press.

Hirschi, Travis. 1969. *Causes of delinquency*. Berkeley, CA: University of California Press.

Holmes, Thomas H., & Masuda, Minoru. 1974. "Life change and illness susceptibility." In B.S. Dohrenwend & B.P. Dohrenwend (Eds.), *Stressful life events: Their nature and effects* (Pp. 45–72). New York: Wiley.

Kanin, Eugene J. 1965. "Male sex aggression and three psychiatric hypotheses." *Journal of Sex Research* 1:227–29.

———. 1967. "An examination of sexual aggression as a response to sexual frustration." *Journal of Marriage and the Family* 29:429–33.

———. 1983. "Rape as a function of relative sexual frustration." *Psychology Reports* 52:133–34.

———. 1985. "Date rapists: Differential sexual socialization and relative deprivation." *Archives of Sexual Behavior* 6:67–76.

Kennedy, Leslie W. 1990. *On the borders of crime: Conflict management and criminology*. White Plains, NY: Longman.

Kennedy, Leslie W., & Forde, David R. 1990. "Routine activities and crime: An analysis of victimization in Canada." *Criminology* 28:137–52.

Larrance, D.T., & Twentyman, C.T. 1983. "Maternal attributions and child abuse." *Journal of Abnormal Psychology* 92:449–57.

Lockwood, Daniel. 1980. *Prison sexual violence*. NY: Elsevier.

Luckenbill, David F. 1977. "Criminal homicide as a situated transaction." *Social Problems* 25:176–86.

———. 1980. "Patterns of force in robbery." *Deviant Behavior* 1:361–78.

Melburg, Valerie, & Tedeschi, James T. 1989. "Displaced aggression: Frustration or impression management." *European Journal of Social Psychology* 19:139–45.

Messner, Steve. 1988. "Research on cultural and socioeconomic factors in criminal violence." *Psychiatric Clinics of North America* 11:511–25.

Miethe, Terance D., Stafford, Mark C., & Long, J. Scott. 1987. "Social differentiation in criminal victimization: A test of routine activities/lifestyle theories." *American Sociological Review* 52:184–94.

Motowidlo, Stephan, Packard, John S., & Manning, Michael R. 1986. "Occupational stress: Its causes and consequences for job performance." *Journal of Applied Psychology* 71:618–29.

Mueller, Charles W. 1983. "Environmental stressors and aggressive behavior." In R.G. Geen & E.I. Donnerstein (Eds.), *Aggression: Theoretical and empirical reviews* (Vol. 2). New York: Academic Press.

Nacci, Peter L., & Tedeschi, James T. 1977. "Displaced aggression: Drive reduction or equity restoration." *Human Relations* 30:1157–67.

Olweus, Dan. 1978. *Aggression in the schools: Bullies and whipping boys*. Washington, DC: Hemisphere.

Palmer, Craig T. 1988. "Twelve reasons why rape is not sexually motivated: A skeptical examination. *The Journal of Sex Research* 25:512–30.

Parke, Ross D., & Collmer, Candace W. 1975. "Child abuse: An interdisciplinary analysis." In E. Mavis Hetherington (Ed.), *Review of child development research* (Vol. 5). Chicago: University of Chicago Press.

Shields, William M., & Shields, Lea M. 1983. "Forcible rape: An evolutionary perspective." *Ethology and Sociobiology* 4:115–36.

Shuck, J., & Pisor, K. 1974. "Evaluating an aggression experiment by the use of simulating subjects." *Journal of Personality and Social Psychology* 29:181–86.

Straus, Murray A. 1980. "Stress and child abuse." In C.H. Kempe & R.F. Helfer (Eds.), *The battered child* (3rd ed., pp. 86–103). Chicago: University of Chicago Press.

Symons, D. 1979. *The evolution of human sexuality.* New York: Oxford University Press.

Tedeschi, J.T. 1970. "Threats and promises." In P. Swingle (Ed.), *The structure of conflict.* New York: Academic Press.

Tedeschi, J.T., Gaes, J., & Rivera, A.N. 1977. "Aggression and the use of coercive power." *Journal of Social Issues* 33:101–25.

Tedeschi, J.T. & Norman, Nancy M. 1985. "A social psychological interpretation of displaced aggression." *Advances in Group Processes* 2:29–56.

Tedeschi, J.T., Smith, R.B., III, & Brown, R.C., Jr. 1974. "A reinterpretation of research on aggression." *Psychological Bulletin* 89:540–63.

Thornhill, Randy & Thornhill, Nancy W. 1983. "Human rape: An evolutionary analysis." *Ethology and Sociobiology* 4:137–73.

Toch, Hans. 1969. *Violent men: An inquiry into the psychology of violence.* Chicago: Aldine.

Westley, W.A. 1970. *Violence and the police: A sociological study of law, custom and morality.* Cambridge: M.I.T. Press.

Widom, Cathy S. 1989. "Does violence beget violence? A critical examination of the literature." *Psychological Bulletin* 106:3–28.

Wilson, James Q., & Herrnstein, Richard J. 1985. *Crime and human nature: The definitive study of the causes of crime.* New York: Simon and Schuster.

Wolfe, David A. 1985. "Child-abusive parents: An empirical review and analysis." *Psychological Bulletin* 97:483–96.

Wolfgang, Marvin E. 1958. *Patterns in criminal homicide.* Philadelphia: University of Pennsylania Press.

6

Tinderbox Criminal Violence: Neurogenic Impulsivity, Risk-taking, and the Phenomenology of Rational Choice

Nathaniel J. Pallone and James J. Hennessy

It is a fair assessment to say that, from the perspective of scientific psychology and psychiatry, the principal advance in criminologic theory during the past decade has been the marshaling of hard evidence that leads compellingly to the proposition that impulsive violence is attributable to neurogenic sources in a preponderance (perhaps even an overwhelming preponderance) of cases. That proposition would seem to yield the conclusion that criminal violence is rarely the product of cool deliberation, much less "choice."

From a sociological perspective as well as that of the policy sciences, however, the principal advance has surely been the formulation and elaboration of rational choice theory (Clarke 1984, 1985; Clarke and Cornish 1985; Clarke and Mayhew 1989; Cornish and Clarke 1986), which seems to insist that criminal behavior is rarely the product of anything but rather cool deliberation in interaction with the opportunity to behave. Are these seemingly conflicting perspectives irreconcilable? If not, what points of empirical and conceptual agreement might contribute to a *rapprochement*?

We believe both that reconciliation is possible (and desirable) and that what might be construed as an interactionist conceptual position, emphasizing (in simplest terms) that behavior is a function of intrapsychic variables interacting with stimulus characteristics, represents the soundest conceptual foundation for such a *rapprochement*. This chapter represents an effort at such a reconciliation by presenting a conceptual model that addresses the neurology, demography, and phenomenology associated with impulsive criminal violence.

Three Pivotal Propositions

The model herein described pivots on three fundamental propositions:

- A substantial preponderance of the criminal homicides that occur in this country each year (and, very likely, of the episodes of assault as well) are of the "tinderbox" variety, in that they occur between people reasonably well-known to each other, ostensibly to settle long-standing or emerging disputes; victims and offenders are essentially similar to each other in a variety of characteristics; and whether one emerges as one sort of homicide statistic rather than another may essentially be a matter of "chance."
- There is now very sound scientific reason to believe that neurologic or neuro-psychological dysfunction underlies impulsivity and that such impulsivity constitutes a principal contributing factor in tinderbox violence.[1]
- There is reason to believe that actors with a high taste for risk, which may itself be construed as the product of neurogenic impulsivity, *self-select* those psychosocial environments that are peopled by like-minded (and likely also neurogenically impulsive) others. Such self-selection in essence constitutes "rational choice" on the part of such actors that functions so as to *create* the proximate opportunity for criminal violence.

Characteristics of Tinderbox Homicide

As portrayed in official data sets (Bureau of Justice Statistics 1988; Flanagan and Jamieson 1988; Maguire and Flanagan 1991), the circumstances surrounding the prototypical homicide in the United States clearly depict what we construe as "tinderbox" circumstances. In those cases in which the relationship is known (67% of all homicides), in only 1 of 5 are victim and slayer strangers to each other; official police accounts overwhelmingly cite arguments and/or disputes as precipitants; in nearly two-thirds of the cases, a readily available firearm provides the means to murder; according to their *post-hoc* self-reports, more than half the *convicted* homicide offenders were actively "under the influence" of alcohol or drugs at the time of the killing.

The conjecture that victim and slayer are, in the prototypical case, essentially similar is supported by a wide array of data from a variety of sources. National data indicate that criminal homicide is tightly bound within racial groups, with only 11% of the murders in a year interracial, with only 23% of the victims female, and with half the victims young adults aged 20–34. Blacks, who constitute about 12% of the nation's population, represent half its homicide victims; fully 45% of all cases of criminal homicide involve victim-slayer pairs in which both are black; another 42% involve victim and slayer pairs in which both are white; moreover, as Wood (1990) and O'Carroll (1990) have observed, homicide now represents a *leading* cause of death among black adolescents and young adults.

Among investigations of less than national scope, a study by Budd (1982), of the Los Angeles Coroner's office, reported that toxic levels of alcohol were found at autopsy in the blood samples of 61% of murder *victims,* with similar findings reported by Abel (1986, 1987) in investigations of homicide victims in Erie County (Buffalo), New York, over a 12-year period; and, in a more detailed inquiry utilizing the same data set, Welte and Abel (1989) found that higher levels were found in young male adults and among black victims. Most tellingly, in a study that compared black women who committed homicide with their victims on a number of social characteristics, McClain (1982) concluded that the two groups "exhibit essentially similar behavior patterns that increase their probability of involvement in homicide." Similarly, in his remarkable study of the characteristics of inmates who aggress against other inmates in contrast to those who become the victims of aggression while incarcerated (i.e., the "violent vs. the victimized" in state prison populations), Wright (1991) found that the "most deviant personality types" (those with the most significant psychopathology) were "clearly *over*-represented among the *victimized.*" Accordingly, Wright concluded (pp. 3, 6) that, "*victims . . . may be aggressors who lose in contests of wills.*"

Hence, we construe as elements of tinderbox circumstances: (1) two actors, (2) known to each other, and (3) similar to each other in a variety of ways — particularly (4) age, (5) race, and (6) gender; (7) emergent or long-standing disputes; and the ready availability of (8) lethal weapons and (9) mood-altering substances, obtained licitly or illicitly. Under these circumstances, it is not difficult to understand that who emerges as victim and who as offender may be attributable to the "luck of the draw" in a specific behavioral interaction, especially when alcohol or drugs lubricate emergent conflicts or strike a spark in the tinderbox of long-standing conflicts. More intriguing questions emerge, however, when we inquire into the characteristics of those actors who find themselves, *or elect to place themselves,* in tinderbox circumstances.

Neurogenic Impulsivity

Within the past 25 years, major technological advances in the neurosciences have made it possible to record brain activity and later to map that activity through technologically powerful imaging devices (Rosse, Owen, and Morisha 1987; Volkow and Tancredi 1991). Concomitantly, an explosion of knowledge in psychopharmacology and psychoendocrinology has yielded new understandings of a panoply of interactions between brain morphology and functioning, neurochemistry, and emotional and behavioral disorder. According to distinguished neuropsychiatrist Joseph Coyle (1988:23–24) of Johns Hopkins, the "nearly logarithmic growth in neuroscience research over the last decade" has yielded a major paradigm shift in the mental health sciences, producing in the process "new methods for diagnosing psychiatric disorders, clarifying their pathophysiology, and developing more specific and effective therapies." The net effect, according to Herman Van Praag (1988) of Albert Einstein College of Medicine, has been to "enable psychiatry to be a medical rather than a social science," united (or, more properly, reunited) with biology as its governing discipline.

Because disordered brain and neurochemical processes often eventuate in violent behavior, and because subjects with a history of violence are to be found in great profusion in prison populations, many studies—typically involving either extensive laboratory protocols (e.g., for technologically sophisticated computerized imaging of the brain and its functions) or surgical procedures (e.g., studies of the metabolism of neural transmitting enzymes typically require samples of spinal fluid, available only through lumbar puncture)—of the relationship between neurological disorder and violence have been conducted within correctional settings, with offenders convicted of violent crimes as subjects. These studies have contributed directly to the emerging picture of the neurogenesis of violence. At the conceptual level, a persuasive (if not yet quite compelling) case can now be made linking dysfunction, anomaly, or abnormality in the neurological substratum to *impulsive* displays of violence and/or aggression. Because statistical data on homicide as it is actually committed reveal a high incidence of slayings in what we have called "tinderbox" circumstances (in contrast to those slayings that are carefully deliberated and could hardly be denominated as "impulsive" events, including many felony murders), such a linkage appears to hold promise for understanding variables at work in some large proportion of episodes of violent crime.

Social Science's Posture of Skepticism toward Neuroscience

Yet it is a reasonable assessment to say that the paradigm shift at the conceptual and empirical levels of which Coyle has spoken is still imprecisely understood by many in the disciplines of psychology and psychiatry. Small wonder, then, that scholars outside these disciplines display little understanding of (or sympathy for) the fund of knowledge thus newly generated. Indeed, there lingers among many social scientists an attitude of suspicion toward the application of knowledge from the neurosciences to theories of criminogenesis — as if that body of exploding knowledge amounted to no more than Lombroso or Kretschmer revisited on their worst days.

Some are even willing to dismiss solid neuroscientific data rather derisively. The consistent finding, for example, that brain wave patterns recorded by electroencephalograph (EEG) among offenders incarcerated for crimes of violence consistently reveal anomalies in bioelectrical activity (Bell 1986; Blackburn 1975a, 1979; Bonkalo 1967; Gorenstein 1982; Gorenstein and Newman 1980; Gunn 1978; Hart 1987; Hindler 1989; Howard 1984; Langevin, Ben-Aron, Wortzman, and Dickey 1987; Lewis, Shanok, Grant, and Ritvo 1983; Martinius 1984; Raine and Venables 1988; Volavka 1991; Wettstein 1987; Whitman et al. 1984; Williams 1969; Yeudall and Fromm-Auch 1979; Yeudall, Fedora, and Fromm 1987) is lampooned with some frequency by asserting that such abnormalities *result from* habituation to mind-numbing prison routines *rather than* contribute to the genesis of that criminal behavior that has yielded incarceration in its wake.

But even this comfortably skeptical interpretation is countered in two Scandinavian studies. In a rare instance in which both evidence of brain dysfunction and longitudinal data were available on a large birth cohort, Petersen et al. (1982) reported that EEG abnormalities diagnosed in childhood or early adolescence were followed by criminal behavior in adulthood. Similarly, Virkkunen, Nuutila & Huusko (1976) followed a sample of brain-injured World War II veterans for nearly 30 years, finding (as expected) more frequent criminality than among control subjects and concluding that the relative frequency of criminality following injury is particularly associated with impairment in the fronto-temporal region; most important, they found that "the criminal acts very often happened only after several decades following the head injury."

The Allure of Interspecific Evidence

The evidence we find most persuasive, however, is that which remains congruent between clinical and laboratory observations within the human species and simultaneously congruent across species. If the clinical observations of neurologists and neuropsychiatrists say that Behavior A is related to Neurological Condition B and if empirical data seem to corroborate that association in a wide array of subjects (thus seeming to control for the selective perception endemic to clinical observation) and if research in comparative psychobiology yields the finding that a behavior analogous to A on the part of laboratory animals is associated with neurological condition B in those animals, who are we to remain skeptical about an association between A and B?

Let us take as a case in point the evidence that links damage or dysfunction in the frontal lobes of the brain to impulsive violence both among humans and in laboratory animals. The frontal lobes are generally held to be the "seat" of such mental functions as cognition, memory, abstraction, concentration, and judgment. Both clinical (Cicerone and Wood 1987; Joseph 1990; Wood 1987) and empirical evidence (Gorenstein 1982) linking frontal lobe dysfunction (whether as the result of injury or of congenital anomaly) among humans is sufficient to warrant the inclusion of frontal lobe syndrome as a distinct organic mental disorder in the current edition of the International Classification of Diseases (U.S. Public Health Service 1989). According to that source, at least when engendered by an identifiable injury to the brain (so that baseline data can be inspected for purposes of contrast), the "principal manifestations" of the disorder include

> general diminution of self-control, foresight, creativity, and spontaneity . . . manifest[ed] as increased irritability, selfishness, restlessness, and lack of concern for others . . . [with] a change toward impulsiveness, boastfulness, temper outbursts . . . [although] measurable deterioration of intellect or memory is not necessarily present.[2]

Many social scientists will recognize in that litany precisely those characteristics that have been held, at least from Cleckey onward, to be the distinguishing attributes of persons labeled *psychopathically deviant* (Blackburn and Maybury 1985); but that is another topic for another time. Instead, let's consider some evidence from infrahuman species.

The naturally occurring rate of generational maturation in such laboratory species as the white rat coupled with the wide availability and relatively low cost of videotape equipment enables animal experimenters to record every moment of the life of a laboratory animal, including the animal's learning history (or, if one insists on anthropomorphism, "pattern of socialization" to reinforcers and contingency conditions of various sorts) from birth onward (or at least until the point of an experimental intervention) — a set of conditions under which the usual academic debate about nature vs. nurture essentially evaporates. Rather, it is possible to specify with high precision those conditions under which a laboratory animal has been trained or "nurtured" — for example, to behave aggressively or peaceably to intrusion or attack by another animal; and the very character of the laboratory itself permits the induction of a target dysfunction in ways that are simply not possible in research on human subjects.

Under these conditions, we can determine what happens when we deliberately damage the frontal lobes of the brain in laboratory rats who have been reared to respond peaceably or aggressively. According to distinguished neuropsychopharmacologists Robert Feldman and Linda Quenzer (1984:248–52), the consequences are uniform, whether the animals had been "socialized" to respond aggressively or nonaggressively to intrusion or attack. Not only did the deliberately brain-damaged animals respond with lethal aggression, but with a particularly virulent form thereof:

> ... the topography of the killing is different in that ... [animals] with frontal lobe lesions are particularly vicious and ferocious, biting the [victim] again and again even though the victim is dead.

It is hardly surprising, then, that Feldman and Quenzer conclude that "each form of aggression has a *particular* anatomical and endocrine basis." Nor is there, in this experiment, much tolerance for the customary chicken-and-egg discussion about what preceded what or which is the causative and which the resultant variable.

Possible/Probable Neurogenic Sources of Impulsive Violence

We have elsewhere reviewed in some detail both the clinical and empirical evidence that links impulsive violence to neurogenic sources (Pallone & Hennessy 1992:137–60, 349–61). Those sources have been identified as

- head trauma (closed or open head injury) and its effects (Fletcher et al., 1990; Silver, Yudofsky and Hales 1987; Stoudemire 1986);
- brain function anomalies, including such bioelectrical anomalies as epilepsy, brain wave abnormality, and other forms of neuropathology (citations *supra*);
- neurochemical anomalies, including anomalies in the metabolism of ethanol (Virkkunen et al. 1987);[3] dysfunction in the metabolism of glucose (Virkkunen et al. 1982a, 1982b, 1983a, 1984, 1986, 1987, 1989), an excess of which produces "manic" states; abnormal metabolism of monoamine oxidase (Boulton et al. 1983; Lidberg 1985; Virkkunen et al. 1987), an important neural transmitter that regulates mood; abnormalities in the regulation of serotonin (Coccaro et al. 1989; Feldman and Quenzer 1984; Virkkunen and

Narvanen 1987), another powerful neurotransmitter related to depression; and abnormally high concentrations of testosterone (Bradford and McLean 1984; Dabbs et al. 1987; Gandelman 1980; Rada and Kellner 1976; Rada et al. 1983; Virkkunen 1985).[4]

Taste for Risk and Self-Selection of Risky Environments

In the statistically prototypical homicide, most victims and offenders are known to each other; that prototypical homicide occurs under "tinderbox" circumstances in which arguments or disputes erupt into lethal violence, often under a set of stimulus determinants (including biochemical lubricants) that at least potentiate intraperson variables that dispose a behaver toward violence — and that may also dispose him or her toward self-selecting those psychosocial environments that resemble tinderboxes.

A distinguishing characteristic of those tinderboxes is the recurrent threat of impulsive violence. Impulsivity is a frequent consequence of even relatively minor neurologic injury; whether neurogenic or not, impulsivity as psychometrically inventoried appears to reliably differentiate violent offenders both from nonviolent offenders and from nonoffenders (Pallone and Hennessy 1992:178–83). Patterns of violence can be learned intrafamilially and intergenerationally and can be reinforced or extinguished by long-distance vicarious learning and conditioning (Ibid., pp. 205–67).

Young Males and the Choreography of the Dare

Wolfgang and Ferracuti (1967) early identified a "subculture of violence" as linked to chronological age. Congruently, Holinger (1979) nominated "fatal violence" (through homicide, suicide, or accident) as the leading cause of death among victims from the age of 19–34 in the United States. Marohn and associates (1982) observed a similar, very strong confluence between homicide, suicide, and accidental death among adolescents.

Such propensity toward fatal violence has been interpreted by Wilson and Daly (1985) as indicative of a "young male syndrome," in which "status competition, 'taste for risk,' dare-devilry and gambling" are said to be principal features. Observing that the data from homicides in Detroit demonstrate that "victim and offender populations were almost identical, with unemployed, unmarried young men greatly over-represented," these investigators propose that the "taste for risk" is "primarily a masculine attribute and is socially facilitated by the *presence of peers* in pursuit of the same goals."

As if to underscore the impact of the normative expectations held by one's peers, Steadman (1982) confirmed that the presence of third parties in a conflict situation tends to potentiate the probability of violence both among mental patients and among criminal offenders. Felson and Steadman (1983) indeed identified what they described as a "systematic pattern" in what we have called tinderbox homicides in a study of such episodes:

> They began with identity attacks, followed by attempts and failures to influence the antagonists. Threats [are] made, and finally the verbal conflict end[s] in physical attack . . . retaliation is a key principle in the escalation of these incidents, in that aggressive actions by the victim [are] associated with aggressive actions by the offender and [potentiate] the likelihood that the victim [will] be killed.

Following Goffman (1967), Luckenbill (1977) has termed this phenomenon a "character contest," in which both the prospective victim and the prospective offender stipulate to violence as a means of conflict resolution. Conceptually, the notion of the character contest has much in common with what Redl and Wineman (1957) had, in a somewhat different context, termed "the choreography of the dare" and with Farley's (1986) empirically derived description of the thrill-seeking personality. It is also quite congruent with the description that Feldman and Quenzer (1984:248–52) provide of what is termed "intermale aggression" among members of infrahuman species.

Strong empirical validation for the suppositions that undergird the notion of the choreography of the dare is found in a study by Fishbain and associates (1987) which contrasted some 20 subjects who had died while playing Russian roulette with 95 who had committed suicide, with both characterized by high levels of risk-taking behavior. Similarly, in a study that compared black women who committed homicide with their victims on a number of social characteristics, McClain (1982) concluded that the two groups "exhibit essentially similar behavior patterns that increase their probability of involvement in homicide," so that who became the victim and who the offender was indeed essentially a matter of the luck of the draw in a specific behavioral interaction. Similar findings were reported by Mann (1990): "Black female homicide offenders . . . kill those closest to them in homicides that are intraracial and intrafamilial."

Those results echo the findings of Jarvinen (1977) in a study in Finland of violent offenders versus psychiatric patients who had attempted suicide, which reported essentially similar personality structures and characteristics between the two; and those of Stewart and Helmsley (1979, 1984) in investigations on risk-taking in prospective criminal behavior situations among convicted offenders, which reported that risk-taking varied in concert with psychoticism as measured by the Eysenck Personality Inventory and with unrealistic "expectancy of gain" — that is, that risk-takers characteristically misconstrued costs and benefits in a stimulus situation in which criminal behavior was construed as normative.

A Tinderbox Peopled by Risk-Takers

A behavioral situation in which both participants agree to violence, and in which both lubricate themselves for that violence by means of alcohol or drugs, surely sounds like "tinderbox" circumstances writ large and peopled by the "risk takers" described by Silver, Yudofsky, and Hales (1987), whose propensities for violence are said to inhere in neurologic dysfunction. Indeed, a major study conducted at the medical faculty of Semmelweiss University of Budapest produced strongly congruent cross-national evidence, among victims of violence, of a neurogenic impairment in the capacity to inhibit violent behavioral responses. Demeter and associates (1988, 1989) conducted postmortem examinations of the brains of homicide victims and of control subjects; they found among homicide victims consistent morphological anomalies in brain structures involved in the metabolism of serotonin, so that the inhibiting effect of that substance was compromised.

Surely it is not difficult to understand the process by which both participants construe violence as normal and normative, with such construing indeed mutually reinforcing; to the extent that one participant construes violence as normal and normative, he or she is likely to search out and to self-select those psychosocial environments peopled by like-minded others.

An Age-Related Decline in the Taste for Risk?

Clarke (1985) and other commentators have opined that such a "taste for risk" likely declines with advancing age. Such an interpretation seems consistent with the findings of Loeber (1982), Ageton (1983), Holland and McGarvey (1985), Blumstein and Cohen (1987), and Hare, McPherson, and Forth (1988) on the age-related decline in the emission of violent behavior; with those of Colligan and associates (1988) on the age-related decline in scores on the mania and psychopathic deviation scales to emanate from the Mayo Clinic restandardization of the Minnesota Multiphasic Personality Inventory; and with those of Farley (1986) on thrill-seeking as a function of age.

From an alternate perspective, however, it might be argued that most males who are likely to kill have already done so by age 35 and, in consequence of the high ratio of apprehension and prosecution for homicide (in contrast to those for other felony crimes), are serving prison sentences thereafter; and all those "essentially similar" risk-takers who are likely to become victims are already dead.

Self-Selection of Environments as the Creation of Opportunity for Criminal Violence

Opportunity is a key construct in rational choice theory. Too often, the notion is interpreted simplistically: The offender-to-be "happens upon" an unattended (and unlocked) bicycle, an automobile left running, a woman disrobing, etc. But Clarke (1984) clearly regards opportunity as rather a complex stimulus determinant for criminal behavior, not merely the unidimensional availability of an unguarded target:

> Opportunity is not merely the necessary condition for offending, but it can provoke crime and can also be sought and created by those with the necessary motivation . . . opportunity is a rather more complex concept than implied by simple counts of available targets. Whether opportunities are acted upon depends upon their ease and attractiveness, and these qualities must be subjectively perceived and evaluated. Moreover, these subjective processes are affected by motivation as well as knowledge and experience — which explains why opportunities may not only provide the cue for offending in those with an established propensity (as when an untended handbag tempts the sneak thief), but may also provoke crime in the previously law-abiding (as when an accounting loop-hole proves to be the bank clerk's downfall). In addition opportunities are not merely presented and perceived, but can also be sought. [Thus] not only can crimes be the result of presented or sought opportunities, but they can also be the outcome of opportunities which have been created or "planned" . . .

It is our contention that the self-selection of an environment with high tolerance for risk, in which impulsive violence is perceived as normal and normative, indeed constitutes a "rational" choice for the person with a high taste for risk — and that, in making that choice, he or she thereby "creates" the opportunity for discharging impulse into behavior.

A Stepwise Conceptual Model Linking Neurogenic Impulsivity to the Phenomenology of Choice

We have characterized some rather large proportion of criminal homicides as occurring under what we have termed "tinderbox" circumstances — that is, circumstances in which offender and victim are not strangers to each other and in which disputes or arguments (rather than instrumental means to perpetrating another felony crime) are reported as triggering lethal violence. It is likely that a large proportion of other crimes of violence take place under similar tinderbox circumstances. To assess one dimension only: Large-scale victimization studies suggest that offender and victim are known to each other in well over half the rapes, aggravated assaults (i.e., those in which a weapon is used), and simple assaults committed annually, whether these are formally reported to law enforcement officials or not (Flanagan and Jamieson 1988:235).

We have speculated that the essential components in such tinderbox circumstances are two actors, known to each other, each of whom has a taste for risk, and an environment that regards the taking of risks as normal or normative, so that the social milieu that envelopes both actors reinforces risky behavior. We have also opined that some (perhaps quite large) proportion of episodes have their origins in disordered neurology that inclines toward impulsivity.

Neurogenesis vs. Social Learning: An Analogy

In a review of the research evidence that links alcoholism with "biological markers and precursors," the prestigious Group for the Advancement of Psychiatry (1991) observed that it has now been clearly established that, in some people, alcoholism is virtually an inherited disease and that "efforts to map the gene or genes that convey a vulnerability to alcoholism are underway." Moreover, what may be congenital, if not hereditary, dysfunctions in the neurohormonal system have also been firmly linked to alcoholism.

Suppose, for the sake of analogy, that Person X has indeed inherited the gene that yields that vulnerability to alcoholism and that he or she also suffers those neurohormonal dysfunctions that predispose to alcoholism — but that he or she has been raised in a traditionally strict Moslem culture, in which neither role models for the ingestion of beverage alcohol nor purchasable beverage alcohol are available. Would we expect that person to become an alcoholic? Or is it not more reasonable to suppose that the biological precursors are, at best, necessary but not sufficient conditions for the development of alcoholism? If that is so, Person X may remain forever prone to alcoholism — but, in the absence of socially conditioned role models and the availability of the substance itself, forever free of that addiction.

Analogically, that situation may not be very different from the linkage between neuropathology and what we have called tinderbox criminal violence.

Neurogenesis, Socialization, Channelization

The present state of the evidence in the neurosciences inclines us strongly to the belief that a taste for risk may have its origins in brain function anomalies of one or another sort, whether structural, neurochemical, or bioelectrical. For us, the case is attractively persuasive, but not yet compelling. The evidence is not so clear that it can as yet be posited axiomatically that such anomalies lead invariably to violent behavior — for it may be the case that some very large proportion of the cases of tinderbox violence have their origin in brain dysfunction; but it may not be the case that nearly all instances of brain dysfunction lead to such violence.

What intervenes, of course, is the complex process of socialization; and that process incorporates such elements as the influence of role models within and outside the family, the intergenerational transmission of patterns of behaving, long-distance vicarious influences, social imitation, *in vivo* exposure to environments that elicit and/or constrain behaviors of various sorts.

In the course of development, some people are socialized into quite peaceable and prosocial environments, so that whatever proclivities one may feel toward the emission of antisocial, aggressive, or violent behavior is quickly either suppressed or channelized into pathways the sociocultural envelope deems positive (Zaleski 1984). Others are socialized into antisocial, or at least asocial environments, in which antisocial, aggressive, and violent behavior is readily modeled and easily learned by social imitation. To judge by the enormous popularity of motion pictures in which even "good guy" heroes, ranging from "Dirty Harry" Callahan to "The Terminator," behave in incredibly violent ways (and often in direct violation of constraints laid down for them by their acknowledged superordinates) in order to achieve purposes that are presented and widely perceived as essentially not antisocial, one can only conclude that the central thrust of the society at large is toward the image of the frontiersman who defines the law for himself. That image, as American cultural historians such as Frederick Jackson Turner have said for a century, conveys the portrait of the invincible hero who constitutes himself the sole arbiter of the good, the true, and the just, who sets himself beyond the formal requirements of the law — and who may well, as Farley (1986) intimates, thrive on thrill-seeking for its own sake. Shorn of its romanticism, of course, that portrait reveals a set of beliefs and behaviors deeply corrosive to societal order through the rule of law.

Some interpreters will assert that diametric sociocultural milieux are sufficient in and of themselves to account for diametric differences in behavior. We assert, not quite to the contrary, that the interaction between a sociocultural environment of the antisocial or asocial sort and a neurogenic proclivity toward impulsivity yields a geometric progression in which one potentiates the other. Moreover, we assert that a sufficiently compelling neurogenic proclivity will propel one to self-select an environment that one construes as encouraging the discharge of impulse into behavior. Nonetheless, it is patently not the case that all, or perhaps not even the majority, of those persons who suffer neurologic dysfunction will eventually behave in violently criminal ways; and, quite clearly, socialization and channelization are key constructs in understanding why they do not.

The Experience of Restlessness

But, proceeding from what we have clearly labeled as a belief, there appears to us a characteristic developmental sequence flowing from neurologic dysfunction that yields in its path psychological and social consequences of substantial import.

It is reasonable to believe that the person who suffers brain function anomaly — especially at a subclinical level of severity that is not the subject of medical attention — experiences that anomaly merely as "restlessness," as an inability to concentrate on a particular or single topic for an appreciable length of time; as a result, he or she is propelled constantly to seek serial sources of stimulation and excitement. Inevitably, the constant search for serial stimulation in order to relieve restlessness in the here-and-now rivets the person to the present, precluding consideration of the future. But he or she construes such restlessness not as something alien to how he or she construes the self, but rather as part and parcel of the self — as what our psychodynamicist colleagues would term *ego-syntonic,* rather than *ego-alien,* characteristics of the self. Indeed, the prototypical person here described may be volubly proud that he/she "can't sit still — have to be up and doing," with little or no awareness of how distant such a pattern of behavior is from that of most members of the relevant age cohort. In its turn, an inability to concentrate impedes the capacity to construe long-term goals and objectives and the capacity to construe the means to achieve those goals and objectives; these very capacities are generally conceded to form the foundation for that *planfulness* that characterizes self-sufficient, responsible adults who are able to postpone gratification of momentary impulses in favor of achieving long-term goals.

Observers will say that the subject of our exemplary sequence has a short attention span; because of that limited capacity to concentrate coupled with the propulsion toward constant craving for sources of stimulation, he or she is likely to experience school learning problems, often formally diagnosed as "attention deficit disorder." Differential psychologists might want to group the composite of anomalous brain function and its sequelae under the trait-label "impulsivity," believing that, once such a trait has been named, it acquires some metaphysical reality apart from the aggregate behaviors for which it is a label. In its turn, that behavior that results from impulsivity rather than from planfulness is typically described as "violent," whether criminally or not.

The Continual Search for Stimulation

Phenomenologically, the person we have described will experience "boredom" with great regularity; and, to combat boredom, will constantly and serially seek new sources of stimulation, either or both in the form of novel activities or new people with whom to engage in those activities. Indeed, a quarter century ago Quay (1965) saw in the need for constant stimulation the seeds of psychopathy; what is novel in the current discussion is the burgeoning evidence that such a need has neurogenic roots. By early adolescence, those efforts will almost surely lead to experimentation with mood-altering substances, particularly the central nervous system stimulants. In using such substances, he or she may actually be choosing a form of self-medication for an undiagnosed neurological disorder. But people who use mood-altering substances, whether central nervous system stimulants or depressants, are at risk for both closed and open head injury, the result of which will almost certainly be an exacerbation of an underlying neurological disorder. Attempts to change the behavior of the person thus described, especially through aversive means, typically fail to produce positive results. Instead, it seems to be the case that such aversive treatment may in itself be greeted as a novel form of stimulation (Hare 1982).

Substantial empirical evidence links such early learning problems as "attention deficit disorder" to the later emission of criminal behavior; early learning problems are held, in turn, to be precursors to the development of psychopathic deviation in adolescence (Lilienfeld and Waldman 1990); impulsivity and psychopathic deviation are highly correlated, as are impulsivity, psychopathic deviation, habituation to mood-altering substances, and certain forms of neurological anomaly; those who score high on measures of psychopathy customarily have few friendships (and these are often quite shallow) and are typically described as "unable to profit from experience," so that even the aversive treatment of penal incarceration appears to affect their behavior minimally.

Perhaps because those of us who are not impulsive and/or do not experience a strong taste for risk tend to shun the company of those who are and who do, the latter soon enough encounter others like themselves, even if they have not been socialized in environments that reflect a culture of violence and/or a taste for risk. That conjugation is certain to produce a social environment in which impulsive behavior is construed as normal or perhaps even as desirable—an environment in which the satiation of one's taste for risk through impulsive and violent behavior is a normative expectation, especially when biochemical lubricants are added and weapons are available. Such environments, with their high tolerance for risky behavior, present unprecedented opportunity to behave without deterrence and with the full expectation of impunity; they systematically reinforce the mis-construing of costs, risks, and benefits associated with behavior.

The Like-Minded Playmate Who Becomes a Victim

Interpersonal disputes are inevitable in any social environment, and perhaps more so in the environments peopled by the neurogenic risk-takers we have just described. Such disputes may (by mutual agreement between the protagonists) in fact be kept alive rather than reconciled, precisely because those disputes provide the rationale for a fine bout of "mixing it up" with one's "playmates"—that is to say, they may be kept at a "simmering" point by relatively conscious and deliberate decision on the part of both disputants.

But those deliberately simmering disputes add the final element to the tinderbox that what observers may construe as merely a "chance spark" may ignite into criminal violence; since an analogy to sheer internal combustion implies only one actor rather than two or several, it seems inapplicable here. Yet only a subset of those disputes between contending actors are in fact ignited into lethal violence—or even into such aggravated assault as comes to the attention of law enforcement authorities. Why? Given a behavioral situation in which the elements for conflagration have been aggregated into a tinderbox, what accounts for an episode of lethal violence at *this* moment, but not at some prior moment?

The intellectual shorthand, of course, is *acute potentiation,* typically of one or more intraperson variables, typically by the introduction of a new and powerful stimulus determinant or environmental contingency *or* because the salience of one or more determinant or contingency has rapidly escalated, perhaps because new observers have been added to the audience to a long-enacted "dance of the dare"—with such potentiation sufficient to interactively transform those intraperson variables Cattell (1980) would call "traits" into a "state" of readiness-to-act. Though that process is in fact quite orderly, at least at the point of postdictive reconstruing, phenomenologically it is frequently not experienced as the product of conscious deliberation or what most of us would regard as "decision."

Indeed—and here we must stress the speculative nature of our conjecture—it seems likely that the denizens of such risky environments regard each other not as "enemies," but in fact (and consistent with what the psychodynamicists would term "fixation" at a preadult level of psychosocial development) rather as "playmates." Now, one surely wants to "mix it up" with one's playmates, often in very stimulating rough-and-tumble ways, but not to harm them in any significant, much less life-threatening, way. Indeed, if our conjectures to this point are not woefully off the mark, to resolve a long-standing dispute (whether murderously or not) would be, for the risk-taker, quite counterproductive—for a long-standing dispute, with recurrent violent exchanges between the disputants, is in itself precisely the source of stimulation risk-takers seek when they self-select what we have termed "risky environments."

In the final irony, the person who, driven by disordered neurology and spurred by impulsivity and the self-selection of risky environments, has committed lethal tinderbox criminal violence will characteristically denominate his or her behavior as unintentional, as an "accident." Phenomenologically, he or she may be offering us quite an accurate interpretation of how he or she has construed the situation. And, as we have seen, in such tinderbox circumstances who emerges as victim and who as offender may turn on the luck of the draw.

Our conjectural schematic linking disordered neurology to tinderbox criminal violence is portrayed graphically in Figure 6.1.

The Frizzle: The Phenomenology of Risk

Many malefactors we have known over the course of the years, in and outside of correctional institutions, have spoken of the exhilaration they have experienced, particularly when they have eluded detection under "close call" conditions; a large proportion of them have referred to that exhilaration as "the Frizzle," that special feeling that arises when one knows he or she has "gotten over" on another—and preferably, on someone in a position of formal authority. Certainly, few who have so described that exhilaration have troubled to trace the term etymologically, so that they are unlikely to know that in an earlier time it denoted "that which has been fried." Though the specific referent is substance abuse, the description given by medical pharmacologist Renata Bluhm of Vanderbilt (Roueche 1991:73) is quite apt: "Adrenalin is turned on by more than the drug itself. [Users] know there is a risk—anything might happen—and *that risk is part of the experience.* There is an excitement in a jump into the unknown." The term, which may be related to the Old

FIGURE 6.1
From Neurogenic Impulsivity to Tinderbox Criminal Violence –
A Stepwise, Mutually Reinforcing Progression

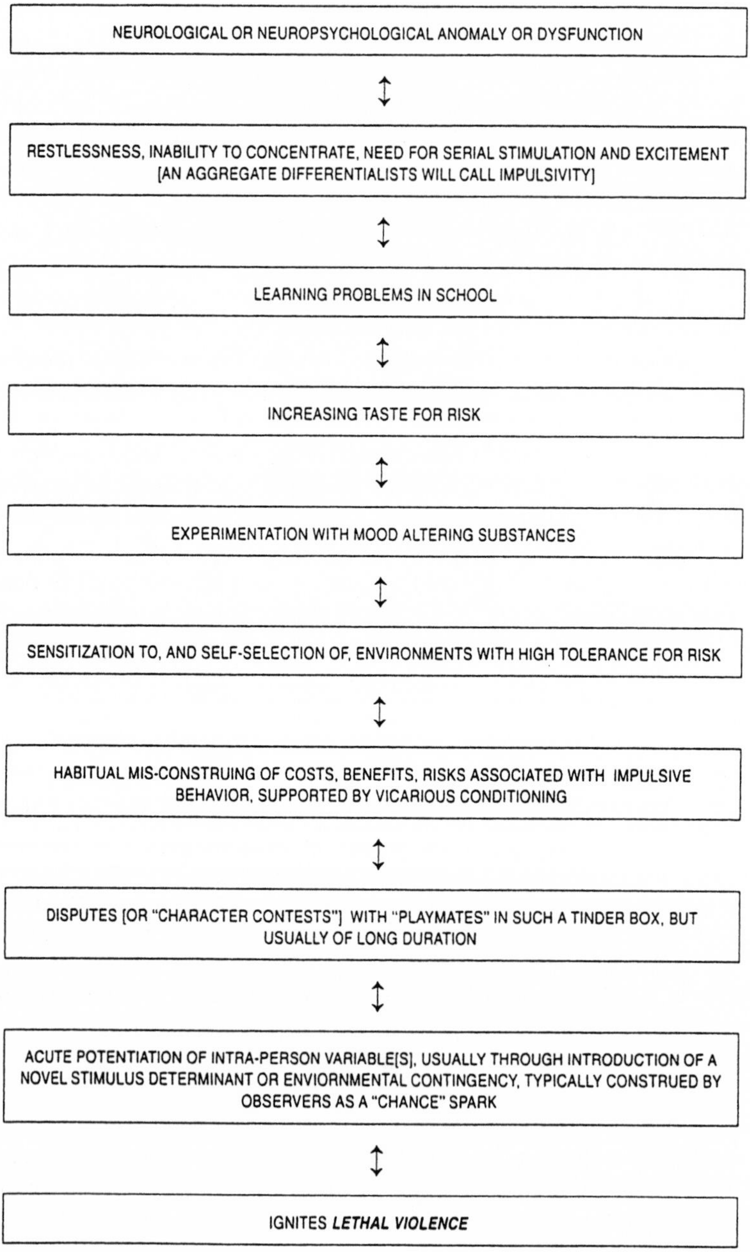

NEUROLOGICAL OR NEUROPSYCHOLOGICAL ANOMALY OR DYSFUNCTION

↕

RESTLESSNESS, INABILITY TO CONCENTRATE, NEED FOR SERIAL STIMULATION AND EXCITEMENT
[AN AGGREGATE DIFFERENTIALISTS WILL CALL IMPULSIVITY]

↕

LEARNING PROBLEMS IN SCHOOL

↕

INCREASING TASTE FOR RISK

↕

EXPERIMENTATION WITH MOOD ALTERING SUBSTANCES

↕

SENSITIZATION TO, AND SELF-SELECTION OF, ENVIRONMENTS WITH HIGH TOLERANCE FOR RISK

↕

HABITUAL MIS-CONSTRUING OF COSTS, BENEFITS, RISKS ASSOCIATED WITH IMPULSIVE
BEHAVIOR, SUPPORTED BY VICARIOUS CONDITIONING

↕

DISPUTES [OR "CHARACTER CONTESTS"] WITH "PLAYMATES" IN SUCH A TINDER BOX, BUT
USUALLY OF LONG DURATION

↕

ACUTE POTENTIATION OF INTRA-PERSON VARIABLE[S], USUALLY THROUGH INTRODUCTION OF A
NOVEL STIMULUS DETERMINANT OR ENVIORNMENTAL CONTINGENCY, TYPICALLY CONSTRUED BY
OBSERVERS AS A "CHANCE" SPARK

↕

IGNITES *LETHAL VIOLENCE*

French gerund *frisson,* (translated roughly as "apprehensive excitement") may be as convenient an intellectual shorthand as any other to describe the phenomenology of risk.

Central to our explanation of tinderbox criminal violence is the notion that those prone to the taking of risks self-select those environments in which risky behavior is not unusual, but quite normative — those environments in which, in Wright's (1991) description, "the prospect and often the reality of violence are facts of everyday life." Now, how in the world does such a choice, patently irrational to you and to me, come to be construed as normative or desirable?

At bottom, the pivot that guides the behavior of those persons who are labeled, on the basis of psychometric tests, as psychopathically deviate is essentially the *mis-construing* of the costs, benefits, and risks associated with behavior — invariably in the direction of *under*-estimating costs and risks and of *over*-estimating benefits. What requires further elaboration is the matter of how risks are construed and particularly how risks are *experienced.*

We do not know you, but we would wager a guess that you and we would not behave terribly differently from each other in some situations. At 3:00 A.M. and fully sober, I daresay both of us would be willing to risk breaking the law by running a red light in a nonresidential area. The process of construing that stimulus situation would for each of us doubtless include consideration of the sanction attached to the behavior — that is, breaking a law that speaks to a behavior that is *mala prohibita* rather than *mala in se,* with a sanction that is typically limited to a fine, but with no prospect (given the hour and some small vigilance on our part) of instant deterrence and but little probability of detection thereafter. Neither you nor we are likely to construe our *physical* safety as in jeopardy. To the extent that we construe the prospect of arrest and prosecution as unlikely *and* construe our physical safety as not likely to be compromised, we are behaving rather like the "reasonable adventurer" described by Harvey (1962) or the "eternally optimistic gambler" described by Atlas and Peterson (1990), who in essence is willing to place bets only when losing seems to have a markedly low probability and winning seems to have, on objective and publicly verifiable criteria, a substantially better than even probability.

Reasonable and Unreasonable Adventurers

Our belief is that the habitual risk-takers we have described, especially when their risk-taking habits have a neurogenic etiology, are quite unreasonable adventurers.

Were you or we to wander into the sort of environment we have denominated as part of the tinderbox circumstance — say, a dingy bar whose denizens appear at least alcohol-inebriated if not drug-intoxicated as well, with many of them brandishing weapons, and with loud arguments on the periphery — each of us would likely experience a threat to our physical safety. That experience will doubtless involve the classic physiological indicators of apprehension, stress, anxiety — clammy palms, lowering of peripheral body temperature (a combination that many, quite accurately, describe as "breaking out into a cold sweat"), increased heart rate, the elements indeed of "The Frizzle." For most, that experience is quite unpleasant; your behavioral response or ours is likely to be *flight,* as we seek to distance ourselves from those fear-provoking stimuli and circumstances. On the other hand, and usually only long after we have fled from those noxious stimuli and achieved sufficient physical safety to permit rumination, if we are genuinely honest with ourselves, we may admit that, for a moment back there, The Frizzle felt kind of good — but only for a moment, mind you.

Our contention is that, for the unreasonable adventurer, the habitual risk-taker, the phenomenology of The Frizzle is assuredly not as (at best) momentarily positive but quickly to be terminated, but rather as pleasurable in and of itself — and therefore to be prolonged. Perhaps anticipating the work of Farley on thrill-seeking behavior, novelist Aldous Huxley aptly described such phenomenology in his 1955 *The Genius and the Goddess;* "You want some special kind of thrill, and you deliberately work away at yourself until you get it — a green or bruise-colored lump of fear; for fear, of course, is a thrill like any other; fear is a hideous kind of fun."

Moreover, for the unreasonable adventurer for whom risk-taking issues from a neurogenic etiology, it may be that the threshold for the phenomenology of The Frizzle (in a very real sense, and as a result of neurological anomaly) is substantially higher than for you and for us; the findings of Farley and Sewell (1976) on thrill-seeking and sensation-seeking among juvenile delinquents certainly seem to argue in that direction. If that conjecture is anywhere near the mark, then we might expect both that the habitual risk-taker not only does not perceive danger to physical safety in situations that would provoke apprehension followed by flight in most of us but also that, once he or she has penetrated the risky environment sufficiently to step over his or her own ipsative threshold for apprehensive anxiety, he or she construes the adrenalin-pumping experience of stress as pleasurable — and thus behaves in ways so as to continue or increase the sense of risk.[5]

Unreasonable Adventurers Seeking The Frizzle

Just as one might become habituated to the normal dosages in prescription medication and thus require ever-escalating dosages in order to achieve the medically therapeutic effect, so it may also be the case that the threshold for the apprehension of risk escalates for habitual risk-takers, who will in turn require ever-greater and more palpable threat to physical safety before the pleasurable experience of The Frizzle is engaged. One attractive competing hypothesis might argue that, among at least some unreasonable adventurers whose habitual risk-taking behavior has a neurogenic etiology, the experience of stress, tension, anxiety, or fear is neurochemically inhibited in very direct ways as a consequence of neurologic anomaly or dysfunction; another might argue that those responses are inhibited in consequence of social imitation of fearless "macho" figures.

To the extent that he or she is successful in avoiding painful physical or social consequences even as the threshold escalates, at some extreme point a third-party observer might be tempted to characterize the successful unreasonable adventurer as feeling immune to the negative consequences of risky behavior; and, in common with such usage in the behavioral sciences, to attribute such a feeling of immunity to *grandiosity,* understood as an internal quality or characteristic of personality. For us, such a feeling of immunity (or indeed of grandiosity, if one prefers) results from behavior that has been positively reinforced; and, even though in a kind of intellectual shorthand, one might describe that immunity or grandiosity as a driving force for ever-greater escalation in future risky behavior, to assert that the "trait" preexists behavior in any meaningful way (as a "potentiality" to behave that preexists behavior) is simply to mis-construe the interactive calculus.

Risk Experienced as Visceral

Thus far, we have described the phenomenology of risk-taking as largely *visceral and emotional* for the unreasonable adventurer, but as essentially *cognitive* for you and me. Now, if that conjecture is not woefully inadequate, we may have reached a nexus that connects the person who habitually or persistently commits crimes of violence with little regard for the consequences of that behavior and the person who repeatedly commits crimes against property but has successfully eluded sanction. In the first case, sanctions will have little deterrent value, since what might be called motivation is largely visceral and emotional; in the second case, sanctions will have major deterrent value, since motivation is largely cognitive, not visceral and emotional.

Neurogenesis: A Necessary or a Sufficient Condition?

Neuropathology (or, at least, neurologic anomaly) is very likely a contributory factor in a very large proportion of cases of tinderbox criminal violence (and, indeed, were transitory states of organic dementia consequent upon the ingestion of mood-altering drugs to be added to the grouping, perhaps in very nearly all such cases). But it is our contention that neuropathology alone may serve as a "necessary" (but not "sufficient," except in cases of very sudden-onset violence clearly issuing from instant injury) antecedent condition to criminal violence of the tinderbox variety.

Nor do we hold, for that matter, that social imitation alone constitutes either a necessary or a sufficient condition for violence, whether criminal or prosocial. Not every citizen who applauds Clint Eastwood's celebrated "Go ahead, kid; make my day" statement in the film *Sudden Impact* is, by virtue of the force of social imitation and vicarious conditioning alone, destined to arm himself or herself with an appropriately menacing Smith & Wesson revolver and walk the San Francisco waterfront (or its analogue elsewhere) in search of societal predators worthy of execution by a rogue cop who has become by self-warrant the singular arbiter of the good, the true, and the just.

Instead, the issue turns on the interaction between significant neuropathology (perhaps indeed experienced as restlessness, but construed as fearlessness in the face of societal predators) and an attractively violent role model (perhaps presented via a popular entertainment medium) on the one hand, and, on the other, the availability of a weapon in a sociocultural atmosphere that invites or tolerates violence. That interactive mix may indeed yield a sufficient condition for lethal violence — undertaken for what the actor construes as society's betterment when the role model is positive and prosocial, so that the actor construes himself or herself among the "good guys," but undertaken for quite contrary purposes when the actor construes himself or herself and his or her role model in diametrically different ways.

Neurogenic Violence and Criminal Culpability

Though the evidence for a statistical association (technically, no more than a correlative relationship) between bioelectrical or neurochemical anomalies and violent criminal behavior is relatively strong, the state of the evidence does not yet permit specification of "cause and effect" relationships. Such determination would require, as Heinrichs and Buchanan (1988) have observed in regard to the evidence on the neurogenesis of schizophrenia, clear indication that neurophysiological dysfunction "predates" criminal violence. The directionality of the relationship is complicated by the relative insensitivity of even highly sophisticated measuring devices to the time of onset of brain dysfunction, except perhaps in cases of very recent head trauma, typically independently verifiable from physical evidence of concussion. Though most knowledgeable commentators would regard neurochemical anomalies as constitutional or congenital rather than acquired through accident or injury, the regulation of neurotransmitting fluids may be decisively affected by brain dysfunctions consequent to injury sustained during violent behavior; thus, the issue of directionality may apply as well to anomalies in neurochemical processing.

There is also the issue of the interaction between brain dysfunction, substance abuse, and violence, as Virkkunen and associates (1987) have suggested. Hence, people who overimbibe alcohol (or use psychotomimetic drugs) tend to find themselves in violence-prone situations; people in violence-prone situations are susceptible to head injury, whether from fights with others also intoxicated or from injuries attendant upon arrest; alternately, simple intoxication may lead to falls that engender head injury or compound preexisting dysfunctions.

Hence, the scientific picture on the neurogenesis (as distinct from the biogenesis, at least in the sense of inherited constitutional predispositions, as Herrnstein [1990] uses the term) of violence is currently richly suggestive but not yet definitive. Given what is currently either known or hypothesized about brain and neurochemical anomalies thought to "control" impulsivity and aggression, and in light of at least fragmentary evidence about the incidence of anomalies in brain and neurochemical functioning among violent offenders, it may well be the case that future research will demonstrate conclusively that criminally aggressive behavior is "triggered" by very primitive neurophysiological or neurochemical processes over which the individual can be expected to exert little *volitional* control. Some rather silly academic debates about antecedent and consequent conditions — concerning whether, for example, such personality traits as are measurable through psychometric or clinical instruments result from disordered neuropsychological processes or whether such traits (presumably acquired as the remnants of disordered developmental or learning processes) dictate disordered neuropsychological processes — might then be expected. But the more salient debates will concern the implications of revolutionized understandings of the genesis of violent behavior that is formally criminal for societal and legislative notions of culpability.

The matter of directionality may not be particularly pertinent in fixing culpability for a specific offense, unless it be the case that the putatively "triggering" brain or neurochemical anomaly can be demonstrated to have arisen consequent to that offense. Consider a situation, for example, in which earlier, documented episodes of criminal violence have yielded neuropsychological anomalies of such character that the emission of violent behavior is virtually beyond the control of the individual, and in which there is also documented evidence that the individual in question was free of such anomalies prior to those earlier episodes. In an instant case of criminal violence subsequent to the onset of such anomalies, what degree of culpability should attach to that individual? In that situation, whether earlier episodes of violent behavior that "caused" such anomalies themselves constituted "willful misconduct" may be quite irrelevant to the determination of *current* culpability.[6]

Notes

1. The imputation of violent criminal behavior to disordered neurology is hardly new. In fact, it dates very nearly to the time of Bentham and Beccaria — specifically, to the trial of one John Hadfield. who had attempted to assassinate George III while the monarch sat in the royal box at the Drury Lane Theatre. Hadfield's acquittal on the grounds of "lunacy" attributable directly to neurological disorder led directly, four decades before judicial formulation of the M'Naghten Standard, to enactment of the Trial of Lunatics Act of 1800. In that case, and in thousands of others in the past 190 years, disordered neurology has been invoked to *exculpate* in the exceptional case; what is new in 1992 is that disordered neurology now emerges to *explain* criminal violence in the nonexceptional case. In fact, if one accepts the paradigm of ethologist Henri-Marie Laborit, violent aggression became attributable not to disordered neurology — but instead to the mere *fact* of neurology itself. Laborit's paradigm runs this way: The only source of energy in our universe is the sun. Transformed solar energy is necessary to sustain life. Plants absorb energy directly from the sun and therefore do not "need" to move about. Animals lack the capacity to synthesize solar energy directly but must instead consume plants, which have absorbed and transformed solar energy, and/or other (typically smaller and weaker) animals which have already consumed plants. Thus, animals "need" the capacity to move about. To provide that capacity, the process of evolution has inexorably produced in animals a central nervous system, *the very purpose of which is to permit aggression* against other forms of life. Hence, aggression is very nearly the very purpose of neurology — and, within our context, the question is not whether aggression follows neurology, but how destructive that aggression is to other forms of life.
2. Some very responsible neuroscientists construe habituation to alcohol itself (typically attributed by social scientists to the availability of role models and other "predisposing" psychosocial variables) as *itself* the product of neurologic anomaly or dysfunction — and, since ethanol biochemically lowers the threshold for seizure, particularly of subclinical epilepsy. Thus, Virkkunen et al. (1987) observed a high rate of alcoholism among violent offenders in whom they had also observed anomalies in regulation of neural transmitters and opined that, because ingestion of alcohol represents a temporary corrective to abnormal metabolism of monoamine oxidase, "*alcohol abuse* in these individuals . . . *may represent an effort to self-*

medicate," even though "alcohol only makes the situation worse by further impairing impulse control." In other studies, Virkkunen and his colleagues have observed a relationship between habitual violence and abnormal metabolism of cholesterol (1983) and abnormal metabolism of glucose (1987) *under the influence of* alcohol. Nonetheless, it will patently be the case that, whether at the scene of a crime or in later studies that rely solely on social history variables, violent behavior will be attributed to alcohol ingestion; the issue of why it seems to a particular abuser of alcohol that he or she "feels better" when drinking (i.e., the issue of whether alcohol use or abuse is itself an effort to self-medicate and thus *secondary* to a naturally occurring neuro-anomaly) will scarcely be raised. As a further obfuscation in a chicken-and-egg argument, of course, it is a reasonable assumption that those role models from whom, let's say, a child "learns" through modeling that alcohol ingestion to excess is normative themselves behave violently toward those in their social sphere—in other words, that in those very environments that are sometimes construed as a sufficient explanation for alcoholism, abusive child-rearing practices may result in precisely those neurological anomalies which predispose toward alcoholism.

3. Stoudemire (1987:134–35) distinguishes two categories of organic personality syndrome, labeled respectively "pseudo-psychopathic (characterized by emotional lability, impulsivity, socially inappropriate behavior, and hostility) and pseudo-depressive (characterized by apathy, indifference, and social disconnectedness)" with both varieties "marked by indifference for the consequences of behavior and an inability to perceive appropriately the effects of such behavior on others." Importantly, whether head trauma results in pseudo-psychopathy or in pseudo-depression is apparently *not* particularly related to "predisposing" psychosocial variables—as the episodes of clearly neurogenic violence in previously quite positively socialized persons who had suffered head injuries reported by Wood (1987) seems to attest. While organic personality syndrome of the pseudo-depressive variety is routinely encountered in medical settings as a consequence to head injury, it is a reasonable assumption that the pseudo-psychopathic variety is more often encountered in criminal justice settings.

4. The finding of higher concentrations of testosterone among such offenders is quite independent of (and the research proceeds on quite a different basis than that which was once believed to support) the now largely discarded hypothesis concerning the XYY karyotype, which sought to attribute persistent violent criminality to the anomalous presence of an "extra" male chromosome in certain offenders (Finlay et al. 1973).

5. Again, there is corroborative evidence from the laboratory of the neuroscientists. Nearly three decades ago, Kimble (1963:336–38) reported "the rather remarkable findings that rats will press a lever in order to deliver . . . electric shocks to parts of their hypothalamus and limbic system through permanently implanted electrodes . . . as often as five thousand times per hour. . . . The inference is, of course, that these shocks are rewarding to the animal. . . . If these rats are allowed to 'self-stimulate,' they continue to deliver . . . shocks to the brain, often choosing these shocks in preference to food or other 'rewards.' . . . Successive experiments using the self-stimulation method have shown that rats and other animals will run mazes, will cross electrified grids, or will press levers solely for the opportunity to stimulate parts of the limbic system. . . . The areas of the brain which yield high self-stimulation rates are *not* in the cortex, but deep . . . in subcortical structures, such as the amygdala."

6. Elsewhere, we have discussed the implications of the emerging picture on the

neurogenesis of violence for current legal and conceptual definitions of "insanity" (Pallone and Hennessy 1992:158–60).

References

Abel, Ernest L. 1986. Guns and blood alcohol levels among homicide victims. *Drug & Alcohol Dependence* 18:253–57.

———. 1987. Drugs and homicide in Erie County, New York. *International Journal of the Addictions* 22:195–200.

Ageton, Suzanne S. 1983. The dynamics of female delinquency, 1976–1980. *Criminology* 21:555–84.

Atlas, Gordon D., & Peterson, Christopher. 1990. Explanatory style and gambling: How pessimists respond to losing wagers. *Behaviour Research & Therapy* 28:523–29.

Bell, Carl C. 1986. Coma and the etiology of violence. *Journal of the National Medical Association* 78:1167–76.

Blackburn, Ronald. 1975a. Aggression and the EEG: A quantitative analysis. *Journal of Abnormal Psychology* 84:359–65.

———. 1975b. An empirical classification of psychopathic personality. *British Journal of Psychiatry* 127:456–60.

———. 1979. Cortical and autonomic arousal in primary and secondary psychopaths. *Psychophysiology* 16:143–50.

Blackburn, Ronald, & Maybury, Clive. 1985. Identifying the psychopath: The relation of Cleckey's criteria to the interpersonal domain. *Personality & Individual Differences* 6:375–86.

Blumstein, Alfred, & Cohen, Jacqueline. 1987. Characterizing criminal careers. *Science* 237:985–91.

Bonkalo, A. 1967. Electroencephalograpy in criminology. *Canadian Psychiatric Association Journal* 12:281–86.

Boulton, Alan A., Davis, Bruce A., Yu, Peter H., Wormith, Stephen, & Addington, Donald. 1983. Trace acid levels in the plasma and MAO activity in the platelets of violent offenders. *Psychiatry Research* 8:19–23.

Bradford, John M., & McLean, D. 1984. Sexual offenders, violence, and testosterone: A clinical study. *Canadian Journal of Psychiatry* 29:335–43.

Budd, Robert D. 1982. The incidence of alcohol use in Los Angeles county homicide victims. *American Journal of Drug & Alcohol Abuse* 9:105–11.

Bureau of Justice Statistics. 1988. *Criminal victimization in the United States: Trends.* Washington, DC: U.S. Department of Justice.

Cattell, Raymond B. 1980. *Personality and learning theory: The structure of personality in its environment.* New York: Springer.

Cicerone, Keith D., & Wood, Jeanne C. 1987. Planning disorder after closed head injury: A case study. *Archives of Physical Medicine & Rehabilitation* 68:111–15.

Clarke, Ronald V. 1984. Opportunity-based crime rates: The difficulties of further refinement. *British Journal of Criminology* 24: 80–93.

———. 1985. Delinquency, environment, and intervention. *Child Psychology & Psychiatry* 26:505–23.

Clarke, Ronald V., & Cornish, Derek B. 1985. Modeling offenders' decisions. In Michael Tonry & Norval Morris (Eds.), *Crime & justice* (Vol. 6, 147–85). Chicago: University of Chicago Press.

Clarke, Ronald V., & Mayhew, Patricia M. 1989. Crime as opportunity: A note on domestic gas suicide in Britain and the Netherlands. *British Journal of Criminology* 29: 35–46.

Coccarro, Emil F., Siever, Larry J., Klar, Howard M., & Mauer, Gail. 1989. Serotonergic studies in patients with affective and personality disorders: Correlates with suicidal and impulsive aggressive behavior. *Archives of General Psychiatry* 46:587–99.

Colligan, Robert C., Osborne, David, Swenson, Wendell M., & Offord, Kenneth P. 1988. *The MMPI: A contemporary normative study* (2nd ed.). Odessa, FL: Psychological Assessment Resources.

Cornish, Derek B., & Clarke, Ronald V. 1986. *The reasoning criminal.* New York: Springer-Verlag.

Coyle, Joseph T. 1988. Neuroscience and psychiatry. In John A. Talbott, Robert E. Hales, and Stuart C. Yudofsky (Eds.), *American psychiatric press textbook of psychiatry,* (Pp. 3–32). Washington, DC: American Psychiatric Press.

Dabbs, James M., Frady, Robert L., Carr, Timothy S., & Besch, Norma F. 1987. Saliva testosterone and criminal violence in young adult prison inmates. *Psychosomatic Medicine* 49:174–82.

Demeter, Erzsebet, Tekes, Kornelia, Jaorossy, Kalman, Palkovitz, Miklos 1988. Does -sup-3H-imipramine binding asymmetry indicate psychiatric illness? *Acta Psychiatrica Scandinavica* 77:746–47.

———. 1989. The asymmetry of -sup-3H impramine binding may predict psychiatric illness. *Life Sciences* 44:1403–10.

Farley, Frank. 1986, May. The big T in personality, *Psychology Today,* pp. 44–52.

Farley, Frank, & Sewell, Thomas. 1976. Test of an arousal theory of delinquency. *Criminal Justice & Behavior* 3:315–20.

Feldman, Robert S., & Quenzer, Linda F. 1984. *Fundamentals of neuro-psycho-pharmacology.* Sunderland, MA: Sinauer.

Felson, Richard B., & Steadman, Henry J. 1983. Situational factors in disputes leading to criminal violence. *Criminology* 21:59–74.

Finlay, Wayne H., McDanal, Clarence E., Finley, Sara C., & Rosecrans, Clarence J. 1973. Prison survey for the XYY karyotype in tall inmates. *Behavior Genetics* 1:97–100.

Fishbain, David A., Fletcher, James R., Aldrich, Timothy E., & Davis, Joseph H. 1987. Relationship between Russian roulette deaths and risk-taking behavior: A controlled study. *American Journal of Psychiatry* 144:563–67.

Flanagan, Timothy J., & Jamieson, Katherine M. 1988. *Sourcebook of criminal justice statistics.* Washington, DC: Bureau of Justice Statistics, U.S. Department of Justice.

Fletcher, Jack M., Ewing-Cobbs, Linda, Miner, Michael E., Levin, Harvey S., & Eisenberg, Lauren. 1990. Behavioral changes after closed head injury in children. *Journal of Consulting & Clinical Psychology* 1990:58, 93–98.

Gandelman, Ronald. 1980. Gonadal hormones and the induction of intraspecific fighting in mice. *Neuroscience & Biobehavioral Reviews* 4:133–40.

Goffman, Erving. 1967. *Interaction ritual: Essays on face-to-face behavior.* Garden City, NY: Anchor.

Gorenstein, Ethan E. 1982. Frontal lobe functions in psychopaths. *Journal of Abnormal Psychology* 91:368–79.

Gorenstein, Ethan E., & Newman, Joseph P. 1980. Disinhibitory psychopathology: A new perspective and model for research. *Psychological Review* 87:301–15.

Gunn, John C. 1978. Epileptic homicide: A case report. *British Journal of Psychiatry* 132:510–13.

Group for the Advancement of Psychiatry, Committee on Alcoholism and the Addictions. 1991. Substance abuse disorders: A psychiatric priority. *American Journal of Psychiatry* 148:1291–300.

Hare, Robert D. 1982. Psychopathy and physiological activity during anticipation of an aversive stimulus in a distraction paradigm. *Psychophysiology* 19:266–71.

Hare, Robert D., McPherson, Leslie M., & Forth, Adele E. 1988. Male psychopaths and their criminal careers. *Journal of Consulting & Clinical Psychology* 56:710–14.

Hart, Cedric J. 1987. The relevance of a test of speech comprehension deficit to persistent aggressiveness. *Personality & Individual Differences* 8:371–84.

Harvey, O.J. 1962. Personality factors in resolution of conceptual incongruities. *Sociometry* 25:336–52.

Heinrichs, Douglas W., & Buchanan, Robert W. 1988. Significance and meaning of neurological signs in schizophrenia. *American Journal of Psychiatry* 145:11–18.

Herrnstein, Richard. 1990. Biology and crime. In Larry J. Siegel (Ed.), *American justice: Research of the National Institute of Justice* (pp. 11–14). St. Paul, MN: West.

Hindler, C.G. 1989. Epilepsy and violence. *British Journal of Psychiatry* 155:246–49.

Holland, Terrill R., & McGarvey, Bill. 1985. Crime specialization, seriousness progression, and Markov chains. *Journal of Consulting & Clinical Psychology* 52:837–40.

Holinger, Paul C. 1979. Violent deaths among the young: Recent trends in suicide, homicide, and accidents. *American Journal of Psychiatry* 136:1144–47.

Howard, Richard C. 1984. The clinical EEG and personality in mentally abnormal offenders. *Psychological Medicine* 14:569–80.

Jarvinen, Liisa [*sic*]. 1977. Personality characteristics of violent offenders and suicidal individuals. *Annals of the Finnish Academy of Sciences*, pp. 19–30.

Joseph, Rhawn. 1990. *Neuropsychology, neuropsychiatry, and behavioral neurology*. New York: Plenum.

Kimble, Daniel P. 1963. *Physiological psychology*. Reading, MA: Addison-Wesley.

Langevin, Ron, Ben-Aron, Mark, Wortzman, George, & Dickey, Robert. 1987. Brain damage, diagnosis, and substance abuse among violent offenders. *Behavioral Sciences & the Law* 5:77–94.

Loeber, Rolf. 1982. The stability of antisocial and delinquent child behavior: A review. *Child Development* 53:1431–46.

Lewis, Dorothy O., Shanok, Shelley S., Grant, Madeline, & Ritvo, Eva. 1983. Homicidally aggressive young children: Neuropsychiatric and experiential correlates. *American Journal of Psychiatry* 140:148–53.

Lidberg, Lars. 1985. Platelet monoamine oxidase activity and psychopathy. *Psychiatry Research* 16:339–43.

Lilienfeld, Scott O., & Waldman, Irwin D. 1990. The relationship between childhood attention-deficit hyperactivity disorder and adult antisocial behavior reexamined: The problem of heterogeneity. *Clinical Psychology Review* 10:699–725.

Luckenbill, David F. 1977. Criminal homicide as a situated transaction. *Social Problems* 25:175–86.

Maguire, Kathleen, & Flanagan, Timothy J. 1991. *Sourcebook of criminal justice statistics*. Washington, DC: Bureau of Justice Statistics, U.S. Department of Justice.

Mann, Coramae R. 1990. Black female homicide in the United States. *Journal of Interpersonal Violence* 5:176–201.

Marohn, Richard C., Locke, Ellen M., Rosenthal, Ronald, & Curtiss, Glenn. 1982. Juvenile delinquents and violent death. *Adolescent Psychiatry* 10:147–70.

Martinius, Joest. 1983. Homicide of an aggressive adolescent boy with right temporal lesion. *Neuroscience & BioBehavioral Reviews* 7:419–22.

McClain, Paula D. 1982. Black female homicide offenders and victims: Are they from the same population? *Death Education* 6:265–78.

Megargee, Edwin I., & Bohn, Martin J. 1979. *Classifying criminal offenders: A new system based on the MMPI.* Beverly Hills: Sage.

O'Carroll, Patrick W. 1990. Homicides among black males 15–24 years of age, 1970–84. *Public Health Surveillance of 1990: Injury Control Objectives of the Nation* 37:53–60.

Pallone, Nathaniel J., & Hennessy, James J. 1992. *Criminal behavior. A process psychology analysis.* New Brunswick, NJ: Transaction Publishers.

Petersen, K.G. Ingemar, Matousek, M., Mednick, Sarnoff A., Volavka, J., & Pollock, V. 1982. EEG antecedents of thievery. *Acta Psychiatrica Scandinavica* 65:331–38.

Quay, Herbert C. 1965. Psychopathic personality as pathological stimulation seeking. *American Journal of Psychiatry* 122:180–83.

Rada, Richard T., & Kellner, Robert. 1976. Thiothixene in the treatment of geriatric patients with chronic organic brain syndrome. *Journal of the American Geriatrics Society* 24:105–7.

Rada, Richard, Laws, D.R., Kellner, Robert, Stivasta, Laxmi, & Peake, Glenn. 1983. Plasma androgens in violent and non-violent sex offenders. *Bulletin of the American Academy of Psychiatry & the Law* 11:149–58.

Raine, Adrian, & Venables, Peter H. 1988. Enhanced P3 evoked potentials and longer P3 recovery times in psychopaths. *Psychophysiology* 25:30–38.

Redl, Fritz, & Wineman, David. 1957. *The aggressive child.* [Single volume combined edition of *Children who hate: The disorganization and breakdown of behavior controls,* 1951. & *Controls from within: Techniques for the treatment of the aggressive child,* 1952]. New York: Free Press.

Rosse, Richard B., Owen, Cynthia M., & Morisha, John M. 1987. Brain imaging and laboratory testing in neuropsychiatry. In Robert E. Hales and Stuart C. Yudofsky (Eds.), *American psychiatric press textbook of neuropsychiatry.* (pp. 17–40). Washington, DC: American Psychiatric Press.

Roueche, Berton. 1991, 11, March. Annals of medicine: A good, safe tan. *New Yorker,* pp. 69–74.

Silver, Jonathan M., Yudofsky, Stuart C., and Hales, Robert E. 1987. Neuropsychiatric aspects of traumatic brain injury. In Robert E. Hales and Stuart C. Yudofsky (Eds.), *American psychiatric press textbook of neuropsychiatry* (pp. 179–190). Washington, DC: American Psychiatric Press.

Steadman, Henry J. 1982. A situational approach to violence. *International Journal of Law & Psychiatry* 5:171–86.

Stewart, C.H.M., & Helmsley, D.R. 1979. Risk perception and likelihood of action in criminal offenders. *British Journal of Criminology* 19:105–19.

Stewart, C.H., & Helmsley, D.R. 1984. Personality factors in the taking of criminal risks. *Personality & Individual Differences* 5:119–22.

Stoudemire, G. Alan. 1987. Selected organic mental disorders. In Robert E. Hales and Stuart C. Yudofsky (Eds.), *American psychiatric press textbook of neuropsychiatry.* (pp. 125–140). Washington, DC: American Psychiatric Press.

U.S. Public Health Service. 1989. *International classification of diseases, 9th Revision, clinical modification: Third edition.* Washington: U.S. Department of Health & Human Services. Publication No. (PHS) 89–1260.

Van Praag, Herman M. 1988. Biological psychiatry audited. *Journal of Nervous & Mental Disease* 176:195–99.

Virkkunen, Matti. 1974. Suicide linked to homicide. *Psychiatric Quarterly* 48:276–82.

———. 1979. Alcoholism and antisocial personality. *Acta Psychiatrica Scandinavica* 59:493–501

———. 1982*a*. Evidence for abnormal glucose tolerance test among violent offenders. Neuropsychobiology 8:30–34.

———. 1982*b*. Reactive hypoglycemic tendency among habitually violent offenders: A further study by means of the glucose tolerance test. *Neuropsychobiology* 8:35–40.

———. 1983*a*. Insulin secretion during the glucose tolerance test in antisocial personality. *British Journal of Psychiatry* 142:598–604.

———. 1983*b*. Serum cholesterol levels in homicidal offenders: A low cholesterol level is connected with a habitually violent tendency under the influence of alcohol. *Neuropsychobiology* 10:65–69.

———. 1984. Reactive hypoglycemic tendency among arsonists. *Acta Psychiatrica Scandinavica* 69:445–52.

———. 1985. Urinary free cortisol secretion in habitually violent offenders. *Acta Psychiatrica Scandinavica* 72:40–44.

———. 1986. Insulin secretion during the glucose tolerance test among habitually violent and impulsive offenders. *Aggressive Behavior* 12:303–10.

Virkkunen, Matti, Horrobin, David F., Jenkins, Douglas K., & Manku, Mehar S. 1987. Plasma phospholipid essentially fatty acids and prostaglandins in alcoholic, habitually violent, and impulsive offenders. *Biological Psychiatry* 22:1087–96.

Virkkunen, Matti, & Huttunen, M.O. 1982. Evidence for abnormal glucose tolerance test among violent offenders. *Neuropsychobiology* 8:30–34.

Virkkunen, Matti, de Jong, Judith, Bartko, John J., & Goodwin, Frederick K. 1989. Relationship of psychobiological variables to recidivism in violent offenders and impulsive fire setters: A follow-up study. *Archives of General Psychiatry* 46:600–3.

Virkkunen, Matti, & Kallilo, Eila. 1987. Low blood glucose nadir in the glucose tolerance test and homicidal spouse abuse. *Aggressive Behavior* 13:59–66.

Virkkunen, Matti, & Narvanen, S. 1987. Plasma insulin, tryptophan, and serotonin levels during the glucose tolerance test among habitually violent and impulsive offenders. *Neuropsychobiobiology* 17:19–23.

Virkkunen, Matti, Nuutila, Arto, Goodwin, Frederick K., and Linnoila, Markku 1987. Cerebrospinal fluid monamine metabolite levels in male arsonists. *Archives of General Psychiatry* 44:241–47.

Virkkunen, Matti, Nuutila, rto, & Huusko, Simo. 1976. Effect of brain injury on social adaptability: Longitidinal study on frequency of criminality. *Acta Psychiatrica Scandinavica* 53:168–72.

Volavka, Jan. 1991. Aggression. electroencephalography, and evoked potentials: A critical review. *Neuropsychiatry, Neuropsychology & Behavioral Neurology* 3:249–59.

Volkow, Nora D., & Tancredi, Laurence R. 1991. Biological correlates of mental activity studied with PET [positron emission tomography]. *American Journal of Psychiatry* 148:439–43.

Welte, John W., & Abel, Ernest L. 1989. Homicide: Drinking by the victim. *Journal of Studies on Alcohol* 50:197–201.

Wettstein, Robert M. 1987. Legal aspects of neuropsychiatry. In Robert E. Hales, and Stuart C. Yudofsky (Eds.), *American psychiatric press textbook of neuropsychiatry* (pp. 451–463). Washington, DC: American Psychiatric Press.

———. 1988. Psychiatry and the law. In John A. Talbott, Robert E. Hales, and Stuart C. Yudofsky (Eds.), *American psychiatric press textbook of psychiatry* (pp. 1059–1084). Washington, DC: American Psychiatric Press.

Whitman, Steven, Coleman, Tina E., Patmon, Cecil, Desai, Bindu T., Cohen, Robert, & King, Lambert N. 1984. Epilepsy in prison: Elevated prevalence and no relationship to violence. *Neurology* 34:775–82.

Williams, Denis. 1969. Neural factors related to habitual aggression: Consideration of differences between those habitual aggressives and others who have committed crimes of violence. *Brain* 92:501–20.

Wilson, James Q., & Herrnstein, Richard J. 1985. *Crime & human nature: The definitive study of the causes of crime.* New York: Simon & Schuster.

Wilson, Margo, & Daly, Martin. 1985. Competitiveness, risk taking, and violence: The young male syndrome. *Ethology & Sociobiology* 6:59–73.

Wolfgang, Marvin E., & Ferracuti, Franco. 1967. *The subculture of violence.* London: Tavistock.

Wood, Nollie P. 1990. Black homicide: A public health crisis. *Journal of Interpersonal Violence* 5:147–50.

Wood, Rodger Llewellyn. 1987. *Brain injury rehabilitation: A neurobehavioral approach.* Rockville, MD: Aspen.

Wright, Kevin N. 1991. The violent and the victimized in the male prison. *Journal of Offender Rehabilitation* 16:1–25.

Yeudall, Lorne T., & Fromm-Auch, D. 1979. Neuropsychological impairments in various psychopathological populations. In John Gruzelier and Pierre Flor-Henry (Eds.), *Hemisphere asymmetries of function in psychopathology.* (pp. 401–428). Amsterdam: Elsevier/North Holland Biomedical Press.

Yeudall, Lorne T., Fedora, Orestes, & Fromm, DaLee. 1987. A neuropsychological theory of persistent criminality: Implications for assessment and treatment. *Advances in Forensic Psychology & Psychiatry* 2:119–91.

Zaleski, Zbigniew. 1984. Sensation-seeking and risk-taking behavior. *Personality & Individual Differences* 5:607–8.

7

Rational Choice, Behavior Analysis, and Political Violence

Max Taylor

In what is perhaps the most systematic account of the application of rational choice theory to offending, Cornish & Clarke (1986) noted that the rational choice perspective offers a potentially exciting conceptual framework for bringing a range of approaches to bear on the problems of offending and deviant behavior. The significance of this should not be underestimated. The analysis of social problems presents enormous difficulties, in part caused by the fragmentation of knowledge within the social sciences. One of the salutary experiences discipline practitioners have when attempting to apply their discipline outside of the laboratory or classroom is the realization that particular discipline insights are generally insufficient to deal with the multifaceted nature of social problems.

This applies in principle to most areas of application, but it becomes particularly evident when attempting to understand the nature and features of crimes associated with political protest, especially terrorism. The teasing out of relevant aspects of relationships between approaches to political violence, and the creation of conceptual frameworks that enable different approaches to interact, is an endeavor of enormous potential importance. The notion of "rational choice" (and what that might imply) offers advantages over other approaches to understanding crimes related to political activity for both methodological and conceptual reasons. In methodological terms, its strength is that it is primarily focused on what individuals do, rather than what they think or intend, and it offers accounts that relate to the observable context to an individual's behavior. In conceptual terms, it offers a framework that complements other approaches, enabling diverse and sometimes conflicting approaches to come together when addressing a particular behavioral issue.

This chapter is written from a radical behaviorist perspective; that is to say it takes its principal conceptual position from the writings of B.F. Skinner. From that perspective, the rational choice approach to offending offers a fruitful complementary conceptual framework with the potential for bringing together insights from different traditions, which while not necessarily sharing conceptual assumptions, serve to complement each other at a behavioral level. For example, it has been argued that it offers a context in which macro qualities of political theory such as millenarianism, public space, and others can be integrated with more micro behavioral analyses (Taylor 1991). This chapter explores areas of potential conceptual congruence between the rational choice perspective and contemporary approaches to radical behaviorism. Surprisingly there has been little direct exploration of such links, either in the specific criminological or the more general behavioral literature. Such analyses that do exist either relate to less scientific interpretations of behavioral approaches (as in social learning theory, for example, Akers 1990), or reject the appropriateness of such exploration altogether (Simon 1980; Skinner 1985).

This chapter seeks at a general level to renew exploration of areas of fundamental commonality between the conceptual bases of the rational choice perspective and radical behavior analysis (termed in the following *behavior analysis*). Initially, a brief discussion of some general conceptual issues explores the notion of rationality, and establishes areas of conceptual congruence. Later, the application of both approaches to the problems of crime related to political violence (such as terrorism) are discussed with particular reference to the role of ideology.

Rational Choice and Behavior Analysis

The radical behaviorist approach to psychology asserts the primacy of causal environmental accounts of behavior. This is a distinctive conceptual approach within psychology, which seeks above all to create a basic science of human behavior, characterized by an emphasis on the relationship between relevant consequences of behavior and events associated with those consequences. The most important consequence to behavior is reinforcement, and behavior that is followed by reinforcement tends to have an increased probability of occurrence. Events associated with behavior are largely (but not necessarily) features of the organisms' environment, and can be thought of as stimuli. One important class of stimuli (discriminative stimuli) set the occasion for responding; that is to say, when the stimulus occurs, the appropriate behavior follows if that behavior has in the past been reinforced. Such stimuli may be said to "control" behavior.

Explanations in behavior analysis are expressed in terms of the environmental features of behavior, and tend to be presented in atheoretical terms. Behavior analysis is often characterized (and criticized) as a positivist approach. In this respect, an important dividing line between radical behaviorists and other methodological behaviorists relates to the significance given to "covert" or cognitive factors in explanations of behavior. Radical behaviorists tend to maintain their level of analysis at what organisms do, rather than speculate about internal mediating conditions related to behavior. This gives great empirical and methodological strength to the approach, but does not necessarily exclude consideration of more complex competence-related variables, as we will discuss below (Reese 1989b). Another dividing line relates to the sense in which an organism might be said to exercise "free will" in choice and to have autonomy of action independent of its history and the context in which behavior occurs, a view largely rejected by behavior analysts (for a discussion of this, see Skinner 1971).

We can identify 4 fundamental features of both the rational choice perspective[1] and behavior analysis that suggest a capacity for a largely unacknowledged and provocative degree of commonality in approach.

1. Both focus on behavior as the *primary* data for analysis; that is to say, what people do (rather than think or intend) is the principal subject of analysis[2] (this is the case even though Simon introduced into the rational choice framework issues related to competence, cognitive structure, and information processing in Newell and Simon [1972] that has subsequently been extended at great length by other authors).
2. Both emphasize the importance of the consequences of behavior in the context of the situation in which it occurs.
3. Because of the above, for both the causes of behavior are essentially "knowable" in terms of the events associated with behavior. There is therefore no need to generate special accounts of behavior, either in terms of presumed personal inner states or vacuous concepts of social structure.
4. By stressing the importance of the situational context to behavior (rather than disposition or intention) both emphasize the significance of the features and qualities of the environment in which people live as determinants of behavior.

It has to be said, however, that neither Simon nor Skinner would necessarily agree with the above. Both have argued (Simon 1980; Skinner

1985) that their different approaches do have fundamental differences that relate to the complexity of behavior analyzed and the need for and nature of cognitive qualities underlying behavior. At the practical level, however, these essentially theoretical differences diminish in significance.

The position adopted in this chapter is that in conceptual terms, the qualities that the rational choice and behavioral approaches have in common extend beyond the methodological. Taking offending as an example, conceptualizing the criminal as a knowable person *subject to the same sort of influences* as noncriminals enables us to bring to bear on the study of offending behavior essentially empirical insights that have proved their utility in other areas of behavioral investigation. This serves to advance the debate away, for example, from notions of "pathology" or "abnormality." By associating the rational choice perspective with a behavioral approach, we bring together a powerful conceptual structure with an equally powerful technology for effecting behavior change. Exploration of this coming together at a practical level may offer an enhanced capacity for developing strategies for intervention.

This is of particular significance when we try to understand political violence and terrorism. Bringing the debate about political violence into the realm of the addressable marks a major advance toward establishing a basis from which to develop understanding (Taylor 1988). Policy-related discussions of political violence are often related to crisis management and particular dramas, rather than developing from a coherent conceptual base. The area is characterized by ad hoc solutions, rather than systematically worked through analysis.

If areas of fundamental conceptual affinity can be identified, why have they not been more clearly expressed and developed in either the behavior analysis or rational choice literature concerned with offending? We will identify three broad issues that are relevant to this. The first is that behavior analysis approaches to offending are themselves relatively poorly developed at both empirical and conceptual levels. Discussions on offending, as distinct from the management of convicted offenders, are sparse and of limited breadth. A small number of studies have attempted to evaluate ways of changing specific criminal or undesirable behavior (for example, Van Houten et al. [1980] examined behavioral factors related to vehicle speeding; Schnelle et al. [1975] examined police patrolling strategies) but these studies generally lack a coherent focus and framework. From a broader perspective, Skinner (1953) discusses the nature of the law, social agencies associated with the law, and how these might relate to behavior; this is further elaborated in Skinner (1971). However, the discussion in both rarely rises above the general, and conspicuously fails to address the complexity of offending behavior. Nietzel and Himelein

(1987) do extend the discussion further, but nevertheless there is a striking lack in the contemporary behavior analysis literature in this area.

The second issue we can identify is of somewhat broader significance, and concerns the generally collective approach to behavior of the rational choice perspective, in contrast to the essentially individual focus of the behavioral approach. At least in terms of the typical economic analysis underlying rational choice concepts, the individual appears to receive sparse attention, with the focus being on the aggregate. The behavior analysis approach adopts an almost opposite perspective in this respect, with very little empirical or conceptual attention being paid to distinctive qualities of collective behavior.

The third issue is probably the most important reason for a failure to develop conceptual links, and this relates to a problem at a fundamental conceptual level. A significant difficulty that has undoubtedly deterred behavior analysts from exploring the rational choice paradigm relates to what might be meant by the term *rational,* and unease at the assumption of "inner" explanations of behavior this might imply. Conversely, the behavior analyst's emphasis on the *environment* selecting behavior in circumstances of choice, rather than the individual processing information to enable choice, seems to constitute an irreconcilable difference.[3]

We can discern two senses from the rational choice literature in which *rational* is used to characterize behavior. It is sometimes used to refer to the *process* of choice, and sometimes to the *bases* of choice. In an everyday sense, we probably most readily use the concept of "rational" to imply a cognitive intervening variable that effects a form of internal control over behavior. By this view, the presumed cognitive structure constitutes all (or part) of the *bases* of choice (although other factors may be necessary to complete the account). This point of view is clearly at odds with the environmental analysis developed within behavior analysis that emphasizes contingency selection as the bases of choice. If *rational* is used to refer to the *process* of choice, however, this usage appears to raise issues about free will that are equally antithetical to a behavioral approach. This apparent lack of conceptual consistency between rational choice approaches and behavior analysis has undoubtedly hindered further exploration of commonalities. It has led, for example, to Morris's (1987) limited acknowledgement of the significance of rational choice approaches to behavior analysis in his discussion of conceptual issues in behavior analytic approaches to crime and delinquency.

The relationship between other less methodologically rigorous behavioral approaches and the rational choice perspective have been developed, however, notably with respect to Bandura's formulation of social learning theory (Bandura 1986). This may be because the conceptual difficulties associated with notions of rationality as a cognitive quality of an individual presents less difficulty to Bandura. In Bandura's terms, "stimuli that either signify events to come or indicate probable response consequences" give rise to a "cognitive representation of the contingencies" (Bandura 1977). Thus explanations of behavior in Bandura's terms necessarily relate to presumed cognitive structures, but because of that, of course, effectively lose whatever methodological strength a behavioral approach might bring. Efforts to apply Bandura's notions to offending behavior can be seen in Akers (1985) (extended and critically discussed in the context of rational choice theory in Akers 1990).

However, when we examine further how rational choice theorists use the term *rationality,* the apparently fundamental difficulties between behavior analysis and rational choice diminishes in significance. The concept of rationality relates essentially to assumptions made about the motivation of individuals and how we try to explain why they choose to do particular things. In the rather crude economic thinking from which the rational choice perspective has emerged, an individual is assumed to be a "self interested, purposeful, maximizing being" (Petracca 1991). Purposefulness and rationality and their correlate, maximization, are often used both in economic discussions and in areas of application of rational choice theory in the narrow sense described by Simon (1978) to imply maximization in the sense of extreme calculating self-interest.

Notions of self-interest do not present any insurmountable obstacle to understanding the rational choice perspective for a behavior analyst. To say that behavior is controlled by its consequences (as a behavior analyst might) can be argued to be nothing more than a technical and neutral way of referring to self-interest. Assumptions from the different perspectives about the origins of that self-interest, however, are more problematic. Discussions of this essentially psychological issue from a general economic perspective (in the absence of more explicitly relevant offender-related discussions) have tended to lack conceptual development. Despite this, areas of commonality between economic and behavior analysis approaches to understanding choice behavior at a general level have been identified by Hursh (1984). But this contrasts with crude and unsophisticated economic notions of maximization that are given psychological clothing with simple-minded speculations of underlying cognitive processing, that do little to convince workers outside of the discipline of economics.

In fact, although some later economics-oriented literature on rational choice does him little justice in this respect, Simon (1978) recognized the difficulties in the relationship between economics and the other social sciences caused by a narrow use of rationality to imply simply crude maximization. In recognizing and discussing this difficultly, he also goes some way toward offering a model of rationality that is quite consistent with current conceptions in behavior analysis. Indeed, he notes that even from an economic perspective, substituting a less narrow, everyday sense of rationality, for a strong assumption of maximization does no harm to economic analysis, and has the virtue of more readily enabling links to be developed with disciplines outside of economics.

The key issue in this respect is Simon's introduction of a relationship between what he means by rationality and the concept of "functionality." Simon uses *rationality* to refer to circumstances in which there is a sense of function to behavior, which refers to the movement of behavior systems toward stable equilibria. Recognizing that the factors that influence behavior shift and change, he further notes that functionality in complex systems might relate to the establishment of temporary, rather than permanent equilibria (thereby introducing an avenue for developing a more personal focus). The critical issue as far as this chapter is concerned is that *at the level of the individual,* functionality in Simon's terms appears to be expressed in terms of the responsiveness of behavior to its consequences. It might be argued that in a dynamically changing environment, the introduction of the notion of equilibrium may be unnecessary, implying the attainment of an illusory final state. However, the use of the concept of equilibrium presumably relates to the provision of a mechanism to account for the directed qualities of behavior, in that attainment of an equilibrium is assumed to motivate behavior. (This seems to be little more than a variant of homeostatic models of motivation using economic rather than physiological forces to impel behavior change). There are other ways of conceptualizing the direction to behavior, however, as we will note below.

If "functionality" in this sense is what is meant by *rationality,* then the links between behavior analysis and rational choice perspectives become much clearer and stronger. There appears to be no necessary reason for concepts like "intention" or "conscious processing" to be invoked in explanations, but rather the emphasis is upon the consequences of behavior as they impinge on the individual. To the behavior analyst, this now has a very familiar ring, and the functional analysis described by Skinner (1953) readily accommodates to Simon's similar concepts. It then becomes a matter of empirical exploration to establish the kinds of events that influence behavior, and there need be no necessary reason to seek explanations outside of this broad functional framework.

As noted earlier, Hursh (1984) has presented a useful starting point examining the links between general economic and behavioral concepts in terms of functional relationships. However, this discussion needs to be developed further within the specific context of rational choice perspectives on offending. To some extent, Taylor and Nee (1988) have made a start on this in their discussion of the environmental cues used by residential burglars when making decisions about choice of which property to victimize. They characterized in behavioral terms the functional environmental features to which the burglar is sensitive in making such choices as discriminative stimuli that "set the occasion" for the response of burglary. The simulation paradigm they employed was sufficiently close to the free responding situation used in typical behavior analysis studies to enable the commonality of explanations to emerge.

While the above discussion is broadly consistent with Simon (1978), influential but earlier more clearly psychological formulations associated with Simon do not so readily lend themselves to interpretation in behavioral terms. In particular Newell and Simon (1972) seek to distinguish between behavior directly related to the task environment that illustrates maximization, and behavior imperfectly related to the task environment, in which they suggest that " (t)he explanation must lie inside the subject" in terms of processes of problem solving expressed in terms of information processing (a view of rationality as an intervening variable related to the *bases* of choice). This theme has been subsequently extensively developed by Simon in studies rejecting the appropriateness of the positivist approach of behavioral analysis. Simon refers to the sense of imperfection in choice as illustrating "bounded rationality" (Simon 1983). It is worth noting that Newell and Simon (1972) do not overemphasize the importance of cognitive elements (what they term "the psychology of the subject"), and they note that environment and the "psychology of the subject" are like figure and ground, dependant on the perspective adopted. Later formulations by Simon, however, are less hesitant in their assertion of the exclusively cognitive bases of imperfect choice.

From the determinist and positivist perspective of a radical behaviorism, behavior cannot be imperfectly related to its environment, and this seems to recreate the conceptual impasse noted above. Indeed, from a behavioral perspective, explanation of "imperfections" by the qualification of bounded to rationality might be argued to do little to aid conceptual clarity, and might properly be regarded as an explanatory fiction (Skinner 1953)—it purports to explain, but simply restates the problem in more complex terms. Reference to "optimal" states (as distinct from a process of maximization) begs too many psychological questions.

As an alternative, however, it is perfectly reasonable to assume that the array of circumstances that we term "environmental influence" embraces not simply immediate contingencies, but also an organism's competence factors related to its complex previous history of environmental events. If we return to our earlier discussion of the meaning of rationality as the *bases* of choice, there is no necessary reason to equate rationality with a form of cognitive intervening variable. An equally tenable view is that the logic of choice (which we might refer to as demonstrating rationality) relates to the organism's behavioral history. Deviation from some optimal outcome may be seen as an imperfection of environmental control, or alternatively it may more usefully be seen not to be deviation at all, but a reflection of the differential history of that individual expressible in competence-related behavioral terms.

Political Violence

If we now turn our attention to political violence, themes of functionality and maximization recur as important issues in conceptual analysis. At first sight many features of political violence (such as terrorist behavior or participation in political protest) seem to resist understanding in terms of maximizing utility at the individual and even at the collective level. This is even more the case when we consider an extreme example of political violence, where the individual deliberately damages, or even kills, himself as part of a politically violent act. The hunger striker and the Shi'ite suicide bomber seem to defy explanation in terms of personal utility as behavior controlled by its consequences. Seeking explanations of such behavior (which in one sense is clearly irrational) by reference to notions of rationality seems contradictory and inappropriate, and the nature of political violence often seems to be more readily located within the context of abnormality and psychopathology, rather than in any sense of normal behavior. In the case of terrorism, for example, the choice of victims rarely relates in any obvious sense to expressed political aims; the means of expressing violence is frequently excessive; and the characteristic lack of regard for the well-being of innocents appears to place such behavior outside the bounds of what we might accept as normal behavior. How else can we understand and accommodate to what is frequently repulsive and grossly excessive behavior?[4]

One weakness of the rational choice perspective in aiding our understanding of the factors influencing political violence is that it has tended to assume the primacy of collective rather than individual consequences for behavior. (A more general point related to this has been noted above.) For example, authors such as Chalmers and Shelton (1975) and Mason (1984), have discussed at length riot or civil disorder situations, and have attempted to examine the nature of the consequences to such behavior. Because rational choice approaches tend to assume collective consequences to behavior (the public goods referred to by economists), discussions of most forms of political violence face the immediate difficulty of identifying such consequences to behavior such as riot when the individuals concerned derive no apparent material gain. Sometimes the "spoils" of rioting (as looting) are drawn upon, but this is a manifestly weak explanation at variance with what we know about rioting behavior. More typically, the debate has focused on the relative status of "private interest" versus "public" goods (see for example Muller and Opp 1986).

The challenge of political violence to both rational choice and behavior analysis approaches is quite clear — how can an individual who shows self-interest (or expressed in more technical behavioral terms, whose behavior is environmentally structured and controlled by its consequences) engage in political activities such a riots, bombings, or hunger strikes that appear to be of no apparent self-interest, or where the consequences to such behavior (such as the downfall of a regime and creation of a new society) may be very distant and unspecific. We will attempt to address this challenge by discussing three interrelated issues: the dynamic of behavior; the role of ideology as a form of rule governance; and the distinction between involvement and events in politically extreme behavior.

The Dynamic of Behavior in Political Violence

How do we conceptualize the process of development and change of behavior? In the sense used by Simon (1978), the concept of rationality he draws on implies an orderly process, in which the end product of balance or equilibrium is attained by the organism in some sense maximizing the utility of the various consequences to behavior. Leaving aside the necessity of assuming maximization, rational choice theorists have been quite unclear how the forces or processes that impel behavior toward stability operate on the individual. Indeed, in Simon's discussion (Simon 1978), he notes that the "interest lies not in *how* decisions are made but in *what* decisions are made." Where a more complex account is necessary, appeal is most frequently made to notions analogous to biological concepts of natural selection. In contrast, behavioral approaches have explored these process issues at great length, relating change to contingency variables (for an example of this, see Skinner 1986).

As far as discussions of offending behavior are concerned, Cornish and Clarke (1986) to some extent do go beyond a focus on decisional outcomes, and this has been extended further by some authors, for example, Lattimore and Witte (1986) and Tuck and Riley (1986). There have been limited efforts, however, to capitalize on thinking from a behavior analysis perspective to attempt to understand how criminal choices might be made, and there have been no any attempts to extend the analysis to similar problems of political violence. However, insofar as political violence is concerned, the need for this lies not simply in an urge for theoretical consistency or completeness. Unlike criminal behavior, in which the behavior (theft of something, for example) might be characterized as being primarily for a personal end (the sale of the item stolen to realize cash), political behavior is characterized as being directed toward some ulterior explicit end. Political behavior gains its *social political* relevance not so much from itself or from the consequences for the individual concerned, but by reference to the political framework in which it belongs — we might term this framework *ideology*. Individual acts gain their meaning and coherence by reference to this ideological framework. The intense discussion by politically violent groups that frequently precedes acts of violence is a simple illustration of this, and analyses of the communications from terrorist groups similarly illustrate this (Cordes 1988).

At first sight rational choice assertions of maximization seem to have little to offer here. A characteristic of the extreme politically committed is their sense of certainty and righteousness, regardless of the utility of their behavior in any objective sense (Taylor 1991). If a notion of utility is necessary, it is essentially related to the overriding ideological context. The issue here, therefore, is not whether choice is perfect or imperfect — choice is "controlled" by a clear and explicit context that is largely insensitive to other pressures.

How then might we think of the dynamic of behavior in the context of political violence? Is behavior pulled along by its consequences? If so, do we characterize its directed qualities, its apparent integrity and cohesion, through post hoc analysis and description? Or is behavior structured and directed in some way toward particular ends; pushed along certain directions through the influence of ideology? In the above, if we chose the former case, the principal difficulty encountered is how to explain the influence of distant ideological ends on immediate behavior. If we chose the latter, the problem of how does ideology influence future behavior is raised.

A brief discussion of the issue of suicide may help to develop the argument further. Rational choice theorists have addressed the above problem in considering suicide, but in many ways have rather evaded the issue by focusing on the immediate circumstances surrounding the suicidal event itself and the methods used (see for example Lester 1988 and Lester 1990). Either psychopathology in some form is assumed to account for the initiating suicidal state, or, alternatively, the utility of suicide as a release from pain or distress is assumed. This approach is not sufficient, however, when thinking of superficially similar acts of political violence (for example a hunger strike). Neither pathology nor the utility of "release" from distress captures the essentially political and ideological commitment underlying such behavior.

One way of attempting to conceptualize in behavioral terms the processes that might be involved has been offered by Taylor and Ryan (1988). In a discussion of fanatical political behavior, they have offered an explanation in terms of "chaining" — particular relationships between behavior and consequence are directly linked through sequences of behavior to the more distant goal. Behavior change and development can be seen as the consequence of incremental change, where the end product gains its coherence through understanding the sequence of events the individual has been exposed to.

The accounts of individual terrorist's life histories, for example, seems to support this view. Kellen (1979) in his discussion of the development of the West German terrorist Michael Baumann (the founder of the 2nd June Movement) describes a process of increasing involvement in a terrorist life-style that readily fits this model. Baumann did not suddenly embark upon a terrorist career. He went through a process of increasing marginalization from society, drifting into political radicalism and terrorism. In the process of this, he became absorbed into a particular kind of society (one that emphasized particular kinds of dress and long hair, ready access to sexual favors, etc.) that proved to be very attractive to him. The Italian Red Brigade terrorist leader, Alberto Francescini, gives a similar account of his incremental development toward terrorism.[5]

These accounts have a great deal in common with the literature on criminal careers, (eg., Farrington 1986), although it is difficult to see how the systematic longitudinal research necessary to establish this might be conducted. An important difference, however, between the development of the terrorist and the development of the criminal is that however random and inconsistent terrorist behavior may appear to the observer, there is a clear sense of direction and purpose to it (Taylor 1988). While the terrorist is undoubtedly influenced by the immediate context of his behavior, there is a more distant sense of organization to behavior lacking in the case of the criminal. Both Baumann and Francescini were highly selective in the things they did, not because they took advantage of events for personal profit or excitement, but because their behavior contributed toward some ultimate objective. Francescini described his own political involvement as "an ethical, civil commitment. I always thought that people should have their own job or occupation, earn their own money, and politics should be something separate." Maintenance of a separation of those things political from the mundane and ordinary can be seen quite clearly in the way other terrorists integrate their terrorist activities with their normal life-style, and is probably a general phenomena of the terrorist living within a broader civil community (as distinct from the guerrilla fighter).

We can see the same issue emerging, although from a different perspective, when we consider terrorist behavior. The variety of tactics employed by the Provisional IRA, for example, in its attacks on the British mainland illustrate how focused and directed such activity is, even though the individual acts themselves may have little *apparent* relationship either with themselves or with the ultimate objectives of the Provisional IRA. Accounts expressed in terms of chains of behavior fail to capture this directed quality to terrorism.

Rule Governance

A useful way of thinking from a behavior analysis perspective about the directed qualities of behavior and about the control exercised by distant outcomes is to think not in terms of relatively mechanistic chains of behavior, but in terms of behavior mediated by rules that relate distant outcomes to particular events (Skinner 1968). In the sense used by Skinner, rules are verbal descriptions of the relationship between behaviors and consequences[6] — they are generalizations about the circumstances that control behavior (both positive and negative) that have applied in the past or will apply in the future, and hold a similar relationship to behavior as do discriminative stimuli.

In conceptual terms, the notion of rule following might serve as an important bridge between Simon's cognitive assumptions in rational choice theory and a more radical behavioral approach. What Skinner describes as rule following can be seen as little more than an expression in behavioral terms of the process of problem solving, a theme developed further by Skinner (1968, 1985). Contemporary developments in the area of cognitive science, and the growing recognition of conceptual relationships between cognitive psychology and radical behaviorism (eg., Reese 1989a, Barnes and Keenan 1991) further illustrate this point. Furthermore, the notions of rule following may also be consistent with Bandura's theory of social learning if a consistent environmental account is maintained and we substitute the essentially *verbal* qualities of rules for what Bandura assumes to be *cognitive* factors (Poppen 1989).

The chain analysis of behavior noted earlier emphasizes the importance of immediate acting circumstances in the control of behavior. In such an analysis, distant outcomes in themselves need have no necessary relationship with immediately controlling events. The individual might drift toward something (like involvement with terrorism) but that eventual state has no necessary relationship with the particular circumstances that affect the individual at any given time. Nor need the starting point have any necessary immediate relationship with later behavior. In contrast, an analysis in terms of rule governance emphasizes the relationship between present behavior and deferred or distant consequences; the rule effectively mediates between present behavior and distant consequences. The significance of this redirection of analysis is that it draws upon the same explanatory and conceptual framework to explain both immediate and distant effects—a significant conceptual advance over other approaches. Returning to our earlier discussion of the meaning of rationality, we might, therefore, see rule governance as the *bases* of "rationality," generating the logic and direction of choice. The issue of imperfections in choice, therefore, as "bounded rationality" no longer arises in issues of substantive choice.

The source of the rules that affect and determine political behavior is ideology (it is worth noting that the same analysis may well equally apply to religion). Consistent with the approach taken here, Rokeach (1968) has defined ideology as "a common and broadly agreed set of rules to which an individual subscribes which help to regulate and determine behaviour." The source of ideology is generally some written material of some form; the content of ideology specifies the particular rules that might apply at any given time. For the politically committed, ideology provides the conceptual framework within which behavior is developed. In a sense, therefore, we might argue that at least with respect to political violence rule governance describes the process of functional rationality referred to by Simon (1978). It remains a matter for speculation whether this analysis will apply as readily to criminal behavior. Ideology provides a particularly public and explicit basis for the development of behavioral rules. Less clearly articulated forces (such as perhaps subcultural effects, family context, etc.) may need to be drawn on to identify the origins of rule governance in criminal behavior.

Involvement and Event

Cornish and Clarke (1986) note the utility of making a distinction between criminal involvement, and criminal events. They point out that different influences may well affect the involvement decisions of an individual in contrast to those factors influencing the circumstances surrounding particular events. Put simply, involvement in crime may well draw upon different processes from the circumstances that surround and "explain" the commission of a particular crime. This same distinction has been used by Taylor (1991) in his discussion of political violence, in which he argues that the reasons for the expression of a particular violent political behavior can be distinguished from the process whereby the individual might develop into a violent political activist.

Factors influencing a particular behavior tend at one level of analysis to be essentially short term. They relate in this sense to opportunity, the immediate consequences to behavior, and the nature of the special learning processes that have preceded the particular event. But for these factors to be effective, we must also assume a facilitating context, an engagement with the processes that lead the individual to this particular situation. To extend our discussion further, and to draw together the discussion above, we might speculate that this important distinction is mirrored in the differential control over behavior exercised by rule governance versus immediate consequences.

Within the political context, we have already noted that engagement with terrorism, for example, does not occur suddenly. There is a long period of initiation into terrorist life-styles and culture. For many terrorists, that engagement begins very early in life, and relates to family involvement. The number of families in Northern Ireland, for example who have had brothers, uncles, and grandparents engage in terrorist activity at some point in their lives is considerable.

Perhaps more importantly, however, the basis to this lies not so much in actual engagement in terrorism, but familiarity with the ideological bases of such behavior. This early exposure to a facilitating ideological context that enables terrorist behavior to later develop is a striking feature of many accounts of terrorists. Alberto Francescini makes the point well: "I learned politics from them. For my parents my interests and involvement in politics, in communism, was a fundamental part of life." Francescini's grandfather had been one of the founders of the Communist party in Italy, his family used to live in the same building as the trade union offices where his grandfather and father worked; communism was an essential part of his early life.

It may be, however, that when used with respect to political activity, "involvement" factors take on a much more directive quality than implied by Cornish and Clarke in their discussion of offending. If we think of such involvement as an example of rule governance over behavior, then the content of the rules relate to ideological principles. The direction, the "purpose" to action, therefore, gains meaning through reference to these ideological qualities.

In contrast, the factors that lead to the commission of a particular terrorist act certainly gain their meaning by reference to ideology, but the choice of a particular activity (such as a bombing or shooting) and the circumstances in which it might occur are affected by much more local issues. My own unpublished work in this area on the analysis of particular terrorist incidents suggests that situational factors similar to those that have emerged from the study of residential burglary are important. In a study of some 60 "low-level" terrorist incidents in the Belfast and Armagh areas of Northern Ireland that occurred in the period 1984–1986, opportunity and a facilitating local environment (cover, lack of surveillance, etc.) emerged as critical issues that determined the choice of terrorist action. Twenty percent of the incidents could be described as truly opportunistic, the remainder showing evidence of some degree of structure and planning. The overwhelming common feature of all incidents was the availability of escape for the terrorists, either in the sense of locating themselves away from the immediate scene or having clearly accessible avenues of escape from the incident. (If we were to pursue this analysis in detail, however, it would be necessary to distinguish between kinds of terrorist behavior. The varieties of behavior included within the general concept of "terrorism" lack homogeneity). Notwithstanding the above, however, we might speculate that particular terrorist behavior might show a much greater influence of "involvement" factors than criminal behavior.

The above account can be contrasted with Bandura's discussion of the origins of terrorist behavior (Bandura 1990), in terms of moral disengagement. His account proposes various mediating conditions that impede the function of self-sanctioning that in Bandura's view facilitates terrorist violence. His emphasis on the importance of language in the development and maintenance of terrorism is both revealing and important. But reliance on concepts such as "self-deception," and a failure to distinguish factors influencing the individuals contextual engagement with terrorism from those related to the events of terrorism, diminish the significance of his comments. Indeed, in many ways his paper illustrates the conceptual problems that arise when an apparently behavioral approach looses rigor through speculation involving intervening variables.

Conclusion

The above discussion of course leaves unanswered many important issues, and it suggests compromises rather than resolutions to fundamental conceptual differences. Nor does it "explain" politically violent behavior through the provision of simple predictive criteria. Indeed, why should there be a single coherent explanation of terrorist behavior (or criminal behaviour)? Many life choices for people are related to random events, the juxtaposition of opportunity and facilitating circumstance that might owe nothing to logic and all to chance. Given this, the private logic of events may be much more important than the public appearance of behavior. This is certainly the case when we seek to explain career and job choice, for example. Why should terrorist (or criminal) careers be any different? Indeed, we might conclude that the question "what causes terrorist behavior" is rather pointless.

A more appropriate way of addressing the issue would be to ask "how do we change terrorist behavior?" Perhaps the greatest conceptual contribution of the rational choice perspective in this area is that it facilitates this reformulation. The rational choice perspective directs our attention to the utility of terrorist behavior and its orderliness. It offers a way of structuring behavior in terms of its broader environmental context, facilitating ways of conceptualizing preventative strategies. The behavioral approach offers what has been argued to be a complementary conceptual framework that is associated with powerful techniques for the management and control of behavior. Modification of the situational contingencies that control terrorist behavior gives focus and meaning to intervention strategies. It would be wrong, however, to see terrorist behavior, and political violence in general, as something apart from analyses of other criminal behaviors. While there may be conceptual differences, their practical significance may be limited.

The virtue of the rational choice approach to the problems of political violence, therefore, is that it gives a methodological and conceptual framework from which to develop some form of understanding and offers avenues to empirically explore initiatives to effect change. As in the case of crime-related analyses, that framework can help to inform the policy process in an empirical and systematic way. While ideology as an involvement factor might be argued to have a greater influence on the nature of politically violent events than is the case in a criminal context, the parallels we can identify are both striking and provocative. Drawing a behavioral approach into this powerful conceptual framework makes available an array of well-established techniques for analysis that may serve to extend and enhance the utility of both.

Notes

1. While there are very many accounts exploring rational choice approaches to understanding behavior, one of the most influential was that published by Simon (1978); much of the following is taken from that paper.
2. This is not to say that evidence from interviews in which people might be invited to speculate on their reasons for doing things, or to describe events that have happened, are not relevant and useful. We should note, however, "that descriptions of contingencies do not have the same effect as the contingencies themselves" (Skinner 1985).
3. The issues here go beyond the scope of this chapter. Further discussion can be found in Simon (1980) and Skinner (1985). The approach adopted here is that the differences may prove to be less of substance than of form when dealing with

specific problems, and that useful areas of commonality can be identified at empirical and practical levels.

4. Explaining behavior in terms of psychopathology is of course entirely appropriate provided we do not use such concepts to evade explanation. Issues related to this have been discussed at length with respect to terrorism in Taylor (1988) and with respect to more general political violence in Taylor (1991).

5. Unpublished interview with the author, October 1991.

6. This is a complex area of behavior analysis. For more information see Malott (1988), Hayes (1989), Skinner (1985), Skinner (1989) and Vaughan (1987). See Taylor (1991) for a specific discussion of rule governance as it might relate to political behavior, fanaticism, and ideology. The relevance of this for the following discussion is that rule governance may offer a means of reconciling a major conceptual fissure in psychology between radical behavioral accounts of behavior and cognitive science and information-processing accounts. While raising issues, however, the following discussion does not address in any detail the many outstanding areas of conceptual disagreement between notions of rule governance and parallel accounts in cognitive psychology.

References

Akers, R.L. 1985. *Deviant behavior: A social learning approach* (3rd ed.). Boulder, CO: Westmount.

———. 1990. "Rational choice, deterrence, and social learning theory in criminology: The path not taken." *Journal of Criminal Law and Criminology* 81:653–67.

Bandura, A. 1977. "Self-efficacy: Towards a unifying theory of behavior change." *Psychological Bulletin* 84:191–215.

———. 1986. *Social foundations of thought and action: A social cognitive theory.* Englewood Cliffs, NJ: Prentice-Hall.

———. 1990 "Mechanisms of moral disengagement." In W. Reich (Ed.), *Origins of terrorism, psychologies, ideologies, theologies, states of mind.* Cambridge: Cambridge University Press.

Barnes, D., & Keenan, M. 1991. "Radical behaviorism, stimulus equivalence and human cognition." *The Psychological Record* 41:19–31.

Chalmers, J.A., & Shelton, R.B. 1975. "An economic analysis of riot participation." *Economic Inquiry* 13:321–36.

Cordes, B. 1988. "When terrorists do the talking: Reflections on terrorist literature." In D.C. Rapoport (Ed.), *Inside terrorist organisations.* London: Frank Cass and Co.

Cornish, D.B., & Clarke, R.V. 1986. Introduction. In D.B. Cornish & R.V. Clarke (Eds.), *The reasoning criminal. Rational choice perspectives on offending.* New York: Springer-Verlag.

Farrington, D. 1986. "Stepping stones to adult criminal careers." In D. Olweus, J. Block, & M.R. Yarrow (Eds.), *Development of antisocial and prosocial behavior.* New York: Academic Press.

Hayes, S.C. (Ed.) 1989. *Rule-governed behavior. Cognition, contingencies and instructional control.* New York: Plenum Press.

Hursh, S.R. 1984. "Behavioral economics." *Journal of the Experimental Analysis of Behavior* 42:435–52.

Kellen, K. 1979. *Terrorists — What are they like? Some terrorists describe their world and actions.* Santa Monica, CA: Rand Corporation.

Lattimore, P., & Witte, A. 1986. "Models of decision making under uncertainty: The criminal choice." In D.B. Cornish & R.V. Clarke (Eds.), *The reasoning criminal. Rational choice perspectives on offending.* New York: Springer-Verlag.

Lester, D. 1988. "Why do people choose particular methods for suicide?" *Activitas Nervosa Superior* 30:312–14.

———. 1990. "An economic theory of choice and its implications for suicide." *Psychological Reports* 66:1112–14.

Malott, R.W. 1988. "Rule governed behavior and behavioral anthropology." *The Behavior Analyst* 11:181-200.

Mason, D. 1984. "Individual participation in collective racial violence: A rational choice perspective." *American Political Science Review* 78:1040–56.

Morris, E.K. 1987. "Introductory comments: Applied behavior analysis in crime and delinquency: Focus on prevention." *The Behavior Analyst* 10:67–68.

Muller, E.N., & Opp, K.-D. 1986. "Rational choice and rebellious collective action." *American Political Science Review* 80:471–87.

Newell, A., & Simon, H.A. 1972. *Human problem solving.* Englewood Cliffs, NJ: Prentice-Hall.

Nietzel, M.T., & Himelein, M.J. 1987. "Crime prevention through social and physical environmental change." *The Behavior Analyst* 10:69–74.

Petracca, M.P. 1991. "The rational choice approach to politics: A challenge to democratic theory." *The Review of Politics* 53:289–319.

Poppen, R.L. 1989. "Some clinical implications of rule governed behavior." In S.C. Hayes (Ed.), *Rule-governed behavior. Cognition, contingencies, and instructional control.* New York: Plenum.

Reese, H.W. 1989a. "The nature and place of behavioral analyses of rule-governed behaviour." In S.C. Hayes (Ed.), *Rule-governed behavior. Cognition, contingencies and instructional control.* New York: Plenum.

———. 1989b. "Rules and rule-governance. Cognitive and behavioristic views." In S.C. Hayes (Ed.), *Rule-governed behavior. Cognition, contingencies and instructional control.* New York: Plenum.

Rokeach, M. 1968. *Belief, attitude and value.* San Francisco: Jossey-Bass.

Schnelle, J.F., Kirchner, R.E., McNees, M.P., & Lawler, J.M. 1975. "Social evaluation research: The evaluation of two police patrolling strategies." *Journal of Applied Behavior Analysis* 8:353–65.

Simon, H.A. 1978. "Rationality as process and as product of thought." *American Economic Review* 8:1–16.

Simon, H.A. 1980. "The behavioral and social sciences." *Science* 209:76.

———. 1983. *Reason in human affairs.* Oxford: Blackwell.

Skinner, B.F. 1953. *Science and human behavior.* London: Collier-Macmillan Ltd.

———. 1968. *Contingencies of reinforcement.* New York: Appleton-Century-Crofts.

———. 1971. *Beyond freedom and dignity.* Harmondsworth, Middx.: Penguin Books.

———. 1985. "Cognitive science and behaviorism" *British Journal of Psychology* 76:291–301.

———. 1986. "The evolution of verbal behavior" *Journal of the Experimental Analysis of Behavior* 45:115–22.

————. 1989. *The behavior of the listener.* In S.C. Hayes (Ed.), *Rule-governed behavior. Cognition, contingencies and instructional control.* New York: Plenum Press.

Taylor, M. 1988. *The terrorists.* London: Brassey's Defence Publishers Ltd.

————. 1991. *The fanatics. A behavioural approach to political violence.* London: Brassey's (UK).

Taylor, M., & Nee, C. 1988. "The role of cues in simulated residential burglary." *British Journal of Criminology* 28:396–402.

Taylor, M., & Ryan, H. 1988. "Fanaticism, political suicide and terrorism." *Terrorism* 11:91–100.

Tuck, M., & Riley, D. 1986. "The theory of reasoned action: A decision theory of crime." In D.B. Cornish & R.V. Clarke (Eds.), *The reasoning criminal. Rational choice perspectives on offending.* New York: Springer-Verlag.

Van Houten, R., Nau, P., & Martini, Z. 1980. "An analysis of public posting in reducing speeding behavior on an urban highway." *Journal of Applied Behavior Analysis* 13:385–95.

Vaughan, M. 1987. Rule-governed behavior and higher mental processes. In S. Modgil and C. Mogdil (Eds.), *BF Skinner: Consensus and controversy.* New York: Falmer Press.

8

Ransom Kidnapping in Sardinia, Subcultural Theory and Rational Choice

Pietro Marongiu and Ronald V. Clarke

During the last 25 years, kidnapping has been a major preoccupation for the Italian authorities. More than 600 "ransom" kidnappings (designed to obtain money by threatening the life or well-being of hostages) occurred in the country between 1968 and 1989 alone. Compared to the rest of Europe and to the Western world in general, this constitutes an unusually high rate for this crime (Rudas and Marongiu 1988; Luberto and Manganelli 1990). For instance, apart from its reappearance in the 1970s with the sensational Hearst case, kidnapping has been almost absent from the American scene since the wave of ransom kidnappings during the 1920s and 1930s (Alix 1978).

Kidnapping is a highly visible crime, likely to produce strong social reaction and extensive media coverage, especially when prominent members of the community are involved as victims or when it occurs as a part of a terrorist attack. Even so, systematic information on kidnapping is difficult to obtain. Official crime statistics may not make a clear distinction between kidnapping and other crimes such as robbery and extortion, and they rarely take account of the different forms this crime can take.

Indeed, the term *kidnapping* is used to describe a wide range of unlawful behaviors. Some 15 different forms of kidnapping have been identified, ranging from a child being seized by one of the parties in a custody dispute to white slavery (Alix 1978).[1] But all of these different forms share the basic notion of illegal taking and detention of a person against his or her will.

179

The motives, objectives, strategies, dynamics, and structure of kidnapping can vary considerably according to the different forms of the crime and, because of these variations, each form requires its own crime-specific analysis. We are here interested in "classic" ransom kidnapping, the main purpose of which is to obtain money through extortion by threatening the life of hostages. In its typical form this is a violent crime carried out by a group of organized criminals.

This form of kidnapping has a long tradition in Italy, particularly on the island of Sardinia, where there is evidence of its occurrence since the 15th century (Rudas and Marongiu 1988). Until the 1970s, when kidnapping began to spread to the mainland, it had been regarded as a typical expression of the subculture of inner rural areas of Sardinia. Ten out of 13 episodes that occurred in Italy in 1968 (76.9%) took place on the island, while in 1977, when this crime reached its peak nationwide, only 4 out of 75 episodes (5.3%) were reported in Sardinia (Luberto and Manganelli 1984) (see fig. 8.1). This phenomenon cannot therefore be regarded simply as a local problem specifically linked to particular social and geohistorical conditions. The so-called internal or rural-pastoral Sardinian ransom kidnapping has thus been considered a "prototype," out of which the mainland variety has subsequently derived. In 1985, however, Sardinia was again among the regions showing the highest kidnapping rates, with 4 episodes out of a total of 9 (Luberto and Manganelli 1984).

Note on Sardinia

An island of approximately 24,000 square kilometers, Sardinia is located in the central section of the Mediterranean, equidistant from northern Africa and continental Italy. It has a low population density (in 1989, 68.7 inhabitants per sq. km.), with a total of 1,655,859 persons. Most of these live in urban centers, with the result that large portions of the countryside, in particular the central-eastern mountainous area characterized by a sheep-raising nomadic economy, are almost deserted (Pinna 1970). These inner rural areas have a long history of isolation and are characterized by a violence-oriented social organization as first shown in the pioneering work of Alfredo Niceforo (1897), who identified a geographical area (the "delinquent zone") with an extremely high rate of violent crime, including homicide, assault, rustling, and kidnapping.

Socio-historical approaches have usually emphasized two forms of conflict that have helped to shape the culture of the delinquent zone. The first of these is an endemic "political" conflict between the inhabitants of the central areas of the island and the invaders who dominated Sardinia from the time of the Phoenicians (800 B.C.). The native inner populations

FIGURE 8.1
Ransom Kidnappings in Italy and Sardinia
(1968–1989)

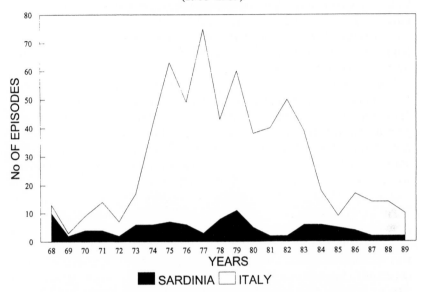

of the island have developed very little economic, social, and cultural exchange with the different colonizers, resulting in different sociocultural traditions and distinct dialects. Distrust, antagonism, and hostility toward the "invading" civilizations have been traditional features of the isolated "Barbagia" (from the name *civitates barbariae,* or "cities of barbarians," given by the Romans to the settlements in the internal mountainous part of the island). This conflict has resulted in a continuing struggle between the inhabitants of the isolated inner areas and the police and the military. Second, there is "internal" conflict due to the constant search for grazing between the shepherds of the central areas and the surrounding agrarian society. This latter conflict has been seen to be the principal cause of blood feuds.

Sardinia is one of twenty regions of Italy and is administratively divided into four districts or *provincie*: Cagliari, Sassari, Nuoro and Oristano. Nuoro covers the pastoral areas where most kidnappings take place.

Subcultural and Rational Choice Approaches

Although no detailed theoretical treatments exist of Sardinian ransom kidnapping, most discussions of this topic make reference to the subculture of violence thesis (Wolfgang and Ferracuti 1967; Ferracuti, Lazzari, and Wolfgang 1970). This was originally developed to explain explosive violent crimes in urban lower-class groups and holds that in certain sociocultural settings the system of values and related norms of conduct exhibit a "potent theme of violence . . . that make up the life-style, the socialization process, the interpersonal relationships of individuals living in similar conditions" (Wolfgang and Ferracuti 1967: 140). Since these values represent "normative standards that are part of the repertoire of response that an individual may use as alternatives for action" (Wolfgang and Ferracuti 1967: 114), violence is either expected or required in some kinds of social interaction. Sardinian pastoral society seems, in fact, to accept and support the use of violence under specific circumstances as a problem-solving mechanism. In vengeful murder, for instance, aggressive, albeit "regulated" behavior is socially required according to subcultural values specifically aimed to preserve individual or group honor.[2]

The subcultural approach assumes that subcultural affiliation takes place through primary and secondary socialization processes, and provides a detailed analysis of the content and transmission of violence-oriented values and norms. The usefulness of a social learning perspective in explaining the mechanisms of subcultural transmission is asserted. Direct behavioral observation, in particular, is seen as an important mechanism of transmission of values and attitudes. Under this perspective, the process of social identification with kidnappers as local leaders can be seen as provoking and reinforcing criminally learned responses in a number of individuals (Wolfgang and Ferracuti 1967).

Subcultural explanations of involvement in ransom kidnapping would also focus on specific patterns of culturally defined and accepted violent behavior. Rustling, for instance, has been traditionally regarded as a "normal" activity occurring in "enemy" territory and victims may be seen as "deserving it" simply because of their privileged social position or involvement in internal conflicts. Similar justifications are present in kidnapping and, indeed, kidnapping is generally regarded as having evolved from rustling.

The successful outcome of kidnapping (collecting the ransom and avoiding identification and conviction) is, of course, a reinforcing factor in relation to persistence in this crime. Given the social origins of most kidnappers, ransom money is mainly invested locally in land, cattle, and housing. Again, this reflects cultural attitudes, which are quite different in rural and urban environments. Financial advantages are therefore enjoyed by the community as a whole and social support and imitation processes are presumably enhanced.

Rational Choice

Like other major theoretical approaches in criminology, the subculture of violence thesis is basically a theory of criminality, rather than a theory of crime (Hirschi 1986: 113). It appears to explain quite adequately the reasons for the prevalence of ransom kidnapping in Sardinia, but it seems to be less successful in explaining why here, as in other nonsubculturally-oriented environments, only particular individuals are involved in kidnapping and other similar violent crimes. A second limitation is that it does not explain fluctuations in the rate of kidnapping or the changing nature of the crime; for example, more foreign visitors to the island have been seized in recent times. Finally, subcultural theory does not adequately reflect the fact that much violence in many subcultural contexts is carefully calculated and in this sense, "rational." Indeed, if we consider two major forms of Sardinian violent crime, retaliatory killing and ransom kidnapping, the image of a reasoning, nonpathological offender is pregnantly present (Ferracuti, Lazzari, and Wolfgang 1970).

The presence of instrumental motives and structured decision-making processes renders ransom kidnapping apparently suitable for a rational choice analysis, under which crime is held to be the result of decisions and choices made by offenders in pursuit of their own self-interest. Although developed in order to provide an explanatory framework for all forms of crime, the extent to which the model can be applied to violent offenses is still unclear (Cornish and Clarke 1986; Trasler 1986).

The rational choice perspective stresses the "limited" rationality and situated nature of much offending (Clarke and Cornish 1985; Cornish and Clarke 1986). It also emphasizes the need for separate analysis of the decision processes leading to an individual's involvement in crime (initial involvement, persistence, and desistance) and those resulting in the commission of a particular criminal event. (This distinction between involvement and event mirrors Gottfredson and Hirschi's [1990] distinction between theories of crime and criminality.) Finally, it requires the development of separate explanatory models for specific categories of crime. This is because many of the variables influencing decisions about kidnapping, for example, might be quite different from those for rustling, even if these forms of crime are related.

A rational choice approach would reinterpret subcultural background as an decision-orienting factor leading to criminal involvement (Cornish and Clarke 1986) and would stress the importance of the choice-structuring properties of this particular crime (Cornish and Clarke 1987). These are the characteristic features of the crime in question (such as type and amount of payoff, perceived risk, skills needed, and so forth) that render it attractive to particular offenders. As we shall see when looking into the structure of kidnapping, the choice-structuring properties common to offenses designed to yield cash for the offender, such as awareness of method and accessibility of targets, along with specifically related opportunities, such as the availability of fugitives as possible guardians and extensive knowledge of the terrain, appear to be essential in explaining and understanding the dynamics of kidnapping events.

The necessity of adopting a crime-specific focus is also evident, considering the many forms that kidnapping can take (Alix 1978). In the case of Sardinian ransom kidnappings, for example, it is clear that those events that involve a hostage foreign to the island will be more difficult and risky, as well as more financially rewarding, than in cases where the hostage is a native resident. The fact that decisions to become involved in crime and to commit particular offenses are highly influenced by a change in the opportunity structure for crime may help to explain changes in rates of kidnapping and changes in the nature of the crimes reported. This line of theoretical reasoning will be developed in the Conclusions, but first it is necessary to consider some of the main features of Sardinian ransom kidnappings.

Ransom Kidnappings in Sardinia

Some 132 cases of "classic" ransom kidnapping, occurring between January 1, 1966 and December 31, 1990, were analyzed to assist the theoretical analysis. Data were drawn from the files provided by the Regional Criminalpol Unit of Sardinia,[3] and included almost all cases occurring in the island during the period.[4] The use of Criminalpol files allowed each case to be examined as a single event, including the essential information on hostages, kidnappers (where available), the dynamics of the crime, the progress of investigations, and subsequent legal processes.

Classification of Kidnappings

Although all ransom kidnappings have in common a basic structure in which hostages are captured and a ransom demanded, preliminary analysis of Sardinian data suggested that a satisfactory explanation would not result from treating ransom kidnappings as an unitary phenomenon. In fact, the dynamics of the crime require division into two basic types:[5]

1. "Internal" ransom kidnappings (57 of the total of 132 incidents studied) which usually take place in the inner pastoral areas of Sardinia and always involve both kidnappers and victims belonging to the same geographical, social, and cultural environment.

2. The "external" type (75 of the 132 incidents), in which hostages are chosen from among the wealthy group of Sardinian (and non-Sardinian) industrialists, businessmen, and professionals (and their relatives) and from among visitors to the island, whether for business or vacation.

The possibility of extorting a much higher ransom is obviously present in external kidnappings, and it is these events in particular that have brought the problem of Sardinian kidnapping to international attention. As we shall see when examining the separate stages of kidnapping, "external" episodes display a rather complicated structure, requiring more persons and resources, in comparison with traditional "internal" ones. The move to external kidnappings seems to have entailed a considerable amount of adaptive organizational effort, since this development occurred in a relatively short period of time. By preserving basic elements, such as the custody of the hostages in the inner areas of the island, it may be assumed that external kidnapping constitutes an evolution of the internal type, rather than constituting an altogether "different" category of crime.

General Features

The distribution of ransom kidnapping in Sardinia during 1966–90 shows a cyclical trend (table 8.1). The two 5-year periods with the highest number of cases were 1966–70 and 1976–80 (over 50% of all episodes), with peaks in 1966 and 1979 (both with 11 kidnappings). The majority of episodes in the first of these periods were internal, while external hostages were much more frequent in the second. Internal kidnappings tended to decrease over the period, being progressively outnumbered by the other type. There was a marked decrease in both kinds of kidnapping in the final period (1986-90).

Most of the hostages are seized in the Nuoro District, though external episodes also frequently occur in Sassari where the exclusive seaside tourist resorts (such as the Costa Smeralda) are located (fig. 8.2). Internal victims are invariably seized in the open country or in their usual place of work (farm or fold), while isolated country mansions frequently provide the venue for the external type (18 out of 75 events). This obviously reflects the differences in hostages' occupations and social position: mostly breeders, farmers, or landowners in one case (51 out of the 57 "principal" hostages) and urban industrialists or professionals in the other. (Only 10 of the 75 principal "external" hostages fell into the category of breeders, farmers, or landowners.)[6]

Wherever the hostages are seized, they are almost always recovered in the Nuoro District (90 out of the 109 who were released, escaped, or were

TABLE 8.1
Ransom Kidnappings in Sardinia by 5-Year Periods and Type of Event

Years	Internal	External	Total
1966–1970(*)	24	16	40
1971–1975	14	11	25
1976–1980	9	24	33
1981–1986	7	15	22
1986–1990	3	9	12
Total	57	75	132

(*) The 1966/1970 five year period includes one episode (Nuoro District) which actually occurred in 1965.

freed by the police). According to hostages' reports, they are also nearly always held in this same district. Of the 90 hostages released, nearly all were recovered in the countryside, usually during the night, thus allowing the kidnappers to vanish undetected.

Available data on 181 sentenced kidnappers show that 144 of them (79.5%) were born in the Nuoro District. It should be noted, however, that many of the kidnappers born in other districts came from villages located on the fringe of the Nuoro District and thus share the cultural traditions of this area.

Given the presence of more external targets in the holiday season (May-November), it is not surprising that these months (accounting for 56 out of the 75 external events), are favored for external kidnappings. The evening hours of 6:00–12:00PM are also generally chosen, especially in external kidnappings (43 out of 75), for reasons related to the secure transfer of hostages to the inner regions of the island.

Hostages are most commonly males (female victims were involved in only 17 kidnappings out of a total 132 episodes). Age seems also to be a choice-structuring factor since individuals aged less than 20 were taken in only 11 of the 132 episodes. While children may be less likely to identify their captors or the places where they have been held and thus present a reduced risk for the kidnappers, they pose certain difficulties as hostages. In particular, they more easily get sick and show distress. They may need to be cared for by women, which complicates the operation, while cultural factors may also inhibit the taking of child hostages. In fact, some 60% of the principal hostages were over 40 years old at the time of the capture. Older victims (over 60) are more likely to be involved in external episodes. As far as age and sex are concerned, it can be said that the "ideal" hostage is male and young enough to survive custody.

The length of victims' imprisonment is shorter in the internal kidnappings (less than one month in two thirds of cases) while nearly 60

FIGURE 8.2
**Random Kidnapping in Sardinia (1966–1990) by Place of Capture
and Type of Event**

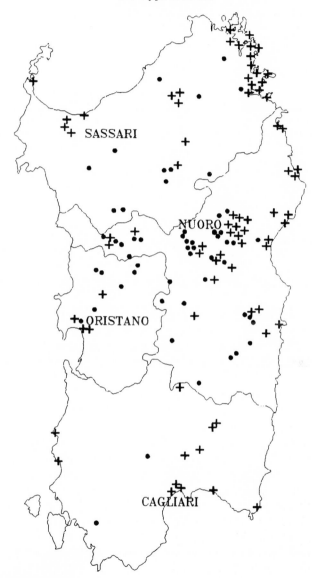

- **Internal Kidnappings**
+ **External Kidnappings**

(*) Place of capture was not reported in one internal episode.

TABLE 8.2
Ransom Kidnappings by Outcome (Principal Hostages) and Type of Event

Outcome	Internal	External
Release	38	52
Escape	5	3
Freed by police	3	8
Death	11	12
Total	57	75

percent of the external victims were held for more than one month. The duration of custody appears to be influenced by the nature of the negotiations, which are more complicated when "foreign" parties and higher ransoms are involved. The amount of ransom paid is actually substantially higher in external kidnapping (table 8.3), where in 12 cases, occurring mostly in Sassari during 1976-80, ransoms of between U.S. $1 million and U.S. $4.39 million were paid.

Release is the most frequent outcome (table 8.2), though other outcomes are possible. In particular, victims manage to escape or are set free by police in about 14 percent of kidnappings and deaths occur in about 17 percent of cases. In almost half of these cases, hostage deaths occurred after payment of the ransom.

Kidnappers were much more likely to be apprehended in external cases: Police investigations led to arrests and subsequent convictions in more than twice as many (52% or 39 out of 75) of these cases as the internal ones (19% or 11 out of 57). In 1976-80, as many as 75 percent of external kidnappings resulted in arrests and convictions, reflecting the high risks of these crimes.

The Stages of Kidnapping

Although the two types of kidnapping show considerable differences, the basic stages are similar and can be classified as follows: (1) planning, (2) hostage seizing and transfer, (3) custody, (4) contacts and negotiations, (5) outcome.

Planning. In ransom kidnapping, opportunities are evidently sought or created through a systematic monitoring of possible targets and their accessibility by kidnapping gangs. Gangs tend to be formed by local criminal families who, on the one hand, may have extensive contacts with possible informants and, on the other, may be supporting a fugitive bandit, whose role is vital in a successful kidnapping (see below).

As noted, the number of potential external targets is higher during the summer period but accessibility to them is apparently more difficult than

TABLE 8.3
Ransoms Paid in Lire(*), 5-Year Periods and Type of Kidnapping

Years	Internal		External	
	Average Payment	No. of Ransoms Paid	Average Payment	No. of Ransoms Paid
1966–1970	94 million	15	633 million	14
1971–1975	283 million	10	1274 million	10
1976–1980	1132 million	3	1699 million	16
1981–1985	408 million	3	1035 million	10
1986–1990	–	0	1124 million	5
Total	286 million	31	1177 million	55

*Figures are standardized for 1990 values (1 million lire = U.S. $833)

in internal episodes. The victims' accessibility is assessed through systematic observation of their habits and movements over a sufficient period of time in a suitable geographical area. A certain degree of regularity in these habits and movements (which can vary according to the reasons for the victim's presence in the area, whether work, residence, or vacation) is required to effectively plan the seizure.

The larger amount of information needed when external hostages are involved increases the possibility of error concerning the victim's circumstances and thus the logistics of the capture. The role of informants, many of whom come from the Nuoro District and are domestic servants or workmen in the new villas, can therefore be very important in external kidnappings. They have to provide reliable facts about the victim's economic situation and accurate information about movements and habits, as well as a physical description of the place where kidnapping will take place.

Kidnappers may decide that transfer to and from the place of ambush is too risky (depending upon location) or information about the victim's movements is insufficient. They may also be aware of lacking expertise needed to neutralize bodyguards or protective devices (armored cars, alarm systems, etc.) and shift their attention to less protected targets. Finally, the risks of detection become greater when the number of people involved as informants increases.

Target selection and, at a more general level, the decision to carry out a kidnapping, will depend, however, on an assessment of the expected cost of the entire operation and the likely cash yield per crime. The financial investment can indeed be rather large in terms of the resources required. The higher ransoms obtainable in external kidnapping will have to be shared among more people, and the cost of money laundering can severely reduce the net yield.[7] Internal kidnapping, on the other hand, is even less economically profitable and, no matter how subculturally "justified," may lead to violent reaction from the victim's family. Subcultural influences, as noted, may also inhibit the taking of women and children while "encouraging" the taking of external hostages, who may be seen as "invaders," exploiting the Sardinian people and economy.

Seizing of hostages and transfer. A commando group, usually of 4 or 5 persons, equipped with firearms, ambushes the victim. Witnesses will be tied up or taken away. Kidnappers will wear masks to avoid identification and act as rapidly and suddenly as possible. Cool nerves and instrumental violence are required at this crucial moment. Hostages and witnesses are often beaten to facilitate the capture. When a conflict occurs during a confrontation with the victims or due to external intervention (by police or others), injuries or death are possible.

The methods used in internal kidnappings and the expertise required are often rudimentary in character, while in external kidnapping these have to be continuously refined in order to overcome increasing sophistication in target protection.

Transfer of the hostage to the place of custody will follow the safest possible itinerary in order to avoid detection by the police. A careful assessment of the means and the time required to make the transfer is necessary since the risk of apprehension is relatively high at this stage. The risk is apparently increased when the ambush takes place outside the internal areas of custody, which helps to explain why most kidnappings occur in the central-eastern section of the island from where it is easier to reach such areas without crossing busy roads or highways. This may also account for the time of the day chosen for seizing victims. For external episodes, the evening hours will mean less visibility during the transfer of the hostage. For the internal variety, this condition is less important since hostages are ambushed in the countryside where they usually spend the entire day in isolated farms or sheep folds, closer to the custody areas.

During the transfer, one or more stopovers are usually required to reach the final place of custody. The commando group, which undertook the capture of the hostage, now hands over the hostage to the guardians. These guardians are generally fugitive bandits, that is, convicted criminals who have escaped or suspects with a high probability of conviction who have evaded arrest. Some of these fugitives have managed to avoid capture for up to 15 years. Their assistance in guarding the hostages at night is vital since the continued absence from their homes of the shepherds involved in the kidnapping would be noticed.[8,9]

The time needed to complete the transfer and the choice of the safest itinerary may also become crucial factors influencing decisions. If the alarm is raised immediately after seizure of the hostage, police intervention with intensive patrolling and roadblocks may greatly increase the risk of apprehension. Under such circumstances, kidnappers may actually decide to abandon the hostage to ensure a safe escape.

Custody. The inner pastoral areas of the island, where hostages are nearly always held, provide a number of advantages for the kidnappers. This is territory with which they are very familiar and which in a sense they control. They will arouse no suspicion if encountered there by the authorities. They are surrounded by informants who will warn them of approaching police. They are used to provisioning themselves to sustain long periods of absence from home. Finally, they are intimately acquainted with the terrain, which enables them to choose natural shelters like caves in which to hide the hostage.

Despite their convenience, caves have the disadvantage that they can retain physical signs of a prolonged stay. Not infrequently a temporary shelter may therefore be constructed by covering a fissure in rocks with a makeshift roof consisting of branches and foliage. Since this roof can be removed and destroyed, the identification of the place will be more difficult once the kidnapping is over.

It is often necessary to move hostages during custody, for example when police searches are getting dangerously close or when boar hunting parties are in the area. Custody in towns or villages is almost never considered as this is seen to make an emergency escape more difficult.

The conditions of custody are generally quite hard. Hostages are often forced to wear hoods and are kept tied or chained most of the time. On the other hand, conditions are not generally so poor as to result in death since this would jeopardize payment of the ransom and would lead to more severe sentences in case of arrest and conviction. Hostages may be beaten, sexually assaulted, or otherwise brutalized, however, and the threat of death is always present. Cutting off part of the ear and sending it to the family in order to back up ransom demands is sometimes reported. While most of this violence is instrumental and carefully calculated not to jeopardize hostages' lives, a certain amount of superfluous "hostile" violence has been reported in some kidnapping cases.[10] This may require deeper psychological explanation of the violent attitudes of Sardinian kidnappers, involving the notion of "ambivalence" toward the hostage.[11]

Negotiation. Ransom kidnapping can be regarded as a process of negotiation, the outcome of which is to trade a person for a price. The parties metaphorically sitting at the negotiation table are only two, in a condition of "bilateral monopoly" (Rudas and Marongiu 1988). Notwithstanding the extreme asymmetry of the negotiation, by forcing the family to "buy" the victim the kidnappers are compelled to "sell" to the only party that attributes an economic value to the hostage. If for any reason the family does not comply, the entire transaction is worthless.

The negotiation stage is obviously very painful for the family, which is put in the position of regarding its relative as an economic good to be traded at the minimum possible price. To pay more than is necessary could be to jeopardize the future financial security of the family as a whole. The instrumental nature of kidnapping is therefore clearly apparent at this stage of the crime. Depersonalization and instrumental use of the victim, while common in many types of crime, is probably *the* essential feature of ransom kidnapping.

A first telephone call, confirming the capture, usually advises the family not to collaborate with the police. Ransom demands and death threats can also be communicated at this point. A calculated lapse of time is then allowed to prepare the family to negotiate by increasing the anxiety about the hostage's life. Communication may take the form of letters or phone calls, while sometimes direct meetings between negotiators from both parties are arranged.

The role of negotiators is crucial. Family negotiators can be taken in exchange when the hostage is released in order to ensure the completion of payment. While they are usually hostage's relatives, they may be designated by kidnappers. Most commonly, negotiators meet in the inner areas of the island. Several itineraries are followed to avoid police detection and allow the payment of ransom. Violence may be committed against the family's negotiators and additional requests for money may be formulated.

Notwithstanding the precautions adopted, custody remains a risky stage for kidnappers. Negotiations tend to be more complicated when external hostages are involved and high ransoms are demanded, therefore increasing the length of custody and the perceived risk of apprehension.[12]

Long-drawn-out negotiations, such as those common in external kidnapping are likely to increase the anxiety of the families. On the other hand, the greater amount of contact required in this kind of transaction increases the chances of detection.

Outcome. Release after payment is the objective of the crime and, therefore, the normal outcome. Sometimes, however, hostages manage to escape, are freed by the police, or are released without payment. Release without payment is commonly due to errors in planning, leading to seizure of the wrong person or overestimation of financial possibilities. Premature release of the hostage may also be due to action by the police who have become increasingly successful in identifying the kidnappers or the place where the hostage is being held.

The effectiveness of the extortion depends upon the credibility of the kidnapper's death threats. For this reason the recent Italian law preventing the payment of ransoms by freezing family assets and bank accounts has been criticized for putting hostages' lives at risk.[13] It has been argued that this provision may also inhibit the family's collaboration with the authorities and that it tends to favor higher-income families, assumed to be capable of avoiding the prohibition. The probability of short-term[14] and/or unreported kidnappings has been also envisaged, but clear evidence of this kind of displacement has not yet been found.

Payment of the ransom does not invariably guarantee release of the victim. For example, kidnappers can decide to eliminate the hostage when a substantial risk of identification is perceived. However, intentional killings of the hostage are not in the interests of kidnappers since this would reinforce the idea that payment does not avoid the death of the hostage.

Choice-Structuring Properties of Ransom Kidnappings

This discussion of the 5 stages of ransom kidnapping has been informed by Cornish and Clarke's (1987) formulation of choice-structuring properties of crimes designed to yield cash for the offender. It is clear that at all stages of the kidnapping the offenders take considerable care to maximize their chances of success through careful planning and preparation. It is also evident that the "external" form is considerably more complicated than the traditional variety and that kidnappers have had to substantially modify their methods to be successful in these cases. This greater complexity is illustrated in table 8.4, which is an adaptation of Cornish and Clarke's (1987) original table for offences designed to yield cash. It will be seen that most choice-structuring properties favor the commission of internal rather than external kidnappings.

It is perhaps instructive that the larger ransoms and greater social cachet of external kidnappings appear to have been sufficient to outweigh the greater difficulties and risks attaching to this form of kidnapping, with the result that it came largely to replace the original variety. However, the risks of external kidnappings not only increased as the authorities improved their countermeasures, but may also have become better known with greater experience of the crime, with the result that external kidnappings decreased markedly toward the end of the period studied.

Conclusions

In our discussion of the subcultural approach to kidnapping we noted its usefulness in explaining the prevalence of this form of crime in Sardinia and in accounting for some of its principal features. Selection of hostages is apparently justified in subcultural terms by their privileged social posi-

TABLE 8.4
Comparison of Choice Structuring Properties for "Internal"
and "External" Ransom Kidnappings

	Choice Structuring Property	Kidnapping Favored
1.	Knowledge of methods	Internal
2.	No. of hostages available	Internal
3.	Accessibility of hostages	Internal
4.	Protection of hostages	Internal
5.	Availability of informants	Internal
6.	Skills needed	Internal
7.	Planning necessary	Internal
8.	Resources required	Internal
9.	No. of associates needed	Internal
10.	Logistics of capture	Internal
11.	Cool nerves required	Neither
12.	Instrumental violence needed	Neither
13.	Physical danger	Neither
14.	Availability of fugitives	Neither
15.	Severity of punishment	Neither
16.	Risks of apprehension	Internal
17.	Revenge from victim's family	External
18.	Moral evaluation	External
19.	Social cachet for kidnappers	External
20.	Amount of ransom	External
21.	Complexity of negotiations	Internal
22.	Time to collection of ransom	Internal
23.	Money laundering needed	Internal

tion, while the entire modus operandi of the crime from the seizing of hostages to the transfer, custody, and negotiation stages appears also to be influenced by the subcultural context. Techniques of seizure and transfer, for instance, can be seen as a development of increasingly refined patterns in a long tradition of rustling. Custody is facilitated by the presence of a network of support and complicity furnished by the subculture of inner Sardinia. These conditions also permit safer negotiation and collection of ransoms. Hostile violence to victims is consistent with their social and financial positions, which also furnished the initial justification for their selection.

As we also noted in our account of the subcultural interpretation of ransom kidnapping, the image of a purposive, rational offender is implicit in the details of the modus operandi, and our description of the 5 stages of kidnapping has emphasized this aspect. Indeed, the main purpose of the present analysis was to see whether application of the rational choice perspective would permit the fuller explanation of some of the well-known features of ransom kidnapping as well as assist in the identification of some new features.

A characteristic of ransom kidnapping not adequately addressed in subcultural theory relates to the instrumental nature of most of the violence (which is carefully calculated to extort the ransom), whereas this instrumentality would be entirely consistent with the rational choice perspective. A more serious limitation of subcultural explanations is that they do not adequately account for changes in crime patterns, such as the varying rates of offending observed over different time periods. Under the rational choice perspective, such changes are entirely to be expected and represent the offender's changing judgements about the viability of the crime in question — its difficulty, risks and rewards — in the face of changing external conditions. Under a rational choice view, it would also be expected that different forms of the crime would exist that would represent differential responses to variations in the opportunity structure for the offense.

Consistent with this expectation, two main forms within the basic category of Sardinian ransom kidnapping — a traditional "internal" and a much more recent "external" form — each with its own characteristic features, have been identified in the present study. This classification, essentially based on the nature of the hostages involved, seems useful in providing an explanation of the "evolution" of ransom kidnapping during the last 25 years. During this period, there was an initial increase with substantial shifting from internal to external episodes. At the same time, there is no reason to think that kidnappers were being drawn from a different social group, since they almost always come from the Nuoro District and frequently from the same group of criminal families. There is also evidence that some kidnappers have been involved in both kinds episodes, though more of the younger generation of kidnappers have been involved in external episodes. It therefore seems unlikely that the "evolution" of kidnapping can be ascribed to variations in the violence-oriented set of subcultural values and related norms of conduct, since these can only be modified as the result of long-term and complex social processes. Rather, in our view, this evolution reflected the fact that there was a substantial increase in the number of attractive, "foreign" targets on the island during the 1970s as a result of its development as an exclusive tourist resort. The resultant increased visibility of kidnapping as a lucrative form of extortion may be part of the explanation for the spread of the crime to the mainland. (There is also evidence that some of the mainland kidnappings were either committed by Sardinians who had learned their skills in their home island, or were committed by local criminals with advice from Sardinians.)

The more recent substantial decline of both kinds of kidnapping, both in the island and on the mainland reflects, in our view, a remarkable improvement in police intervention, especially at the stages of transfer and negotiation. The various branches of the police (Polizia di Stato, Carabinieri, and Guardia di Finanza) have formed contingency plans to deal with kidnapping and have coordinated their response to permit more rapid intervention and better control of territory. They have also improved their information networks and have concentrated on identifying potential informants. As we have seen, ransoms are not paid in a substantial number of episodes and over 50% of external cases studied were followed by arrest and conviction of at least one member of the organization.

The higher rate of conviction for external kidnappings is probably related to several conditions. In internal kidnappings, subcultural pressures militate against collaboration with the police. In external kidnappings, however, factors such as the length and complexity of negotiations and the need to involve more persons at different stages of the crime, increase investigators' opportunities to detect organization members.

One weakness of the subcultural position not addressed in our study, which has been concerned largely with the commission of the criminal event, concerns the question of involvement in kidnapping. Subcultural theory does not adequately explain why only some individuals exposed to subcultural influences become involved in crime. For rational choice theorists this point does not usually constitute a serious problem. Leaving aside small differences in background and experience that could easily affect decisions about involvement, the opportunity structure for crime is never identical for any two individuals. To take a simple example, it is entirely conceivable that a Sardinian youth with an uncle who had been involved in a successful kidnapping might be considerably more likely to entertain the idea of committing the crime himself. The best way of gaining insight into involvement decisions would be through detailed interviewing of those involved in kidnapping and this might be the subject of further research.

Policy Implications

In contrast to the dispositional view of subcultural theory, the main policy implication of a rational choice analysis is that the kidnapper is responsive to changes in his environment. Just as he may exploit new opportunities for crime, he is also sensitive to increased risk and difficulty. We have already mentioned that the decline in ransom kidnappings may be partly a result of increased police effectiveness, which has reduced the chances of collecting the ransom and increased the chances of arrest, particularly in the more complex external cases. Vulnerable individuals might also be increasingly varying their routines and investing in more sophisticated security. In addition, we believe that, despite the criticism these have attracted, the recently enacted laws making it harder for victim's families to cooperate in payment of the ransom may have achieved their purpose. Finally, the Gregoriani case, in which a Sardinian bandit who had played a leading role in a number of kidnappings was persuaded to reveal the identity of his collaborators in exchange for more lenient treatment by the courts, suggests that greater use of plea bargaining as a weapon against kidnapping should be considered. This strategy is more likely to be effective in Sardinia where kidnappers do not belong to a structured criminal organization such as the Mafia, which would constitute a deterrent to collaboration with the authorities. The strategy may be particularly productive in external cases where the likelihood of revenge being taken against the kidnapper by the victim's family is much smaller than in the traditional form of the crime.

Notes

1. Alix does not include terrorist "political" kidnapping as a separate category. Differences in motivation apparently make these forms of "political" crime quite dissimilar to their "ordinary" counterparts, ransom kidnapping and hostage-taking for robbery. It should be noted however, that ideological, subcultural, and plainly criminal motivations and justifications can happily coexist in both categories. Terrorists, in fact, do not always seem to work for the "cause," but also for personal gain, just as ordinary kidnappers may act in subcultural contexts and provide ideological justifications for their crimes.
2. A customary but highly formalized code of vengeance (*codice della vendetta barbaricina*) regulates feuds as well as individual vengeance in the inner areas of the island (Pigliaru 1975; Marongiu and Newman 1987). By defining "offenses" as intentional acts aimed to damage someone else's dignity and honor, this code compels the offended person or group to punish the offenders by implementing vengeance. A number of subculturally defined offenses, ranging from murder to breaking a promise of marriage (Pigliaru 1975: 123–24) may provoke blood retaliation, which in turn constitutes a new motive for revenge. At each stage of this exchange violence is apparently increased, thus leading to highly destructive consequences for the community.
3. The authors would like to extend their deep appreciation to Dr. Silla Lissia, chief of the unit and to inspectors Giancarlo Nanni and Raffaele Cireddu, for providing the files. We also thank Dr. Emilio Pazzi, Questore (chief of police) of the Province of Cagliari for many helpful suggestions, deriving from his 30-years experience in fighting ransom kidnapping.
4. All cases available to the police were included with the exception of: (1) a few cases in which too little information was available; (2) minor cases of ransom kidnappings, which did not involve planning and execution by organized groups of criminals, but which were carried out by lone individuals, usually for very short periods of time; (3) attempted kidnappings (given the considerable difficulties of

determining the actual purpose of the attack which, for example, might have been homicide or robbery); and (4) pseudo-kidnappings (criminal homicide disguised as kidnapping).

5. Further classification is necessary when analyzing ransom kidnapping in its manifestation outside Sardinia. At least two other main types have been identified: Mafia kidnappings and "metropolitan" kidnappings (Rudas and Marongiu 1988).

6. In 25 of the 132 kidnappings, more than one hostage was seized. Unless otherwise noted, data reported in the paper relate to the "principal" hostage for each kidnapping.

7. Little is known about the dynamics of ransom money laundering. In traditional kidnapping each member of the gang had to take care of this problem. Big amounts of cash and modern detection systems have subsequently required contacts with national and international criminal organizations.

8. It is interesting to note that the commando group very rarely includes fugitives among its members, because it would be too risky for them to travel outside the internal area of the island. Losing a fugitive in this way could also jeopardize the possibility of other kidnappings since only persons whose presence is by definition not required can take care of the hostages without their absence being noticed.

9. According to the Regional Criminalpol Unit of Sardinia, a number of fugitives ranging from 5 to 29, listed as "dangerous" and probably involved in kidnapping and other serious crime, are reported as being at large from 1967 to 1991. No correlation was found between the number of fugitives and variations in the number of kidnappings in different periods. The reason may be that not all fugitives are available for the role of jailer or they may not wish to be involved in kidnappings.

10. Indeed, death is intended in cases of pseudo-kidnapping, incidents often motivated by revenge, aimed both at killing the victim and obtaining the ransom.

11. The possibility of an "envious" motivation in kidnapping in Sardinia has been hypothesized, in order to explain this kind of seemingly " irrational violence," not readily understandable in utilitarian-opportunistic terms (Rudas and Marongiu 1988). Many violent subcultures appear to rely on a "reciprocity model" (Newman 1977), not allowing the members of the group to break a basic "egalitarian pact" by accumulating wealth and power. This could explain the presence of strong "vengeful" and "envious" patterns in these subcultural organizations. According to this approach, a great deal of envious hostility (due to the privileged position of the victim) can be involved in the kidnapper-kidnapped relationship, leading to the final destruction of the envied object, (economically, physically, and psychologically), thereby making him no longer "enviable" (Rudas and Marongiu 1988). The personal psychological makeup of kidnappers is probably significant from this point of view, but some general mechanism of justification of aggression, on subcultural or ideological basis is probably also involved. Legitimization of violence by blaming the victim, for instance, is commonly asserted in terrorist episodes (Fattah 1979). By holding hostages responsible for political, social, or economic misdeeds, kidnappers may regard themselves as "victims" entitled to exact retribution. Depersonalization of the victims (a common technique in political and racial aggression) will naturally follow these premises. If hostages are not considered "human" they can be legitimately brutalized and traded for a price.

12. Repeated contacts between negotiators during collection of the ransom is probably the weakest point in a kidnapping transaction and generally in extortion crimes. This point emphasizes the differences between ransom and political episodes, where, for instance, release of prisoners is demanded and media coverage (viewed as damaging in ransom kidnapping) is very important.

13. The law also prohibits kidnapping insurance and negotiating on a family's behalf.
14. It has been hypothesized (though without supporting evidence) that in the very few episodes where hostages were released after a few hours, immediately after the kidnapping was reported to the police, a quick negotiation followed by ransom payment might have occurred.

References

Alix, K.E. 1978. *Ransom kidnapping in America, 1874-1974.* Carbondale IL: Southern Illinois University Press.

Clarke, R.V., & Cornish, D.B. 1985. Modeling offender's decisions: A framework for research and policy. In Michael Tonry and Norval Morris (Eds.), *Crime and justice* (Vol. 6). Chicago: University of Chicago Press .

Cornish, D.B., & Clarke, R.V. (Eds.). 1986. *The reasoning criminal.* New York: Springer-Verlag.

————. 1987. Understanding crime displacement: An application of rational choice theory. *Criminology* 25:933–47.

Fattah, E.A. 1979. Some reflections on the victimology of terrorism. *Terrorism: An International Journal* 3 (1–2).

Ferracuti, F., Lazzari, R., & Wolfgang, M.E. (Eds.). 1970. *Violence in Sardinia.* Rome: Bulzoni.

Gottfredson, M.R., & Hirschi, T. 1990. *A general theory of crime,* Stanford, CA: Stanford University Press.

Hirschi, T. 1986. On the compatibility of rational choice and social control theories of crime. In D.B. Cornish & R.V. Clarke (Eds.), *The reasoning criminal.* New York: Springer-Verlag.

Luberto, S., & Manganelli, A. 1984. *I Sequestri di Persona a scopo di Estorsione.* Padova: CEDAM.

————. 1990. *I Sequestri di Persona a scopo di Estorsione.* Padova: CEDAM.

Marongiu, P., & Newman, G. 1987. *Vengeance. The fight against injustice.* Totowa, NJ: Rowman & Littlefield.

Newman, G. 1977. *The punishment response,* Philadelphia, PA: Lippincott.

Niceforo, A. 1897. *La delinquenza in Sardegna, con prefazione di Enrico Ferri. Note di Sociologia Criminale.* Palermo: Sandron.

Pigliaru, A. 1975. *Il Banditismo in Sardegna.* Milano: Giuffre.

Pinna, L. 1970. Sardinia in historical and sociological perspective. In F. Ferracuti, R. Lazzari, & M.E. Wolfgang (Eds.), *Violence in Sardinia.* Rome: Bulzoni.

Rudas, N., & Marongiu, P. 1988. Il sequestro di persona in Italia. In F. Ferracuti (Ed.), *Trattato di Criminologia, Medicina Criminologica e Psichiatria Forense* 9 Milano: Giuffre'.

Trasler, G. 1986. Situational crime control and rational choice: A critique. In K. Heal & G. Laycock (Eds.), *Situational crime prevention: From theory into practice.* London: H.M.S.O.

Wolfgang, Marvin E., & Ferracuti, Franco. 1967. *The subculture of violence: Towards an integrated theory in criminology.* London: Tavistock Publications.

9

"Successful" Criminal Careers: Toward an Ethnography within the Rational Choice Perspective

Bruce D. Johnson, Mangai Natarajan, and Harry Sanabria

During the past decade, research on career criminals has made considerable progress in documenting very high rates of offending and considerable versatility of crimes committed (Blumstein et al. 1986; Chaiken and Chaiken 1982, 1985, 1987). In other respects, the situation has changed little since 25 years ago when Becker (1963:166) commented: "Very few [studies] tell us in detail what a juvenile delinquent [or criminal] does in his daily round of activity and what he thinks about himself, society and his activities." In particular, few studies (see Glassner and Carpenter 1985) have been undertaken that analyze the actual criminal practices of property offenders who are at liberty in the community, who "successfully" commit a large number of property offenses, and who earn and spend criminal returns, but who have little or no contact with the police and the criminal justice system. Yet Chaiken and Chaiken (1985) report that a whole class of offenders may be considered quite "successful" in that they actually engage in high-rate and serious criminality, but generally avoid arrest and prison sentences. This success may be a major reason for their persistence in criminal careers.

Employing a rational choice perspective (Cornish and Clarke 1986), this chapter suggests ways in which ethnography could provide new information about how high-rate property offenders continue their careers and conduct their "criminal" business. It considers (from the offender's perspective) how "successful" careers in property offending develop and how such offenders commit numerous specific criminal episodes while generally avoiding detection and arrest. Such information would be of direct relevance to the criminal justice system. For example, Walsh's (1978, 1980, 1986a) three books on shoplifting, residential burglary, and commercial burglary and robbery each contain concluding chapters that are filled with suggestions for target hardening, improved police tactics, construction of communities with few criminal opportunities, and the deterrent impact of various sentencing options. Ethnographic studies could also show how satisfying offenders consider their crimes to be (Katz 1988) and whether and how they maintain and change their self-images during a given time period and in response to legal pressures. The potential outcome of such research might be a series of suggestions and recommendations which would assist the criminal justice system in more systematically and effectively dealing with offenders.

Ethnographic Methods in Crime Episode Research

Ethnographic methods are primarily designed to improve scientific understanding of a phenomenon, and to generate new hypotheses for testing and or modeling (but not for testing hypotheses). Ethnographers have developed skills in the following critical areas: (1) in locating and gaining access to persons who exhibit the phenomenon of interest (in this case, active criminals); (2) in gaining fully informed consent of criminals to become research subjects and in building strong rapport and trust with subjects; (3) in conducting in-depth interviews with subjects about virtually any topic and exploring questions that occur to either party (such interviews can be tape-recorded and transcribed verbatim, so the subjects' exact wording and mind-set can be subsequently analyzed); (4) in unobtrusively and safely spending time with subjects as they go about their normal routines, making direct observations, listening to conversations, and asking informal questions (Williams et al. 1992); (5) in subsequently writing detailed field notes about such observations and conversations, so as to describe in detail the processes observed.

The field notes and transcripts of ethnographers constitute the data from which analyses are subsequently written. A key analytic approach is the constant comparative method, in which, for example, the different crime episodes are examined for the presence or absence of various elements, such as those proposed below (e.g., "drug need," "casing," "targeting," etc.).

Particularly in studying crime episodes, major ethical and legal issues arise (Cromwell et al. 1991). The principal ethical issue is whether ethnographers can or should try to study criminals and observe them commit crimes. If it is decided that they should, the question then becomes one of the seriousness of crime. Thus it may be appropriate to observe shoplifting or drug sales, but ethically inappropriate to observe intentional robbery or homicide. It would to seem to the present authors that the need for an improved scientific understanding of how property offenders choose targets and commit crimes justifies such direct observation; the offender's description of their actions after the event may miss too much. Far too many different factors may influence the offender's action in the environment, especially the many avoided victims or targets, which are critical to a comparative method and which will provide critical insights about why targets are selected.

The main legal issue concerns ethnographers' status as accomplices to crime if they are arrested while studying a criminal during a crime event. Generally, this would not be a major problem since arrests for any specific crime are rare. It is even less likely that the police would charge a nonparticipant, especially if the ethnographer has appropriate legal protection, such as a federal certificate of confidentiality. These issues have been addressed by prior researchers and it would seem that the way is clear for ethnographers to begin to focus upon delineating the characteristics of crime events, especially property crimes, in which the rational choices made by offenders would be most evident.

Key Questions

The following discussion suggests several major questions of interest to policymakers in the criminal justice system that could be illuminated by ethnographic studies.

How and Why Do Property Offenders Continue "Successful" Careers?

A variety of studies (Akerstrom 1983; Bennett and Wright 1984; Rengert and Wasilchick 1985; Shover 1973; Walsh 1978, 1980, 1986a, 1986b; Cromwell et al. 1991) have directly addressed questions of criminal careers and "how" property crime is committed, but virtually all of these rely upon retrospective accounts of crimes provided by prison and jail inmates. In retrospective recollection, subjects are most likely to report, and perhaps exaggerate their more successful crimes, while forgetting the aborted or less successful ones. Also the many different details of numerous crime episodes may be combined during such retrospective descriptions of events. Cromwell et al. (1991) have also identified "a tendency of burglars (and other persons) to describe past events as though they were performed in the ideal or proper fashion" (p. 51), a tendency they term "rational reconstruction."

Clearly, the criminal justice system needs to know much more (from the offender's viewpoint) both about successful criminal careers and their numerous successful criminal episodes. Ethnographic methods are well developed to locate high-rate offenders at liberty in the community, gain their rapport, and obtain details about how they view their careers and methods of operation.

What General Strategies Do Offenders Employ in Committing Crime?

"Decisions to offend are influenced by the characteristics of both offenses and offenders, and are the product of interactions between the two" (Cornish and Clarke 1987:902). Ethnographic research could be carefully designed to provide greatly improved information about how mid-career property offenders organize their lives (offender characteristics) so as to repeatedly commit crimes (Rengert and Wasilchick 1985; Shover and Honaker in press) and how they make the difficult, quick, and complex decisions needed to successfully execute specific crime episodes (offense characteristics). Such information will also reveal much about the interactions of offender and offense characteristics.

The theoretical and empirical literature on offender characteristics such as demographics, age of onset in crime, and range of criminal activities is extremely large and diverse. Ethnographic research could examine certain offender characteristics that are relatively little studied. These include several important parameters of property-offending careers, such as initiation into offending (Biron and Ladoucer 1991); frequency of offending; dependence on co-offenders or criminal networks (Cromwell et al. 1991); criminal incomes and expenditures for drugs and alcohol (Johnson et al. 1985, 1988; Johnson and Kaplan 1989) (especially the relationship between criminal income and expensive "party" life-styles [Shover and Honaker in press]); periods of remission, escalation, on desistance in their criminal and drug use careers; the effect of drug and alcohol abuse on decision making and target selection (Carpenter et al. 1988; Cromwell et al. 1991); offenders' thinking and responses to arrests and incarcerations (Shover and Honaker in press).

By focusing upon a variety of concepts suggested by the rational choice perspective (Clarke and Cornish 1985; Cornish and Clarke 1986) and systematic studies of imprisoned burglars, robbers, and shoplifters (Walsh 1978; 1980, 1986b; Rengert and Wasilchick 1985; Bennett and Wright 1984; Shover and Honaker in press), property offenders might be asked to describe their "standing" decisions concerning their favored crimes and other offenses they commit, how they view such crimes, and the advantages and disadvantages of each . Likewise, they might be asked about their general strategies of crime commission in order to clarify both their characteristic "style" (Maguire 1980) and the "templates" (Brantingham and Brantingham 1984:432) of offending that they employ.

Concerning criminal "style," they could be questioned about whether this is primarily to s*eize* opportunities (commit crimes mainly when an appropriate target presents itself), to *seek* opportunities (study several locales and pick the best available target), or to *develop* opportunities (choose a particularly rewarding target based upon prior information, then carefully plan and execute the crime) (Maguire 1980).

Crime templates are relatively enduring "patterns of categories and experiences [from prior crimes] that make it possible to recognize and anticipate or innovate during the search for a target and commission of an offense" (Brantingham and Brantingham 1984:432). Offenders draw upon these templates to guide themselves during all aspects of the crime episode. These templates govern what the offender perceives in the physical and social environment at the crime scene, and help direct ways in which the "flow of action" (decisions made and behaviors enacted almost instantaneously) will occur as the offender interacts with the victim, departs the crime scene, and disposes of the stolen property. Potential targets and victims are compared to preexisting templates and either accepted or rejected.

Crime templates are virtually identical to what police call the modus operandi, except that police are likely to learn only about a small fraction of an offender's crime template. While templates are likely to contain many complex elements (cues, cue clusters, awareness spaces, temporal ordering), each offender is likely to have a limited number of templates, which are relatively enduring for a specific offense class. Such templates may be carefully constructed and considered by the offender, but may also "develop in an unconscious, cybernetic fashion so that the offender can not easily articulate it" (Brantingham and Brantingham 1984).

Because crime templates tend to "emerge" from prior experiences rather than being carefully planned and thoughtfully constructed, the various crime templates of an individual offender are likely to be unique to that person. Thus, across several offenders committing a specific offense class (e.g., burglary), none will report or exhibit crime templates that are essentially similar for most elements; rather each offender's template will differ in many elements from those of other offenders.

A careful delineation of criminal styles and templates used by experienced offenders is essential to improving criminal justice practices. Knowing more about the diversity of actual templates among serious offenders, will clarify and provide specificity about the modus operandi to police and judges who routinely work to prove the offender's intentions, motives, and actions in court by inferring the accused person's modus operandi. The closer a particular arrestee's actions may fit one or more offender templates, the easier it may be for complex legal decisions about guilt and disposition to be made by appropriate authorities.

What Factors Influence Choices and Actions Made by Career Criminals during Specific Crime Episodes of Robbery, Burglary, and Shoplifting?

An effective ethnography could provide greatly improved information about the offender's perspectives, choices, and actual behaviors by studying crime episodes in detail. Remarkably little research has been conducted on the commission of crime episodes (Bennett and Wright 1984; Carroll and Weaver 1986; Walsh 1978, 1980, 1986a, 1986b; Rengert and Wasilchick 1985; Johnson and Wish 1982, 1987; Feeney 1986; Gibbs and Shelly 1982; Brantingham and Brantingham 1978, 1984; West 1978; Cromwell et al. 1991). In particular, a search of this literature revealed only two efforts to diagram or graphically display what happens during the criminal episode; Cornish and Clarke (1986) and Walsh (1980:144–45) provide brief models of the burglary event.

In short, no reasonably complete theoretical model of burglary episodes is available, nor are such models evident for other offenses (robbery, shoplifting, fencing), nor is a general model of criminal episodes applicable to all offense classes available. Nevertheless, the existing knowledge base provides several good starting points, particularly in the emerging rationale choice perspective (Cornish and Clarke 1986) to which we turn below.

A Rational Choice Framework for Ethnographic Research

The rational choice perspective (Cornish and Clarke 1986) begins with the "assumption that offenders seek to benefit themselves by their criminal behavior; that this involves the making of decisions and of choices, however rudimentary on occasions these processes may be; and that these processes exhibit a measure of rationality, albeit constrained by limits of time and ability and the availability of relevant information" (Cornish and Clarke 1986:1). The rational choice perspective draws from a variety of different theoretical traditions, including concepts from criminology (conflict, control, deterrence, and incapacitation), economics (expected utility, reasoned action, bounded rationality), and psychology (social learning, risky decision making). It is not an integrated theory of criminality. Rather, it emphasizes the heuristic value (i.e., asking the right questions for focusing observations) of various theories rather than their intrinsic utility (i.e., providing testable hypotheses and systematic integration).

While the rational choice perspective (Cornish and Clarke 1986) addresses issues of how and why persons become property offenders, the main value of an ethnographic study is likely to emerge by focusing upon "successful" offenders committing "successful" crimes (from the offender's perspective) in which goods or money were obtained, and detection and arrest did not occur.

Thus, the thrust of this chapter is to focus conceptual, theoretical, and methodological attention upon understanding how seasoned offenders commit crime episodes on a regular basis. That is, how do they formulate and conceptualize criminal intent? How do they select targets and victims? How do they evaluate the circumstances at the crime scene? What tactics do they employ to commit crimes? How do they "fence" stolen goods? What do they purchase with criminal income?

In the development of a conceptual model of specific crime episodes, we have adapted and expanded the Cornish and Clarke (1986) and Walsh (1980, 1986) sequences for decision making for specific crimes. The general model shown in figure 9.1 involves several major dimensions of decisions that are "episode specific" prior to, during, and after the crime. Even if the actor's behavior in each dimension is committed rapidly and without clear consciousness by the offender, prior experience and skills help the offender make nearly instantaneous choices on each dimension (like a skilled surgeon must make immediate choices and use all his training and skills to keep an emergency victim alive). Figure 9.1 shows the general conceptual model for any crime episode.

Conceptualizing "Success" in Offending: The "Dependent" Variables in the Rational Choice Perspective

Any ethnographic research should be designed to provide a clearer understanding of offenders' perspectives on their specific crimes and lifestyle. As such, primary analytic attention will focus upon the end product of crime episodes. These are represented in the lower right corner of figure 9.1 and include: the dollar income, purchase of goods, services, or drugs-alcohol, and "satisficing" (see below) of specific and general needs. Such desired outcomes are conceptualized as the rough equivalent of dependent variables in a quantitative study; what the offender wishes to maximizes (and research to understand).

Criminal returns are usually measured in the number of dollars earned from the crime; such income includes both money taken and dollars obtained after the sale of stolen goods. Most offenders, however, do not

FIGURE 9.1
**Rational Choice Perspectives and Concepts for Commission of
Specific Crime Episodes**

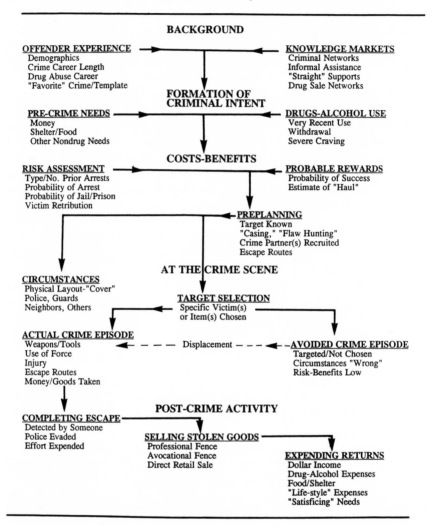

"accumulate" or "save" crime dollars for subsequent days. Most criminal income is expended on the same day to maintain a "party" life-style (Shover and Honaker in press), that is, to purchase specific services and goods, particularly illicit drugs (Johnson et al. 1985; Johnson, Kaplan & Schneidler, 1990; Johnson, Wish & Anderson 1988).

Offenders may "satisfice" (Simon 1957; Cornish and Clarke 1986:181–82) rather than optimize their returns and needs . That is, they may select a crime from among the first few alternatives considered, rather than consider a longer set of alternatives, several of which would provide greater returns. This "satisficing" concept can also be extended to the purchases made with criminal income and the priority given to meeting several important "needs." That is, an offender with $100 in criminal income may satisfice his desires by expending $90 for his drug "needs" and $10 in food for his hunger "needs," rather than optimize his expenditures across a variety of "needs" (for shelter, clothes, personal health, etc.). In addition, as vividly portrayed by Katz's (1988) *Seductions of Crime,* an offender may also commonly satisfice a variety of noneconomic needs (e.g., excitement, expression of rage/anger, having a good time, dominating others, increasing peer group status, or a combination of these).

Conceptualizing Offender's Choices before, during, and after the Criminal Episode: The "Independent" Variables in the Rational Choice Perspective

From the offender's perspective, all other dimensions given in figure 9.1 are primarily factors associated with the "means" to the "ends." That is, the type of crime, and all legal elements (intent, motive, and actual act) of the crime episode involve important decisions among a wide variety of choices. Thus, all dimensions (except the lower right) in figure 9.1 are like independent variables in quantitative research. Each of these dimensions is described in more detail in the Appendix.

The "Flow of Action" during Criminal Episodes

The general model of criminal episodes specified in figure 9.1, and discussed in detail in the Appendix, can now be combined into a dynamic model (figure 9.2) of continuing careers and "process tracing" during criminal episodes (Carroll and Weaver 1986). In the example depicted in figure 9.2, drawn from previous research in New York City (Johnson et al. 1985; Johnson and Wish 1987) on criminal drug abusers, it is assumed that the offender is a near-daily user of cocaine, heroin, alcohol, and a less regular user of marijuana and pills. It is also assumed that the offender is a violent predator (Chaiken and Chaiken 1982) and a high-rate robber.

FIGURE 9.2
Rational Choice Perspectives for a Robber Committing a Robbery Episode

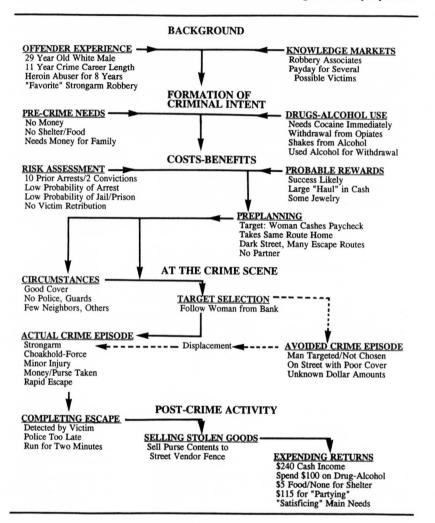

During a three-month period, this offender may commit 4-5 robberies, 6-8 burglaries, and 15-18 shopliftings, and possibly 10 other property offenses (general thefts, cons, forgeries, sales of stolen goods, etc).

During an initial ethnographic interview, such an offender could be asked to report crime templates for each offense class. The robbery template includes selecting victims who work in a nearby office and typically cash their paychecks at a local bank and then walk home. More detailed subsequent interviews may result in "process tracing" diagrams like those presented in figure 9.2. The robbery episode involves selecting a woman who has just cashed her paycheck at a bank, and following and robbing her in a dark street on her way home.

Across several such crime episodes in the same offense class, the actual decisions and outcomes can be compared with the crime templates reported in the initial ethnographic interview. Also each actual crime episode reported can be compared with others to address issues discussed above.

The Contribution of Ethnography

Most of the foregoing section of this chapter has drawn concepts from criminology, a discipline noted for heavy reliance upon quantitative techniques and large samples of representative groups of offenders. Although the recent theoretical and empirical emphasis of criminology has been on initiation of crime careers and estimates of crime rates, several recent contributors (Blumstein et al. 1986; Cornish and Clarke 1986, 1987) have outlined research agendas calling for a greatly improved understanding of how criminal careers unfold, and of how specific crimes occur.

This emphasis on how criminals commit crimes provides a major new opening and opportunity for anthropologists and ethnographers to become more central contributors to mainstream criminology, and in the process begin to educate police, judges, and other criminal policymakers about how criminals think and work.

Ethnographic techniques and qualitative methodologies are particularly well designed to study the issues delineated above — which are rarely a focus of existent criminology. Specifically, trained ethnographers in most urban areas would be able to easily locate, recruit, and repeatedly interview high rate offenders who successfully avoid arrest for the vast majority of their crimes. Such offenders are eager to tell their story to impartial observers who will protect their identity. Rapport is usually not difficult to achieve and a large network of other criminal subjects should quickly become available.

Qualitative interviewing techniques will permit the flexibility to pursue particular topics as well as related issues and themes that the subjects choose. New ideas and understandings on criminal careers and ways specific crimes are committed are certain to emerge from both open-ended questions and extensive interviews with offenders. The key contribution of ethnographers will come when they reduce offender complexity to key themes and findings accessible to criminal policymakers.

Fortunately, the major audiences (police, prosecutors, judges, defense attorneys, corrections staff) for ethnographic research may be considered as ethnographers-in-different clothing. That is, they are very strongly case-oriented, highly attuned to individual differences in motivation and skills, and very interested (for legal reasons) in all aspects of the specific criminal events, and the careers of offenders. Ethnographic information discussed within their frames of reference (e.g., modus operandi instead of crime templates) could provide them with new insights and understandings that they could and would likely apply to the cases and offenders they process.

In short, ethnographers have an opening to increasingly participate in and affect the complex world of criminals, and make major contributions to criminology and the entire criminal justice system.

APPENDIX
Offenders' Choices Relating to the Criminal Episode

This appendix describes in detail the various concepts included diagrammatically in figure 9.1 that relate to the offender's choices before, during, and after the criminal episode (i.e., the "independent" variables of the rational choice perspective). The "dependent" variables of "Expending returns" in the lower right hand corner of figure 9.1 are discussed in the text.

Background for Crime Episode

No crime episode occurs in a vacuum but is the product of many complex factors. Two of the most important are what prior experiences and skills an offender has, and the "knowledge markets" (Walsh 1986:44) within which the offender operates.

Offender experience is a convenient concept that summarizes all the life history, activities, beliefs, and values the person has toward crime prior to committing a crime episode. This includes his/her:

Demographics — sex, age, education, family ties, and many standard sociological variables.

Crime career length and complexity — Includes all forms of illegal behavior, frequencies of involvement, and skills learned during many prior crime episodes.

"Favorite" crime(s) and templates — Is the offense class that the offender likes the most, and generally commits at the highest frequencies. This is the crime in which he/she is most "expert" and may have several "crime templates" that contain well-developed strategies, tactics, and decision making for acting rapidly and decisively in the crime setting. This favorite crime may be only one of several offense classes in which he is active.

Drug use/abuse career — Includes the patterns of use and extensive use of illegal substances and alcohol; among high rate property offenders such patterns are frequently parallel to their criminal careers.

Knowledge markets are the sources of information about potentially profitable criminal targets other than the offender's direct observations (Walsh 1986a, 1986b). Other person(s) or media provide direct or indirect statements about some specific persons, structures, or items that may be further investigated by the offender and include:

Criminal networks — Offenders frequently associate with each other, share information, and recruit each other to participate in some criminal opportunities.

Informal assistance networks — Persons who do not themselves commit crimes, will seek out or tell known offenders about lucrative crime targets, with expectation of some kind of payback.

"Straight" networks — Noncriminals and the media inadvertently provide information to an offender about good criminal targets.

Drug distribution networks — Organized distribution groups frequently have elaborate role structures (of steerers, touts, lookouts, runners) to encourage sales and provide networks of rapid information about potential targets for property crime; they can often warn of police presence in the area.

Central to property crimes is the formation of criminal intent and motive for committing crime. The desired end or "need" is divided into substance and nonsubstance needs. This division is necessary due to the pharmacological properties of drugs (see below). In short, drug "needs" are only "satisficed" for short time periods, while food and shelter needs persist longer or may be delayed for longer periods.

Precrime (nondrug) needs are offender's commonly expressed (nondrug) "needs" and frequently reflect what are also socially acceptable, without specific statements of how things will change if these are gained.

Money — Generally means "cash" to property offenders, not savings, credit, or investments. Such cash is generally expended within a short period of time (usually within 24 hours); it is rarely "held" or "saved" or valued for itself.

Shelter/Food/Family — Many property offenders generally lack a home or comfortable shelter and do not eat adequate and nourishing food; in this sense offenders express a "need" for such items.

Specific goods — Property offenders may state that they need certain goods or material possessions, yet they seldom are the ultimate consumer of such goods. They typically sell (fence) such goods for cash.

"Life-style" — Property offender may "need" partying, gambling, and good times for which money is believed essential; these needs typically reflect the subcultural expectations.

Noneconomic — Property offenders mention quasi-psychological needs such as excitement, expression of anger, a desire to harm others, to control or dominate others. These needs generally cannot be satisfied by money.

Drugs-alcohol use/abuse involves the consumption of some substance near the time of the specific crime episode. Cocaine, heroin, and alcohol are believed (by offenders and others) to induce "needs" (or cravings) that demand rapid satisfaction, take higher priority than other (nondrug) needs, and induce another cycle of "needs" even after the desired drug is consumed.

Very recent use or intoxication — Generally involves being "high" or in a euphoric state or (with alcohol, opiates, sedatives) being unaware of the surroundings and one's actions. For stimulants such as cocaine, intoxication may be associated with paranoia and various hallucinogens that distort perceptions.

Withdrawal — Involves a relatively longer period between repeated administrations of a drug; physiological changes lead to pain and convulsions when drug is not administered regularly.

Severe craving — Pharmacological property of most substances that create a very strong desire to have another dose of the drug (independent of withdrawal). The desire is so predictable and powerful, especially with cocaine and crack, that it may become the highest priority for the offender.

Gain "courage" — Offenders frequently report consuming alcohol and drugs prior to commission of crimes. They report doing so to reduce or suppress fears of getting caught/ being detected, as well as to instill "courage" to solidify their intent to commit the crime.

In short, the pharmacological properties of several substances may create very strong motives to obtain another dosage quickly and rapidly. In the absence of existing cash, the property offender quickly forms clear criminal intent. Or, knowing that he will soon experience withdrawal or severe craving, a nearly continuous criminal intent develops, so that opportunities for crime that may arise when he is not seeking such, will be acted upon almost immediately.

Cost-Benefit Calculations

Every offender must weigh, however quickly or imperfectly, whether the various anticipated economic and noneconomic benefits are worth the risks of arrest and confinement or retribution by the victim. Sometimes these decisions are made instantaneously, and at other times involve careful planning and searching.

Risk assessment involves assessment of the likelihood of contact with and injury from victim(s), the probability of arrest, and severity of punishment if arrested.

Probability of arrest — The probability of contact with police and an arrest must be informally considered by the offender .

Probability of jail/prison given an arrest — if arrested, each offender also faces a probability of conviction, and if convicted, sentences of different length to jail or prison.

Type and number of priors — The offender's prior arrest record ("rap sheet") and felony convictions (i.e., predicate felon eligible) are the primary factors, other than the offense itself, for which a severe penalty, rather than a light one is likely to be imposed.

Victim retribution — Offenders need also consider the probability of being detected by the victim, and being harmed or injured by the targeted person, especially when the victim is another "deviant" or criminal.

Probable rewards are, according to the offenders informed judgments, the economic value of the property and money they are likely to obtain if the crime is successful.

Estimate of "haul" — Informal expectations or careful screening of targets will lead to expectations of "how much" they are likely to obtain. Frequently, experienced offenders (especially burglars and shoplifters) will consider the "cash" value of goods after resale to a fence or "street" consumer.

Probability of success — Offenders must also make an estimate of the likelihood that they will be able to take the money/goods and get away from the crime scene.

Preplanning involves some (but not all) offenders' further attempts to improve the odds by engaging in various precrime planning activities.

Target known — Identification of a specific target (via information obtained from the knowledge market) may greatly increase the probability of a large "haul."

Searching behavior — In the absence of specific advance information from knowledge markets about large hauls, offenders may engage in careful searching behavior for potential targets that fit their preexisting "templates" (cues, cue clusters, and cue sequences [Brantingham and Brantingham 1984]) for appropriate victims.

"Casing," "flaw hunting," and "windows of vulnerability" — When a particular target has been selected, offenders may repeatedly observe or "case" it (especially relatively stationary targets like houses or stores) to seek various cues about how to commit the crime. They may engage in "flaw hunting" — searching for chinks in impregnable security systems, or for "windows of vulnerability" — the one feature the target custodians have neglected to provide for (Walsh 1980, 1986a, 1986b).

Weapons and tools — offenders will typically decide what (if any) weapons (guns, knives, objects) and "tools" (burglary instruments, gloves, jackets with large pockets, cars, etc.) they will take to the crime scene.

Crime partner(s) — Offenders may feel that they need help for specific crimes and recruit (or be recruited by others). Such partners can be both an asset (spread risk, gain control, carry more goods), but also a liability (may "mess up," split the proceeds, be "turned" if arrested).

Escape routes — Offenders may also carefully plan a variety of routes by which to exit from the crime scene. They particularly need multiple exits, and options afterwards.

Careful planning and preparation prior to entry into the crime scene may increase the probability of success (to the perpetrator) and may further reduce the probability of detection and arrest.

At the Crime Scene

Circumstances, at the crime scene, despite all the preplanning that may go into the commission of a crime, will often play a major role in determining whether a crime is actually committed and what tactics will be employed.

Physical layout-"cover" — The physical layout or the "cover" afforded the offender often provides a "feel" to the advisability of actually engaging in a crime or not. Particularly when the offender is searching among several alternatives (i.e., homes for burglary, items for shoplifting), his perception of physical concealment of the criminal act may be a priority for the crime.

Police, guards — The presence or absence of police or guards will almost certainly influence the decision-making process. In cases in which much preplanning has been done and elaborate security is present, the offender will need to have plans about how to handle encounters with guards and police, as well as contingency plans if these expectations prove false.

Neighbors, others — The presence or absence of neighbors or other significant persons (e.g., shopkeepers, mailmen, housewives, children) at the time of the crime event will also influence the decision to commit or and where to commit a specific crime.

Target selection refers to the specific persons, stores, physical structures, and items that will be the actual objects of the crime.

Specific victim(s) — The choice of specific victims actually chosen is necessarily the confluence of preplanning, the circumstances at the crime scene, and the offender's choice at the time of the actual event.

Item(s) chosen — Items stolen during the actual event will necessarily involve the preferences of the offender toward particular items (e.g., money, jewelry, cars, appliances) as well as their availability afforded during the event.

Actual Crime Episode

Tactics will be selected once a target has been selected and the circumstances of the situation assessed. An offender may then consider what specific tactics will be appropriate for the particular crime.

Weapons/tools — On the basis of preplanning, an offender will bring whatever weapons and/or tools are deemed necessary. Often they may bring more than is necessary to compensate for unexpected events or circumstances. The choice and use of particular weapons and/or tools will vary depending upon the type of crime being committed and the preferences of the offender.

Use of force — The use of force may be either premeditated or the result of unexpected events. In either case, the offender must consider the manner and degree of force used in a crime episode.

Injury — The probability of injury to either the victim or the offender is great given certain types of crime, especially robbery. The willingness of an offender to risk injury will often depend upon the type of crime being committed, the circumstances of the episode itself and the offender's previous experiences with violence and injury, and "need" to dominate others.

Money/goods taken — What is actually taken during a crime episode is a function of the offender's intent and template formed before the episode itself. Typically, the offender has a hierarchy of money and goods that he prefers to take. For example, many burglars prefer to steal VCRs (they are quickly fenced with high returns) while other household appliances that had been popular in the past (TVs, stereos) are left behind. In houses lacking VCRs, these other appliances are almost always taken.

Escape routes—Offenders may use two types of exits. First, if the crime episode goes as planned, the planned escape routes will be followed. Second, if the crime does not go as planned, and planned exits are blocked, he will need to improvise other escape routes. Such routes are typically chosen when the offender senses that detection and/or apprehension is likely.

Avoided Crime Episode

In trying to reach some assessment of how a reasoning offender decides to commit a crime, it is equally important to know what are the circumstances under which they nearly choose some targets for crime, but choose another target for the actual crime.

Targeted/not chosen victims are spared for various reasons or there may be a variety of factors that lead the offender to choose other victims. Careful documentation of the reasons why particular targets are not ultimately chosen despite their desirability will lead to a better understanding of how offenders themselves prioritize risks and benefits and "displace" their actual crimes.

Circumstances "wrong"—Even though a potential and very lucrative target may be located, the wrong circumstances may lead to that victim not being chosen. These circumstances may include: lack of adequate "cover," few escape opportunities, the presence of police, or guards, neighbors, or other significant persons who might become involved or be witnesses in court.

Risk-benefits low—Some crime episodes may be avoided because the risks involved clearly outweigh the potential benefits or the "haul" may be considered too low. This assessment is made by the offender on personal observations of the potential victim, his or her circumstances, and information acquired from the knowledge market.

Postcrime Activity

Completing escape is an important component for the offender. Following specific plans for escape that contain multiple exits and options will almost certainly be considered by the offender. The actual route may vary depending upon detection and circumstances of the crime episode.

Detected by someone — In the event of detection, the offender's mode of escape may differ significantly from what was originally planned. This may be done to minimize the risk of immediate apprehension or to avoid identification (which might mean apprehension at a later time). Detection and observation by another person increases the risk for the offender.

Police evaded — Ultimately, evading apprehension and arrest by the police is one important goal of a successful escape. Even though an offender might be detected by other persons, this does not always mean that they will be identified and/or apprehended. Evading the police entails a successful escape from the crime location as well as avoiding the police while trying to dispose of stolen goods.

Effort expended — Managing a successful escape can entail as much or more effort than the crime event itself. The escape often involves a great deal of planning and coordination (especially when the crime is not committed alone) and may impinge significantly on an offender's cost/benefit reasoning on whether or not to commit a crime.

Selling stolen goods is the final step in completing a successful property crime. Stealing cash avoids having to go through this step (unless the money can be identified in some way) . Disposing of stolen goods may be accomplished in a variety of ways. Property offenders may use all three of the following methods of disposal depending upon opportunity, experience, personal preference, and customer networks:

Professional fence — A person who frequently has legal or quasi-legal ways of selling stolen merchandise. They provide cash quickly, but provide a relatively low dollar return relative to the value of the stolen goods. Professionals often buy items that would be difficult to sell otherwise because of their distinctiveness (for example, personal jewelry) or manageability (cars or trucks).

Amateur or avocational fence — Cromwell et al.'s (1991) sample of burglars reported that 60-70% of the property they stole was disposed of through amateur fences. These amateurs came from a wide background and included schoolteachers, plumbers, restauranteurs, and students. Frequently such amateurs are local shop owners or bar owners who will buy low-cost goods that they know will sell well to regular customers. The range of goods willingly handled by these "grocery" fences is more limited than that accepted by the professional fence, but they usually pay a higher "fence factor" than a professional.

Direct retail sale — The offender sells directly to the ultimate consumer. This usually provides the best monetary return for the goods, but finding a customer who wants a specific item and has enough money is always problematic and takes much more time.

References

Akerstrom, M. 1983. *Crooks and squares: Lifestyles of thieves and addicts in comparison to conventional people.* Sweden: Studentlitteratur.

Ball, J.C., Rosen, L., Flueck, J.A., & Nurco, D.N. 1981. "The criminality of heroin addicts when addicted and when off opiates." In J.A. Inciardi (Ed.), *The drugs-crime connection* (39–65). Beverly Hills, CA: Sage.

———. 1982. "Lifetime criminality of heroin addicts in the United States." *Journal of Drug Issues* 3:225–39.

Becker, H. 1963. *Outsiders.* New York: Free Press.

Bennett, T., & Wright, R. 1984. *Burglars on burglary.* Hampshire, England: Gower.

Biron, L.L., & Ladoucer, C. 1991. "The boy next door: Local teen-age burglars in Montreal." *Security Journal* 2:200–04.

Blumstein, A., Cohen, J., Roth, J.A., & Visher, C.A. (Eds.). 1986. *Criminal careers and "career criminals."* Washington, DC: National Academy Press.

Brantingham, P.J., & Brantingham, P.L. 1978. "A theoretical model of crime site selection." In M.D. Krohn & R.L. Akers (Eds.), *Crime, law and sanctions* (105–18). Beverly Hills, CA: Sage.

Brantingham, P.J., & Brantingham, P. L. 1984. *Patterns in crime.* New York: Macmillan.

Carpenter, C., Glassner, B., Johnson, B. & Loughlin, J. 1988. *Kids, drugs, and crime.* Lexington, MA: Lexington Books.

Carroll, J., & Weaver, F. 1986. "Shoplifter's perceptions of crime opportunities: A process-tracing study." In D.B. Cornish & R.V. Clarke (Eds.), *The reasoning criminal: Rational choice perspectives on offending* (19–38). New York: Springer-Verlag.

Chaiken, J., & Chaiken, M. 1982. *Varieties of criminal behaviour.* Santa Monica, CA: Rand Corporation.

Chaiken, J., & Chaiken, M. 1985. *Who gets caught doing crime?* Bureau of Justice Statistics Discussion Paper. Washington, DC: Bureau of Justice Statistics.

Chaiken, J., & Chaiken, M. 1987. *Selecting "career criminals" for priority prosecution.* Final Report to National Institute of Justice. Cambridge, MA: Abt Associates.

Clarke, R.V., & Cornish, D.B. 1985. "Modeling offenders' decisions: A framework for research and policy." In M. Tonry & N. Morris (Eds.), *Crime and justice: An annual review of research* (Vol. 6, 147–85). Chicago: University of Chicago Press.

Clarke, R.V., & Hope, T. 1983. *Coping with burglary: Research perspectives on policy.* Boston: Kluwer-Nijhoff.

Cornish, D.B., & Clarke, R.V. 1986. *The reasoning criminal: Rational choice perspectives on offending.* New York: Springer-Verlag.

———. 1987. "Understanding crime displacement: An application of rational choice." *Criminology* 25(4):901–16.

Cromwell, P.F., Olson, J.N., & Avary, D.W. 1991. *Breaking and entering: An ethnographic analysis of burglary.* Newbury Park, CA: Sage.

Feeney, F. 1986. "Robbers as decision-makers." In D.B. Cornish & R.V. Clarke (Eds.), *The reasoning criminal: Rational choice perspectives on offending* (53–71). New York: Springer-Verlag.

Gibbs, J.J., & Shelly, P.L. 1982. "Life in the fast lane: A retrospective view by commercial thieves." *Journal of Research in Crime and Delinquency* 19:299–330.

Glassner, B., & Carpenter, C. 1985. *The feasibility of an ethnographic study of adult property offenders.* Report Prepared for the National Institute of Justice. Washington, DC: Department of Justice.

Johnson, B.D., Goldstein, P.J., Preble, E., Schmeidler, J., Lipton, D.S., Spunt, B., & Miller, T. 1985. *Taking care of business: The economics of crime by heroin abusers.* New York: Lexington Books.

Johnson, B.D., Kaplan, M.A., & Schmeidler, J. 1990. "Days with drug distribution: Which drugs? How many transactions? With what returns?" In R.A. Weisheit (Ed.), *Drugs, crime and the criminal justice system* (193–214). Cincinnati: Anderson Publishing Co.

Johnson, B.D., Williams, T., Dei, K. & Sanabria, H. 1990. "Drug abuse and the inner-city: Impact on hard drug users and the community." In M. Tonry & J.Q. Wilson (Eds.), *Drugs and crime* (6–97). Chicago: University of Chicago Press.

Johnson, B.D., & Wish, E. 1986. *Crime rates among drug-abusing offenders. Final report to the National Institute of Justice.* New York: Narcotic and Drug Research, Inc.

———. 1987. *Criminal events among seriously criminal drug abusers. Final report to the National Institute of Justice.* New York: Narcotic and Drug Research, Inc.

Johnson, B.D., Wish, E., & Anderson. K. 1988. "A day in the life of 105 drug abusers: Crimes committed and how the money was spent." *Sociology and Social Research* 72(3): 185–91.

Katz, J. 1988. *Seductions of crime.* New York: Basic Books.

Maguire, M. 1980. *Burglary as opportunity.* Home Office Research Bulletin, No. 10. London: Home Office.

———. 1982. *Burglary in a dwelling.* London: Heinemann.

Rengert, G.R., & Wasilchick, J. 1985. *Surburban burglary: A time and a place for everything.* Springfield, IL: Thomas Books.

Shover, N. 1973. "The social organization of burglary." *Social Problems* 20(4):499–514.

Shover, N., & Honaker, D. (in press). "The socially bounded decision making of persistent property offenders." *Howard Journal of Criminal Justice.*

Simon, H.A. 1957. *Models of man: Social and rational.* New York: Wiley.

Walsh, D.P. 1978. *Shoplifting: Controlling a major crime.* New York: Holmes & Meier.

———. 1980. *Break-ins: Burglary from private houses.* London: Constable and Co.

———. 1986a. *Heavy business: Commercial burglary and robbery.* London: Routledge & Kegan Paul.

———. 1986b. "Victim selection procedures among economic criminals: The rational choice perspective." In D.B. Cornish & R.V. Clarke (Eds.), *The reasoning criminal: Rational choice perspectives on offending* (40–52). New York: Springer-Verlag.

West, W.G. 1978. "The short-term careers of serious thieves." *Canadian Journal of Criminology* 20(2):169–90.

Williams, T., Dunlap, E., Johnson, B.D., & Hamid, A. 1992. "Personal Safety in Dangerous Places." *Journal of Contemporary Ethnography* 21(3):343–74.

Part Two

Bridging the Gaps

10

The Rational Choice/Opportunity Perspectives as a Vehicle for Integrating Criminological and Victimological Theories

Ezzat A. Fattah

The Decline of Positivist Criminology

It is no secret that positivist criminology,[1] despite some recent desperate attempts to stimulate it (such as those by Yochelson and Samenow 1976, 1977; Mednick and Christiansen 1977; Mednick, Moffitt, and Stack 1987), is rapidly losing ground. The reasons for the demise have to do not only with the theories' manifest failure to provide valid, satisfactory, or even plausible explanations for what they set out to explain, namely criminal behavior, but also, and above all, with the questionable postulates underlying those theories. No theory can be valid if based on a false premise and no theory can be sound if its starting point is wrong.

Biogenetic and psychological explanations, popular since the lombrosian era, are currently giving way to some fresh, exciting, and more promising approaches, such as the existentialist approach (Katz 1988); the rational choice perspective (Cornish and Clarke 1986); and the victimological approach (Fattah 1991).

The problems of positivist criminology are many and some of them are well summarized by Katz (1988). Katz deplores positivist criminology's persistent preoccupation with a search for background forces, usually defects in the offenders' psychological backgrounds or social environments, to the neglect of the positive, often wonderful attractions within the lived experience of criminality (p. 3). Katz then goes on to outline some of the irritations to inquiry that the statistical and correlational findings of positivist criminology provide. He writes:

> (1) whatever the validity of the hereditary, psychological, and social-ecological conditions of crime, many of those in the supposedly causal categories do not commit the crime at issue, (2) many who do commit the crime do not fit the causal categories, and (3) and what is most provocative, many who do fit the background categories and later commit the predicted crime go for long stretches without committing the crimes to which theory directs them. Why are people who were not determined to commit a crime one moment determined to do so the next? (1988:3–4).

Some Questionable Premises of Positivist Criminology

It is not my intention to provide a general or a thorough critique of criminological theory. However, since the primary purpose of the chapter is to highlight the need for a new approach to criminal behavior and to propose some possibilities for integrating criminological and victimological perspectives, it is necessary to pinpoint some of the weaknesses of current criminological explanations. To do so, I will examine briefly but critically some of the premises underlying positivist criminology.

The Assumption That Crime Is a Distinct Category of Human Behavior

Positivist theories are based on the assumption that crime is a distinct category of human behavior, that there is an ontological reality of crime. Wilson and Herrnstein (1985), for example, contend that predatory crime, on which they chose to focus, "is condemned in all societies, and in all historical periods, by ancient tradition, moral sentiments, and formal law" (p. 22). They further claim that certain acts such as murder, theft, robbery, and incest are regarded as wrong by every society, preliterate as well as literate. This contention, made in 1985, is not too different from the one made a century earlier by R. Garofalo who claimed that there are "natural crimes" that offend the fundamental altruistic sentiments of pity and probity in the average measure possessed by a given social group. Rather than using Garofalo's term *natural crimes* Wilson and Herrnstein (1985) prefer to call them *universal crimes*. Both claims fly in the face of incontrovertible historical, anthropological, and sociological evidence showing that all the examples used by Garofalo as well as by Wilson and Herrnstein were at one time or another not norm violations but cultural imperatives. In his book, *Comparative Criminality,* Gabriel Tarde (1886) demonstrates over and over again the fact that crime is relative both in time and space.[2]

More recently, in his study of social deviance, Wilkins (1964) has denoted that "at some time or another, some form of society or another has defined almost all forms of behavior that we now call criminal as desirable for the functioning of that form of society" (p. 46). The relativity of crime and the fact that for every behavior defined as criminal and made punishable by the criminal code there are similar or even identical behaviors that are not, clearly indicate that crime is neither unique, exceptional, nor qualitatively different from other categories of behavior. One can give countless examples to substantiate the claim that criminality is neither an intrinsic quality of the behavior so defined nor an innate character of that behavior. Deviance, as Becker (1963) maintained, is *not* a quality of the act but rather a consequence of the application by others of rules and sanctions to an offender. Actually the same material act can be criminal in certain situations but not in others. Killing is allowed in some circumstances, such as war, self-defense, use of the death penalty, and euthanasia. In many cultures the killing of the adulterous wife and her lover is a cultural norm. In many nomadic tribes killing the sick, immobile elderly is a moral obligation. Infanticide of newly born females is a practice dictated by the cultural norms of many societies. Rape is a serious crime that is severely punished and yet, in many jurisdictions, raping one's wife is not a crime. Many acts of violence are criminal while others are condoned, tolerated, and even sanctioned by cultural norms. Until recently the use of physical violence against women and children was culturally legitimate and legally permissible. Sociologists and anthropologists have revised their belief about the "incest taboo."[3] In his comprehensive cross-cultural study of incest, Sumner (1906) concluded that "the instances show that the notion of incest is by no means universal or uniform, or attended by the same intensity of repugnance. It is not by any means traceable to a constant cause."

All this is to say that there is no such thing as "natural crimes" nor "universal crimes" — basic tenets of positivist criminology. The old distinction between acts that are *mala in se* and acts that are *mala prohibita* has long been discredited. In her Hamlyn lectures, Lady Wootton (1963) suggested that actions classified as *mala in se* are really only *mala antiqua* — actions, that is to say, that have been recognized as criminal for a very long time. She adds: "For the origins of the supposed dichotomy between real crimes and quasi-crimes we must undoubtedly look to theology. . . . In the secular climate of the present age, however, the appeal to religious doctrine is unconvincing, and unlikely to be acceptable" (1963: 44–45).

For "positivist" criminology to base its theories on a theological distinction is, no doubt, a contradiction. The fact is, as Hulsman (1986) correctly points out, there is *no ontological reality* of crime. And since behavior patterns are not objectively criminal, "*any* attempt to explain *any* criminal behavior is necessarily fallacious on its face" (Quinney 1975). What positivist criminologists often forget is that at one time all harmful, injurious behaviors were civil torts treated in more or less the same manner. The emergence of the criminal law saw the creation of a new category of behavior believed to be deserving of punishment. The selection of behaviors to be brought under the realm of the criminal law was guided by political, historical, and religious considerations and not by the unique qualities of the behaviors that came to be defined as crimes. As a result, the distinction between crime and tort, between the criminal and the civil code, is both artificial and arbitrary and the demarcation line separating the two is often blurred. Some forms of dishonest behavior are criminal, others are civil torts, and still others are neither. The characteristics that Gottfredson and Hirschi (1990) believe are shared by those who rob banks and those who park illegally in front of fire hydrants, namely "a lack of concern for the interest of others and a disregard for the consequences of one's acts" (p. 43) are common to those who are responsible for crimes and civil torts. Quite frequently the same act is both crime and tort. And yet, as Morris and Hawkins (1969) point out, no research projects have been conducted to search for the primary causes of tort, no one inquires what social or psychological pathologies underlie the incidence of tort in our society, and no one has suggested that those who commit torts are biologically inferior to their fellows. Morris and Hawkins add that a large part of criminal behavior is perfectly "normal" behavior both in the statistical sense and in the sense that it occurs naturally. They write:

> The truth is that almost all adults have at some time in their lives committed criminal acts and it is those who have not who are abnormal. Almost all acts which are defined as criminal in our society have at some time in some society been tolerated and even socially approved. The line between legitimate and illegitimate means of acquiring property is both arbitrary and difficult to define precisely. There are wide differences between states in regard to what sexual behavior is criminal, and considerable variation in the same state at different historical periods. There is no evidence that the bulk of criminal behavior is the result of some pathological mental or somatic conditions which distinguishes criminals in general from noncriminals. (1969:48)[4]

If crime is an artificially created legal category of behavior, how could it be claimed that it has innate, endogenic, or biological causes?

The False Dichotomy between "Criminals" and "Noncriminals"

Another basic assumption of positivist criminology is that criminals are fundamentally different from noncriminals. Hence the primary task is to identify the specific abnormalities, peculiarities, and particularities that differentiate criminals from law-abiding citizens. Wilson and Herrnstein (1985), for example, explain that their book is chiefly concerned with the individual differences between criminals and noncriminals (p. 459). Cornish and Clarke (1986) are critical of criminologists' repeated attempts to identify differences between criminal and noncriminal groups that could explain offending. Such attempts, they feel, have reinforced assumptions that offenders are similar to each other and different from everybody else. The tendency to "overpathologize" offending and offenders and to focus on their supposedly abnormal personality, deviant character, or irrational mode of thinking, discounts the fact that most criminal behavior is of a mundane, opportunistic, and rational nature. It is neither irrational nor purposeless. Senseless crimes are the exception not the rule and are often committed by individuals suffering from some mental imbalance or disorder. But this is only a very small minority of the offender population. The Japanese criminologist Hiroshi Tsutomi (1991) said it best when he wrote: "People commit crimes not because they are pathological or wicked, but because they are normal" (p. 14).

The vast majority of criminals are normal people driven by the same motives that drive all of us. The pursuit of criminal activities is not very different from the pursuit of other risky, dangerous, lustful activities. In many cases such pursuit is motivated by the search for pleasure, thrill, adventure, excitement, or fun. Motives for criminal behavior are therefore essentially the same as those behind everyday legitimate, legal activities. The quest for pleasure, profit, gain, status, power, is the principal driving force behind everyday activities: criminal and noncriminal, legal and illegal. As Sutherland and Cressey (1978) point out, both criminal and noncriminal behavior are expressions of the same needs and values: "Thieves generally steal in order to secure money, but likewise honest laborers work in order to secure money" (p. 82). Whatever difference there may be lies not in the goals being pursued but in the means used to achieve those goals. The common saying "the end justifies the means" is an effective technique of rationalization used by criminals and noncriminals alike. It played a major role in the Watergate Affair and the "crimes" of Colonel Oliver North. It is also the same justification used by individual terrorists and terrorist groups.

Positivist criminologists' assertion that "people who break the law are often psychologically atypical" (Wilson and Herrnstein 1985:173) or that "offenders are . . . atypical in personality" (p. 173) is contradicted by the observation that anyone placed in certain situations, under certain conditions, subjected to certain pressures and constraints, is capable of committing acts of extreme atrocity, cruelty, cupidity, and dishonesty. The experiments of Milgram (1969) and of Zimbardo (1972) prove it. So does Christie's (1952) study of Norwegian guards in concentration camps during the Nazi occupation of Norway, the Mai Lai massacre in Vietnam, to name but a few. The so-called folk crimes, such as lynching or the looting by the masses during civil disturbances, blackouts, or in the aftermath of natural disasters, are proof that it does not take an atypical personality to commit the predatory crimes that seem to be singled out by Wilson and Herrnstein (1985) as being the trademark of "real" criminals. On the contrary, these crimes illustrate the preponderant importance and role situational factors play in crime causation. The assumption that criminals are inherently different from noncriminals is further contradicted by the findings of hidden delinquency studies.

Self-report studies (Wallerstein and Wyle 1947; Elmhorn 1965; Anttila and Jaakkola 1966; Christie et al. 1965; Belson et al. 1968) reveal that the great majority of people have, at one time or another, perpetrated acts that qualify as criminal offenses under existing laws. They show that delinquency, in one form or another, is a "normal," "developmental," and "transitory" phase in the life of most male teenagers (Doleschal 1970).

Most theories of positivist criminology, starting with those of Lombroso, were based on samples or populations of convicted offenders that are not representative of the total universe of offenders. Furthermore, the studies serving as the basis for the theories rarely include those committing white-collar crime, corporate crime, or those whose crimes are committed mainly through abuses of political and economic power.

Surprisingly, the erroneous belief that offenders are abnormal or have atypical personalities continues to persist despite recent surveys showing that family violence, for example, is extremely widespread.[5]

The Artificial Dichotomy between Victims and Offenders

Criminals and victims, in the public's view, are as different as night and day. They are perceived as two distinct populations who have nothing in common — two separate groups — predators and prey. As Singer (1981) points out, "The idea that victims and offenders are part of the same homogeneous population runs contrary to the public's popular impression that criminals are distinct from their innocent victims" (1981:779).

Positivist theories of criminal behavior depart from a very similar viewpoint, thus creating an artificial dichotomy between offenders and victims. This dichotomy is coming under increasing criticism as a result of a growing body of evidence pointing to a strong link between victimization and offending (see Thornberry and Figlio 1972; Singer 1981, 1986; Johnson et. al. 1973; Lauritsen, Sampson, and Laub 1991).[6] The evidence emanating from victimization surveys, birth cohort studies, victimological research, and research on family violence, points to victims' frequent involvement in criminal activities and offenders' frequent victimization.

The positive association observed between violent offending and violent victimization apparently extends to property offenses as well. In two studies of Dutch juveniles, van Dijk and Steinmetz (1984) discovered a substantial overlap between being a victim of various theft offenses and admitting to having committed them. One of the explanations they offer for the observed overlap is the possibility that theft might result from normative curbs being weakened by victimization or because it is a convenient way of recouping losses.

The British Crime Survey (Chambers and Tombs 1984), which included questions about the respondents own criminal activities, revealed that 40% of respondents admitting an assault had themselves been the victim of an assault during the survey period: only 1% of those who did not admit an assault were themselves assault victims during that period.[7]

Commenting on the findings of the British Crime Survey, Mayhew and Elliott (1990) concluded that

> in the broadest terms, the self-report evidence from the BCS, especially Gottfredson's (1984) analysis, bears on thinking about victims insofar as it highlights the inappropriateness of seeing victims and offenders as distinct groups. . . . The fact that men and the young face higher risks of personal crime, especially violence, has been one of the most significant findings of victimization surveys, countering the idea that it is the weakest and most vulnerable who are uniformly sought out by offenders. (p. 20)

Jensen and Brownfield (1986) suggest that criminal or delinquent lifestyles and routines may be the most victimogenic of all routines. Their analysis of victimization data revealed that delinquent activity is positively related to victimization and is more strongly related to victimization than nondelinquent activity (p. 85). This leads them to conclude that the similarity in background characteristics of victims and offenders may be, at least partly, a product of that correlation.

One problem with victimization data, in their present form, is their inability to reveal the chronological order and the time sequence of offending and victimization, thus making it difficult to tell which occurs first. Does offending precede or succeed victimization? It is quite possible that becoming a victim of violence creates the motivation (and justification) for offending (revenge, retaliation, getting even). Van Dijk and Steinmetz (1983) seem to lean toward this explanation for property victimization/offending. But the reverse chronological order is also plausible. That is, violent offending may increase the chances of becoming a victim of retaliatory violence. It could also be that involvement in delinquency and adoption of a delinquent life-style do enhance, in other ways, the likelihood of violent (or property) victimization (Fattah 1991).

That victimization creates the motives and rationalizations for offending and that offending provides the reasons for victimization means that the two activities are closely linked. To look upon them as separate and unrelated activities, or to look upon victims and offenders as two distinct or mutually exclusive populations that have nothing in common, is in direct contradiction to the available empirical evidence.

If it is true that prior victimization is a primary or a major factor in offending, or that victims and offenders are constantly moving between the two roles, then it seems necessary that the tenets of positivist criminology (as well as the theories based on those tenets) be revised to take into account the role victimization plays in the process of primary or secondary offending. Moreover, if the traits and attributes claimed by positivist theories to be characteristic of offenders are common to both offenders and victims, their criminogenic role and their explanatory value as causes of delinquency would be greatly diminished.

Another problem is the current practice of categorizing (and labeling) offenders and victims on the basis of a single event instead of the totality of their life experiences. By so doing, the frequent link between victimization and offending is quite often missed. With the exception of birth cohort studies, very few researchers have used a longitudinal analysis to explore the existence and the nature of the link between victimization and offending experiences.

A further problem with predispositional theories (whether of the biological, constitutional, psychological, or even sociological variety) is that they tend to dissociate criminal behavior from the dynamic situational forces that determine, condition, or shape that behavior, or at least, contribute to its occurrence. By ignoring these forces and omitting situational variables from their explanatory models, they naturally fail to come up with a satisfactory explanation of crime. As Kinberg (1960) points out, when analyzing the genesis of an action to determine its causes, it is not possible to regard certain facts or groups of facts as separate entities. The logical intellectual process requires that the researcher take an overall view of the intricate web of factors that form a tight causal chain, the last link of which is the action being analyzed.

Gibbons (1971) also observes that in many cases criminality may be a response to nothing more temporal than the provocations and attractions bound up in the immediate circumstances. He adds: "It may be that, in some kinds of lawbreaking, understanding of the behavior may require detailed attention to the concatenation of events immediately preceding it.

Little or nothing may be added to this understanding from a close scrutiny of the early development of the person."

Further Empirical Evidence Supporting the Link between
Offending and Victimization

In addition to evidence from birth cohorts and victimization surveys, research on family violence offers further support to the victimization/offending link by documenting what is becoming known as the "cycle of violence." The statement that "abused children grow up to be abusing adults" seems to be widely accepted (Steinmetz 1986). Greven (1991) meticulously documents the behavioral consequences of violent victimization of children. He affirms that physical punishment of children consistently appears as one of the major influences shaping subsequent aggressiveness and delinquency of males (p. 194). He also insists that corporal punishments always figure prominently in the roots of adolescent and adult aggressiveness, especially in those manifestations that take an antisocial form, such as delinquency and criminality (p. 194). Steinmetz (1980) finds the data supporting the cycle of violence to be substantial. She also cites studies by Brownmiller (1975) and by Hartogs (1951) who found a brutalizing childhood to be characteristic of rapists.

As vital as the process of transformation from victim to victimizer or from an offender to victim is to the explanation of many forms of delinquency and crime, it has not been thoroughly investigated by criminologists or victimologists.

So far we have examined the process in which the roles of victim-offender-victim are assumed successively but there are cases in which the move from one role to the other occurs almost simultaneously. Conflict situations are often characterized by reciprocal verbal attacks and by an exchange of blows or other forms of physical violence. Who ends up being the "victim" and who is legally qualified as the "offender" depends quite often on chance factors rather than deliberate action, planning, or intent. Thus victim and offender roles are not necessarily antagonistic but are frequently complementary and interchangeable. This is particularly true of brawls, quarrels, physical disputes, and violent altercations (Fattah 1989: 47).

Role reversal is also characteristic of victim-precipitated violence. Gratuitous violence is the exception rather than the rule. Unless the motive for the aggression is robbery or sex, or unless the attacker is a mentally deranged individual shooting indiscriminately at any person in sight or stabbing anyone close by, it is unlikely that a person will be attacked, killed, or assaulted without any precipitating action on his or her part.

While this precipitating action may take various forms (see Wolfgang 1956, 1958), its role in triggering the victimization is a crucial one (Fattah 1991: 292). Role reversal is also characteristic of situations in which violence is employed in self-defence to stop an imminent or an actual attack.

Even in some property offenses, the roles of victim-offender could be easily reversed. It is not too uncommon in cases of swindle for the person trying to defraud to get fleeced. And not infrequently victimized employees may retaliate against their employer by acts of theft, pilfering, embezzlement, or even sabotage. The practice of doing oneself justice is yet another example of role reversal. Children whose books, articles or supplies are stolen by other children in school may "do themselves justice" by stealing the same or similar articles from other schoolmates.[8] Some "well adjusted," "law abiding" car owners who had some piece or part, such as a hubcap, mirror, hood ornament, or emblem, stolen, may not report their victimization to the police and instead "help themselves" to the same part from a similar car (Fattah 1991: 148–49). By assuming the role of offender they feel they are only righting the wrong done to them.

The Need for an Alternative Approach

Most current theories of criminal behavior, whether attempting to explain causation, statistical association/correlations, offer only static explanations. Since criminal behavior, like other forms of human behavior, is dynamic, it can be explained only through a dynamic approach in which the offender, the act, and the victim are inseparable elements of a total situation that leads to the crime (Fattah 1976).

The traits approach, which seeks the genesis of criminal behavior in the characteristics and attributes of the offender, is a simplistic approach. Theories of offenders' attributes, personalities, constitution, or social background and conditions do not explain why other individuals who have the same traits, same personality type, same constitution, same or similar social background and upbringing do not commit crime or do not persist in a criminal career. They equally fail to explain why the offender committed a particular crime in a particular situation at a given moment against a specific victim. In other words, the traits approach either ignores or deliberately minimizes the importance of situational factors in triggering or actualizing criminal behavior.

Moreover, criminological theories that stress individual traits or offender pathology fail miserably when the task at hand is to explain the temporal and spatial patterns of crime; regional, provincial, intercity, and intracity variations in crime rates; or the changes in those rates over time.

As suggested earlier, theories seeking the genesis of criminal behavior in the abnormality or the psychopathology of the offender ignore the dynamic forces that determine, condition, shape, or influence the offender's behavior in a given situation. Not only do they fail to explain why many of those who share offenders' abnormal or pathological characteristics do not engage in criminal behavior, but they also fail to explain why it is that most of those who commit incest or family violence (to give just one example) confine their sexual coercion or aggression strictly within the family and rarely, if ever, are violent or sexually preying on others outside the home. The theories do not fare any better when it comes to explaining retaliatory behavior committed as a reaction to prior victimization or in response to provocation or precipitation. This is a serious shortcoming because:

1. retaliation is a key principle in violence (Felson and Steadman 1983: 60; Singer 1986: 61–62) and because violence is, in many cases, situationally determined. In other words, it is the result of events and circumstances that cause a conflict to escalate (Felson and Steadman, 1983: 59–60);
2. a nonnegligible part of violence and homicide is victim precipitated (Wolfgang 1958). In such cases, the violent response is more a function of the precipitating behavior of the victim and the "situational determinants" (Felson and Steadman 1983) than it is a function of the characteristics and the background of the respondent.

Another shortcoming of the "positivist" approach is the static way in which it views the personality traits and character attributes believed to be responsible for criminal behavior. Traits such as aggressiveness, callousness, and dishonesty are neither constant nor absolute and, thus alone have very little, if any, explanatory value. Some individuals become aggressive only when under extreme stress, have consumed alcohol, or when provoked. Others may use violence only when they are humiliated or hurt in their vanity. Some men become violent in situations where they feel the need to assert their maleness. Some people may be shy and withdrawn without peer support only to become extremely mean when in the presence of, and under pressure from, their peer group. People may be scrupulously honest in one situation and shamelessly dishonest in another. Many "honest" people, whose moral scruples would never allow them to cheat or steal from a friend or neighbor, a work partner, or in general another human being, become totally unscrupulous when it is a matter of cheating the government, a large corporation, or the general public. They could be totally without inhibitions or compunction when it comes to committing a white-collar crime, such as tax or custom duty evasion, insurance fraud, price fixing, and so forth (Fattah 1991).

An individual's attitudes to others are not indiscriminate. Clifford Olson, the serial killer found guilty of slaying 11 children in British Columbia, and whom the police suspect of having slain even more, was proven to be a loving husband and affectionate father. Yet he had no sympathy or empathy for the several young victims he brutally killed to satisfy his sexual desires. Nor is the case of Olson unique. Many murderers who exhibit extreme cruelty, brutality, and callousness toward their victims, show tender love and compassion for others and even for animals. In one of the murder cases I studied (Fattah 1971) after savagely killing the victim and robbing her house, the killer took utmost care to feed the victim's dog and cat. He even left them enough food for fear that nobody would come to the scene of the crime for some time.

In view of all these serious problems and shortcomings, one might wonder why it is that theories of criminals' psychopathology have maintained their popularity for over a hundred years. The answer is rather simple. The attractiveness of the traits/attributes approach lies in its central (though faulty) premise that criminals and delinquents are different from the rest of us. Propagating the view that some individuals are "bad," "evil," or in some way abnormal, allows the average citizen to perceive offenders as distinct individuals, as different beings capable of committing the terrible crimes that we cannot conceive of ourselves as capable of perpetrating. It is a self-assuring approach that allows the dichotomization of people into the good and the bad, the normal and the abnormal, those who are criminally inclined and those not so inclined.

The rational choice perspective and the victimological approach are based on different premises. Both maintain that crime is more a function of opportunity than pathology, of rational choice than irresistible forces or unchecked impulses, exogenic rather than endogenic factors, of the situation rather than the offender's constitution. Both perspectives raise a host of different questions for criminological research.

If crime is a chosen activity and if a criminal career is a deliberately chosen occupation, then the search for why some individuals commit crime or adopt a criminal career can be no more enlightening than the search for the reasons why some elect to join the police force or become doctors, lawyers, or academics while others choose to become undertakers, bouncers, pimps, or car racers. Becoming a victim is an entirely different matter. In the vast majority of cases, victimization occurs without either the knowledge or consent of those who are victimized and thus does need to be explained. Another reality requiring explanation is the skewed distribution of victimization risks and the clustering of those risks in time, space, and within certain groups. The fact that crime victims do not constitute a representative sample or an unbiased cross-section of the general population indicates that criminals do not choose their victims (targets) at random. This suggests an important area of research: how criminals choose their targets and the criteria they use in such selection. What makes certain targets more popular, more attractive, more vulnerable, or easier to victimize than others? Hence the need for crime-specific analysis. Target selection is therefore another area that links victimology to the rational choice perspective. In fact, the rational choice perspective makes it imperative to incorporate the victim in any explanatory model of criminality.

Rational Choice and Victimology as Alternative Approaches to the Study of Crime

Unlike positivist theories that view criminal behavior as distinct, unique, abnormal, pathological, irrational, purposeless, mindless, or senseless, and that start with the premise that criminals are inherently different from noncriminals, the rational choice perspective (Cornish and Clarke 1986) takes as its point of departure a set of radically different assumptions:

1. It recognizes the mundane, opportunistic, and rational nature of much offending, thus rejecting the view that depicts it as "irremediably alien to ordinary behavior — driven by abnormal motivations, irrational, purposeless, unpredictable, potentially violent, and evil" (Cornish and Clarke 1986: v). The authors affirm that the leitmotif encapsulated in the notion of a "reasoning" offender implies the essentially nonpathological and commonplace nature of much criminal activity (p. 6).
2. Rather than emphasizing whatever differences may exist between criminals and noncriminals, the rational choice perspective stresses some of the similarities. And rather than focusing on the irrational and pathological components in some crimes, it examines more closely the rational and adaptive aspects of offending (Cornish and Clarke 1986: vi).
3. Rather than viewing crime as a unitary phenomenon that could be explained by a general, far-reaching theory, it calls for crime-specific analysis (ibid). Still, the approach is intended to provide a framework for understanding all forms of crime but without attempting to impose a conceptual unity upon divergent criminal behavior (p. 6).
4. Rather than focusing attention solely on the criminal, his attributes, his traits, his background, and the factors governing his involvement in particular crimes, it draws attention to the criminal event itself and the situational factors that influence its commission (Cornish and Clarke 1986: vi). Cornish and Clarke explain that whereas

most existing theories tend to accord little influence to situational variables, the rational choice approach explicitly recognizes their importance in relation to the criminal event, and, furthermore, incorporates similar influences on decisions relating to involvement in crime.

The above-mentioned premises are quite similar to those that have guided research in theoretical victimology. It is not surprising, therefore, that the paths of the two approaches do join at several points in the analysis of criminal behavior. Through its emphasis on situational variables and crime-specific analysis, the rational choice perspective becomes particularly receptive to victimological concepts and explanations. This is so because in many cases the victim (target) is an integral part of the crime situation and the victim's characteristics and behavior are, quite often, important situational variables. Actually, the situational and victimological approaches are being increasingly regarded as two components of the same analytical process. Wikstrom (1991), for example, insists that "Situational and victimological approaches to the study of crime are in part only different aspects of the same thing. What makes a person or object an attractive target for potential offenders creates at the same time a risk of victimization for that person or object" (1991: 100).

Despite their variety, the multitude of criminogenic factors encountered in all criminological theories may be grouped into three broad categories: (a) predisposing factors; (b) situational factors; and (c) triggering, actualizing, or catalytic factors. The most popular criminological theories thus far have been the ones that attempt to explain the etiology of criminal behavior by reference to the offender's personal characteristics and background. The victimological approach, on the other hand, is predicated on the premise that "criminal behavior is dynamic behavior" and cannot therefore be explained by the static theories that have dominated the discipline of criminology for over a century. Victimology thus shifts the research focus from predisposing factors to environmental, situational and catalyzing factors; from the notion of pathology to the concept of opportunity, from causes to motives, from the offender's action to victim-offender interaction. Unlike the traditional criminological perspective, which postulates that the impulses for crime emanate from within the offender and are manifestations of his psychopathology, victimology views criminal behavior as a response to environmental stimuli, stimuli that ineluctably include the characteristics, the behavior of the potential victim and the available opportunities for offending. In the victimological perspective, violent behavior, as an example, is seen not as a unilateral action but as the outcome of dynamic processes of interaction, not as a one-sided behavior but, rather, as a reaction or an overreaction (Fattah 1991). This explains why the victimological approach pays great attention to the contexts in which violent confrontations occur, to the situational dynamics of these contexts, as well as to the verbal and nonverbal exchanges between the involved protagonists themselves, as well as with third parties who might be present. In other words, these violent confrontations are analyzed as situated transactions (Luckenbill 1977).

Rather than viewing criminals and victims as totally distinct and fundamentally different populations, victimology stresses the homogeneity, the affinity, and the similarities between the two populations. Victimology rejects the artificial dichotomy between offenders and victims and postulates that the roles of "victim" and "victimizer" are neither fixed, assigned, nor predetermined, but are mutable and interchangeable and may be assumed simultaneously or consecutively. Victimology claims that the roles are revolving, with many individuals moving alternatingly between the two roles: yesterday's victims becoming today's offenders and today's offenders becoming tomorrow's victims. This observation, backed by substantial empirical evidence, is clearly at odds with popular stereotypes and mental images portraying the two populations as mutually exclusive.

All this shows that the rational choice perspective and the victimological perspective do have much in common and could be easily linked together via some common and potentially unifying concepts such as "rationality/ rationalization," "choice," "risk," "opportunity," "association/exposure," "target selection," and so forth.

Some Commonalities between the Two Approaches

- Both rational choice and victimology see the vast majority of offending not as the outcome or manifestation of some underlying pathology but as a normal and predictable outcome of human interaction; human conflict, as a normal and predictable response to environmental stimuli, opportunities, temptations, provocations, lack of options, etc.

- Both rational choice and victimology posit that immediate environmental variables, including situational inducements and opportunities for crime, play a far greater role in determining delinquency and criminality than the constitutional or psychological traits of individual offenders. Both approaches insist that the former variables are much more important than had previously been thought or is usually acknowledged.

- Both the rational choice perspective and victimology pay much greater attention to the motives of criminal behavior than do positivist theories of criminality. Motives are believed to play a significant role in the choices people make, including the decision to commit a crime and the decision to attack a specific victim/target.

- By stressing the role of situational dynamics and the importance of triggering and catalyzing factors, both approaches reject the implicit determinism of the theories revolving around offenders' psychopathology. This does not mean a return to the classical notion of free will. To stress the deliberate and rational choices offenders make does not mean or imply that these choices are free. Our choices are severely constrained by endogenic and exogenic forces, by a host of personal, situational, and environmental factors. Despite these constraints, we try to do the best with possible and available choices and to pick what appears to be the best among them. The rationality in the cost-benefit calculation of the consequences of the behavior is relative and has to be judged from the point of view of the actor. What may appear as an irrational behavior to the external observer may be the ultimate in rationality from the actor's point of view.
- Both rational choice and victimology logically lead to a different and innovative approach to crime prevention and to a shift of policy emphasis from legal deterrence to situational prevention, target hardening, opportunity reduction, physical deterrents, and so on.

Some Integrative Variables and Concepts

Age

Attempts to explain delinquency or crime by reference to the biological or psychological abnormalities of offenders are unable to account for the early desistance from such activities (Matza 1964). If crime or delinquency is caused by (or is attributable to) some biological or psychological abnormality, why is it then, that most of those who engage in such activities do stop at a relatively early age and have no criminal involvement beyond age 25 or 30? Desistance from delinquency and crime is, on the other hand, quite compatible with the rational choice perspective, which asserts that with advancing age a point is reached when persistence in delinquent or criminal activities is no longer perceived as profitable or rational, hence the decision to desist.

More important still is the fact that both delinquency and victimization start to decline in late adolescence and continue this decline in each subsequent age group. That both criminality and victimization follow exactly the same age curve, reaching their peak and starting their decline at identical points along the age scale, suggests that common factors are at play influencing both the rise and fall of the two phenomena. It seems to indicate further that factors such as association, exposure, opportunity, life-style, and routine activities are far more important to delinquency than the constitutional or psychological abnormalities of individual offenders. The decisive impact age has on offending and on victimization shows clearly how necessary it is to search for the common factors responsible for their decline with age. It also points to the need to develop an integrated model capable of explaining the identical development of both phenomena along the age continuum.

Associations/Exposure/Social Interaction

The concept of association has dominated sociological explanations of offending ever since Sutherland introduced the theory of differential association in 1939 and revised it in 1947. The theory stresses the pivotal role of learning and of the processes of interaction and communication (particularly within intimate personal groups) to the engagement in criminal activities. The theory equally stresses the importance of motives, drives, rationalizations, and attitudes in the genesis of criminal behavior. That the engagement in offending is a deliberate choice is made quite clear in the theory's central statement stipulating that "a person becomes delinquent because of an excess of definitions favorable to violation of law over definitions unfavorable to violation of law. This is the principle of differential association" (Sutherland and Cressey 1978: 81). In addition to his insistence that criminal behavior is learned through the processes of interaction and communication, Sutherland (1937) should be given credit for treating crime as a way of life at a time when other criminological researchers such as E.A. Hooton (1939) were trying to prove that crime is the result of some biological inferiority!

Differential association, interaction, and communication are all important notions in victimological explanations of the differential risks of criminal victimization. One of the tenets of the life-style model (Hindelang, Gottfredson, and Garofalo 1978) is that differential risks of victimization are (at least partially) a function of the differential association with, and differential exposure to, motivated offenders. Since the frequency and intensity of association with potential offenders and since the level and degree of exposure to potential offenders vary according to socio-demographic characteristics such as age, gender, marital status, occupation, unemployment, and income, risks and rates of victimization are bound to vary accordingly. The life-style model also maintains that social activities that increase the level of association with, and exposure to, potential offenders (such as alcohol consumption in public entertainment places) increase the risks and the rates of criminal victimization.

The homogeneity of the victim and offender populations (Singer 1981;

Reiss 1981; Gottfredson 1984; Smith 1986; Fattah 1989, 1991) suggests that differential association is as important to criminal victimization as it is to crime and delinquency. Thus, individuals who are in close proximity to, and in close personal, social, or professional contact with potential delinquents and criminals run a greater risk of being victimized than those who are not. This is confirmed by Cohen, Kluegel, and Land (1981) who found that the chances of victimization increase with increasing interaction with potential offenders. They point out that persons who share potential offenders' socio-demographic characteristics are more likely to interact socially with those potential offenders. In so doing, their chances of being victimized by those offenders increase.

In fact, it is fair to say that both the routine activity approach (Cohen and Felson 1979) and the opportunity model (Cohen, Kluegel, and Land 1981) use differential association as a variable in trying to explain the differential risks of criminal victimization. Both posit that the risk of criminal victimization depends largely on people's life-style and routine activities that bring them (and/or their property) into direct contact with potential offenders in the absence of capable guardians.

Victimological research and theory have always placed a great emphasis on the personal relationships between victims and offenders in violent crime. The intervening variables of interaction and communication explain the important role such relationships play in violent crime. The fact that a great deal of violence occurs within the family and between intimates, peers, and associates shows how important association and interaction are in creating the motives, the conflicts, and the situations that often lead to the use of violence.

Rationality/Rationalization

The rational choice perspective maintains that criminal behavior is rational behavior, that the decision to engage in such behavior is a rational decision. The verbal utterances of delinquents and criminals betray an adherence to the principle of rationality. Their persistent attempts to show how rational their offending is leave little doubt as to their constant preoccupation to prove to themselves and others that they are rational operators behaving according to specific rules and norms. As mentioned earlier, rationality is relative and subjective. Once a behavior is rationalized, it becomes rational in the eyes and the mind of the individual doing the rationalizing. Hence, it is important to examine not only the rationale for the behavior being analyzed but also the techniques used by offenders to rationalize such behavior and to make it possible. Rationalizations make it possible for persons who are seemingly well adjusted and law abiding to commit serious crimes without hurting their self-image and without experiencing feelings of guilt or remorse. Rationalization, as an explanation, is consistent with the belief that offenders are not inherently different from nonoffenders and that everyone is capable of committing crime if the motivation is sufficiently strong and the circumstances are sufficiently propitious. One criminological theory that does not seek the roots of delinquency in the "devils in the mind or stigma of the body" is the "techniques of neutralization" theory (Sykes and Matza 1957). The theory rejects the image of juvenile delinquency "as a form of behavior based on competing or countervailing values and norms" and contends that much delinquency is based on what is essentially an unrecognized extension of defenses to crimes, in the form of justifications for deviance that are seen as valid by the delinquent but not by the legal system or society at large. Sykes and Matza's theory focuses on the techniques of neutralization delinquents use to lessen the effectiveness of social controls. While these behavioral justifications are called "techniques of neutralization" by Sykes and Matza, Redl and Wineman (1951), both psychologists, speak of techniques of "tax evasion from guilt feelings." They also refer to the special tricks or "alibi tricks" that delinquents use to avoid feeling much concern about their behavior or their victims and to keep all phases of delinquent behavior "tax exempt" from feelings of guilt.

Some years ago (Fattah 1976) I made an attempt to link criminological and victimological explanations by analyzing the techniques of neutralization that either refer to the victim or to the delinquent's perception of himself or herself as a victim. More recently (Fattah 1991), I offered a distinction between three mental processes that precede the commission of the crime: neutralization, redefinition/auto-legitimation, and desensitization. Neutralization has the victimizer as its focus, and its main purpose is to enable the victimizer to overcome the moral and cultural barriers that stand in the way to the victimization act. Redefinition and auto-legitimation has the victimization act as its focus, and its main purpose is to redefine, rationalize, and justify the act. The third process, desensitization, has the prospective victim as its focus. Its main aim is to desensitize the victimizer to the pain and suffering inflicted on the victim. The neutralization process operates to render the mechanisms of social control ineffective. The redefinition process operates to strip the act of its delinquent, illegal, or immoral character. The desensitization process makes it possible to hurt, injure, or harm the victim without feeling bad or guilty about it and without suffering postvictimization cognitive dissonance.

The victimizer can use various techniques of desensitization. These techniques are the denial, reification, and depersonalization of the victim; the denial of injury to the victim; the blaming of the victim; and the devaluation of the victim. An extremely popular technique is blaming the victim. In this technique, the victimizer is able to convince himself or herself that the victim has done him or her wrong and that the victim is guilty of some injustice. Once the guilt of the victim is established, any compassion for that victim and any sense of personal culpability can be discarded. Although blaming the victim is a common and often-used technique of desensitization, it is not a process of intentional distortion. In most cases, the victimizer is actually convinced of the victim's guilt. These techniques of desensitization have received a great deal of empirical support in research done in social psychology (Fattah 1991).

One of Sykes and Matza's main assertions is that delinquents make careful and subtle distinctions between appropriate and inappropriate targets. They write: "Juvenile delinquents often draw a sharp line between those who can be victimized and those who cannot. Certain social groups are not to be viewed as 'fair game' in the performance of supposedly approved delinquent acts while others warrant a variety of attacks."

There is a great deal of empirical evidence supporting this contention (Sutherland 1937; Cressey 1953; Redl and Wineman 1951; Robert 1966; Schwendinger and Schwendinger 1967).

Both the rational choice perspective and the techniques of neutralization theory view offenders as rational operators who make deliberate choices to engage in delinquent activities and who carefully choose their targets. Both offer valid qualitative explanations for the differential risks of victimization and for the popularity (or unpopularity) of certain individuals, groups, businesses, or households as targets for victimization. Both try to explain why some targets are particularly prone or vulnerable to being victimized while others are quasi immune to such attacks.

Target Selection

Through its emphasis on target selection and the choices offenders make between potential targets, the rational choice perspective offers a framework that allows the direct linking of criminological and victimological theories. That the majority of offenders do not choose their victims or targets at random is an indisputable reality. Were victims chosen at random we would reasonably expect them to constitute an unbiased cross-section of the entire population. It would also be reasonable to expect the risks as well as the rates of criminal victimization to be evenly divided within the general population. This, evidently, is not the case. The clustering of victimization in certain geographical areas and within certain groups revealed by victimization surveys suggests the existence of some crude or sophisticated selection processes. As rational operators, criminals, particularly those who commit property crime, white-collar crime, and similar types of profit-oriented offences, go about selecting their victims or targets in a carefully considered, circumspect manner approaching rationality. Naturally, some are more rational than others, and some are more choosy and more picky than others. Professionals tend to be more selective than occasional or amateurish criminals. Selection, however, is neither exclusive nor limited to professional or semiprofessional criminals. This is well illustrated in the example given by Wilkins (1964):

> Let any (non-criminal) reader try to imagine himself in the position of being required to commit a crime — say one of the most common crimes like larceny or breaking and entering — within the next twelve hours. Few readers would select the victim completely at random, unskilled at victim selection though they might be. There will be something approaching rationality in the selection of the victim. (P. 75)

To understand the skewed distribution of victimization risks, to understand why certain victims or targets are more attractive, more popular, and more frequently victimized than others, it is necessary to explore offenders' selection processes and the criteria they use in such selection. Certain questions become vital for criminological investigation and research: What attracts a given offender to a specific victim? What exactly do offenders look for and consider when searching for a suitable target? How and why does an offender pick a particular target from the wide array of available ones? Interest in finding answers to these important questions has been growing in recent years, stimulated by the rational choice/opportunity perspectives. This is evidenced by a number of recent studies on target selection (Bennett and Wright 1984; Blazicek 1979; Chappell and James 1986; Hough 1987; Walsh 1986; Wilson 1987; Wright and Logie 1988).

It is obvious that insights gleaned from knowledge about target selection, from an analysis of the selection process, and the criteria used, can be extremely useful in developing policies, strategies, and techniques of protection and prevention and for providing potential victims and vulnerable targets with helpful advice as to how to avoid criminal victimization. It is also invaluable for understanding the displacement phenomenon.

Unfortunately, with the exception of the "techniques of neutralization" theory and the rational choice theory, very few other criminological theories have incorporated target selection in their explanatory schemes. One of these is the routine activity approach (Cohen and Felson 1979), which argues that the occurrence of direct-contact predatory violations is the outcome of the convergence in space and time of three minimal elements: motivated offenders, suitable targets, and absence of capable guardians.

By recognizing "suitable targets" as a principal element, the routine activity approach converges toward victimology and moves beyond conventional criminological theories that consistently ignore the victims and the role they play in the genesis of crime.

Another approach that pays particular attention to the selection of targets, to their spatial distribution, and to the distance offenders travel to commit their crimes is environmental criminology (Brantingham and Brantingham 1981). Since research on target selection demonstrates that the majority of offenders do not travel long distances to select their targets, in line with the "distance decay pattern" (Brantingham and Brantingham 1975; 1981; 1984; LeBeau 1987), environmental criminology stands to make a significant contribution to the understanding and explanation of the differential and skewed distribution of victimization risks and opportunities in time and space. It can also contribute to the understanding of the affinities between the offender and victim populations. Some of these affinities are undoubtedly related to the geographical (and social) proximity of those who offend to those who are victimized.

This geographical proximity of offenders to victims or of victims to offenders is also a key to explaining "spatial vulnerability." Spatial vulnerability is a victimological concept referring to the fact that victimization risks are closely linked to the area of residence. It suggests that those who reside in close proximity to concentrations of potential offenders (young, single, unemployed, lower-class males) have a greater likelihood of being victimized than others. This is precisely why rates of victimization are usually higher for those who reside in the deteriorating parts of the inner city than for those who live in the more affluent peripheral areas (Smith 1986).

Opportunity

Another criminological theory that converges toward victimology is opportunity theory. Opportunity theory is by no means new. The well-known saying "the opportunity makes the thief" (*L'occasion fait le larron*) seems to have been coined by the School of Lyon (Alexandre Lacassagne) in 19th-century France. The theory has been regaining momentum under the impetus of work done by the British Home Office (*Crime as Opportunity*, 1976, by Mayhew, Clarke, Sturman, and Hough) and as a result of the advances made by environmental criminology.

The concept of opportunity carries different meanings in criminology and the relationship between opportunity and crime is manifold. One way of attributing a causal role to opportunity is to talk about an opportunity structure unfavorable to the members of certain groups in society. This is the notion of "differential opportunity" advanced by Cloward and Ohlin (1961) who argued that the equality of opportunity espoused by the democratic ideology creates high aspirations for success. The reality, however, is different. There are enormous barriers to the achievement of success goals in the way of lower-class persons, barriers that deny them access to legitimate opportunities. The resulting discrepancy between aspirations and legitimate opportunities leads some to try to achieve success by illegitimate means: the delinquent solution. In other words, Cloward and Ohlin's theory views lower-class delinquents as victims of the unequal opportunity structure and of a blockage of legitimate opportunities that lower-class members have to face and overcome. The theory also views the delinquent solution as a deliberate choice that depends on the relative availability of illegal alternatives to various potential criminals. In this respect, the theory takes a stand similar to Sutherland's view of criminality as a life-style, and to the one underlying the rational choice perspective. Like differential association, the rational choice perspective, the techniques of neutralization, and the victimological approach, Cloward and Ohlin's theory views the motives and drives of delinquent activities as essentially the same as those behind legal, legitimate activities. The theory equally implies that feelings of injustice and victimization play a major role in the decision to engage in delinquent activities. Thus, a victimological reading (or reinterpretation) of the theory would lead to a statement along the following lines:

The unavailability of opportunities and the obstruction of legitimate channels for success to members of the lower classes create feelings of injustice, frustration, hopelessness, and outright victimization. This, coupled with a perception of relative deprivation and a rejection of society's hollow claim to equal opportunity throw many into delinquent activities not only as a substitute for legal ones but as a last resort, as the only available means of fulfilling the cherished aspirations of the American dream.

Another way of expressing the relationship between opportunity and crime is to refer to an opportunity structure favorable to the commission of certain crimes[9] or one that hinders the effectiveness of deterrents. The popular saying "the opportunity makes the thief" is actually a vulgarization of a theory linking crimes to the opportunities available for committing them. It stresses the importance of environmental and situational variables in the genesis of offending. Usually the criterion used to classify professional and occasional criminals is their attitude to opportunity. Thus, the professional criminal is one who searches for, or creates, the opportunity to commit crime, while the occasional criminal is someone who takes advantage of a criminal opportunity that presents itself.[10] This is similar to

Ferri's (1917) distinction between habitual and occasional criminals. What differentiates the former from the latter is that the first acts upon the environment in order to produce and repeat the opportunity for the commission of crime. In the case of the occasional criminal it is the opportunity that acts intermittently and extraordinarily upon him to cause the crime. Carroll and Weaver (1986) distinguish between "experienced criminals" who actively and rapidly search out and develop crime opportunities and "novices" who respond only to obvious opportunities and spend considerable time thinking them over because each opportunity is novel (p. 23).

To the lay person, opportunity theory is generally presented in terms of number of *potential targets* and the impact their availability has on crime rates. Thus people are reminded that the more cars, television sets, stereos, fur coats, and so on there are, the more are stolen; the more banks and financial institutions, the more hold-ups; the more department stores, the more shoplifting, and so forth. Empirical support for this comes from several studies. A Swedish study (Aspelin et al.1975) found, for example, that the number of car thefts followed closely the number of cars on the streets and increased proportionately to the number of registered motor vehicles. It is also generally believed that the lower crime rates socialist countries enjoy, in comparison to capitalist states, are partially due to the lower crime opportunities available in those countries.

Opportunity theory can also be presented in terms of available *means* to commit crimes. Research aimed at assessing the impact of availability of firearms (or of gun control) on homicide rates or other crimes of violence is usually conducted within the framework of opportunity theory.

Opportunity theory is also a *situational* theory since it places the emphasis not on the characteristics of the offender but on the characteristics of the situation. Employment in a position of trust creates the opportunity (situation) that makes embezzlement, breach of trust possible. Unattended goods in large department stores create a temptation and an opportunity situation that facilitate shoplifting. Hitchhiking creates an opportunity for rape, robbery, theft, or assault. In all these cases and many others, the opportunity (situation) cannot be ignored in any explanatory model.

It should be obvious by now that the concept of opportunity is central to both environmental criminology and to the rational choice perspective. Through the notion of opportunity, their explanations converge with those of victimology. This is so because opportunities are viewed as being greatly influenced by the behavior of potential victims or targets. The collective behavior of potential crime victims is believed to have a strong impact on crime rates and variations in those rates could therefore be explained, at least partially, through differences or changes in victim behavior. The rational choices criminals make, particularly with regard to target selection, are also believed to be strongly influenced by victims' behavior. Victims' presence or rather their absence is also a major explanatory variable in the routine activity approach since in most cases the "capable guardians" are the potential victims.

The rational choice perspective links opportunity theory to victimological theory through the view it holds of offenders. According to this view, many criminals are opportunists who take advantage of situations and environmental opportunities, many of which are created by prospective victims' negligent, careless, imprudent, reckless, or facilitating behavior. That negligence and carelessness of potential victims are important facilitating factors in many property offenses is too well-known to need any documentation (see Baldwin 1974; United States 1979) But there is evidence as well to substantiate the claim that opportunities for crime may be deliberately created by the prospective victims.[11]

Like the explanatory model of victim-precipitation, opportunity theory directly links offenders' behavior to victims' behavior. The behavior of the victim is seen as the environmental stimulus that elicits the criminal response. In the case of spontaneous, impulsive, opportunistic crimes, the behavior of the victim acts as a triggering, or catalyzing factor, while in the case of premeditated, planned crimes it acts more as a facilitating one. Opportunity theory, therefore, provides a sound basis for developing a stimulus-response model of criminal behavior, an interactive model that incorporates the behavior of both parties (offender-victim) into one integrative schema.

Risk

Risk avoidance is generally considered a characteristic of rational behavior. Economic (Becker 1968; Cook 1977, 1980) and rational choice theories (Cornish and Clarke 1986) of crime see risk perception and risk assessment as important factors influencing potential offenders' decisions to engage or not to engage in criminal activities. Risk calculation is the basic tenet of utilitarian theories of punishment and the doctrine of deterrence. It is important to reiterate, however, that rationality is subjective and relative. This explains why for some individuals risk acts as a deterrent while others may be attracted by it. Even for the same individual, the willingness to take risks varies according to the mood and the situation. Maguire and Bennett (1982) note, for example, that personal preferences and reasoning vary considerably among burglars, and an individual's mood on any one day may cause him to take more or less risk than usual (p. 87). Letkemann (1973) points out that when money is desperately needed, the criminal may dispense with careful planning and proceed quickly and at high risk. He adds that "crimes committed shortly after release from prison, when the exconvict is out of money, are the most risky" (p. 143). Be this as it may, it is fair to assume that risk perception, risk assessment, and risk avoidance characterize the attitudes and behavior of both potential offenders and potential victims. The former try to avoid, reduce, or minimize the risk of apprehension and conviction; the latter the risk of victimization.

Considerations of risk figure prominently in the choice of offense and the choice of target. Some criminal activities are more dangerous than others and some targets are riskier than others. Offenses that require face-to-face confrontation with the victim, such as rape, robbery, or mugging involve a much greater risk for the offender than those involving no confrontation. Risk is also an important criterion in target selection. Brantingham and Brantingham (1984) point out that although the characteristics of a target that make it "good" or "bad" might be diverse, they must include an assessment of the risk associated with the choice of a particular target, together with the difficulty of actually succeeding. They write: "There are irrational criminals — those who commit offenses without regard to risk or in the hopes of being apprehended — but most criminals are psychologically normal. Some offenses are so emotional or affective that consideration of risk does not occur, but in most offenses it is clear that the people committing the offenses take some precautions" (p. 363).

When planning the offense and when choosing the victim/target, the offender has two primary concerns: the chances of success or failure in achieving the criminal objective, and the risks and dangers of the criminal situation. It is only natural that predatory criminals will try to work out a plan and select a victim (or target) with the potential to maximize their chances of success and minimize the risk of failure and of being caught. The choice of a vulnerable, unprotected victim (or target) is one way of reducing the probability of a negative outcome. The choice of a victim (or target) from which or whom the offender can easily get away after committing the crime or when something goes wrong is another way of lowering the risks involved. The underlying premise of current policies of target hardening as a means of crime prevention, is that easy targets are preferred, and are more attractive and more often selected than harder ones (Fattah 1991).

Certain categories of victims pose much less risk for the offender than others. Socially stigmatized groups are preferred targets for different types of attacks not only because it is easy to rationalize and legitimize their victimization but also because the risk associated with their victimization is minimal. The laxity in investigating and prosecuting the offenders and the leniency often exhibited by the courts vis à vis them explain why disposable, expendable victims (criminals, outlaws), worthless victims (deviants, outcasts, marginals), and deserving victims (dirty hands victims) (Fattah 1991) are often victimized with impunity.

The concept of risk helps to explain not only the behavior and the choices offenders make but also the differential risks of victimization, the popularity of certain targets, and the unpopularity of others, as well as the proneness or vulnerability of certain victims and the quasi immunity of others. It also helps explain the phenomenon of displacement both technical and geographical.

Conclusion

The major task of theoretical criminology is to explain the differential involvement in delinquency and crime and the uneven distribution of criminality in time and space. The main task of theoretical victimology is to explain the differential risks of victimization and the skewed distribution of victimization in time and space. Attempts to explain these two facets of the same reality have been proceeding in an unrelated, almost parallel fashion as if crime and victimization are two separate phenomena. Ignored has been the fact that they are simply two sides of the same coin. Holistic explanations of the crime/victimization phenomenon require therefore the pooling, the linking, and the integration of criminological and victimological knowledge so that we may better understand who victimizes whom, where, when, and why?

The rational choice perspective provides a useful framework for linking some criminological approaches to the victimological approach and for integrating some criminological theories with theories of victimization. This is so because the rational choice perspective and the victimological approach do have a lot in common and because their paths join at several points of the explanation process. Through this new integrated approach it is hoped that we will be able to develop dynamic, tridimensional models (offender/victim/ situation) to replace the static, unidimensional, and fragmented explanations that currently characterize theoretical criminology.

Notes

1. The adjective *positivist* or *positivistic* can naturally be applied to any theory that "systematically, and in varying degrees, empirically analyzes the causes of crime and delinquency and concludes that personal or social and environmental factors determine criminal behavior" (Shoemaker 1990: 5–6). However, it has become common to apply the term to the pathological perspective, to theories contending that criminals suffer from some pathological or abnormal traits that differentiate them from noncriminals.

Gottfredson and Hirschi (1990) point out that positivism brought with it the idea that criminals differ from noncriminals in radical ways together with the idea that criminals carry within themselves properties peculiarly and positively conducive to crime.

2. Tarde's views were reiterated by Clarence Darrow (1902) who affirms that "one age has pronounced martyrs and worshipped as saints the criminals that another age has put to death . . . it is quite as possible that another generation will look with the same horror on the subjects of our laws as we look upon those of the years that are gone" (1902: 53).

Sellin's (1938) observation is strikingly similar:

Crimes of yesteryear may be legal conduct today, while crime in one contemporary state may be legal conduct in another. This lesson of history makes it a safe prediction . . . that everything the criminal law of any state prohibits today, it will not prohibit at a given future time, unless complete social stagnation sets in, an experience unknown to the social historian.

3. Forward and Buck (1983) give several examples of societies where various forms of incest (father-daughter; mother-son; brother-sister; etc.) are widely practiced.

4. Parker's (1977) account of the historical development that led to the emergence of the criminal law illustrates further the absence of any intrinsic quality that differentiates acts defined as criminal from civil wrongs. He writes:

At this stage of legal development there was no differentiation between what we know as crime or criminal law and tort or civil liability for damage inflicted. All injuries to persons or property were considered as "wrongs." The seriousness of the wrong depended upon the disruption caused to the community or the actual or perceived affront to the injured parties. Slowly, a distinction emerged between wrongs which were private disputes and required payment to the injured party or his kin and wrongs which had a public quality and required compensation to the whole group. (1977: 28)

5. In an American survey cited by Steinmetz (1986:56) spanking, the most prevalent form of family violence, was reported to occur in between 84% and 97% of all American families.

6. Thornberry and Figlio (1972) examined victimization and criminal behavior using a 10% sample of individuals drawn from a 1945 Philadelphia birth cohort. The sample consisted of 975 members, about 60% of whom were found and interviewed. The data revealed that arrest status was strongly and consistently associated with victimization. In *all* 24 comparisons those subjects who had been arrested were more likely than those who had not been arrested to be the victim of a crime. Furthermore, 18 of these 24 comparisons were statistically significant

In the follow-up survey to the Philadelphia birth cohort, a study of self-reported victimization, Singer (1981) examined the extent to which victims are also guilty of serious assault. He reports that cohort members who were shot or stabbed were most often nonwhite, and when they were surveyed they were high school dropouts, unemployed, and single. They were also involved more frequently in official and self-reported criminal activity. Victims of serious assault had the highest probability of having a friend arrested, belonging to a gang, using a weapon, committing a serious assault, and being officially arrested. Singer concluded that his findings, along with those of other studies examining the victim-offender interaction, indicate support for the homogeneity of victim-offender populations involved in serious assaultive conduct.

Johnson et al. (1973) followed up all victims of gunshot and stab wounds admitted to the City of Austin Hospital in Texas during 1968 and 1969. They found that 75% of the male victims had a criminal record, and 54% had a jail record. Savitz, Lalli, and Rosen (1977), using a Philadelphia cohort, also observed an association between official records of having committed assault and assault victimization. And in their London, England, survey, Sparks, Genn, and Dodd (1977) found victims of violent crime to be significantly more likely than nonvictims to self-report the commission of violent crimes.

7. Gottfredson (1984) analyzed the 1982 British Crime Survey data and was struck by the relatively strong interrelationship between offending and victimization. For persons with at least one self-reported violence offense, the likelihood of victimization was 42%, or seven times the likelihood of personal victimization for persons reporting no self-reported violent offenses. Suspecting that the source of the relationship between offending and victimization might be the common association between age and delinquency, Gottfredson controlled for age. The relationship between self-reported delinquencies and self-reported violence and personal victimization persisted despite the controls. And the relationships between self-reported offending and both personal and household victimization also seemed to hold regardless of place of residence. Gottfredson suggests that there is probably a life-style that, for some, includes high probabilities of misfortune, victimization, and offending, due perhaps to where they live, where they go, and with whom they associate. In other words, the social processes that produce high rates of offending in some segments of the population may also be productive to high rates of victimization. Gottfredson went on to test various hypotheses about these interrelationships using the British Crime Survey data. The data strongly suggested that life-styles conducive to victimization of all forms are also conducive to offending.

8. In an attempt to illustrate this point, Singer (1986) makes reference to De Sica's classic film, *The Bicycle Thief,* in which the victim of a bicycle theft steals someone else's bicycle after a fruitless search.

9. Kòhlhorn and Svensson (1982) suggest that the more stringent the measures taken to control the opportunity structure for a particular type of crime, the greater the probability of success in reducing the number of such crimes. They also note that the opportunity structure is determined, inter alia, by the contacts between perpetrator and victim, and factors such as the proximity, attraction, and accessibility of the victim or object to potential criminals play an important role (p. 14).

10. It should be emphasized that the difference between professionals and occasional or amateurish criminals in the way they choose their targets does not reflect a difference in character or personality but simply a difference in their modus operandi.

11. For the sake of brevity one example will suffice to back up this claim. In her study of shoplifting in Chicago, Cameron (1964) points out that the lavish displays of merchandise that department stores exhibit to encourage impulsive buying are, for the experienced pilferer, there for the taking. Gibbens and Prince (1962) reported that a store in England set out to achieve a certain level of shoplifting to demonstrate the adequate lure of the goods on display. If the shoplifting rate fell below the anticipated level, the store rearranged its shelves and counters on the assumption that they were not offering sufficient temptation for impulse buying — and stealing.

References

Anttila, I., & Jaakkola, R. 1966. *Unrecorded criminality in Finland* (Series A:2). Helsinki: Institute of Criminology.

Aspelin, E. et al. 1975. *Some developments in Nordic criminal policy.* Scandinavian Research Council for Criminology.

Baldwin, J. 1974. The role of the victim in certain property offences. *Criminal Law Review,* 353–58.

Becker, H. 1963. *Outsiders.* London: Free Press of Glencoe.

Becker, G.S. 1968. Crime and punishment: An economic approach. *Journal of Political Economy.* 76:169–217.

Belson, W.A., Millerson, G.L. & Didcott, P.J. 1970. *The development of a procedure for eliciting information from boys about the nature and extent of their stealing.* London: London School of Economics - Survey Research Centre.

Bennett,T., & Wright, R. 1984. *Burglars on burglary: prevention and the offender.* Aldershot, Hants: Gower Publishing Co. Ltd.

Blazicek, D.L. 1979. The criminal's victim: A theoretical note on the social psychology of victim selection. *Journal of Crime and Justice* 1:113–31.

Brantingham, P.J., & Brantingham, P.L. 1975. The spatial patterning of burglary. *Howard Journal* 14:11–23.

———. 1981. *Environmental criminology.* Beverly Hills: Sage Publications.

———. 1984. *Patterns in crime.* New York: Macmillan.

Brownmiller, S. 1975. *Against our will: Men, women and rape.* New York: Simon and Schuster.

Cameron, Mary Owen. 1964. *The booster and the snitch: Department store shoplifting.* London: Macmillan Limited.

Carroll, J., & Weaver, F. 1986. Shoplifters' perceptions of crime opportunities: A process-tracing study. In D. Cornish & R. Clarke (Eds.), *The reasoning criminal – Rational choice perspectives on offending.* New York: Springer Verlag.

Chappell, D., & James, J. 1986. Victim selection and apprehension from the rapist's perspective: A preliminary investigation. In K. Miyazawa & M. Ohya (Eds.), *Victimology in comparative perspective.* Tokyo: Seibundo Publishing Co.

Chambers, G., & Tombs, J. (Eds.). 1984. *The British crime survey Scotland* (A Scottish Office Social Research Study). Edinburgh: Her Majesty's Stationery Office.

Christie, N. 1952. Fangevoktere i Konsentrasjonsleire. *Nordisk Tidskrift for Kriminalvidenskap* 41:439–58. (Also published as a book in 1972.)

Christie, N. et al. 1965. A study of self-reported crime. In K.O. Christiansen (Ed.), *Scandinavian studies in criminology* (Vol. 1). London: Tavistock Publications.

Cloward, R.A., & Ohlin, L.E. 1961. *Delinquency and opportunity – A theory of delinquent gangs.* New York: The Free Press.

Cook, P.J. 1977. Punishment and crime: A critique of current findings concerning the preventive effects of punishment. *Law and Contemporary Problems* 41:164–204.

———. 1980. Research in criminal deterrence: Laying the groundwork for the second decade. In N. Morris & M. Tonry (Eds.), *Crime and justice: An annual review of research* (Vol. 2, 211–68). Chicago: University of Chicago Press.

Cohen, L.E., & Felson, M. 1979. Social change and crime rate trends: A routine activities approach. *American Sociological Review* 44:588–608.

Cohen, L.E., Kluegel, J.R., & Land, K.C. 1981, October. Social inequality and predatory criminal victimization: An exposition and test of a formal theory. *American Sociological Review* 46:505–24.

Cornish, D.B., & Clarke, R.V. 1986. *The reasoning criminal: Rational choice perspectives on offending.* New York: Springer Verlag.

Cressey, D. 1953. *Other people's money: A study in the social psychology of embezzlement.* Glencoe, IL: The Free Press.

Darrow, C. 1902. *Resist not evil.* (Reprinted in 1972, Montclair, NJ: Patterson Smith.)

Doleschal, Eugene. 1970. Hidden crime. *Crime and Delinquency Literature* 2:546–72.

Elmhorn, K. 1965. Study in self-reported delinquency among school children in Stockholm. In *Scandinavian Studies in Criminology* 1:117–46. London: Tavistock.

Fattah, E.A. 1971. *La Victime est-elle Coupable?* Montréal: Les Presses de l'Université de Montréal.

———. 1976. The use of the victim as an agent of self-legitimization: Towards a dynamic explanation of criminal behavior. In E.C. Viano (Ed.), *Victims and society.* Washington, DC: Visage Press, Inc.

———. 1989. Victims and victimology: The facts and the rhetoric. *International Review of Victimology* 1(1):43–66.

———. 1991. *Understanding criminal victimization.* Scarborough, Ont.: Prentice Hall.

Felson, R.B., & Steadman, H.J. 1983. Situational factors in disputes leading to criminal violence. *Criminology* 21(1):59–74.

Ferri, E. 1917. *Criminal sociology.* New York: Agathon Press.

Forward, S., & Buck, C. 1983. *Betrayal of innocence – Incest and its devastation.* New York: Penguin Books.

Garofalo, R. 1885. *Criminology* (Translated and published in English by Little Brown).

Gibbons, D.C. 1971. Observations on the study of crime causation. *American Journal of Sociology* 77:262–78.

Gibbens, T.C.N., & Prince, Joyce. 1967. *Shoplifting: A report on research carried out under the auspices of the I.S.T.D.* London: The Institute for the Study and Treatment of Delinquency.

Gottfredson, M.R. 1981. On the etiology of criminal victimization. *Journal of Criminal Law and Criminology* 72(2):714–26.

———. 1984. *Victims of crime: The dimensions of risk* (Home Office Research and Planning Unit Report No. 81). London: HMSO.

Gottfredson, M.R., & Hirschi, T. 1990. *A general theory of crime.* Stanford: Stanford University Press.

Greven, P. 1991. *Spare the child – The religious roots of punishment and the psychological impact of physical abuse.* New York: Alfred A. Knopf.

Hartogs, R. 1951, March. Discipline in the early life of sex delinquents and sex criminals. *Nervous Child* 9:167–73.

Hindelang, M., Gottfredson, M., & Garofalo, J. 1978. *Victims of personal crime: An empirical foundation for a theory of personal victimization.* Cambridge, MA: Ballinger Publishing Company.

Hooton, E.A. 1939. *Crime and the man.* Cambridge, MA: Harvard University Press.

Hough, M. 1987. Offenders' choice of target: Findings from victim surveys. *Journal of Quantitative Criminology* 3(4):355–69.

Hulsman, L. 1986. Critical criminology and the concept of crime. In H. Bianchi & R. Van Swaanigen (Eds.), *Abolitionism: Towards a nonrepressive approach to crime.* Amsterdam: Free University Press.

Jensen, G.F., & Brownfield, D. 1986. Gender, lifestyles, and victimization: Beyond routine activity. *Violence and Victims* 1(2):85–99.

Johnson, J., Kerper, H.B., Hayes, D., & Killinger, G.G. 1973. The recidivist victim: A descriptive study. *Criminal Justice Monographs* 4(1). Huntsville, TX: Sam Houston State University.

Katz, J. 1988. *Seductions of crime*. New York: Basic Books.

Kinberg, O. 1960. *Les problemes fondamentaux de la criminologie*. Paris: Cujas.

Kòhlhorn, E., & Svensson, B. 1982. *Crime prevention*. Stockholm: The National Swedish Council for Crime Prevention.

Lauritsen, J.L., Sampson, R.J., & Laub, J.H. 1991. The link between offending and victimization among adolescents. *Criminology* 29 (2):265–92.

LeBeau, J.L. 1987. The journey to rape: Geographical distance and the rapist's method of approaching the victim. *Journal of Police Science and Administration* 15(2):129–36.

Letkemann, P. 1973. *Crime as work*. Englewood Cliffs, NJ: Prentice Hall.

Luckenbill, D.F. 1977. Criminal homicide as a situated transaction. *Social Problems* 25(2):176–86.

Maguire, M., & Bennett, T. 1982. *Burglary in a dwelling*. London: Heinemann Educational Books Ltd.

Matza, D. 1964. *Delinquency and drift*. New York: John Wiley & Sons.

———. 1969. *Becoming deviant*. Englewood Cliffs, NJ: Prentice Hall.

Mayhew, P., & Elliott, D. 1990. Self-reported offending, victimization, and the British crime survey. *Journal of Violence and Victims* 5(2):83–96.

Mednick, S.A., & Christiansen, K.D. 1977. *Biosocial bases of criminal behavior*. New York: Gardner.

Mednick, S.A., Moffitt, T.E., & Stack, S.A. 1987. *The causes of crime: New biological approaches*. Cambridge: Cambridge University Press.

Milgram, S. 1969. *Obedience to authority: An experimental view*. New York: Harper and Row.

Morris, N., & Hawkins, G. 1969. *The honest politician's guide to crime control*. Chicago: University of Chicago Press.

Parker, G. 1977. *An introduction to criminal law*. Toronto: Methuen.

Quinney, R. 1975. *Criminology: An analysis and critique of crime in America*. Boston: Little Brown.

Redl, F., & Wineman, D. 1951. *Children who hate*. Glencoe, IL: The Free Press.

Reiss, Al., Jr. 1981, Summer. Foreword: Towards a revitalization of theory and research on victimization by crime. *The Journal of Criminal Law and Criminology* 72(2):704–10.

Robert, P. 1966. *Les bandes d'adolescents*. Paris: les Editions Ouvrières.

Savitz, L., Lalli, M. & Rosen, L. 1977. *City life and delinquency—Victimization, fear of crime, and gang membership*. Washington, DC: U.S. Government Printing Office.

Schwendinger, H., & Schwendinger, J. 1967. Delinquent stereotypes of probable victims. In M.W. Klein & B.G. Meyerhoff (Eds.), *Juvenile gangs in context* (91–105). Englewood Cliffs, NJ: Prentice Hall.

Sellin, T. 1938. *Culture conflict and crime*. New York: Social Science Research Council.

Shoemaker, D.J. 1990. *Theories of delinquency* (2nd Ed.). N.Y.: Oxford University Press.

Singer, S. 1981, Summer. Homogeneous victim-offender populations: A review and some research implications. *The Journal of Criminal Law and Criminology* 72(2):779–88.

———. 1986. Victims of serious violence and their criminal behavior: Subcultural theory and beyond. *Victims and Violence* 1 (1):61–70.

Smith, S.J. 1986. *Crime, space and society.* Cambridge: Cambridge University Press.

Sparks, R., Genn, H.G., & Dodd, D.J. 1977. *Surveying victims.* Toronto: John Wiley & Sons.

Steinmetz, Suzanne K. 1980. Violence-prone families. *Annals of the New York Academy of Sciences* 347:251–65.

———. 1986. The violent family. In Mary Lystad (Ed.), *Violence in the home: Interdisciplinary perspectives.* New York: Brunner/Mazel.

Sumner, W.G. 1906. *Folkways. A study of the sociological importance of usages.* New York: Ginn & Co.

Sutherland, E. 1937. *The professional thief.* Chicago: University of Chicago Press.

Sutherland, E., & Cressey, D. 1978. *Criminology* (10th ed.). Philadelphia: Lippincott.

Sykes, G., & Matza, D. 1957. Techniques of neutralization: A theory of delinquency. *American Sociological Review* 22:664–70.

Tarde, G. 1886. *La Criminalitée Comparée.* Paris: Alcan.

Thornberry, T.P., & Figlio, R.M. 1972. *Victimization and criminal behavior in a birth cohort.* Paper presented at the meetings of the American Society of Criminology, Caracas, Venezuela.

Tsutomi, H. 1991. Reformulating Cloward and Ohlin's differential opportunity theory into rational choice perspective: Occupational orientation of Japanese institutionalized delinquents. Paper presented at the ASC meeting in San Francisco.

United States. 1979. *The cost of negligence: Losses from preventable household burglaries.* (NCJISS). Washington, DC: National Criminal Justice Information and Statistics Service, Government Printing Office.

van Dijk, J., & Steinmetz, C.H.D. 1984. The burden of crime in Dutch society, 1973–1979. In Richard Block (Ed.), *Victimization and fear of crime: World perspective* (29–43). Washington, DC: U.S. Dept. of Justice, Bureau of Justice Statistics.

Wallerstein, J.A., & Wyle, C.J. 1947. Our law-abiding lawbreakers. *Federal Probation* 25:107–12.

Walsh, D. 1986. Victim selection procedures among economic criminals: The rational choice perspective. In D.B. Cornish and R.V. Clarke (Eds.), *The reasoning criminal: Rational choice perspectives on offending.* New York: Springer Verlag.

Wikstrom, P-O.H. 1991. *Urban crime, criminals, and victims.* New York: Springer Verlag.

Wilkins, L. 1964. *Social deviance.* London: Tavistock Publications.

Wilson, D.A. 1987. *Target selection in robbery: An exploratory investigation.* Unpublished masters thesis, Simon Fraser University, Burnaby, BC.

Wilson, J.Q., & Herrnstein, R.J. 1985. *Crime and human nature.* New York: Simon and Schuster.

Wolfgang, Marvin. 1958. *Patterns in criminal homicide.* Philadelphia: University of Pennsylvania Press.

———. 1956. Husband-wife homicides. *Journal of Social Therapy* 2:263–71.

————. 1957. Victim-precipitated criminal homicide. *Journal of Criminal Law, Criminology and Police Science* 48(1):1–11.

Wootton, B. 1963. *Crime and the criminal law: Reflections of a magistrate and social scientist.* London: Stevens and Sons.

Wright, R., & Logie, R.H. 1988. How young house burglars choose targets? *The Howard Journal* 27(2):92–104.

Yochelson, S., & Samenow, S.E. 1976, 1977. *The criminal personality* (2 Vol.). New York: Jason Aronson.

Zimbardo, P. 1972. Pathology of punishment. *Trans-Action* 9:4–8.

11

Environment, Routine, and Situation: Toward a Pattern Theory of Crime

Patricia L. Brantingham and Paul J. Brantingham

As a discipline, criminology tries to understand and explain crime and criminal behavior. This poses fascinating and long-standing questions: Why do some people commit crimes while others do not? Why are some people frequently victimized while others suffer only rarely? Why do some places experience a lot of crime while other places experience almost none? The answers to these questions seem, to us, to reside in understanding the patterns formed by the rich complexities of criminal events. Each criminal event is an opportune cross-product of law, offender motivation, and target characteristic arrayed on an environmental backcloth at a particular point in space-time. Each element in the criminal event has some historical trajectory shaped by past experience and future intention, by the routine activities and rhythms of life, and by the constraints of the environment.[1] Patterns within these complexities, considered over many criminal events, should point us toward understandings of crime as a whole.

Unfortunately, despite the inherent complexity in criminal events, most attempts at explanation have been restricted to simple, unicausal models of criminality, for example, Bentham's (1789) hedonistic psychology; Lombroso's (1911) biological predisposition; Sutherland's (1937a) learned attitudes; Lemert's (1951) secondary deviation; Cloward and Ohlin's (1960) blocked social opportunity; Taylor, Walton, and Young's (1973) capitalist socioeconomic structure. Such classic criminological theories have been far too limited, focusing primarily on conceptually constrained origins of the desire or willingness to commit crimes rather than on the complex patterns in crimes. The primary weakness in most criminological theory is a tendency to equate criminality with crime when criminality is but one of the elements contributing to a criminal event. This confusion has frequently been compounded by an insistence that a theory of criminality must lie completely within the domain of a single academic discipline. Thus, for instance, while Sutherland (1937a), and Taylor, Walton, and Young (1973), and Gottfredson and Hirschi (1990) might have agreed about little else, they all insisted that the explanation of criminality must be fundamentally sociological. Moreover, occasional attempts to construct multidisciplinary explanations of criminality have seemed to attract large volumes of criticism from all directions (e.g., Wolfgang and Ferracuti 1967; Wilson and Herrnstein 1986; Jeffery 1990).

Since the early 1970s, an alternative theoretical movement has focused on criminal events. Aimed explicitly at development of conceptual frameworks for explaining crimes and criminal behavior that cross disciplinary boundaries, this theoretical movement has accepted the need to explain crimes as etiologically complex patterns of behavior. The movement has assumed that crimes can be no more easily explained than headaches or backaches. Such classes of events will never be attributable to any single cause or understood through any single explanation. Understandable, interpretable patterns of events may, however, be derived from a diversity of causes. Many different types of spine and muscle difficulties can produce back pain for people who must lift heavy objects. But even perfectly healthy backs can be injured and produce prodigious quantities of pain if improper lifting techniques are used. Many different socioeconomic situations and psychological conditions can result in particular persons engaging in shoplifting, but no single factor will explain all, or even most, shoplifting. No single, simple model explains either back pain or crime. But patterns in events can point toward different etiologies or clusters of etiologies under different conditions.

The set of ideas encompassed by this alternative theoretical movement have developed under a variety of names: rational choice theory (Clarke and Cornish 1985; Cornish and Clarke 1986; Carter and Hill 1979; Walsh 1978; Brantingham and Brantingham 1978); routine activities theory (Felson 1987; Cohen and Felson 1979; Sherman et al. 1989); environmental criminology (Brantingham and Brantingham 1991, 1984, 1981; Herbert and Hyde 1985; Cromwell et. al 1991); strategic analysis (Cusson 1983); or lifestyle theory (Hindelang et al. 1978). Research, application and expansion of these theoretical ideas appear under such names as: crime prevention through environmental design (Jeffery 1971); situational crime prevention (Clarke 1980); hot spot analysis (Block 1990; Illinois

Criminal Justice Information Authority 1989); or opportunity theory (Barlow 1990; Carroll and Weaver 1986). While this group of new theoretical, research, and practical approaches to the study of crime vary in content and in specific focus, they do have several things in common:

- Criminal events are best viewed as the end points in a decision process or sequence of decision steps. This decision process may not always involve conscious and explicit sequential decision making, but does result, in almost all cases, in rationally predictable actions. For example, cars seem to "drive themselves to work" many mornings, but the route "they" follow and the decisions "they" make on the way are the product of conscious decisions that have been made in the past in establishing the pathways routinely used for trips to work. On such mornings, of course, people are really driving without needing to pay much conscious attention to routine decisions. Sometimes, of course, the driving process is fully conscious because the trip is not routine: an accident changes traffic flows; the driver has a meeting at a client's office he or she has not visited before; and so forth. The decisions that take an offender to a particular criminal event may similarly be conscious or subconscious or some mixture, but they are neither random nor unpredictable and they are reconstructible (Clarke and Cornish 1985; Cusson 1983; Brantingham and Brantingham 1978; Walsh 1978; Willmer 1970).[2]

- The decision process leading to the commission of any particular crime begins with someone who is in a state of readiness for crime (Clarke and Cornish 1985), that is, someone who has sufficient current criminal motivation and knowledge both to perceive and to act upon some available criminal opportunity when it is discovered within known activity areas and associated awareness spaces (Brantingham and Brantingham 1984, 1981). Opportunities may be discovered either in the course of ordinary noncriminal activities or through a specific search for criminal targets. Someone who is ready to commit a bank robbery may see a "good" bank serendipitously while eating lunch with a friend (Letkemann 1973) or may find one after careful search and surveillance (Gabor et al. 1987:57–60). Burglars tend to look for targets within familiar areas, starting from a few key activity nodes such as home, a work site, a favorite pub, or a shopping center where they spend a good deal of time (Brantingham and Brantingham 1981; Maguire 1982; Rengert and Wasilchick 1985; Cromwell et al. 1991).

- Particular criminal motivation levels or states of readiness to commit crime come from diverse, but quite understandable, sources. Motivation or readiness may be seen as tied to goals. These goals involve a desire for action or a search for thrills or self-defined fun; or a wish to acquire some object or make a profit; or an inclination toward aggression or highly emotional behavior in defense or in vengeance; or a wish to dominate (Cusson 1983; West 1982).

- Whether a general state of readiness is reflected in criminal acts depends in part on psychological, social, and cultural background states of the individual; the economic environment; a history of past activities; and, to a large extent, the opportunities available.[3] For example, a group of teenagers' desire for "action" may involve a noisy walk down a business street after closing hours when no one is around or it may involve a confrontation with awakened residents of a street in a suburban neighborhood. The confrontation may lead to the teenagers' departure or to more noise or it may result in the teenagers vandalizing fences or stealing bicycles to "get even."

- The number and sequence of decision points in the process that leads to a criminal event vary with the type and quality of crime (Brantingham and Brantingham 1978). Traditional divisions of crimes into violent and property categories are insufficient to addresses these variations. Some violent crimes, such as serial rape, may involve long decision sequences, while others such as bar assaults may involve very short decision sequences. Some property crimes, such as antique burglary (Maguire 1982: 90–121) or store robbery (Gabor et al. 1987:59) may involve long decision sequences, but others, such as teenage burglary, shoplifting, or vandalism may involve very short decision sequences.

- Criminal readiness levels are not constant in any individual but vary over time and place given both the individual's background behavior and site-specific situations. For example, burglary is sometimes the product of changes in mood and perception brought on by drugs or alcohol, but is sometimes undertaken to get money with which to buy drugs (Cromwell et al. 1991; Chaiken and Chaiken 1990; Rengert and Wasilchick 1985; Maguire 1982). Readiness clearly is also related to age (Brantingham 1991; Gottfredson and Hirschi 1990). Criminal activity, in the aggregate, is dominated by the young.

- Neither motivated offenders nor opportunities for crime are uniformly distributed in space and time. Specific types of crime tend to be closely tied to the locations of targets and the regular travel patterns of potential offenders. The locations of targets and of potential offenders usually vary with the time of the day, the characteristics of specific targets, and the site and situation surrounding the targets. Shoplifting is obviously tied to hours the stores are open and places where stores are located. Spousal (or partner) assault is usually an evening or weekend crime occurring at home or in a bar. Car thefts are tied to the locations of unguarded cars, and follow a rhythm associated with commuting patterns during the week and with leisure activities on weekends. Routine activities develop the framework of opportunities for crime (Felson 1987; Cohen and Felson 1979).

Target suitability is tied both to the characteristics of the target and to the characteristics of the target's surroundings. The declining weight of portable television sets over the course of the 1950s and 1960s serves as a good predictor of increasing theft over time (Felson and Cohen 1981). Portable computers may be attractive objects, but they are not suitable targets for theft when they are in use.[4] The same object found unsuitable as a target at one time of day may become a suitable target at a different time of day, when it is not in use, and no one is around. Cars may have been attractive targets early in the century, when they were rare and extremely valuable, and when registration procedures were primitive and uncertain; they became less suitable during the mid-century period when they became commonplace and when registration procedures became more rigorous (Gould 1969; but see Mayhew 1990). A convenience store may be a good robbery target when only a single clerk is present, but may be an unsuitable target when customers or multiple clerks are present (Hunter and Jeffery 1992; Duffala 1976).

The identification of what makes a good or suitable target is itself a multistaged decision process contained within some general environment. The process may involve just a few stages or many. This process, first described in 1978 (Brantingham and Brantingham 1978; Walsh 1978) and well supported by subsequent research (e.g., Walsh 1986; Cromwell et al. 1991), involves several levels tied to actual perception and learning about the surrounding environment.

Individuals develop "images" of what surrounds them. Not all environmental details are recognized in these images; some stand out. The image that is formed depends on the underlying characteristics of the surrounds, but also on what a person is doing. A person engaged in the process of committing a crime will be looking for details, conditions, a "feeling" of correctness that are related to that specific form of crime.

These images, representing a process-based perception of objects within a complex environment, are frequently called *templates*[5] (Brantingham and Brantingham 1978). A template is an aggregate, holistic image that is not always easily analyzed or understood by fragmenting it into discrete parts (Brantingham and Brantingham 1978; Macdonald and Gifford 1989; Cromwell et al. 1991). It is generally formed by developing an array of cues, cue sequences, and cue clusters that identify what should be considered a "good" target in specific sites and situations.[6]

- Templates vary by specific crimes, offenders, and the general context for the crime. What makes a "good" target and crime situation for a robber in central Houston is different from what makes up a "good" target and crime situation for a first-time shoplifter in a suburban mall, yet the templates are understandable. For some they involve evaluating risk and benefits; for others, excitement; for others showing "importance." Yet there is enough similarity in how people engage in crime, how they perceive or grow to have a cognitive image of an environment, that general templates can be "constructed" to help explain specific crime patterns.[7]

Overall, this newer approach to criminology sees crimes as complex, but even assuming high degrees of complexity, finds discernible patterns both for crimes and for criminals at both detailed and general levels of analysis. *Pattern* is a term used to describe recognizable interconnectiveness of objects, processes, or ideas. This interconnectiveness may be physical or conceptual, but recognizing the interconnectiveness involves the cognitive process of "seeing" similarity, of discerning prototypes or exemplars of interconnections within cases distorted by local conditions (Churchland 1989). A pattern is sometimes obvious, but sometimes is discernible only through an initial insight, particularly an insight that is embedded within the environment as a whole.[8] Crimes are patterned; decisions to commit crimes are patterned; and the process of committing a crime is patterned. These patterns are nontrivial, though opaque, when crime is being explained by some unicausal model, but become clear when crimes are viewed as etiologically complex and as occurring within and as a result of a complex surrounding environment.

Pattern Theory

The complementary work being done in this new movement fits together into what could be called pattern theory. Crimes do not occur randomly or uniformly in time or space or society. Crimes do not occur randomly or uniformly across neighborhoods, or social groups, or during an individual's daily activities, or during an individual's lifetime. In fact, arguing a uniformity seems indefensible. Why would 5% or 40% of all Europeans or females or teenage males or residents of Chicago commit a robbery or a theft or an assault every day at 4:00 P.M. or every week on Friday? Neither is an argument for the complete randomness of behavior plausible. Bar fights do occur with greater frequency on Friday nights than on Tuesday afternoons; shoplifting does occur during a restricted set of hours in the day; income tax evasions do cluster around payment due dates; some neighborhoods do have a lot more crime than others. Yet while we accept nonuniformity and the nonrandomness of crime, most theoretical approaches to crime define concepts that point toward uniformity and assume randomness for the impact of all concepts not included in the theory. They fail to provide concepts or models that can be used to account for the patterned nonuniformity and nonrandomness that characterizes real criminal events.

The limitations of most criminological theories come from many sources. We want conceptually limited models. All sciences, social or natural, want understandable theories. In the natural sciences, such as physics or chemistry, theories are developed within a well-defined, closed intellectual environment.[9] The social sciences cannot exist in a closed or limited environment. The concepts in social sciences may never be conceived or viewed, except as a game, without considering how they interact with a highly variable, never static environmental backcloth, that is, an ever-changing set of sociocultural, economic, legal, structural, and physical surroundings that include, among other things, the activities of individuals, of groups, and of organizations. No firm boundary can be placed around particular elements within a theory that can separate them from the backcloth.[10]

Elements of the backcloth are interconnected and never static. Change is a constant condition of the backcloth, but the types of changes, degrees of change, and rates of change among the elements vary. Change is sometimes slow and minimal; sometimes rapid, massive, and dramatic. For example, the general backcloth for theft in Chicago in 1910 and 1990 might not be considered very different if we were to consider only the street network, but when changes in the character of goods (Felson and Cohen 1981), in the composition of the work force (Cohen and Felson 1979), and in the modes of travel are considered, it is clear why Chic Conwell's description of the good places and situations in which to pick pockets (Sutherland 1937b) no longer holds.

A theory of crime must be flexible, able to explain criminal events against diverse variations in the backcloth. To be of much value, a theory must make it possible to recognize and understand both individual and aggregate patterns of behavior at many levels of resolution. Recognizing patterns, however, is not easy when criminologists focus on fixed theoretical concepts that cannot vary as the backcloth varies. An explanation of how criminal behavior changes as the backcloth varies will produce clear patterns, but such an explanation requires a focus on process, that is, on change itself. Crime is an event that is best viewed as an action that occurs within a situation at a site on a nonstatic backcloth. Crime is the product of varying initial conditions under which the decision processes leading to criminal events unfold. The likelihood of a criminal event transpiring depends on the backcloth, the site, the situation, an individual's criminal readiness, routine activity patterns, and the distribution of targets. None of these elements can, independently, be expected to explain criminal events. They must be considered cojointly with special emphasis on how they shape choices.

Crime is an event that occurs when an individual with some criminal readiness level encounters a suitable target in a situation sufficient to activate that readiness potential. This essentially simple model becomes remarkably complex in real applications because all of its elements are variables. Readiness to commit a crime is not constant: it varies from person to person; and it varies for each individual person across time and space as the backcloth varies. It also varies as the awareness of opportunities to commit a crime vary. Targets are not constant. The types of objects and the categories of people that constitute good targets vary in time and space as the backcloth changes. The distributions of targets vary in time and space. The situation required to activate criminal behavior also varies with the backcloth and the distribution of targets and the level of a given individual's readiness to commit a crime. Motivation influences the commission of crimes; the characteristics of targets and decisions about the quality of a given opportunity to commit a crime influence motivation.

To understand more about criminal behavior and crimes, it is perhaps useful to consider (1) the actual process of committing a crime; (2) the general crime templates and activities of offenders at the moment of crime commission; (3) offenders' readiness or willingness to commit a crime; and (4) the interaction of process, template, activity, and readiness as they are arrayed on the environmental backcloth.

Event Process

Figure 11.1 shows a simplified view of the process followed in the commission of a crime by an individual. A person is engaging in some behavior. An event occurs that "triggers" the desire or willingness to commit a crime. The person, depending on the type of criminal behavior, may see a situation and site making the crime possible (immediately) or may engage in search behavior to find a good site and situation (or "place") for the crime. A person could be drinking with friends and someone comes by saying there is a chance to break into the electronics store down the block. This chance may trigger the person into going along to the store and, assuming no problems are encountered, breaking into the store. Or, a man could be drinking with friends when someone he does not like

FIGURE 11.1
Process

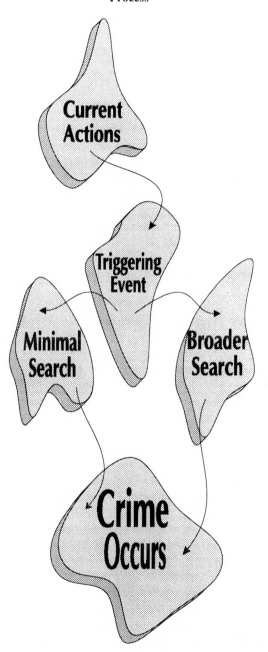

walks by and accidentally spills beer on him. The spilled beer could trigger an angry exchange — vicious words or gestures — leading to a fight.[11]

The process shown in figure 11.1 may be broken down into many steps and considered in detail. The detailed process for shoplifting (Walsh 1978) is different from the detailed process for robbery (Gabor et al. 1987; Feeney 1986). The process for shoplifting in a market (Poyner 1983; Poyner and Webb 1992) is different from the process for shoplifting in a department store (Carroll and Weaver 1986). The process for street robbery is different from the process for store robbery or bank robbery (Gabor et al. 1987; Feeney and Weir 1973; Clarke et al. 1991; Ekblom 1992). Yet, there are common elements in the processes involved in all of these crimes, common elements that produce discernible patterns for each type of crime: decisions or choices occur in the process of committing all crimes. Choices are made and actions follow the choices. The process of decision making and the resulting patterns of decisions must be understood as a prelude to understanding crime (Clarke and Cornish 1985; Cornish and Clarke 1986; Cusson and Pinsonneault 1986).

Template/Activity Backcloth

While forming patterns in the foreground, the event process rests on a general backcloth[12] formed by routine activities (including repeat or routine criminal activities) and on a template that helps identify what a "great" chance is or what a "good" opportunity would be or how to search for chances and opportunities. Almost everyone develops activity routines, a set of repetitive processes that organize most of life's actions. People who commit crimes spend most of their time engaged in noncriminal behavior. These activity routines form a patterned backcloth on which criminal events are played out and against which crime may be studied. As with all patterned behavior, routine activities can be viewed at many levels of analysis or aggregation. At a microlevel, descriptions would involve a minute by minute log of activities and actions. At a mesolevel descriptions would involve the general timing and sequencing of activities in broad categories such as sleep hours, travel time, work hours. Macrodescriptions might look at annual or seasonal patterns of behavior.

Individual patterns at any level of analysis may be aggregated into group patterns spanning many individuals. The aggregate patterns may be viewed temporally or spatially or both. As an extreme example, there are points in any city that are always congested at rush hour, others that are empty during work hours. Both individuals and aggregates display routine activity patterns. (see Chapin 1974; Cohen and Felson 1979; Rengert and Wasilchick 1985; Felson 1987). At all levels of aggregation, actual current activities describing what is happening in a particular instance can be compared to routine activity patterns. Ordinarily, current actions are very strongly related to recent routine activity patterns. Past actions and activities do help "drive" current actions, just as a car might "drive itself" to work or to the supermarket, but unusual events can shape current actions or alter routine activity patterns for a short time.

Routine activities shape an activity space (both in time and in physical space) and, from that activity space, people develop an awareness space (Brantingham and Brantingham 1984). The awareness space is limited, both physically and temporally. Residents do not know their entire city or town. Workers know only a limited space around their workplace. This awareness space is formed by past activities and shapes the time and location of future activities. Routine activity space places people in situations, both physically and temporally, where crime triggering events are more or less likely to occur. If a criminal event is triggered, the awareness space shapes the search area in which targets or victims are sought. For example, routine activities define target search patterns by burglars (Brantingham and Brantingham 1975; Carter and Hill 1979; Maguire 1982; Rengert and Wasilchick 1985; Cromwell et al. 1991) and high activity bars identify centers of violence (Bullock 1955; Engstad 1975; Brantingham and Brantingham 1981; Roncek and Pravatiner 1989; Roncek and Maier 1991).

Routine activities of potential offenders generally define both the areas where and the times when they are likely to commit a crime. The routine activities of potential victims also shape the patterns of crimes (Fattah 1991; Kennedy and Forde 1990; Lasley 1989; Maume 1989). For example, the routine activities in residential areas (many homes are empty during the workday) and of residents (regularly away from home during the workday) and the routine commercial display activities of department stores create the base pattern of opportunities from which potential property offenders who know about the area select sites and targets.[13] The routine activity and awareness spaces of repeat offenders change as a result of their prior crimes. They also change as modes and means of transit change. Suburbanization, mass transit, and new highways alter movement patterns, routine activities, and awareness spaces. Residents' knowledge of areas grows. Exploration in known areas may increase as knowledge grows. At the opposite extreme, burglars from "out of town" rarely seem to pick targets far from the main roads traversing a community (Maguire 1982; Fink 1969). Their local awareness space is limited.[14]

Target selection also depends on mental templates used to shape searches for targets or victims and to predefine the characteristics of a suitable target or suitable place for finding targets. The templates, that is, the sets of cues, cue sequences, or holistic cue clusters used to find and identify suitable targets, vary by crime, by site and situation, and by the offender and his or her reason for the crime. For example, Eck and Spelman (1992) identify the differences in the templates used by a group of white offenders and a group of black offenders who are both stealing from cars parked in the same massive parking lot. Similarly, but using a much more formal procedure for understanding template construction, Macdonald and Gifford (1989) identify cues used by adult and juvenile burglars. They find support for the idea that offenders construct and use holistic templates in identifying suitable targets, but also find that holistic judgment is related to specific crimes and situations in very understandable ways.

Figure 11.2 shows the relationship between the crime process and the backcloth formed by past activity. Routine activities, activity space, awareness space, and crime template may vary by individual, but probably form aggregate patterns for different categories of people and specific types of crimes. While these patterns do vary, they are frequently structured by age, sex, income, home location, friends' locations, work or school locations, the locations of places such as shops, bars, or restaurants that attract visitors, and the sociogeographic and physical structure of an area such as bus routes or highways.

Understanding crime patterns requires an understanding of these activity patterns. For example, the routine activities of juveniles form the base for higher volume crimes. Juveniles frequently hang out around a 24-hour convenience store or a fast-food restaurant. The store becomes a node in their routines and thereby becomes a node in their activity and awareness spaces. Casual, adventitious exploration around the convenience store makes surrounding streets and buildings a better known part of their awareness spaces. Vandalism, thefts from cars, common theft, and burglary are all likely be higher in these awareness spaces. If it happens that the hangout location is not surrounded by "good" targets, then juvenile goals of excitement will probably be expressed in other ways — noise, onsite vandalism, fighting — rather than through property crime. As another example, search patterns and associated awareness spaces and templates vary with experience. First offenders begin within a normal awareness space generated by noncriminal behavior (Brantingham and Brantingham 1984). Little Sidney Blotzman's career as a juvenile delinquent started with a theft of fruit from the corner store and expanded to shoplifting in the big department stores in the Loop as he and his friends gained more mobility by riding public transit (Shaw and Moore 1931). This implies that first offenders have imperfect templates and are at greater risk of error in picking targets and situations than are more experienced offenders. This also implies that beginners run greater risks of getting caught

FIGURE 11.2
Process and Activities

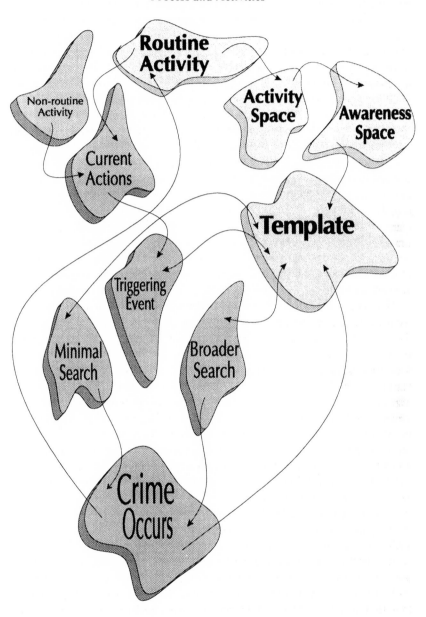

than experienced offenders, a possibility hinted at in the Cambridge co-hort study (West 1982:23).

Generally, individuals create templates used to identify "good" or "bad" or questionable targets. Felson (1987) uses the term *suitable target* to de-scribe targets identified as "good." Whether the offender is a shoplifter or a serial rapist, the potential target or victim and the site and situation surrounding help define what is considered "suitable." As Felson's work makes clear, the presence of a guardian for the target can be a critical situational variable. A shoplifter will not ordinarily try to steal something when a clerk or security guard is standing next to it. A serial rapist does not normally commit the rapes in public. Robbers do commit their robber-ies in public, but usually do not try to rob armed police officers. The presence of a guardian is not always dispositive, however. A fighting drunk may well try to hit a police officer who intervenes in an effort to break up a fight.

Different crimes occur in different behavior settings (Barker 1968) and unfold in different patterns of actions. What is suitable for one crime or crime site or situation is not necessarily suitable for another. Patterned behavior sets appear that define the usual or expected or "normal" actions associated with particular types of crimes and also define abnormal or unexpected actions for that type of crime in that behavior setting. Of course, behaviors that would be abnormal for one offense type would not necessarily be abnormal for another. Overall, it appears that identification of target suitability, that is, judgment of conformance with a template, is a gestalt-like process (Brantingham and Brantingham 1978; Macdonald and Gifford 1989; Cromwell et al. 1991) that is not dependent on some lim-ited number of fixed characteristics, but rather on an overall decision or sequence of decisions at a summary level. Viewed from the opposite direction, however, individual characteristics of the potential target site or situation may make some specific crimes unattractive. Consider Felson's concept of guardianship. A person sitting in a car may make that car and the cars surrounding it safe from theft; but the absence of someone in the car may not be enough to make an otherwise unappealing target crimi-nally attractive. It might, like a rusted-out Yugo, be a generally undesir-able make or model, even to car thieves.

Templates, awareness spaces, and routine activities are all interrelated and influence crime patterns and victimization (Cusson 1989). This is not a unidirectional influence. For first offenders, routine activities and gen-eral views may form a crime template that limits possible targets. Crime becomes a routine activity for repeat offenders who reinforce and change their initial crime templates, that is, build more stable images of target search and target selection processes. The changes in the process are shown with the directional arrows in figure 11.2. The large number of directional arrows represent the process of decision making when a crime is committed by an individual whether for the first time or the nth time. The feedback loops may have less importance for the analysis of aggregate crime patterns, but they are very important for understanding what happens during the commission of the initial crimes by both those who will be repeat offenders and those who will be "scared" off crime by the experience.

Process decisions, site and situation factors, the routine behavior of both the offenders and the potential victims, and availability of targets all help form the patterns of criminal events. There are triggers that actually touch off individual criminal events. These triggers and the consequences of criminal acts are sometimes, though not always, predictable but can be understood retrospectively. This lack of predictability comes in part from nonroutine, unusual, or extraordinary events. Nonroutine events, as noted in figure 11.2, may influence actions and, consequently, affect crime. At the extreme, natural disasters such as hurricanes, earthquakes or floods, or administrative disasters such as police strikes or electric power blackouts may open areas to looting. Large crowds at special events such as soccer matches, rock concerts, movie openings, and civic festivals may push people from boisterousness into riot.[15] In most of these situations, the nonroutine event has no long lasting impact, but has a strong influence on criminal behavior in the short run.

Readiness/Willingness

A particular criminal event depends on an individual being triggered. The triggers are generated or experienced during an activity, an action process. The triggers occur in a nonstatic, though mostly routine, situation. They are shaped by the surrounding environment, past experience, and the crime template. Generally, the commission of a crime is a decision process occurring within a limited activity environment and associated with bounded knowledge of the broader surroundings, but a process that is understandable when explored with event and environmental detail.

The criminal event is not independent of the existence of individuals with a readiness or willingness to commit a crime. As described earlier, much traditional criminology has been devoted to finding some unicausal source of motivation. All research and all well-reasoned arguments point, in our view, toward a complex etiology of the sort depicted in figure 11.3. The origin of the complex etiology seems clear when criminal events are explored within the pattern theory described in this article. There is no single force or single goal behind all crime. Individuals seem clearly tied to a multiplicity of identifiable goals. Cusson (1983) defines a taxonomy for goals of criminal behavior: action; appropriation; aggression; and domination.[16] For example, some may be bored and want excitement; others may be after a specific object; still others may want vengeance or want to gain prestige with their peers. Some may have multiple goals or have their goals change over time. In particular, the action/thrill goal making burglary attractive to young teenagers may change to the goal of appropriating money as the teenager gets older. The act, burglary, stays the same, but the purpose for it changes. The goal is tied or linked to a readiness or willingness to commit a crime (or readiness or willingness to engage in other behavior that satisfies the goal). The link depends on the routine activities of individuals, the range of potential triggering events, and their template of what represents a good target to satisfy their goal. Goals are also tied to the social/psychological and situational backcloth in and upon which a person lives.

It is the interactive nature of the link that is of primary importance. A goal of possession of an object, such as a portable computer, or for a particular type of action/excitement, like theft of a car, is tied to the availability of the object (computer or car) and its accessibility (seen as a suitable target).[17] The transformation of goals into readiness and willingness is tied to routine activities that help identify availability within someone's awareness space and the development of a template that identifies suitable targets. Readiness and willingness associated with goals do have varying levels. Action/excitement may mean a desire for a short thrill; it may mean a desire for a long-lasting thrill. The readiness to steal is also tied to readiness to take risks of being caught. The risks people will accept vary, but probably not in an inexplicable pattern.

Crime Type Variation in Readiness. The level of readiness or willingness necessary to commit a crime varies by type of crime. Stated another way, for certain types of offenses, such as petty thefts, it does not take much readiness for a situation to present a triggering event. For other types of crime, such as a residential break-in or a convenience store robbery, the state of readiness must be much higher before a criminal event can be triggered. Readiness for many crimes may be tied to actual risk. Some risk may lead to excitement; too much risk may lead to deterrent fear.

Feedback Effects. Willingness or readiness to commit a crime is unlikely to be independent of the site and situation of a potential crime or of past criminal events or of the triggering event. A person might steal cash off a table in a restaurant if it were a substantial amount and no one were around the empty table. A juvenile might be afraid and reluctant on his[18] first burglary, but be more comfortable the second time around, when his

FIGURE 11.3
Process, Activities, and Motivation

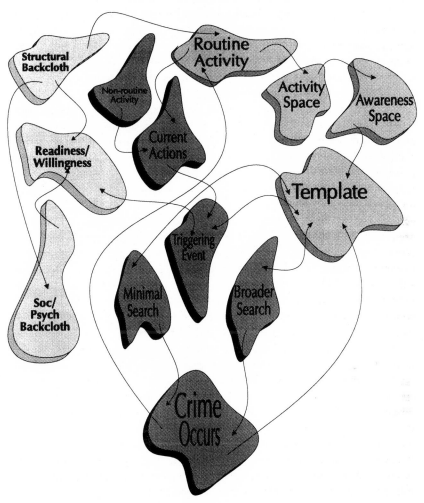

template identifying good targets has been better defined. A burglar might be forced into contact with the owner of a store he has entered and make a better haul as a result. Robbery might start to look easier. A serial rapist might encounter resistance and use excessive force for the first time.

Excessive force might become part of the rape pattern thereafter (Hazelwood et al. 1989). That is, the relationship between readiness and site and situation are mutually nonrecursive over time, with site and situation experiences feeding back into readiness as amplification or suppression loops; and reinforced or suppressed readiness feeding back into the crime template and the assessment of site and situation (Wilkins 1964; Clarke and Cornish 1985; Jeffery 1990; Cromwell et al. 1991).

Temporal Variation. Readiness/willingness is unlikely to stay fixed over long periods of time. The base readiness/willingness of the entire population, whether measured by criminal justice system statistics (Brantingham 1991) or through self-reports (Flanagan and Jamieson 1988:294–318) is known to vary with age, rising sharply in the later teens and into young adulthood, then dropping sharply in the later 20s and early 30s. Despite some small criminal subgroups shown by longitudinal studies to have higher rates of offending regardless of age (Farrington 1986), this general effect appears to be related to changes in both the prevalence of offending and the incidence of offending at different ages (Loeber and Snyder 1990). Moreover, this base variation is mirrored in victimization rates, which vary with age in a pattern similar to that found in offender data (Gottfredson 1986)

In a more proximate arena, the readiness of any given individual will vary with changes in that person's social, economic, and emotional situation. Few burglars work steadily at doing burglaries. A successful and profitable run of crimes will lead to a reduced interest in doing more burglaries, while the money holds out. Few burglars will commit offenses while under obvious police scrutiny. At such times, readiness drops and obvious opportunities will be bypassed unless they form an ideal fit with the individual's crime template. When police scrutiny stops, or the money begins to run out, or simple boredom with life sets in, readiness rises, opportunities are considered more positively, and the offender can be triggered into doing a burglary more easily. At such periods of heightened readiness, the burglar enters a satisficing mode (Cromwell et al. 1991), and settles for crude fits between an opportunity and the crime template. (See, generally, Maguire 1982; Rengert and Wasilchick 1985; Cromwell et al. 1991.) A burglar's readiness and use of a crime template also appears to vary with drug use, rising and allowing riskier behavior with the use of alcohol or cocaine; falling and limiting risky behavior with the use of marijuana and opiates (Cromwell et al. 1991).

Application of Pattern Theory

Pattern theory may appear complex when crime, criminality, and criminal motivation are viewed as fixed objects. Criminologists frequently treat concepts as fixed and nonvarying. Crime, criminality, and criminal motivation are indeed complex if they are seen as invariant and unresponsive to what surrounds them. The elements shown in figure 11.3 are not all equally important in every crime or in every type of crime or to every group of potential offenders, but even when they have relatively less importance in a particular crime they do not disappear. Crime and criminal readiness are better understood as processes, that is, mathematically as functions. When considered as mathematically functional relationships, the variation in the links between different elements and how they interact becomes apparent.[19] Several examples will illustrate some of these functional relationships.

Pilfering of Office Supplies

For example, at one extreme consider the pattern of office supply theft (pens, pencils, pads of paper in small numbers) from the workplace. Pilfering is a common crime, one committed at some time or other by almost everyone who has ever worked within an environment that maintains accessible office supplies.[20] For this type of crime, the basic conditions are:

> *Readiness/willingness* — Almost everyone is willing to take small office supplies home. The goal is the possession of minor goods.

> *Structural backcloth* — All administrative offices maintain inventories of office supplies such as pens, pencils, paper, and envelopes. Businesses are clustered into a few parts of town by zoning rules and economic considerations.

> *Activity backcloth* — A broad socioeconomic range of people work in offices as cleaners, clerks, officers, administrators, managers, and executives. Small office supplies are everywhere. Rarely are there any restrictions on supplies. There are rarely any situational factors that make this crime risky.

> *Event process* — An office worker's children need some extra school supplies. The worker sees a bunch of pens on his or her desk, remembers the "need" at home, puts some of the pens in his or her briefcase, and takes them home to the children.

> *Expected crime pattern* — Spatially, crimes will be clustered in areas with offices. The volume of theft may just reflect the size of offices and, given a commonly accepted view that the mother is responsible for the children's school needs, the concentration of female jobs. Temporally, office supplies will be pilfered at the highest rate in the fall, as school begins, although they will disappear

at some minimal rate all the time. The Christmas season increases the pilfering of cellophane tape for sealing presents.[21]

Relationship of elements — Figure 11.4 shows the relationship between the elements that probably dominate formation of the pattern of a simple crime like pencil theft. The structural backcloth of the town; the routine activities inherent in an office job held by the potential thief; easy access to office supplies; a perceived "need" as a trigger; and the minimal search required to find the wanted supplies in a situation in which they can be taken *all* play roles in forming this fairly uncomplicated pattern.

The relationships between elements in figure 11.4 are presented in a format that tries to maintain their relative location within the larger model shown in figure 11.3. While all of the elements shown in figure 11.3 are present in every crime, only a subset of these elements are likely to dominate the formation of a pattern for any particular crime and therefore to be critical to understanding that crime. The other elements are part of the backcloth and shape the appearance of the crime pattern as it presents to researchers, practitioners, and the public at large.

Household Burglary

Readiness/willingness. Household burglaries are committed for many reasons, but thrill seeking and appropriation of goods appear to be the dominant goals behind most burglaries (Bennett and Wright 1984; Rengert and Wasilchick 1985; Cromwell et al. 1991). The level of readiness to commit a crime and willingness to run risks is substantially higher in residential burglaries than in pilfering of office supplies from work. Many who are after thrills or who are after goods are at their peak level of willingness to take risks when they commit a burglary. Such persons might be ready to commit a crime requiring some lesser risk, such as shoplifting, but might be unwilling to commit a robbery. Other burglars, however, who have aggressive or dominance goals might be ready to commit more confrontational offenses, such as robbery, but be bored by simple theft.

Structural backcloth. Residential areas are not located across the entire city or town. There are, instead, urban mosaics formed by many different land uses. Routine activities create different windows of opportunity in different residential areas. Those with sufficient readiness for household burglary are often clustered in limited parts of town and have limited access to transport (e.g., Baldwin and Bottoms 1976; Shannon 1988).[22]

Activity backcloth. Household burglaries are committed by different types of people who have different routine activities. Yet, the activity and

FIGURE 11.4
Office Theft

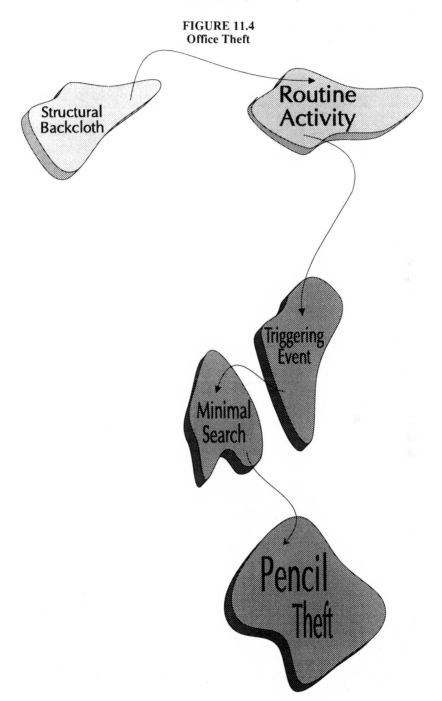

FIGURE 11.5
Burglary

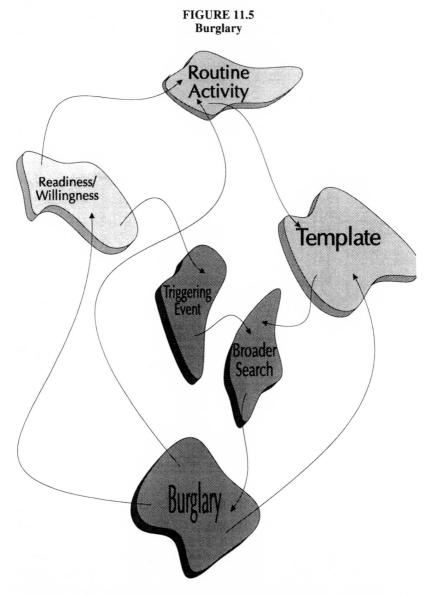

awareness spaces in which they act are frequently limited and, given an urban mosaic as a base, identifiable. From within these limited activity spaces, templates of suitable targets are constructed. What is considered suitable will vary with the individual but should show clear patterns by clustering of some similar offenders. Fifteen year olds living in a suburb of single-family dwellings will develop templates that differ from those developed by young adults living in poor apartment areas located near the center of a city (Reppetto 1974; Waller and Okihiro 1978; Carter and Hill 1979; Maguire 1982; Bennett and Wright 1984; Rengert and Wasilchick 1985; Cromwell et al. 1991). The robber who also does burglaries will develop a crime template that is different from that developed by a house burglar who is never willing to do a planned robbery.

Event process. What triggers the crime will vary with the type of individual committing the offense. For some, the crime will be immediately opportunistic, triggered by noticing an attractive possibility or by the urgings of friends. For others, the crime is more firmly directed at getting money. For the more opportunistic group, the crime may involve a brief search, but is critically dependent on quick discovery of a target that closely conforms to an idealized crime template. For the individuals with a higher level of readiness and a more focused goal of appropriation, the search may be longer and more complex, and a suitable target may require fewer points of congruence with the idealized crime template. But in common with search behavior conducted in noncriminal pursuits, the search patterns in these types of burglaries will be fairly predictable (Brantingham and Brantingham 1991; Rengert and Wasilchick 1985; Cromwell et. al 1991; Capone and Nicols 1976; Costanzo et al. 1986). Those with higher states of readiness may give up for the time being and try later if they fail to find targets that conform in some reasonable way with their crime templates within reasonable time periods, but they are not likely to give up completely. Many of these very ready burglars report giving up for the time being, but going back out on subsequent occasions (Maguire 1982).

Expected crime patterns. Spatially, the burglaries should cluster within restricted activity spaces. At an aggregate level, high activity nodes for teenagers and young adults from certain areas of a city should identify areas where the crimes will occur. When the nodes change the crime patterns change. Shannon (1988) documents the changing spatial distributions of crime in Racine as principal recreation nodes moved from the city center to the periphery in response to increasing automobile use. Rengert and Wasilchick (1990) document the movement of burglary distributions in relation to changes in the location of crack houses in the Philadelphia area. The details of what happens once inside the dwelling, whether mere theft or theft coupled with extensive vandalism, relates back to the goal underlying the crime, but probably does not relate back to the location of the crime.

Temporally, burglaries are, for those for whom burglary is the highest level of acceptable crime, aimed at times when the residence is empty and at residences that are most frequently empty. The emptiness may be based on personal knowledge (the McKinney's are on vacation), on the general observation that mid-afternoons are generally empty times (kids are in school, parents are at work or shopping) or on assumptions derived from routine activities (apartments are empty in mid-morning when everyone is at work). The crimes may, instead, become nighttime crimes for those willing to risk encountering residents or seeking more thrills or excitement. Someone willing to commit nighttime burglaries probably has a readiness for more confrontational and serious offenses such as robbery or rape than someone who commits only daytime breaking and enterings in clearly empty homes (Linedecker 1991; Clarke and Weisburd 1990).

Relationship between elements. In this type of crime the feedback loops between the criminal events and the potential offender's readiness/willingness, routine activities patterns, and, indirectly, triggering events become more important as the criminal behavior pattern develops and should vary in weight or importance as the offenders change from a subgroup of teenagers who break into houses to long-term, repeat burglars.[23]

Serial Rape

Readiness/willingness. Serial rape was chosen as the last example. It is both a nonproperty offense and a rare type of crime. There are few serial rapists. Their goals, in addition to sexual gratification, appear to involve shows of aggression or acts of domination. Serial rapists may repeat their offense behaviors over and over, changing only the particular victim, or they may escalate in frequency and violence as their readiness and willingness is raised to higher levels by the reinforcement of repeated success (Hazelwood et al. 1989; LeBeau 1985, 1987).

Structural backcloth. Since serial rape is a rare criminal behavior pattern, each offender tends to be tied uniquely to the structural backcloth of his own locale. Some underlying commonalities in transportation networks and in the distribution of women and girls in time and space, at schools or shopping malls for instance, may be part of a general backcloth common to many Western or industrialized societies that can be applied to an understanding of the individualized structural backcloths of particular serial rapists.

Activity backcloth. The reported rapes tied to serial offenders do tend to show an activity bias linked to each offender's routine activities and the nodal locations where the offender spends substantial amounts of time (LeBeau 1985, 1987; Maume 1989). The crime template is tied to the special characteristics of the offender's modus operandi and to the character of the triggering events that can touch off a new offense. Yet even

FIGURE 11.6
Serial Rape

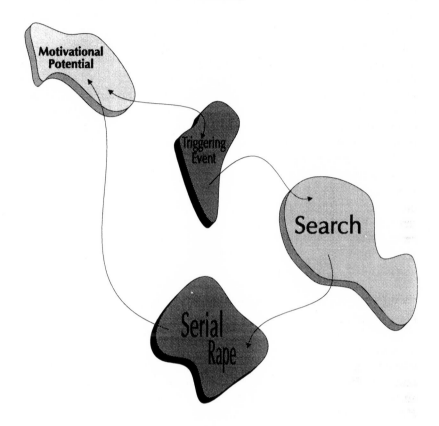

with repetitive events, analysis of individual serial rapists' activity patterns has to be tied to analysis of individual routine activities and awareness spaces. Aggregate analysis is only possible on a transformed "space" representing generic routine activities and awareness spaces.[24] Offense patterns are also tied to the routine activities of potential victims.

Event process. Each actual crime is tied to readiness level, to the triggering event—which could be a fantasy or seeing someone who fits a victim template within a fantasy—and to an individual search process involving a broader, more careful search to find the right target.

Expected crime patterns. Spatially, the patterns may only be analyzed at an individual offender's level. Serial rapists are rare. There is no aggregate cluster pattern, but from an individual perspective there may be a general pattern. Attacks away from main roads or near high activity centers may well mean the area is well-known to the offender, part of his current or past routine daily activities. Attacks near main roads or at high activity nodes such as large shopping malls may well mean that the rapist is being drawn to target concentrations, out of areas he knows well. Temporally, the rapes may well follow a clear pattern: always on the weekend; or always near a holiday. The pattern is shaped in some way by the routine rhythms of daily life. It is also most likely influenced by prior "success" and whatever is the driving force behind the rapes. The time period between successive offenses may well decrease as the offender's behavior is reinforced.

Relationship between elements. This type of crime is underresearched, although LeBeau (1985, 1987) and Hazelwood et al. (1989) have done some work.[25] It appears with this type of crime that process dominates and that no elements are completely static except, perhaps, what is defined by the offender as a suitable target or target situation. The dominant relationships may well be between readiness, triggering event, and search using a clearly defined template.

Conclusions

Pattern theory is derived from the multidisciplinary approaches to understanding crime and criminality found in rational choice theory, routine activities theory, environmental criminology, strategic analysis, life-style theory, crime prevention through environmental design, situational crime prevention, hot spot analysis, and opportunity theory. It explores patterns of crime and criminal behavior. Not all people commit crimes; not all areas experience crimes. The patterns in crime are potentially explicable when the decision process that is crucial to its commission is viewed in conjunction with the actual activity backcloth of offenders and victims, together with general variations in criminal motivation that are themselves not independent of the opportunity backcloth. In some types of offenses triggering events dominate crime patterning. For other types of crimes, past behavioral history, the actual availability of suitable targets, the creation of a decision template, and the current activities of potential offenders drive the pattern.

While the theory is general, it is specifically developed to make it easier to understand patterns of crime and, more specifically, the diversity in patterns of crime. What we "see" is understandable when we look at the specific criminal event, the site, the situation, the activity backcloth, the probable crime templates, the triggering events, and the general factors

TABLE 11.1
Research Topics

Templates

— How do templates vary by past criminal experience?
— Can people who commit crimes be "clustered" by what defines a "good" target? Is this a better way to categorize offenders than using legally defined categories?
— Do templates vary with culture? Are they highly dependent on which country is being studied? If so, is the difference based on varying activity patterns or varying sociocultural patterns?

Triggering Event/Readiness

— How "strong" do triggering events have to be?
— Does their required strength vary by the site and situation or current activity? Are triggers only functional in certain environments or, stated another way, are they non-functional in some situations but not in others?
— Does the trigger change as goals change?
— How do responses to the trigger influence aggravating and mitigating circumstances in sentencing?

Activity Space

— Are activity spaces like ecological niches? Do people feel highly constrained to remain within usual activity spaces?
— Does routine location in or near a perceived high risk alter people's activities leading them to avoid specific places, or indulge in reactive aggression or retreat in the face of specific situations?
— What are the expected crime patterns and down stream costs of policing associated with major changes in the structural backcloth (roads, trains, bridges, etc.) of a locale?
— Are we heading, economically, for more exposure to highly opportunistic crimes?

Readiness

— Do media increase readiness by providing examples?
— Does readiness/willingness stay vague and poorly defined before witnessing or being part of a crime?
— Why are most minor property crime opportunities ignored? Is readiness/willingness strongly tied to goals and associated crime preferences or to goods and easy/frequent activities likely to include triggering events?
— Conversely, since opportunities are so vast, are minor property crimes low because goals like excitement and thrills can be obtained in many other ways?

---

influencing the readiness or willingness of individuals to commit crimes. Aggregate patterns are understandable because they contain some similarity or commonality when viewed from the perspective of the processes in activities and criminal decision making: the use of goals for actions; the construction and use of templates in search behavior; the development of a state of readiness awaiting a triggering event; the process of the triggering event itself. Patterns are based on a more complex view of both crime and criminality than is used by many in the field.

Research strongly supports this approach to looking at crime. Patterns of crime are discernible and understandable. Future research, however, will have to begin to explore alternative analytic techniques. The elements of the decision process, the activity backcloth, the variation in criminal readiness, and the environmental backcloth are interrelated in feedback and iterative loops of a sort to which most of our current analytic tools are poorly suited at best. Future advancements in this field of research may require more reliance on alternative analytic tools such as point-set or algebraic topology, or nonlinear systems models and fractal constructs as well as a continual expansion into alternative methodologies to gain a better understanding of crime occurrence within a cognitive as well as a more objectively defined environment.[26]

Even using current qualitative and quantitative techniques, the elements and interrelationships shown in figure 11.3 may be researched from many perspectives. Table 11.1 contains a short list of possible research questions, some of which have already been mentioned in this article.

Much research has already been conducted in this new criminology. Perhaps most importantly, it already has a strong applied or action research arm.. Crime reduction is possible when crime is viewed from a detailed microperspective (Clarke 1992; Jeffery 1990). Breaking away from the idea that "crime" is generated by some simple, single factor or constitutes some single simple class of behaviors frees criminology to focus on specific types of crime occurring in specific types of situations enfolded in a specific configuration of the environmental backcloth. Looked at in this way, specifically defined problems make it easy to devise focused intervention tactics to deal with concrete criminal situations (see Clarke 1992). Solutions to specific problems can be found[27] by looking at who probably commits the crime; the probable goals behind the crime; whether crimes are related to controllable triggering events; why certain targets or victims, sites and situations are selected; and, how formal changes to the site, situation, or backcloth might alter the "who," the "why," and the "where" of crimes in ways that would reduce their overall prevalence and incidence.

Notes

1. The term *environment* used in this article includes all that surrounds: the sociocultural environment; the economic and legal environment; and the institutional and physical structure of the area. The *environment* may be considered and analyzed at a micro-, meso-, or macrolevel, or at all levels simultaneously.

2. While focus tends to fall on the offender, similar decision processes are assumed to lead the victim or the target, witnesses, and intervenors to the criminal event as well.

3. The critical character of location, setting, situation, and opportunity to delinquency patterns was identified more than 75 years ago by Ernest W. Burgess (1916).

4. While research has not yet been done, we have heard anecdotal information from schools and recreation centers that theft of personal computers has soared as they have started to buy fully portable machines. Even clumsy multicomponent personal computers were being stolen at a high rate before the switch to portables.

5. The terms *prototype* and *place schemata* are also sometimes used in the literature.

6. Templates are not just created to identify "good" targets or "good" sites or situations for crimes. Individuals develop templates for identifying where they want to eat, to live, to shop. General functioning within the infinitely complex cue-emitting environment involves the development of cognitive images and cognitive maps and the use of these images. See Gärling and Golledge (1989) for a general review of theory and research in cognitive images and their use. See Gärling et al (1986) and Genereux et al. (1983) for basic location, orientation, and movement models that are highly relevant to crime pattern analysis.

7. Unfortunately, many research techniques used in studying what forms the template takes must, of necessity, identify one or two characteristics and only study those. In some situations, a crime is straightforward enough that one or two characteristics of targets dominate the template and are accessible through straightforward research. In other situations, the crime itself may be complex, involving many nonrecursive or holistic decisions beyond the capacity of most currently used statistical techniques to address.

8. The environment forms patterns. Ultimately understanding crime, or any behavior, involves understanding patterns within patterns.

9. This is not to say that the concepts in the natural sciences are simple, only that, at a theoretical level the ideas can be developed with fixed initial conditions. The applied sciences may be seen as undertaking the integration of the basic ideas with actual, varying conditions.

10. Praxis and theory are not separable in criminology.

11. This sounds banally simple, but legislation has been adopted to address just such triggering events in bars. In British Columbia, for example, people in bars and pubs may not walk around carrying a drink. Bar fights are common and were seen by the Provincial Legislative Assembly to be often caused by just such spilled drinks. To drink, you must be seated.

12. *Backcloth* is a term used for the variable, ever-changing context that surrounds the daily lives of individuals. While the backcloth changes, it is comprehensible and it forms patterns.

13. See Clarke (1992) for a broad range of examples.

14. While not developed for crime analysis, Gärling et al. (1986) have developed a model of factors influencing spatial navigation consistent with the results of Fink's (1969) analysis and the "edge effect" in target choice (Brantingham and Brantingham 1975; 1978).

15. When the problems at events become regular, they are no longer nonroutine and become predictable. With the predictability comes the possibility of reducing or eliminating the problems (Clarke 1992:14; see Bell and Burke 1992, for cruising).

16. Cusson's *Why Delinquency?* constructs a well-supported taxonomy of the goals of delinquent behavior. Delinquency research has repeatedly found reasonable, understandable goals behind behavior that help explain the variety of crimes that

occur. He also provides a firm basis for identifying the logical and empirically identified flaws in most unicausal theories of criminality.

17. Research into various types of service delivery find that actual usage of a service is tied to three factors: the availability of the service; its accessibility within reasonable limits of effort; and a willingness on the part of the prospective clients to use the service. All three are necessary elements in service utilization. See Brantingham and Brantingham (1984) for a discussion of legal aid utilization. This body of research may prove useful in understanding the way that the elements of a criminal event must come together in the presence of a trigger for the event to actually occur.

18. The gender pattern in burglary in clear. While not exclusively masculine, burglary is predominantly committed by males. Masculine pronouns and adjectives are used in burglary examples to reflect this fact.

19. Conceptually, this is different from using multivariate statistical techniques to show interrelations. The elements shown in figure 11.3 are not independent of crime. They influence crime, but crime influences them. (Similar statements apply for criminality and criminal motivation.) Different elements within the figure can become the focus of a particular crime. Changes in the routine behaviors of criminals may be the focus or triggering events that result in minimal searches; or, they may be the product of past criminal behavior. Pattern theory is not rigid.

20. Other occupational crimes follow more complex patterns, in particular the interaction between perceived need of goods and identification of opportunities. Pretto (1991) explored several occupational crimes and found varying feedbacks between motivation and opportunity. In particular, he explored the theft of bill payments through banks by tellers when they, themselves, get in "over their heads" in debt. Goals, readiness, triggering events, routine activities, and a template for safe targets are all clearly important.

21. Parenthetically, we have been told by constables in a number of different police forces that it is difficult to find operational flashlights, radios, or tape recorders around their offices during the Christmas season. The batteries disappear into toys.

22. Changing the structural transportation backcloth should produce a "sprawl" of residential burglary (Brantingham and Brantingham 1981; Brantingham et al. 1991; Burgess 1925).

23. Cusson (1983) reproduces results of research done by Fréchette and LeBlanc (1978) showing how the goal behind offending may change as teenagers age. Action/excitement as a goal seems to change into appropriation as a goal as repeat offenders age.

24. See Rengert and Wasilchick 1985, for a technique for just such analysis applied to burglar activity patterns.

25. A two-year study of the geographic patterns in serial rape is currently being conducted at the FBI Academy by Roland Reboussin, Robert R. Hazelwood, and Janet I. Warren under National Institute of Justice auspices.

26. Future research may best be placed in cognitive philosophy of science. We do not reason in simple linear ways, or by abduction, but more by prototypes leading to what are called "activation vectors" (Churchland 1989).

27. Or determined to be insoluble because the solution is politically unpalatable. Some crime prevention tactics might force unacceptable changes in noncriminal lifestyles. Some crime prevention tactics might be prohibitively expensive. Some tactics would be unacceptably repressive. Some tactics would be immoral.

References

Baldwin, J., & Bottoms, A.E. 1976. *The urban criminal.* London: Tavistock.

Barker, R.R. 1968. *Ecological psychology.* Stanford: Stanford University Press.

Barlow, H.D. 1990. *Introduction to criminology* (5th ed.). Glenview, IL: Scott, Foresman.

Bell, J., & Burke, B. 1992. Cruising Cooper street. In R.V. Clarke (Ed.), *Situational crime prevention: Successful case studies* (108–12). New York: Harrow and Heston.

Bennett, T., & Wright, R. 1984. *Burglars on burglary: Prevention and the offender.* Brookfield, VT: Gower Publishing Company.

Bentham, J. 1789. *An introduction to the principles of morals and legislation.* London: T. Payne and Son.

Block, C.R. 1990. Hot spots and isocrimes in law enforcement decision making. Paper presented at conference on Police and Community Responses to Drugs, University of Illinois at Chicago.

Bottoms, A., Mawby, R.I., & Xanthos, P. 1989. A tale of two estates. In D. Downes (Ed.), *Crime and the city* (36–87). London: Macmillan Press.

Brantingham, P.J. 1991. Patterns in Canadian crime. In M. Jackson & C. Griffiths (Eds.), *Canadian criminology. Perspectives on crime and criminality* (371–402). Toronto: Harcourt Brace Jovanovich.

Brantingham, P.J., & Brantingham, Jr., P.J. 1991. Niches and predators: Theoretical departures in the ecology of crime. Paper presented at Western Society of Criminology Meetings, Berkeley.

Brantingham, P.J., & Brantingham, P.L. 1978. A theoretical model of crime site selection. In M. Krohn and R. Akers (Eds.), *Crime, law and sanctions* (105–118). Beverly Hills, CA.: Sage Publications.

———. 1981. *Environmental criminology.* Beverly Hills, CA: Sage Publications.

———. 1984. *Patterns in crime.* New York: Macmillan.

———. 1991. *Environmental criminology.* Prospect Heights, IL: Waveland Press.

Brantingham, P.L., & Brantingham, P.J. 1975. Residential burglary and urban form. *Urban Studies* 12:273–84.

———. 1978. A topological technique for regionalization. *Environment and Behavior* 10:335–53.

———. 1981. Mobility, notoriety, and crime: A study in the crime patterns of urban nodal points. *Journal of Environmental Systems* 11:89–99.

———. 1984. *An evaluation of legal aid in British Columbia.* Ottawa: Department of Justice, Canada.

Brantingham, P.L., Brantingham, P.J., & Wong, P.S. 1991. How public transit feeds private crime: Notes on the Vancouver "Skytrain" experience. *Security Journal* 2:91–95.

Bullock, H.A. 1955. Urban homicide in theory and fact. *Journal of Criminal Law, Criminology and Police Science* 45:565–75.

Burgess, E.W. 1916. Juvenile delinquency in a small city. *Journal of the American Institute of Criminal Law and Criminology* 6:724–28.

———. 1925. The growth of the city. In R.E. Park, E.W. Burgess, & R.D. McKenzie (Eds.), *The city* (47–62). Chicago: University of Chicago Press.

Burrows, J. 1988. *Retail crime: Prevention through crime analysis.* (Home Office Crime Prevention Unit Paper # 11). London: HMSO.

Capone, D., & Nichols, W. 1976. Urban structure and criminal mobility. *American*

Behavioral Scientist 20:199–201.

Carroll, J., & Weaver, F. 1986. Shoplifters' perceptions of crime opportunities: A process-tracing study. In D. Cornish & R.V. Clarke (Eds.), *The reasoning criminal* (19–37). New York: Springer-Verlag.

Carter, R., & Hill, K.Q. 1979. *The criminal's image of the city.* New York: Pergamon.

Chaiken, J.M., & Chaiken, M.R. 1990. Drugs and predatory crime. *Crime and Justice: An Annual Review of Research* 13:203–39.

Chapin, F.S. 1974. *Human activity patterns in the city: Things people do in time and space.* New York: Wiley.

Churchland, P.M. 1989. *A neurocomputational perspective on the nature of mind and the structure of science.* Cambridge, MA: MIT Press.

Clarke, R.V. 1992. *Situational crime prevention: Successful case studies.* New York: Harrow and Heston.

Clarke, R.V.G. 1980. Situational crime prevention: Theory and practice. *British Journal of Criminology* 20:136–47.

Clarke, R.V., & Cornish, D.B. 1985. Modeling offenders' decisions: A framework for research and policy. *Crime and Justice: An Annual Review of Research* 6:147–85.

Clarke, R.V., Field, S., & McGrath, G. 1991. Target hardening of banks in Australia and displacement of robberies. *Security Journal* 2:84–90.

Clarke, R.V., & Weisburd, D.L. 1990. On the distribution of deviance. In D.M. Gottfredson & R.V. Clarke (Eds.), *Policy and theory in criminal justice* (10–27). Aldershot: Avebury.

Cloward, R.A., & Ohlin, L.E. 1960. *Delinquency and opportunity: A theory of delinquent gangs.* New York: The Free Press.

Cohen, L.E., & Felson, M. 1979. Social change and crime rate trends: A routine activity approach. *American Sociological Review* 44:588–605.

Cornish, D., & Clarke, R.V. 1986. *The reasoning criminal.* New York: Springer-Verlag.

Costanzo, C.M., Halperin, W.C., & Gale, N. 1986. Criminal mobility and the directional component in journeys to crime. In R. Figlio, S. Hakim, & G. Rengert (Eds.), *Metropolitan crime patterns* (73–96). Monsey, NY: Criminal Justice Press.

Cromwell, P.F., Olson, J.N., & Avary, D.W. 1991. *Breaking and entering: An ethnographic analysis of burglary.* Newbury Park, CA: Sage Publications.

Cusson, M. 1983. *Why delinquency?* Toronto: University of Toronto Press.

———. 1989. Les zones urbaines criminelles, Criminologie 22 (2):95–105.

Cusson, M., & Pinsonneault, P. 1986. The decision to give up crime. 72-82 In D. Cornish & R.V. Clarke, *The Reasoning Criminal.* New York: Springer-Verlag.

Duffala, D.C. 1976. Convenience stores, armed robbery, and physical environmental features. *American Behavioral Scientist* 20:227–46.

Eck, J., & Spelman, W. 1992. Thefts from vehicles in shipyard parking lots. In R. V. Clarke (Ed.), *Situational crime prevention. Successful case studies* (165–73). New York: Harrow and Heston.

Ekblom, P. 1992. Preventing post office robberies in London: Effects and side effects. In R.V. Clarke (Ed.), *Situational crime prevention: Successful case studies* (66–74). New York: Harrow and Heston.

Engstad, P.A. 1975. Environmental opportunities and the ecology of crime. In R. A. Silverman & J.J. Teevan, Jr. (Eds.), *Crime in Canadian society* (193–211). Toronto: Butterworths.

Farrington, D. P. 1986. Age and crime. *Crime and Justice: An Annual Review of Research* 7:189–250.

Fattah, E.A. 1991. *Understanding criminal victimization. An introduction to theoretical victimology.* Scarborough, Ontario: Prentice-Hall.

Feeney, F. 1986. Robbers as decision makers. In D. Cornish & R. Clarke (Eds.), *The reasoning criminal* (53–73). New York: Springer-Verlag.

Feeney, F., & Weir, A. 1973. *The prevention and control of robbery.* Davis: The Center of Administration of Justice, University of California at Davis.

Felson, M.K. 1983. Ecology of crime. In S.H. Kadish (Ed.), *Encyclopedia of crime and justice* (2:665–70). New York: The Free Press.

Felson, M. 1987. Routine activities and crime prevention in the developing metropolis. *Criminology* 25:911–31.

Felson, M., & Cohen, L. 1981. Modeling crime trends: A cumulative opportunity perspective. *Journal of Research in Crime and Delinquency* 18:138–64.

Fink, G. 1969. Einsbruchstatorte vornehmlich an einfallstrassen? *Kriminalistik* 23: 358–60.

Flanagan, T.J., & Jamieson, K.M. 1988. *Sourcebook of criminal justice statistics 1987.* U.S. Department of Justice, Bureau of Justice Statistics. Washington, DC: USGPO.

Fréchette, M., & LeBlanc, M. 1978. *La Délinquance cachée des adolescents montréalais.* Montréal: Groupe de recherché sur l'inadaptation juvenile, Université de Montréal.

Gabor, T., Baril, M., Cusson, M., Elie, D., LeBlanc, M., & Normandeau, A. 1987. *Armed robbery: Cops, robbers, and victims.* Springfield, IL: Charles C. Thomas.

Gärling, T., & Golledge. R.G. 1989. Environmental perception and cognition. In E.H. Zube & G.T. Moore (Eds.), *Advances in environment, behavior, and design: Volume 2* (203–36). New York: Plenum Press.

Gärling, T., Lindberg, E., Carreiras, M., & Böök, A. 1986. Reference systems in cognitive maps. *Journal of Environmental Psychology* 6:1–18.

Genereux, R.L., Ward, L.M., & Russell, J.A. 1983. The behavioral component in the meaning of places. *Journal of Environmental Psychology* 3:43-55.

Gottfredson, M.R. 1986. Substantive contributions of victim surveys. *Crime and Justice: An Annual Review of Research* 7:251–87.

Gottfredson, M., & Hirschi, T. 1990. *The general theory of crime.* Stanford, CA: Stanford University Press.

Gould, L. 1969. The changing structure of crime in an affluent society. *Social Forces* 48:50–59.

Hanawalt, B.A. 1979. *Crime and conflict in English communities: 1300–1348.* Cambridge, MA: Harvard University Press.

Harries, K.D. 1990. *Serious violence.* Springfield, IL: Charles C. Thomas.

Hazelwood, R.R., Reboussin, R., & Warren, J.I. 1989. Series rape: Correlates of increased aggression and the relationship of offender pleasure to victim resistance. *Journal of Interpersonal Violence* 4:65–78.

Herbert, D.T., & Hyde, S.W. 1985. Environmental criminology: testing some area hypotheses. *Transactions: Institute of British Geographers* 10:259–74.

Hindelang, M.J., Gottfredson, M.R., & Garofalo, J. 1978. *Victims of personal crime: An empirical foundation for a theory of personal crime.* Cambridge, MA: Ballinger.

Hope, T., & Hough, M. 1988. Area, crime and incivility: A profile from the British Crime Survey. In T. Hope & M. Shaw (Eds.), *Communities and crime reduction* (30–47). London: HMSO.

Hunter, R.D., & Jeffery, C.R. 1992. Preventing convenience store robbery through environmental design. In R.V. Clarke (Ed.), *Situational crime prevention: Successful case studies* (194–204). New York: Harrow and Heston.

Illinois Criminal Justice Information Authority. 1989. *Spatial and temporal analysis of crime: Users manual/technical manual.* Chicago: Illinois Criminal Justice Information Authority, State of Illinois.

Inciardi, J.A. 1978. *Reflections on crime.* New York: Holt, Rinehart and Winston.

———. 1979. Heroin use and street crime. *Crime and Delinquency* 25:335–46.

Jeffrey, C.R. 1971. *Crime prevention through environmental design.* Beverly Hills, CA: Sage Publications.

Jeffery, C.R. 1990. *Criminology: An interdisciplinary approach.* Englewood Cliffs, NJ: Prentice-Hall.

Kennedy, L.W., & Forde, D.R. 1990. Routine activities and crime: An analysis of victimization in Canada. *Criminology* 28:137–52.

Lasley, J.R. 1989. Drinking routines/lifestyles and predatory victimization: A causal analysis. *Justice Quarterly* 6:529–42.

Lawson, P. 1986. Property crime and hard times in England, 1559–1624. *Law and History Review* 4:95–127.

LeBeau, J.I. 1985. Some problems with measuring and describing rape presented by the serial offender. *Justice Quarterly* 2:385–98.

———. 1987. Patterns of stranger and serial rape offending: Factors distinguishing apprehended and at large offenders. *Journal of Criminal Law and Criminology* 78:309–26.

Lemert, E.M. 1951. *Social pathology.* New York: McGraw-Hill.

Letkemann, P. 1973. *Crime as work.* Englewood Cliffs, NJ: Prentice-Hall.

Linedecker, C.L. 1991. *Night stalker.* New York: St. Martin's Paperbacks.

Loeber, R., & Snyder, H.N. 1990. Rate of offending in criminal careers: Constancy and change in Lambda. *Criminology* 28:97–109.

Lombroso, C. 1911. *Crime: Its causes and remedies.* Boston: Little, Brown.

Macdonald, J.E., & Gifford, R. 1989. Territorial cues and defensible space theory: The burglar's point of view. *Journal of Environmental Psychology* 9:193–205.

Maguire, K., & Flanagan, T.J. 1991. *Sourcebook of criminal justice statistics 1990.* U.S. Department of Justice, Bureau of Justice Statistics. Washington, DC: USGPO.

Maguire, M. 1982. *Burglary in a dwelling.* London: Heinemann.

Maume, D.J. 1989. Inequality and metropolitan rape rates: A routine activities approach. *Justice Quarterly* 6:513–28.

Mayhew, P. 1990. Opportunity and vehicle crime. In D.M. Gottfredson & R.V. Clarke (Eds.), *Policy and theory in criminal justice* (28–50). Aldershot: Avebury.

Poyner, B. 1983. *Design against crime: Beyond defensible space.* London: Butterworths.

Poyner, B., & Webb, B. 1992. Reducing theft from shopping bags in city centre markets. In R.V. Clarke (Ed.), *Situational crime prevention. Successful case studies* (99–107). New York: Harrow and Heston.

Pretto, R. 1991. *Opportunity and occupational crime: A case study of employee property crime in the workplace.* Unpublished master's thesis, School of Criminology, Simon Fraser University, Burnaby.

Rengert, G. 1988. The location of facilities and crime. *Journal of Security Administration* 11(2):12–16.

Rengert, G., & Wasilchick, J. 1985. *Suburban crime: A time and a place for everything.* Springfield, IL: Charles C. Thomas.

Rengert, G., & Wasilchick, J. 1990. *Space, time and crime: Ethnographic insights into residential burglary.* Report Submitted to U.S. Department of Justice, National Institute of Justice, Office of Justice Programs.

Reppetto, T.A. 1974. *Residential crime.* Cambridge, MA: Ballinger.

Roncek, D., & Maier, P.A. 1991. Bars, blocks and crime revisited: Linking the theory of routine activities to the empiricism of hot spots. *Criminology* 29:725–53.

Roncek, D., & Pravatiner, M.A. 1989. Additional evidence that taverns enhance nearby crime. *Sociology and Social Research* 73:185–88.

Rowe, D.C., Osgood, D.W., & Nicewinder, W.A. 1990. A latent trait approach to unifying criminal careers. *Criminology* 28:237–70.

Sacks, H. 1972. Notes on police assessment of moral character. In D. Sudnow (Ed.), *Studies in social interaction* (280–293). New York: Free Press.

Shannon, L.W. 1988. *Criminal career continuity: Its social context.* New York: Human Sciences Press.

Shaw, C.R., & Moore, M.E. 1931. *The natural history of a delinquent career.* Chicago: University of Chicago Press.

Sherman, L.W., Gartin, P.R., & Buerger, M.E. 1989. Hot spots of predatory crime: Routine activities and the criminology of place. *Criminology* 27:27–55.

Sloan, J.H., Kellerman, A.L., Reay, D.T., Ferris, J.A., Koepsell, T., Rivera, F.P., Rice, C., Gray, L., & Logerfo, J. 1988. Handgun regulations, crime, assaults, and homicide. *New England Journal of Medicine* 319:1256.

Sutherland, E. 1937a. *Principles of criminology* (3d ed.). Philadelphia: Lippincott.

————. 1937b. *The professional thief.* Chicago: University of Chicago Press.

Taylor, I., Walton, P., & Young, J. 1973. *The new criminology.* London: Routledge and Kegan Paul.

Taylor, R. 1988. *Human territorial functioning.* Cambridge: Cambridge University Press.

van Dijk, J.J.M., Mayhew, P. & Killias, M. 1990. *Experiences of crime across the world: Key findings from the 1989 international crime survey.* Deventer: Kluwer Law and Taxation Publishers.

Waller, I., & Okihiro, N. 1978. *Burglary: The victim and the public.* Toronto: University of Toronto Press.

Walsh, D. 1978. *Shoplifting: Controlling a major crime.* London: Macmillan.

————. 1986. Victim selection procedures among economic criminals: The rational choice perspective. In D. Cornish & R.V. Clarke (Eds.), *The reasoning criminal* (38–56). New York: Springer-Verlag.

Warr, M., & Stafford, M. 1991. The influence of delinquent peers: What they think or what they do? *Criminology* 29:851–66.

Weisburd, D.L. 1992. Contrasting crime general and crime specific theory: The case of hot spots of crime. In Freda Adler & William S. Laufer (Eds.), *Advances in Criminological Theory* (vol. 4, 45–70). New Brunswick, NJ: Transaction.

Weisburd, D.L., Wheeler, S., & Waring, E. 1991. *Crimes of the middle classes.* New Haven: Yale University Press.

West, D.J. 1982. *Delinquency: Its roots, careers and prospects.* London: Heinemann Educational Books.

Wheeler, S., Weisburd, D.L., Waring, E., & Bode, N. 1988. White collar crimes and criminals. *American Criminal Law Review* 25:331–57.

Wikstrom, P.-O.H. 1991. *Urban crime, criminals, and victims: The Swedish ex-*

perience in an Anglo-American comparative perspective. New York: Springer-Verlag.

Wilkins, L.T. 1964. *Social deviance.* London: Tavistock.

Willmer, M.A.P. 1970. *Crime and information theory.* Edinburgh: Edinburgh University Press.

Wilson, J.Q., & Herrnstein, R.J. 1986. *Crime and human nature.* New York: Touchstone Books.

Wolfgang, M.E., & Ferracuti, F. 1967. *The subculture of violence. Towards an integrated theory in criminology.* London: Social Science Paperbacks.

12

A Strategic Analysis of Crime: Criminal Tactics as Responses to Precriminal Situations

Maurice Cusson

The rational choice perspective includes theories; it is not in itself a theory. More important, it is a way of thinking about crime in strategic terms, a way of seeing it as calculating behavior in the context of conflict. To do this, we need a conceptual toolbox. The one we have already contains some very useful ideas: limited rationality, opportunities, routine activities, choice structuring properties, and so on. The next step would be to make finer distinctions and formulate more analytical concepts. This chapter has two parts. In the first, I distinguish three components in a criminal event: the search, the precriminal situation, and the criminal tactics. In the second part, I use these components to explain the proliferation of mundane predatory crime over the last 40 years.

Search, Precriminal Situation, and Criminal Tactics

According to Ekblom (1988:3-4) a crime pattern is a series of crimes sharing common features, clustering in time and place, having specific targets, and "committed by a particular range of methods" (p. 4). Put in strategic terms, a predatory crime pattern can be seen as having three elements: the offenders' maneuver in a *search* to find suitable *precriminal situations* in which they use similar *tactics*. This gives us three interrelated concepts to define.

The *search* occurs when the offender is looking for a suitable precriminal situation. In some cases, he might find one without much effort. In other cases, having found one, he might have to find a weak spot in the target's protective system. Finally, in still other cases, he might have to create the precriminal situation.

The importance of the search is best exemplified in burglary. Bennett and Wright (1984) and Maguire (1988), have shown that most burglars are searchers. They do not come upon opportunities inadvertently but tour an area, eyes open, looking for vulnerable houses. The search follows "obvious routes" (Felson 1988): the break-in man looks for suitable targets around familiar places, or just off the usual paths to such places (Brantingham and Brantingham 1984; Rengert and Wasilchick 1985:69). Sometimes offenders gather information from secondary sources. They get "tips" from informers, in bars and restaurants, from friends or ordinary citizens.

The concept of a *precriminal situation* is not new. It was used for years by continental criminologists like Kinberg (1935:154), Pinatel (1975:261–67) and Gassin (1988:495–503). But it has been ignored by rational choice theorists. The concept could be useful when the analyst wants to distinguish in a crime pattern what is due to the offender's decisions and what is due to the situation itself.

The authors do not agree on a definition of the *precriminal situation*; mine would be the following: it is *the set of outside circumstances immediately preceding and surrounding the criminal event and making the offense more or less difficult, risky, and profitable.* For example, a precriminal situation favorable for joyriding would be a sports car with the keys left in the ignition. It would not include the fact that one of the kids contemplating the joyride knows how to drive or the fact that he has the nerve to take another person's car. At a minimum, a precriminal situation exists if it brings together the necessary conditions for a crime to occur, what Gottfredson and Hirschi (1990:22) call "the minimal elements necessary (and collectively sufficient) for a crime to occur." The concept of precriminal situation should be distinguished from his closest neighbor: opportunity. The latter is a *favorable* situation for committing an offense. It is what makes possible and even probable the occurrence of a crime. In the precriminal situation notion, we do not presume that the circumstances are favorable; they might be, they might not be.

In military parlance, *tactics* is "the science and art of disposing and maneuvering forces in combat." The common language includes another meaning: "a system or mode of procedure" (*Webster*). I would define criminal tactics as *the sequence of choices and actions made by the offender during the criminal event, including his use of available means to reach his ends in the precriminal situation.*

Offenders tend to repeat their successful moves and the successes of one offender tend to be repeated by others. This means that most criminal tactics are not unique: ways become customary and they crystallize into modes of procedure. When such a pattern comes to be associated with an individual offender, detectives speak of the "modus operandi." Often a number of offenders tend to operate in approximately the same manner, in which case, one could speak of the tactical elements of a crime pattern.

"Criminal tactics" is a descriptive concept. It asks the question: How can we describe the offenders moves? As a guide, the criminologist studying a predatory crime can look for what the offenders do to solve the two basic problems that have to be solved for the success of most predatory crimes: the neutralization of the target's protection and the escape from pursuit, identification, and punishment.

Many precriminal situations result from the offender's search and, in turn, they structure (or shape) his tactics. For example, Quebec robbers show a marked preference for commercial targets over individual victims on the street. In a sample of 1,266 armed robberies committed in 1979–80, 19% of the targets were banks, 21% were convenience stores, 14% pharmacies and groceries, 11% restaurants and bars, 8% jewellers and liquor stores, and 7% service stations. Seventeen percent of the targets were individual victims (Gabor et al. 1987:32). This contrasts with the U.S. situation where a good number of robberies are muggings aimed at individuals on the street. Not unsurprisingly, in 72% of the 1,266 armed robberies studied in Quebec, a firearm was the weapon used (p. 31). Forty-one percent of the incidents were solo endeavors and 46% were committed in pairs, whereas in the United States, 33% of all robberies are committed by three or more offenders. Quebec robbers prefer businesses where there are few people to control: in 48% of the robberies, there was only one attendant and no customer during the event; in 28% of the incidents, only one employee and one customer were present. The event usually lasted less than a minute.

These facts show that the precriminal situation of choice for our robbers is a small business, having only one employee on the premises, at a time when there are very few or no customers. It must be added that robbery victims who manage to grab a gun and shoot back are extremely rare in Quebec—much more rare than in the United States. These small businesses are vulnerable targets for robbery. Quebec robbers' chances of having at least some success are fairly good: in 90% of the cases, the robber(s) managed to escape with a reasonable amount of money (around $500).

In such a precriminal situation, the tactics required are very simple: a lone offender or two individuals with a gun wait for a small store to be just about empty; they hold up the place, staying inside less than one minute, and make a quick getaway, often on foot.

This crime pattern has tended to proliferate in Montreal because it is a city where a potential offender can find an abundance of retail stores, open long hours, attended by only one person unwilling to shoot robbers. The availability of such vulnerable targets is one reason why there are very few muggings in Montreal: there is no need to attack pedestrians in the hope that they are carrying enough money when jewelry stores, convenience stores, and the like are defenseless. (Another reason is our winter: in January, hanging around in the street waiting for a pedestrian to pass by is a bit too uncomfortable for a mugger, but this is not true in summertime).

Contemporary Crime as a Strategic Adaptation to Changes in the Targets and to the Evolution of Policing

The concepts of search, of precriminal situation, and of criminal tactics are not only useful in crime analysis; at a macroscopic level, they can be of some help in the study of crime trends. The following, is an effort to use those concepts to demonstrate how the emergence of new precriminal situations came to structure contemporary crime.

Characteristics of Contemporary Crime

In their recent book, Gottfredson and Hirschi (1990) argue that most crime is unsophisticated and trivial. "The vast majority of criminal acts are trivial and mundane affairs that result in little loss and less gain. These are events that require little preparation, leave few lasting consequences, and often do not produce the result intended by the offender" (p. 16). They continue, arguing that "ordinary crimes require little in the way of effort, planning, preparation, or skill" (p. 17) and that they are "usually of little lasting or substantial benefit to the offender" (p. 21).

The central thesis of Gottfredson and Hirschi is that these crime characteristics result from the offender's lack of self-control. The very characteristics of his criminal behavior are evidence of his impulsiveness, his insensitivity, his short-sightedness, his intolerance of frustration, his temerity, and his low intelligence.

I do not disagree with the picture Gottfredson and Hirschi give of most criminal acts and repeat offenders. But it can be argued that this picture lacks historical perspective. It might give us a valid description of most contemporary crime but not of the crimes of the past. Another related point can be made. It is debatable that the pettiness and simplicity of today's crime can be explained only by the offender's poor self-control. One can argue that they are instead the result of the precriminal situations easily found by contemporary offenders in societies where they can find an abundance of small vulnerable targets. First, as we shall see, crime changed considerably over the last century.

When we compare what we know of contemporary crime as described by Gottfredson and Hirschi and what we know of crime 40 years ago, the contrast is inescapable. Offenders of the past were more sophisticated and skilled than the ones of today. They could commit carefully planned crimes. Sutherland's (1937) professional thief is probably an exaggeration, but it is difficult to argue that he invented all the criminal skills he wrote about. The reason why this picture (and many others) differs so much from what we see today is that there has been a relative decline in professional theft during the last 50 years or so.

Already in 1958, Lemert noted a decline in professional check forgery. He began his research looking for professionals, but the best he could find were "systematic check forgers." The latter distinguished themselves from other forgers by their special techniques and by organizing their lives around this kind of crime. But these men did not have a businesslike attitude, nor elaborate technical skills; they lacked "social organization, occupational orientation, careful planning, common rules, a code of behavior, and a special language" (p. 121). Compared to the systematic check forgers of the past, those of the 1950s did less planning, used less complex procedures, and sought smaller amounts of money. In the late 1950s, passing checks had become easy and there was neither a need to resort to an associate nor a need to employ sophisticated procedures. Yet, with the progress made in bank security and policing, check forgers had become much more vulnerable to arrest. Lemert's conclusion is worth citing: "Organized forgery is a hazardous type of crime, difficult to professionalize under modern conditions" (p. 114). In 1964, D.W. Maurer detected a similar trend in pickpocketing. According to his estimates, in 1945, there were about five or six thousand "class cannons" (expert pickpockets) in the United States and, in 1955, the figure was down to one thousand (p. 171). Among other types of professional crime that have disappeared during the past 50 years are safe burglary, bank sneaking (in which a thief would get in a bank within reach of the cash and take the money when the attention of bank personnel was diverted by an accomplice), and pennyweighting (the substitution of imitation jewelry for the genuine) (Inciardi 1975). The de-professionalization of burglary is another obvious fact. Even better than average burglars, like the ones described in Rengert and Wasilchick (1985), are no match for the professional burglars of the past (Walsh 1980). Today's bank robbery, another type of professional crime, does not have the sophistication of the jobs done by the expert robbers of the 1930s (like the ones described in Karpis and Trent 1971; Letkemann 1973; Haran and Martin, 1977). During the 1960s, the "career" robbers studied by Einstadter (1969:80) were not confident enough to attack banks and fell back on retail liquor stores with takes of $20, $50, or $100. Most robbers described by Conklin (1972) were opportunists, addicts, or alcoholics (see also Feeney 1986). Bank robbers do not gain as much as they did yesterday. "In 1932, the average loss was $5,583, compared with $3,654 in 1981" (Barlow 1987:196). In Montreal, only 26% of robbery suspects use some kind of disguise (Gabor et al. 1987:34). This is not to say that carefully planned and sophisticated crimes have disappeared; only that they are now swamped by the vast increase in the number of small opportunist offenses. Perhaps Inciardi (1975:76) was right when he concluded that "professional crime began to decline in the early 1940's with a sharp reduction in the number of specialized career criminals." What is obvious is the proliferation of small rudimentary thefts after World War II.

It follows that the lack of sophistication and skills of contemporary criminals is not a timeless characteristic, resulting only from the offender's low self-control, but the result of a historical trend. As an alternative thesis to that of Gottfredson and Hirschi, one could argue that contemporary crime is petty, easy, and unsophisticated because very simple ways of operating are effective in most precriminal situations found by offenders today. Criminal tactics that are simple and quick are efficient solutions because the most interesting targets for contemporary offenders are small and easy to get at. This situation is the result of two historical changes: (1) the evolution of target protection and (2) the emergence of modern policing.

Easy but Small Targets

During the last 30 years, changes in the economy, in technology, and in the security industry have confronted offenders with the need to change their tactics. With the advent of the cashless society, it has become increasingly difficult to find large amounts of cash in houses and businesses. The proliferation of bank branches, night depositories, credit cards, safety deposit boxes, and automatic tellers have rendered obsolete the holding of large quantities of cash. For their part, banks and the related industries in the transportation of funds, which have to keep and carry huge amounts of valuables, have greatly improved their security. It is now impossible for the vast majority of thieves to steal the contents of a bank's vault or to attack a Brink's armored truck. More generally, with improvements in the architecture of banks, and in the technology of safes, of alarm systems, of time locks and the like, any large amount of money or valuables can be made practically untouchable. Due to these changes, bank burglars, safe-breakers, and bank sneaks have been driven out of business (a historical testimony to the impact of situational crime prevention).

In turn, economic and social changes have caused the proliferation of easy targets with low or moderate value. More specifically, after World War II, there was a growth in the mass production of durable goods of some value: radios, TV's, sound systems, cars, and so on. Simultaneously, people's routine activities changed, one of the results being a greater number of unoccupied homes during the day (Cohen and Felson 1979). For a potential thief, these developments meant more vulnerable targets of moderate value. In short, during the last 40 years, property offenders have witnessed *the hardening of big targets and the softening of small ones.*

The Superiority of Police Forces

Professional criminals and big gangs of robbers cannot survive without some degree of impunity. Before the 20th century, highwaymen, cattle thieves, and other bandits could flourish because they were out of reach of the law: either their zones of operation were not policed or they could disappear into impregnable sanctuaries that those pursuing did not dare enter (Hobsbawm 1969; Inciardi 1975). In big cities of the past, like London, a distinct underworld with its argot could organize itself inside rookeries that enjoyed a high degree of immunity from the forces of order (Chesney 1970; McMullan 1984). With the progress of political centralization and the creation of modern policing in the 20th century, the superiority of the forces of order over the gangs of rogues became overwhelming, and sanctuaries disappeared. Nowadays, property offenders are facing centralized police organizations equipped with cars, weapons, and communication systems. Because they are so numerous, omnipresent, and mobile, contemporary police forces have a tremendous potential for quick action, so that any gang of bandits can be outnumbered in a matter of minutes, especially in an urban environment. The parallel development of techniques for the identification of known criminals, especially through fingerprints, means that from the standpoint of a professional criminal, each new arrest is put on file, increasing the probability of a conviction and the risk of a heavy sentence the next time. In such a context, predatory criminals become vulnerable to arrest if they stay visible too long; they can no longer afford to attract police attention; and they face very strict time constraints the moment they enter into action. Consequently, speedy and unobtrusive tactics become vital for the offender wanting to stay on the street.

Lacking immunity from police action, contemporary criminals are better off melting into the crowd and looking like any other civilian. In this context, one can understand why the visible urban underworlds of the past are no longer found today. (Among today's juvenile gangs, there is no way to distinguish the delinquent groups from the others.) Staying together in big gangs and speaking their own argot is now dangerous. So contemporary criminals have to opt for a kind of *tactical unorganization*: working alone or with a few co-offenders, and avoiding argot or any distinctive behavior. In doing so, however, they lose their symbols of belonging, and the groups become smaller and less durable.

The Offender's Tactical Response: Crude Quantity Thieving

Given these changes, burglary as a sophisticated craft and robbery as a carefully planned project[1] have become outdated and out of the question. The organization required and the time and money needed are beyond the resources of most criminals. Any attempts to muster the needed organization and resources would make the offenders more visible and attract police attention. In this regard, the Great Train Robbery is really an exception.

Today's offenders, however, can find an abundance of vulnerable small targets. These are easy to find and easy to steal. This is the key to the pettiness and the simplicity of contemporary criminal tactics. The time needed to find a suitable precriminal situation is short and no effort is required to commit the crime. All the offender who wants to make a certain amount of money has to do is to carry out numerous rudimentary thefts—what Tremblay (1986) calls "quantity thieving." Instead of making a few well-prepared big scores, he commits a lot of small thefts, each having a low return. The tactics that evolved in this context are characterized by simplicity and speed. This procedure is a sensible answer to the opportunities found in affluent societies and it gives a reasonable degree of impunity because it takes very little time to do a single job and does not attract intensive police investigation. And since no individual victim suffers great harm, there is a lack of will to wage an energetic war against these offenders.

Conclusion

Useful as it is for situational crime prevention, the rational choice perspective, can also be of some use in achieving a better understanding of the contemporary crime scene. The latter's characteristics have less to do with the offender's psychology than with the situational aspects of crime. And to analyze the impact of the situations on crime patterns, we need to distinguish clearly the situational component of the crime from its tactical aspect.

As Hirschi (1986:115) warned us, we should not over emphasize the rationality and intellectual sophistication of the offenders. On the other hand, neither should we underestimate their capacity as a group for rational adaptation to social change. As big targets became out of reach, 20th-century offenders made the strategic move to hit the small and vulnerable targets they could find in abundance. As modern police became omnipresent and increasingly powerful, criminals evolved from big gangs to loose networks of co-offenders. And since in affluent societies, victims perceive small thefts more as a nuisance than wicked acts, offenders have a fair chance of escaping punishment if they confine themselves to petty crime. Any single offender does not have to be very rational or very intelligent to adopt these tactics. They were probably discovered by trial and error. A considerable number of criminal incidents as measured by victims surveys are only *attempts* to commit crime (according to Hough 1988, 42% of burglaries reported in the British Crime Survey are, in fact, attempts). This means that offenders constantly try things; they drop the ones that fail and repeat their successful moves. Since a strong majority of offenders work at least occasionally with co-offenders and are part of a network of offenders, the successful tactics can be imitated or verbally communicated. This sets in motion a diffusion process of the most effective tactics and a progressive elimination of the ones that are too risky, too difficult, or not sufficiently profitable. At the term of this evolution, the dominant criminal tactics in a given society seem quite effective, not out of a clear reasoning on the part of offenders but as a result of a natural selection process.

Note

1. See McIntosh's (1975) distinction between craft organization and project organization.

References

Barlow, H. 1987. *Introduction to criminology.* Boston: Little, Brown.
Bennett, T., & Wright, R. 1984. *Burglars on burglary: Prevention and the offender.* Aldershot: Gower.
Brantingham, P.L., & Brantingham, P.J. 1984. *Patterns in crime.* New York: Macmillan.
Chesney, K. 1970. *The Victorian underworld.* London: T. Smith.

Cohen, L.E., & Felson, M. 1979. Social change and crime ratio trends: A routine activity approach. *American Sociological Review* 44:588–608.

Conklin, J.E. 1972. *Robbery and the criminal justice system.* New York: Lippincott.

Einstadter, W.J. 1969. The social organization of armed robbery, *Social Problems* 17 (1):64–82.

Ekblom, P. 1988. *Getting the best out of crime analysis.* London: Home Office Crime Prevention Unit Paper 10.

Feeney, F. 1986. Robbers as decision-makers. In D.B. Cornish, & R.V. Clarke (Eds.), *The reasoning criminal* (53–71). New York: Springer-Verlag.

Felson, M. 1988. The changing ecology of security. *Journal of Security Administration* 11:8–11.

Gabor, T., Baril, M., Cusson, M., Elie, D., LeBlanc, M., & Normandeau, A. 1987. *Armed robbery, cops, robbers, and victims.* Springfield, IL: Charles C. Thomas.

Gassin, R. 1988. *Criminologie.* Paris: Dalloz.

Gottfredson, M., & Hirschi, T. 1990. *A general theory of crime.* Stanford, CA: Stanford University Press.

Haran, J.F., & Martin, J.M. 1977. The imprisonment of bank robbers: The issue of deterrence. *Federal Probation* 41–42:28–30.

Hirschi, T. 1986. On the compatibility of rational choice and social control theories of crime. In D.B. Cornish & R.V. Clarke (Eds.), *The Reasoning Criminal* (105–118). New York: Springer-Verlag.

Hobsbawm, E.J. 1969. *Bandits.* London: George Weidenfeld & Nicoloson.

Hough, M. 1987. Offenders' choice of target: Finding from victim surveys. *Journal of Quantitative Criminology* 3:355–70.

Inciardi, J.A. 1975. *Careers in crime.* Chicago: Rand McNally.

Karpis, A., & Trent, B. 1971. *Public enemy number one.* Toronto-Montréal: McCulland and Stewart Ltd.

Kinberg, O. 1935. *Les problèmes fondamentaux de la criminologie.* Paris: Cujas. (Traduction française 1959)

Lemert, E.M. 1958. The behavior of the systematic check forger. *Social Problem* (Fall): 141–48 (Reprinted in Lemert, E.M. 1967. *Human deviance, social problem and social control.* Englewood Cliffs, NJ: Prentice-Hall).

Letkemann, P. 1973. *Crime as work.* Englewood Cliffs, NJ: Prentice-Hall.

Maguire, M. 1988. Searchers and opportunists: Offender behaviour and burglary prevention. *Journal of Security Administration* 11:70–77.

Maurer, D.W. 1964. *Whiz mob.* New Haven, CT: College and University Press.

McIntosh, Mary. 1975. *The organisation of crime.* London: Macmillan Press.

McMullan, J.L. 1984. *The canting crew: London's criminal underworld, 1550–1700.* New Brunswick, NJ: Rutger University Press.

Pinatel, J. 1975. *Traité de droit pénal et de criminologie T III: La Criminologie.* Paris: Dalloz (1ère édition 1963)

Rengert, G., & Wasilchick, J. 1985. *Suburban burglary.* Springfield, IL: Charles C. Thomas.

Sutherland, E.H. 1937. *The professional thief.* Chicago: University of Chicago Press.

Tremblay, P. 1986. Designing crime. The short life expectancy and the working of a recent wave of credit card bank fraud. *British Journal of Criminology* 26(3):234–53.

Walsh, D.P. 1980. *Break-ins: Burglary from private house.* London: Constable.

13

Conscience, Opportunity, Rational Choice, and Crime

Gordon Trasler

In their early essays in rational choice theory, Ronald Clarke and Derek Cornish emphasized their dissatisfaction with contemporary explanations of delinquency and criminality, because these had not generated effective methods of controlling or modifying the conduct of offenders or useful social policies in relation to crime. By contrast, the group of strategies described as "situational crime prevention" did seem to have some impact on certain kinds of crime, within the limits set by the phenomena of displacement.

I shall endeavor to argue in this chapter that rational choice theory, which has been largely developed by economists as a characterization of the decision processes that prompt economic behavior, does not give a complete account of the mechanisms involved in criminality or the decision to commit or to refrain from particular crimes (to borrow Wilkins's useful distinction between crime and criminality), and needs to be supplemented, but not supplanted, by a "dispositional," theory. I shall try to examine the connections between conscience and rational choice, relying upon the notion of "bounded rationality," Davidson's conception of akratic behavior, and Tyler's recent study of the nature of normative commitment to obey the law.

Situational Crime Prevention

Situational crime control was developed originally in response to the realization that "dispositional" conceptions of criminality were not of much help in attempts to reduce the incidence of predatory crime. Endeavors directed at crime prevention through the treatment or retraining of convicted offenders had proved ineffective. In particular, confidence that the achievement of greater understanding of the etiology of criminality would lead to the development of better strategies for remediation seemed to have been misplaced. While we understood—or thought we understood—what caused people to join the ranks of those "known to the police," we had no effective strategies for rescuing individuals from this category. In respect to treatment, retraining, or rehabilitation, it appeared that "nothing worked."

This was, perhaps, an excessively harsh conclusion, but it was also a salutary corrective to the prevailing beliefs that in order to curb the incidence of crime, one needed only to modify the behavior of convicted offenders, and that we already possessed the technology to achieve this. The treatment strategies of the time simply did not restrain the identified offender or deflect the potential offender from a criminal career.

Situational crime control originated as a quiverful of practical tactics: fitting steering column locks to cars, strengthening coin boxes in telephone booths, installing closed-circuit video cameras in stores and underground railway stations, paying wages by bank transfer rather than in cash, and modifying the design of housing complexes to ensure that entrances were in full view of dwellings so that intruders were conspicuous. Such tactics were promising in their potential for reducing certain kinds of crime, and in some cases seem to have secured very substantial and lasting changes in vandalism, in the pattern of motor vehicle theft, and in such noncriminal activities as suicide by carbon monoxide poisoning (Clarke and Mayhew 1988) and causing obstruction of the public roads by the practice of "cruising"—that is, driving aimlessly around in automobiles, an activity that is apparently common among adolescents of both sexes in the United States (Bell and Burke 1992:108–12). Some of the more conspicuous successes for situational prevention are reported in Clarke (1992).

Other practical measures have been less successful. In a thoughtful paper, Berry and Carter (1992) suggest that certain crime prevention initiatives "follow a finite life cycle," becoming less effective and requiring renewal or replacement by a different type of intervention after a while. Some—such as improving street lighting—seem to diminish fear of victimization without affecting risk (Atkins, Husain and Storey 1991; Ramsay 1991; Tien et al. 1979). There are a few clear-cut examples of displacement, and rather more disputed instances (see, for example, Mayhew, Clarke, and Hough in Clarke 1992:52–65; Webb and Laycock 1992a;

Challinger 1991:81). [Clarke presents an interesting analysis of displacement effects, extending the discussion to the phenomenon of "diffusion of benefits," remarking that "the debate about effectiveness may take an altogether different turn with the newly growing realization that situational prevention can sometimes produce the 'complete reverse' of displacement (Poyner 1988), a reduction in crimes not directly addressed by the preventive measures" (Clarke 1992:25). On the other hand, methods intended to frustrate offenders sometimes appear to encourage them by presenting new and exciting challenges (Webb and Laycock 1992b).

These practical measures were not initially informed by an explicit theory of criminal behavior. Insofar as they represented a new emphasis upon the environmental cues that seemed to encourage or deter criminal activity, they relied on the notion that, other things being equal, some individuals seek to maximize personal gain or satisfaction through acquisitive crime or illegal expressive activities such as vandalism or aggressive violence, and to minimize the risk of negative consequences, such as arrest and judicial penalty. Thus in *The Reasoning Criminal* (1986a), Cornish and Clarke explain that the starting point of the rational choice perspective on criminal behavior was "the assumption that offenders seek to benefit themselves by their criminal behavior; that this involves the making of decisions and of choices, however rudimentary on occasion these choices might be; and that these processes exhibit a measure of rationality, albeit constrained by limits of time and ability and the availability of relevant information . . . even in the case of offenses that seemed to be pathologically motivated or impulsively executed . . . it was felt that the identification and description of these might have lessons for crime-control policy" (Cornish and Clarke 1986a:1–2). The notion of rational choice is not, of course, novel: it is characteristic of economic theories designed to account for the behavior of consumers and investors, and has already made one rather unfortunate appearance in criminology as the basis of Isaac Ehrlich's (1975) analysis of the deterrent effect of capital punishment. There are (I would suggest) two basic questions to be asked of the rational choice model. First, do the notions of rationality and conscious choice furnish a recognizable characterization of what happens at the time of the commission of a crime? Second, does this theoretical stance enable us to make better predictions about the occurrence of crime, or to devise better ways of curbing crime, or both?

In its most robust form, a rational choice model is based on the assumption that the individual actor is, at the relevant time, in possession of full and accurate information concerning the risks and potential gains that attend a given course of action, and that he will process all of this information logically and with precision, in deciding whether to proceed (see

Becker's seminal paper, published in 1968). In a more recent formulation, Elster says:

> Rational choice theory appeals to three distinct elements in the choice situation. The first element is the feasible set, i.e., the set of all courses of action which (are rationally believed to) satisfy various logical, physical and economic constraints. The second is (a set of rational beliefs about) the causal structure of the situation, which determines what courses of action will lead to what outcomes. The third is a subjective ranking of the feasible alternatives, derived from a ranking of the outcomes to which they (are expected to) lead. To act rationally, then, simply means to choose the highest-ranked element in the feasible set." (Elster 1986:4)

There are several aspects of this description that are of particular significance. It refers to the choices and decisions of individuals in specific situations, rather than categories of situations; it implies simultaneous processing of information, rather than serial processing; and it attributes to the individual the capacity to handle what may be complex information in the form of probabilities. As Cornish and Clarke, and indeed many other authors, have pointed out, these circumstances are very unlikely to obtain in relation to criminal activities. To the extent that people employ subjective rather than objective probabilities in arriving at decisions, allowance must presumably be made for individual differences (for instance, in appreciation of risks) which may be substantial. Studies that have sought to test the adequacy of the expected utility model against aggregate data are, for that reason, misconceived; however, they, and the handful of studies that have used individual data, "provide only very weak support for the expected utility model" (Lattimer and Witte 1986: 131). (Another version of the rational choice model, the "prospect theory model" of Kahneman and Tversky (1984) is as yet untested in relation to criminal behavior [Johnson and Payne 1986:179].)

Apart from the problem of identifying the variables to be entered into the decision equations (Lattimore and Witte rather oddly portray the potential burglar as weighing the prospect of a gain in wealth against the risk of a loss of leisure) there are difficulties about representing the potential offender as a rational, dispassionate, calculating decision maker. For one thing, many offenders seem to be very vague about such matters as the probability of being apprehended, the likelihood, in that event, of being convicted, and the "going rate" of penalties for such a crime. Some exponents of rational choice theory are undismayed by this, arguing that while the potential criminal may be mistaken in his assessments of the consequences and probabilities contingent upon an action, he may still act rationally in the sense that he derives a logical inference from the data available to him. What is meant by rationality, in this sense, is spelled out by Carroll and Weaver: "Did the subjects make decisions . . . consistent with a normative economic model of optimal decisions? . . . Did the subjects go about deciding in a rational way, collecting relevant information, carefully weighing it in a systematic and effective manner, and acting consistently with their decisions?" (Carroll and Weaver 1986:31). Their study suggests that, among their group of shoplifters, these criteria were not met: they certainly estimated the risk of being detected with some care, but paid little heed to what was likely to happen to them if they should get caught.

Imperfect Rationality

In his fascinating and exhaustive analysis of decision making under conditions of uncertainty, Watkins (1970) makes some important points that are relevant to the analysis of decisions leading to the commission of a crime. Watkins distinguishes between three kinds of decisions: those made "under conditions of certainty," where the decision maker "proceeds as if he knew (a) all of the alternative decisions open to him. . . . and (b) the outcome for him that would infallibly follow from each of these possible decisions" (p. 179); those made under conditions of risk where the decision maker "is again assumed to know all the alternative decisions that are open to him. . . . while he does not know that outcome a decision would have he does know, in the case of each possible decision, each of the possible outcomes it might have . . . casinos and lotteries may provide conditions of risk in this sense, but horse-racing does not." (Watkins 1970:181). The third category of decisions consists of those made under conditions of uncertainty, in which "the decision-maker is again assumed to know all the alternative decisions open to him . . . and, for each possible decision, all the alternative outcomes it might have; but though he may judge one outcome to be more, or less, or equally likely than another, he is *not* able to assign to each outcome a non-arbitrary numerical probability" (Watkins 1970:193). It is this third category that seems to offer the best approximation to the circumstances in which people embark upon the commission of a crime.

Most empirical researchers in this field seem to take the view that a more modest conception of rationality provides a more convincing model of the ways in which offenders decide to commit crimes. The notions of "limited" or "bounded" rationality diverge from the expected utility maximization theory in two ways. First, arriving at the decision to act, as described by burglars or shoplifters, for example, is typically a serial process — deciding to look around for potential targets, reviewing hazards and vulnerable features of the target, and guessing at the possible yield;

watchfully approaching the target, and finally taking the plunge — often still with the possibility of aborting the venture if signs of trouble should appear. Second, some of the elements that would appear in a formal decision model are treated as data — "standing decisions," as Cook (1980) calls them: the individual relies upon decisions taken on previous occasions (presumably with a successful outcome) as to whether the presence of a dog in the house or of human occupants or locks or burglar alarms, presents too high a risk, or whether shoplifting is too risky if there are video cameras in the store. It is clear, from case studies of offenders, that such "standing decisions" vary considerably from one person to another.

While "bounded rationality" models are a great deal more convincing, they lack the elegance and precision of the expected utility maximization model, and one can hardly recognize them as devices for framing policies for crime prevention — the principal role for which rational choice theory was designed, having regard in particular to Lattimore and Witte's (1986) insistence that such models are designed to operate at the level of individuals, not of groups or aggregates.

One of the attractions of expected utility theory in modeling economic behavior is that — at least in principle — it is possible to enter into the equations appropriate values for the information available to the actor concerning the probabilities of particular outcomes. But in the case of criminal actions it is surely impossible to do this: we do not know whether the potential offender was, at the time of committing (or not committing) the crime, in possession of sufficient, accurate information to allow him to make a good bet on the likely outcomes of action or inaction, or to estimate the extent to which the information available to him fell short of what would have been needed to make such an estimation. Since we do not know what information the individual had, it is a matter of lesser importance than it might seem, whether he processed this information with optimal efficiency.

It may be objected that this information might be secured by interrogating the individual after the event. But this presents formidable problems of the accuracy of recall and of rationalization. It is least available in instances in which the individual decided against committing the crime, or — if he did go ahead with it — managed to evade detection; and it is by no means certain that offenders have an accurate grasp of their own decision processes (see Cusson and Pinsonneault 1986). Again, it is not clear whether the rational choice model is intended to account for particular crimes committed, or not completed, by people who have already elected to participate in criminal activities, and is therefore inapplicable to those who have not so elected (in which case it encounters problems with the distinctly fragile distinction between criminals and noncriminals), or whether the inadequacies of their decision-making skills are in some way a contributory cause of the criminal orientation of active offenders — a predisposing condition. If that is the case, the intriguing possibility arises that improvement in decision skills might bring with it not just a reduced likelihood of getting caught, but cessation from crime.

Irrational Behavior

Watkins enumerates several other features of decision making under conditions of uncertainty that represent significant departures from the conventional conception of rational decision making, as reflected, for example, in the expected utility maximization model.

> An actual decision-scheme is usually built up bit by bit, so that the arrival of an isolated bit of situational information may have a quite disproportional influence. And even when all the evidence is in, the practical significance of different parts of it may wax and wane as the decision-maker attends now to this factor, now to that. Not only is an actual decision-scheme more or less vague and fragmentary compared with the ideal, but the agent will usually *reduce and simplify it further* as he proceeds towards a decision. Instead of the complete enumeration of possibilities demanded by normative theory, we usually seize upon a few features and pick out a few interesting possibilities in the given problem-situation.

> In "one-person games" also there is often a compelling need to *narrow* one's attention, to reduce very drastically the possibilities to be taken seriously. ... Where the situation offers a fairly continuous range of possibilities, the decision-maker will often, in the interests of psychological determinacy, *create* discontinuities by drawing more or less arbitrary lines. We dislike having things hovering around our threshold of practical significance. Faced by a small probability of a large calamity the average decision-maker is likely *either* to treat it as if its probability were zero and to exclude it from his decision scheme, *or* to treat it as if its probability were significantly higher than it is. (Watkins 1970:206–8)

Finally, Watkins points out that although the decision taker has made a competent appraisal of the situation that confronts him and arrived at a rational decision, he may subsequently change his mind. "If my prediction [of another's conduct] is to follow logically I must add the further assumption that he will act rationally. It looks trivial; perhaps it *is* trivial, but we need it if we are logically to derive predictions about actions from premisses about the agents' situations" (Watkins 1970:173).

Akrasia

A form of irrationality that might prove to be of particular interest to criminologists has been termed *akratic behavior* (Davidson 1980). Elster (1986) provides a succinct account of this notion:

> Akrasia is characterized by the following features. (l) There is a *prima facie* judgment that X is good; (2) There is a *prima facie* judgment that Y is good; (3) There is an all-things-considered judgment that X is best; (4) There is the fact that Y is chosen. Taking a drink against one's better judgment is a familiar example. (P. 15)

Elster's example demonstrates two important attributes of akratic behavior concerning "the relation between desires and behaviour, or weakness of the will" (Elster 1986: 15). These are (1) the sequential nature of decision making: the observation that considerations that are distant in temporal terms from the situation in which a certain kind of behavior is a viable option may have less weight than those that obtain at the relevant time—one may jettison long-term principles for short-term gratification; and (2) that appetites or temptations may override long-term strategic decisions, but typically in circumstances in which the long-term decisions are rational, and the immediate temptations are visceral or emotional. (Although it would be difficult to dispute this analysis of responses to temptation, the general thrust of this essay is that it is more usually the case that long-term, strategic decisions or orientations reflect strong affective ["moral"] postures, and that responses to immediate temptation involve short-term, superficial or opportunistic reactions to immediate cues.) In writing about akratic decision making, Elster notes that

> when comparing, well ahead of the time of choice, a later larger reward X with an earlier smaller reward Y, the agent thinks X is best. This is his calm, reflected judgment of what is best, all things considered. When the time of choice approaches, however, the imminent availability of Y disturbs his judgment, there occurs a preference reversal, and Y is chosen. (P.15)

This analysis draws attention to the conflict between long-term or "standing" decisions and immediate or "tactical" decisions that often seem to be present before the commission of a crime. Elster is concerned about demonstrating that what is called "akratic" behavior is intentional but irrational; that it is the outcome of a conflict between a general orientation or strategic decision and the temptations or pressures of immediate opportunities. In doing so he draws attention to the serial nature of some forms of decision making, in contrast to the conception of a single, simultaneous review of available opportunities and risks that represents the starting point of expected-utility models of rational choice.

Normative Decisions and Rationality

In its simplest form, rational choice theory seems to imply that every individual must engage in a review of the possibility of gain and the risk of undesirable consequences whenever he encounters an opportunity for theft or some other kind of illegal gratification. This unlikely prospect is modified by Cook's notion of "standing decisions," which presumably cause many people to ignore opportunities for profitable, illegal behavior most of the time: they have made a "standing decision" to obey the law. The relations between standing decisions, which can broadly be described as strategic in nature, and the tactical decisions that cause less law-abiding people to seize or to reject particular opportunities for crime, is less than clear. An orthodox interpretation of expected utility theory would imply that standing decisions would be arrived at by an evaluation of the probable gains and risks of engaging in crime, in general terms, in a way that parallels the potential offender's calculations in relation to a particular opportunity for crime. Yet Tyler's (1990) study of "why people obey the law" does not support such an interpretation. Tyler makes a distinction between *instrumental* and *normative* mechanisms of conformity; the first of these corresponding fairly closely with the model presented by rational choice theory:

> The instrumental perspective on the citizen underlies what is known as the deterrence literature: people are viewed as shaping their behavior to respond to changes in the tangible, immediate incentives and penalties associated with following the law — to judgments about the personal gains and losses resulting from different kinds of behavior . . . a normative perspective . . . is concerned with the influence of what people regard as just and moral as opposed to what is in their self-interest. . . . If people view compliance with the law as appropriate because of their attitudes about how they should behave, they will voluntarily assume the obligation to follow legal rules. They will feel personally committed to obeying the law, irrespective of whether they risk punishment for breaking the law. (Tyler 1990:3–4)

Tyler found, in his Chicago sample, that normative mechanisms were more important in securing conformity with the law than instrumental mechanisms — in other words, that personal morality, or recognition of the legitimate authority of the law, rather than the fear of punishment was the usual reason for refraining from crime (a finding that is consistent with that of the earlier study of Piliavin et al. 1986; see also Tittle 1977, 1980; Grasmick and Green 1980).

The two sources of conformity described by Tyler — "normative judgments through personal morality," and "normative judgments through legitimacy" — reflect several of the characteristics of what is commonly called "conscience." They do not depend upon the threat of punishment or calculations of the gains that might be secured by a criminal act (to use the psychologist's terminology, they are "situation independent" rather than "situation dependent"); they represent a general orientation, in the sense that they effectively remove certain classes or types of behavior from the individual's repertoire. This implies that they are "temporally prior" to any decisions concerning the commission of any particular crime for which there may be an opportunity, essentially preempting such decisions — a feature that is consistent with the notion of sequential decision making rather than simultaneous decision making; they involve convictions (not simply opinions) about what is right and what is wrong. But they share with rational choice theory an exclusive emphasis on cognitive processes and a corresponding neglect of the affective aspect of conscientious behavior. An adequate description of what is experienced as conscience must surely embrace *feelings* of obligation, aversion, self-regard, and the anticipation of guiltiness.

This essentially informal or intuitive notion about the nature of what are sometimes called "gut feelings" of right and wrong — the mechanisms that can, and often do, override "rational" considerations of the prospect of personal gain and risk — is strongly supported by a substantial body of experimental research into what has come to be called "aversive inhibitory conditioning" — what was, in the animal laboratory, termed "passive avoidance conditioning": that is to say, the process by which punishments and threats secure the blocking of highly motivated behavior. The existence of such a mechanism is, of course, the basic requirement of a "dispositional" theory of criminality, which has the task of explaining how it is that individuals are induced to develop an antipathy to illegal, immoral, or dishonest behavior that causes them to ignore, or even not to perceive, opportunities for gain or gratification. In the strict terms of the expected utility model, as described by Elster (1986) the posture of the individual who insists that, whatever the possibilities of personal gain and the remoteness of risk, he will refrain from criminal opportunities, is clearly irrational. He ought, in theory, to weigh the consequences of neglecting his moral principles against the expectation of gain, and — given contemporary conditions in which the probability of being apprehended for an offense of any of the more common categories is low — he might be expected, on rational grounds, to decide that the prospect of gain was more attractive than the possibility of moral censure.

The work of Tuck and Riley (1986) is an attempt to accommodate essentially noneconomic variables of this kind in a rational choice model, making use of the theoretical scheme offered by Ajzen and Fishbein (1980). The essential difficulty about this seems to be that one cannot conceive of the demands of noneconomic considerations being placed in the balance against purely economic elements: "It would be wrong to do this" is not a statement of probability or of degree, but a categorical statement that necessarily takes precedence over a quantitative estimate of the likely advantage to be secured from a course of action. It might be argued that these differences in the significance of moral and practical considerations are also represented as temporal differences: we first determine what kinds of information we are prepared to admit to the decision-making process, and we then proceed to a decision on the basis of a limited set of data. The "moral" individual does not admit to his decision-set considerations that are inconsistent with his moral stance. (The term *moral* is intended to subsume what Tyler [1990] refers to as "normative . . . through personal morality.")

Dispositional Theories of Criminality

"Dispositional" theories imply that whether or not an individual commits a crime on a given occasion is largely determined by his personal characteristics or attributes—they seek to explain criminality rather than criminal acts. Psychologists have been impressed by the immunity to temptation (often amounting to an inability to perceive opportunities for illicit gain or satisfaction) that characterizes the ordinary, well-socialized person, and have consequently concentrated their attention upon those circumstances in which socialization, in this sense, fails. It is clear that inadequate parenting (poor parent-child bonding, inefficient child-training procedures) and the conflicting influences of delinquent subcultures are implicated in failures of socialization. Such analyses, however, take little account of the possibility that individuals differ in their responsiveness to the ways in which parents seek to socialize them. It has, of course, been demonstrated that the absence or the disruption of an affectional bond between parents and child, upon which socialization depends, will retard the suppression of delinquent, predatory behavior. But what of the individual who fails to respond to what appear to be normal conditions of upbringing in a stable and affectionate family? The extreme example of such unresponsiveness is what has come to be known as the primary psychopath (or sociopath)—the person who seems to be wholly lacking in the capacity to experience genuine affection or the obligations of personal loyalty, who shows no sign of compunction or remorse in exploiting and deceiving others, and consequently breaks laws and social conventions whenever it is to his advantage to do so. Recent research (Hare and Schalling 1978) has made considerable progress in identifying the reasons for the refractoriness to ordinary strategies of socialization practiced by parents that characterizes the primary psychopath as an inability to respond to signals of impending punishment, having its origin in what is possibly a constitutional defect of autonomic nervous system functioning. Since, in our culture at least, training children to inhibit aggressive, dishonest, and predatory behavior is normally accomplished by associating early instances of such behavior with punishment, in the form of parental rebukes and expressions of disapproval, such a defect would clearly frustrate attempts to curb these forms of behavior.

Hare's and Schalling's work has made a considerable impact upon the psychology of criminal behavior, playing a part in the revival of biological models of criminality that has been evident during the last decade. Yet its implications for the explanation of nonpsychopathic criminality have been misinterpreted. It is a mistake to regard the psychopath as the type case of criminality. Most offenders, including some of the most persistent, are in general reasonably responsive to the rules, norms, and obligations of the society to which they belong. Their propensity to break the law is fairly specific, in contrast to the habitual disregard of all rules that characterizes the psychopath. It is probable that responsiveness to aversive inhibitory conditioning (that is, the ability to inhibit behavior previously followed by punishment or the threat of it) is a matter of degree (Fowles 1980; Gray 1975; Trasler 1978, 1987). But the main contribution of Hare's work has been to construct a much more precise specification of optimal and less than optimal conditions for the acquisition of those learned inhibitory responses that normally ensure law-abiding behavior.

The most sophisticated of the biological perspectives on criminality to emerge in recent years is Sarnoff Mednick's "biosocial" theory (Mednick et al. 1974). The principal empirical basis of Mednick's work consists of plausible, but not yet conclusive, evidence of a connection between criminality (as indexed by formal convictions) and some enduring characteristic that is distributed across several generations, and among blood relations, in ways that strongly suggest genetic transmission. He presents data from twin studies, from comprehensive police records, and from cross-fostering studies, in support of this proposition.

In order to sustain a case for biological influences upon the disposition to commit crimes, it is necessary to identify the characteristic that mediates this effect and is, by implication, transmitted by the mechanisms of genetics. Mednick's solution to this problem is based upon a version of Mowrer's (1960) two-factor theory of passive avoidance learning. Mednick advances the proposition that "the psychopath and the criminal [may] have some defect in avoidance learning which interferes with their ability to learn to inhibit asocial responses" (Mednick et al. 1974: 2). The requirements for the acquisition and maintenance of such inhibitions are a "censuring agent" (usually a parent or parents); an adequate fear response; the ability to experience fear in anticipation of an asocial action; and fast dissipation of fear, which will produce maximally effective reinforcement of the conditioned inhibitory response. Mednick endeavored to translate this theoretical model into operational terms, so that it could be tested in the laboratory, adopting as his index of changes in arousal (that is, responses to punishment and to the threat of punishment) changes in skin conductance. He argued that the electrodermal response reflects the onset and offset of fear; the amplitude of the response indicates the intensity of the fear reaction; while the rapidity with which skin conductance returns to the basal level (the recovery half-time) is a measure of the rate of fear dissipation. Rapid electrodermal recovery, according to this view, means effective reinforcement of the acquired inhibitory response; slow recovery, on the other hand, implies poor capacity for forming and maintaining inhibitory responses.

There are indications in the literature that undersocialized, delinquent individuals do indeed tend to show slow electrodermal recovery in the laboratory. Hare (1978) found this to be true, in certain conditions, of primary psychopaths. Levander and others (Levander et al. 1980) reported similar findings in a sample of male offenders, and Siddle (Siddle et al. 1977) also found that a tendency to slow electrodermal recovery distinguished between strongly antisocial, incarcerated adolescent offenders and their less delinquent peers. Mednick's own laboratory has provided further data in support of this proposition. In short, the notion that socially conforming behavior depends upon affective processes as well as cognitive (rational) processes seems to attract some support from experimental evidence that individuals who are conspicuously lacking in conformity tend to possess some deficits in the physiological mechanisms that mediate emotional responses to conditioned or "signal" stimuli. The connection is a remote one, but not without significance.

There are problems about the Mednick model (Trasler 1980), but it would not be appropriate to discuss them in this essay. What is important, for present purposes, is to note that Mednick's theory, and the empirical evidence presented in support of it, suggests that the establishment of a general tendency to refrain from illegal and antisocial activities depends upon a conditioned emotional response rather than a rational calculation, and that this response is the consequence of training or "socialization" by parents or other agents within the framework of a dependent affectional relationship. In short, what is being argued is that the trait or disposition of criminality, and its antithesis (inelegantly termed *law-abidingness* by some writers, but meaning conformity with the laws and moral rules of society) is not a matter of rational calculation, but of the conditioning that is brought about by parental training. It follows that individual differences in the propensity to commit crimes are to be sought in variations in sensitiveness to conditioning and in the capacity to respond emotionally to punishment and the threat of punishment (using the term broadly to include the prospect of parental disapproval).

Although dispositional theories have, in the view of the writer, achieved reasonable success in explaining why some individuals are persistently and indiscriminately criminal, and why others refrain absolutely from criminal conduct, they do have major weaknesses, some of which have been exposed by modern studies of criminal careers. It has become clear, for example, that most criminal careers are comparatively short—an observation that creates major difficulties for a theory that attempts to relate childhood events to adult criminality or compliance with the law (see Cusson and Pinsonneault 1986). There are also problems that derive from the fact that many people—perhaps a majority of male citizens—occasionally break the law, and indeed that more than half of the male population can expect to incur a criminal conviction during their lifetimes (Farrington 1981)—an observation that is very difficult to reconcile with the assertion that a criminal conviction is evidence of a failure of socialization. On the other hand, some data relating to displacement effects, and evidence that comparatively few persistent offenders are specialists in the kinds of crime in which they are involved, tend to support the case for dispositional theories, while not necessarily detracting from the explanatory value of the rational choice perspective. One significant contention concerns the applicability of rational choice analysis beyond its original "range of convenience" to acquisitive crimes. This writer offered the suggestion that the rational choice model made sense in relation to "instrumental" offenses, but not in relation to "expressive" crimes, including the passionate offenses of homicide, for example, or wounding, where the notion of a rational calculus was unconvincing (Trasler 1986). This criticism was parried by Cornish and Clarke (1986a:14) on the grounds that studies of violent offenses "suggest that many such offenses do indeed exhibit a substantial degree of rationality." This is an issue that will repay further research. Some violent offenses (including robberies) are clearly instrumental rather than expressive in nature, and involve very little more violence than is necessary to achieve their purpose of extracting valuable property (Feeney 1986). Others are quite clearly explosive and wholly destructive, representing a demonstrative rejection of all restraints upon aggressive behavior, and require a very different kind of explanation. There are some—and Clarke and Cornish (1985) cite the work of the Dobash partnership—that seem to involve nice balancing of aggressive impulses against predictions of the response of the criminal justice system, posing major problems for exponents of the rational choice perspective, and certainly for dispositional theorists. It is arguable, however, that the essential distinction is not between predatory and aggressive crimes, but between instrumental and expressive crimes. Robbery is an example of an instrumental crime that involves violence, but arguably minimal violence (Feeney 1986); whether domestic violence involves any kind of calculus as to its consequences is another matter of major significance to the viability of rational choice perspectives.

Conclusion

Rational choice theories are mainly concerned with explaining the conditions in which an individual who is not in principle averse to criminal conduct will respond to opportunities to gratify his needs. Dispositional theories of criminality, on the other hand, are concerned with those mechanisms that cause many people to eschew criminal activities, no matter how attractive they may be in terms of their potential for gratification and how remote the risk of penal consequences may be. (The reader may be surprised that this negative form of words is used: the fact is that the most satisfactory formulations of such theories seek to explain how one acquires a disposition to inhibit criminal conduct rather than to account for the acquisition of a tendency to commit crimes.) Although rational choice and dispositional approaches have been represented as being in competition, they are in fact intended to explain different aspects of criminal activity, and are essentially complementary rather than incompatible: it is contended that research directed at the relationship between the two is likely to be fruitful, both in theoretical terms and in developing practical means of countering the damage done by criminal activities. Cornish and Clarke, who are the initiators of what has proved to be an important debate in criminological theory, clearly recognize that the simultaneous processing model that is implied by strict expected-utility theory is inappropriate in explaining criminal activities: some form of serial decision making is needed. The thrust of this chapter is that this modification of classical expected-utility theory must also take account of qualitative differences between tactical decisions that may be wholly rational in the sense that they reflect balancing of expected gains against anticipated risks, and long-term "standing decisions" or orientations that involve nonrational, affective components that are best described as moral or normative decisions, and are not responsive to the immediate contingencies of arrest and escape.

References

Ajzen, I., & Fishbein, M. 1980. *Understanding attitudes and predicting social behavior.* Englewood Cliffs, NJ: Prentice-Hall.

Atkins, S., Husain, S., & Storey, A. 1991. *The influence of street lighting on crime and fear of crime.* Crime Prevention Unit: Paper 28. London: Home Office.

Becker, G.S. 1968. Crime and punishment: An economic approach. *Journal of Political Economy* 78:169–217.

Bell, J., & Burke, B. 1992. Cruising Cooper street. In R.V. Clarke (Ed.), *Situational crime prevention: Successful case studies.* New York: Harrow and Heston.

Berry, G., & Carter, M. 1992. *Assessing crime prevention initiatives: The first steps* (Crime Prevention Unit: Paper 31). London: Home Office.

Carroll, J., & Weaver, F. 1986. Shoplifters' perceptions of crime opportunities: A process-tracing study. In D.B. Cornish & R.V. Clarke (Eds.), *The reasoning criminal.* New York: Springer-Verlag.

Challinger, D. 1991. Less telephone vandalism: How did it happen? *Security Journal* 2:111–19. (Reprinted in R.V. Clarke [Ed.], Situational crime prevention: Successful case studies [75–88]). New York: Harrow and Heston.

Clarke, R.V. (Ed.). 1992. *Situational crime prevention: Successful case studies.* New York: Harrow and Heston.

Clarke, R.V., & Mayhew, P. 1988. The British gas suicide story and its criminological implications. In M. Tonry & N. Morris (Eds.), *Crime and justice* (Vol. 10, 79–116). Chicago: Chicago University Press.

Cook, P.J. 1980. Research in criminal deterrence: Laying the groundwork for the second decade. In N. Morris & M. Tonry (Eds.), *Crime and justice: An annual review of research* (Vol. 2). Chicago: University of Chicago Press.

Cornish, D.B., & Clarke, R.V. (Eds.), 1986a. *The reasoning criminal.* New York: Springer-Verlag.

Cornish, D.B., & Clarke, R.V. 1986b. Situational prevention, displacement of crime and rational choice theory. In K. Heal & G. Laycock (Eds.), *Situational crime prevention* (1–16). London: HMSO.

Cusson, M., & Pinsonneault, P. 1986. The decision to give up crime. In D.B. Cornish, & R.V. Clarke (Eds.), *The reasoning criminal* (72–82). New York: Springer-Verlag.

Davidson, D. 1980. *Essays on actions and events.* Oxford, England: Oxford University Press.

Ehrlich, I. 1975. The deterrent effect of capital punishment: A question of life and death. *American Economic Review* 65: 397–417.

Elster, J. 1986. *Rational choice.* Oxford: Blackwell.

Farrington, D.P. 1981. The prevalence of convictions. *British Journal of Criminology* 21:173–75.

Feeney, F. 1986. Robbers as decision-makers. In D.B. Cornish & R.V. Clarke, (Eds.), *The reasoning criminal* 53–71. New York: Springer-Verlag.

Fowles, D.C. 1980. The three arousal model: Implications of Gray's two-factor learning theory for heart rate, electrodermal activity, and psychopathy. *Psychophysiology* 17:87–104.

Grasmick, H.G., & Green, D.E. 1980. Legal punishment, social disapproval and internalisation as inhibitors of illegal behavior. *Journal of Criminal Law and Criminology* 71:325–35.

Gray, J.A. 1975. *Elements of a two-process theory of learning.* New York. Academic Press.

Hare, R.D. 1978. Electrodermal and cardiovascular correlates of psychopathy. In R.D. Hare & D. Schalling (Eds.), *Psychopathic behaviour: Approaches to research* (107–143). New York: Wiley.

Hare, R. D., & Schalling, D. 1978. *Psychopathic behavior: Approaches to research.* Chichester, England: John Wiley & Sons.

Johnson, E., & Payne, J. 1986. The decision to commit a crime: An information-processing analysis. In D.B. Cornish & R.V. Clarke (Eds.), *The reasoning criminal* (170–85). New York: Springer-Verlag.

Kahneman, D., & Tversky, A. 1984. Choices, values, and frames. *American Psychologist* 39:341–50.

Lattimore, P., & Witte, A. 1986. Models of decision making under uncertainty, The criminal choice. In D.B. Cornish & R.V. Clarke (Eds.), *The reasoning criminal* (129–155). New York: Springer-Verlag.

Levander, S.E., Schalling, D.S., Lidberg, L., Bartfai, A., & Lidberg, Y. 1980. Skin conductance recovery time and personality in a group of criminals. *Psychophysiology* 17:105–11.

Mayhew, P., Clarke, R.V., & Hough, M. 1976. Steering column locks and car theft. (Reprinted in R.V. Clarke (Ed.), *Situational crime prevention: Successful case studies.* Albany, NY: Harrow and Heston.)

Mednick, S.A., Schulsinger, F., Higgins, J., & Bell, B. 1974. *Genetics, environment and psychopathology.* New York: North Holland.

Mowrer, O.H. 1960. *Learning theory and behavior.* New York: Wiley.

Piliavin, I., Thornton, C., Gartner, R., & Matsueda, R.L. 1986. Crime, deterrence, and rational choice. *American Sociological Review* 51:101–19.

Poyner, B. 1986. A model for action. In K. Heal & G. Laycock (Eds.), *Situational crime prevention: From theory into practice.* London: HMSO.

———. 1988. Video cameras and bus vandalism. *Journal of Security Administration* 11:44–51.

Ramsay, M. 1991. *The effect of better street lighting on crime and fear: A review* (Crime Prevention Unit: Paper 29). London: Home Office.

Siddle, D.A.T., Mednick, S.A., Nicol, A.R., & Foggitt, R.H. 1977. Skin conductance recovery in anti-social adolescents. In S.A. Mednick & K.O. Christiansen (Eds.), *Biosocial bases of criminal behavior* (213–216). New York: Gardner.

Tien, J., O'Donnell, V.F., Barnett, A., & Mirchandani, P.B. 1979. *Street lighting projects. National Evaluation Program. Phase 1 Report.* Washington, DC: National Institute of Law Enforcement and Criminal Justice.

Tittle, C.R. 1977. Sanction fear and the maintenance of social order. *Social Forces* 55:579–96.

———. 1980. *Sanctions and social deviance.* New York: Praeger.

Trasler, G.B. 1978. Relations between psychopathy and persistent criminality: Methodological and theoretical issues. In R.D. Hare & D. Schalling (Eds.), *Psychopathic behaviour: Approaches to research* (273–98). New York: Wiley.

———. 1980. *Crime, conscience and electrodermal recovery.* Paper presented at the 32nd Annual Meeting of the American Society of Criminology at San Francisco, CA.

———. 1987. Biogenetic factors. In H.C. Quay (Ed.), *Handbook of juvenile delinquency* (184–215). New York: Wiley.

————. 1986. Situational crime prevention and rational choice: A critique. In K. Heal & G. Laycock (Eds.), *Situational crime prevention* (17–24). London: HMSO.

————. in press. Crime, conscience and electrodermal recovery. (Manuscript available from the author)

Tuck, M., & Riley, D. 1986. The theory of reasoned action. In D.B. Cornish & R.V. Clarke (Eds.), *The reasoning criminal* (156–69). New York: Springer-Verlag.

Tversky, A., & Kahneman, D. 1981. The framing of decisions and the psychology of choice. *Science* 211:453–58. (Reprinted in Elster, J. 1986. *Rational choice.* Oxford, England: Blackwell, 1986)

Tyler, T. 1990. *Why do people obey the law?* New Haven: Yale University Press.

Watkins, J.W.N. 1970. Imperfect rationality. In R. Borger & F. Cioffi (Eds.), *Explanation in the behavioural sciences* (167–217). Cambridge: Cambridge University Press.

Webb, B., & Laycock, G. 1992a. *Reducing crime on the London Underground* (Crime Prevention Unit: Paper 30). London: Home Office.

Webb, B., & Laycock, G. 1992b. *Tackling car crime: The nature and extent of the problem* (Crime Prevention Unit: Paper 32). London: Home Office.

14

Crime Prevention through Environmental Design, Opportunity Theory, and Rational Choice Models

C. Ray Jeffery and Diane L. Zahm

The purpose of this chapter is to outline the theoretical underpinnings for crime prevention programs, to compare and contrast various approaches, and to show the relationship of crime prevention to criminological theory in general and to political policy as it relates to crime control.

Numerous basic approaches to crime prevention have emerged since 1971 when Jeffery (1971) published *Crime Prevention Through Environmental Design* (CPTED). In 1972 Newman (1972) published *Defensible Space,* to be followed by the work of Clarke, Mayhew, and others at the Home Office, London. The latter's work was based on a situational approach to crime prevention that resembled in most ways the CPTED approach. Later, Clarke and others moved to a rational choice model that was not contained in the earlier model by Jeffery. Several writers in the 1970s borrowed heavily from economics to discuss crime and the opportunity structure, by which they meant the perceived value of a crime target. This included the evaluation of pain and pleasure, or benefit and cost, of the behavior involved in the commission of a crime. From economic theory the discussion moved naturally to a rational choice model as put forth by Clarke and others. Cohen, Felson, and Land published a series of articles in which they argued that routine activities of individuals as they go to work, or to shopping or entertainment centers, determine the opportunity structure for crime.

The theoretical systems in place for organizing this discussion about crime prevention include a great deal of overlap and commonality, but at the same time apply differing assumptions as to human nature and the nature of criminal behavior. It is the problem of contradictory assumptions that troubles the writers of this chapter, and these assumptions will be its focus.

The conflict is between the classical legal view of human nature based on free will, moral responsibility, and rational choice; and the positive scientific view of human nature based on determinism as found in biology, psychology, and sociology. The classical view is found in social control theory, routine activities, opportunity theory, and rational choice models of human nature and crime prevention.

Crime Prevention and the History of Criminology

The Classical School of Criminology

Criminal justice developed out of a legal system based on revenge and just deserts. The classical school of criminology attempted to replace naked revenge with punishment for deterrence purposes. Its utilitarian model of criminal justice was based on the administration of pain, or a hedonistic model of pleasure and pain as driving forces controlling human behavior. Founded in the Hobbesian philosophy of a violent state of nature, this political ideology was based on a "war of all against all," in which the power of the state was necessary for political and social order (Jeffery 1990; Radzinowicz 1966; Rennie 1978; Jenkins 1984; Jones 1986; Mannheim 1970).

The Lockean doctrine of a social contract to protect the inalienable rights to "life, liberty and property" added to the development of the classical model. A third element in the model was the utilitarian idea of "the greatest happiness for the greatest number" through the maximization of pleasure and the minimization of pain for the members of the social contract. Individual offenders could be punished in order to deter criminal activities and to protect society. This was in direct contradiction to the Kantian idea that no individual can be punished for the good of the group.

The classical school was based on the idea of pain and pleasure as basic to human behavior, which is also true of Freudian psychology, behaviorism as found in Pavlov and Skinner, and modern physiological psychology. Such a model is also basic to the crime prevention through environmental design, routine activities, and rational choice models of crime prevention.

One thread throughout the history of crime control and criminology is that of pain and pleasure. However, the manner in which the various approaches to crime prevention utilize these concepts differ drastically as we shall see.

The Positive School of Criminology

The positive school of criminology developed in the nineteenth and twentieth centuries as a response to the emergence of science and empiricism found in the positivism of Newton, Bacon, Mill, Darwin, Comte, Freud, and Pavlov. The development of a science of human behavior as applied to criminal behavior belongs to the medical profession (Lombroso and Freud), joined by psychologists, sociologists, and lawyers. The positive school replaced punishment with treatment and therapies, and the prison was replaced with the medical clinic as seen in the work of Enrico Ferri (Mannheim 1970; Jeffery 1990; Radzinowicz 1966; Jenkins 1984; Jones 1986; Rennie 1978).

The positive school's scientific study of behavior replaced the classical school's legal system based on free will and moral responsibility. Two major branches of treatment emerged. One model was based on the study of offenders in psychology and psychiatry, where the purpose of science was to rehabilitate the sick individual through a medical model. The second model came from sociology and Marxian ideology, where reforms were aimed at the sick society and not the individual offender. Both of these models of treatment failed during the twentieth-century experiment with the "rehabilitative ideal," to be replaced after 1968 in the United States with a return to just deserts, retribution, and executions.

The positive or scientific school contains the seeds of prevention; however, two aspects of positivism work against crime prevention. Positivism places emphasis on the individual offender and not upon the environment within which crimes occur. It also places emphasis on those individuals who are already offenders and are caught in the criminal justice system rather than on preventing children from becoming offenders. Once an individual is an offender it is impossible to prevent the crimes that person has already committed. It is only possible to prevent the future commission of crimes. The only possible prevention then is from therapies that cure individuals who are already sick. Later on we will suggest that a better strategy is to identify high-risk individuals at an early age (birth to 6) and thereby prevent the emergence of antisocial behaviors.

In summary, we arrive at 1992 with a legalistic model, as found in the classical school, and a behavioral model, as found in the positivistic school, neither of which places any emphasis on preventing crime before it occurs. The antiprevention bias of criminal justice and criminology programs is to be found in the history of the disciplines.

Three Models of Behavior

The first model of behavior is based upon Cartesian dualism of mind and body. The mind produces behavior in an *environment-mind-behavior* model. This model is basic to introspective mentalistic psychology (Jeffery 1990).

The second model of behavior is based on the behaviorism of Pavlov, Watson, and Skinner. Behaviorism rejects mentalistic concepts and seeks a science of behavior based on a stimulus-response psychology without a mind or brain. This is a "black box" approach to behavior, without any analysis of internal events such as consciousness, thought, rationality, or decision making. This is an *environment-behavior* model.

The third model is an interdisciplinary model based on modern genetics and the brain sciences. Information from the environment enters the brain through sensory processes and is changed into biochemical codes that, in turn, control motor activities called "behavior." This is an *environment-brain-behavior* model.

Sociology, Social Ecology, and Crime Prevention

Sociological criminology was a product of Durkheim's rejection of biological and psychological factors in favor of a social explanation of human behavior, including criminal behavior. This orientation was expressed in the sociological models developed at the University of Chicago in the 1910–1930 era that came to dominate American criminology until the emergence of the Harvard school around Parsons in the 1940–1970 era.

The University of Chicago school was dominated by the social psychology of George Herbert Mead, and was based upon a philosophical concept of mind, self, and society. The individual came from social interaction based on symbolism. Although Mead recognized the role of physiological psychology in human behavior, people such as Blumer disregarded biology in their development of symbolic interactionism. Symbolic interactionism became differential association in the hands of E.H. Sutherland with emphasis upon social learning and cultural norms. People were criminals because of their association with criminal attitudes and values (Jeffery 1990).

The Chicago sociologists Park, Burgess, Shaw, and McKay also developed a social-ecological approach to behavior. This model was based not on human ecology but on social ecology. Shaw and McKay studied the residences of criminals, not crime sites. They ignored the physical environment in favor of the social environment, or social disorganization and differential cultural norms. Their work was basic to Sutherland's concept of differential association. The model was one of a *nonphysical individual* interacting with a *nonphysical environment* (Brantingham and Brantingham 1981; Jeffery 1990).

Sociologists used the concept of social area analysis to extend the work of the social ecologists in the study of crime. Shevsky and Bell (1955) used three social variables — social rank, urbanization, and ethnic segregation — to explain crime rates. Such studies produced examples of ecological fallacies and totally ignored the physical environment. Brantingham and Brantingham (1984) note that studies of social space led to the abandonment of space and location in sociological studies of crime, and therefore such studies have contributed little or nothing to our knowledge of the field.

A recent book by Byrne and Sampson (1986) on social ecology and crime states that social ecology is not environmental criminology as found in Harries, Georges-Abeyie, and the Brantinghams, and they go on to state that social ecology must be distinguished from geography since it places emphasis on the social and not upon the physical environment. The writers disagree with the position taken by Byrne and Sampson and place emphasis upon the physical environment as related to crime.

Baldwin (1979; see also Baldwin and Bottoms 1976; and Morris 1957) is critical of the sociological studies of crime based on the social environment and on the individual offender rather than upon the distribution of crime in space and time. As Baldwin notes, such studies ignore the biological substructure of ecology and human behavior.

Other developments in environmental psychology have relevance for environmental criminology (see Stokols 1977; Ittelson et al. 1974; Esser 1971; Altman 1975). The important difference between the environmental psychology approach and the approach used by the present writers is that environmental psychology regards the individual within a mentalistic and nonphysical framework in which perception and cognition rather than the brain govern the response of individuals to the physical environment. This approach utilizes the work of Kevin Lynch, in which he refers to the "images of the city" or the cognitive maps people carry around with them of the physical environment (Stokols 1977:259; Ittelson at al. 1974:288). Brantingham and Brantingham (1981) refer to these images of the environment inside the heads of individuals as "templates," while an article by Nichols in Georges-Abeyie and Harries (1980) refers to them as mental maps and another article by Smith and Patterson discusses cognitive mapping and subjective geography. Downs and Stea's book (1973) is entitled *Image and Environment: Cognitive Mapping and Spatial Behavior*. Mentalistic psychology is very much a part of environmental psychology and environmental criminology. The model is one of *environment → organism (mind) → behavior.*

Several sociologists have been developing an environmental sociology in recent years, and by *environment* they mean the physical rather than the social environment (Dunlap 1980; Dunlap and Catton 1979; Catton and Dunlap 1978). They argue that sociology must take into account the physical as well as the social environment within which human behavior occurs.

The model of ecology developed in biology is one of the interaction of a physical organism with a physical environment. Ecology is an overarching concept that unites biology, psychology, sociology, geography, and urban planning (Michelson 1976; Boulding 1978; Odum 1975; Ehrlich, Ehrlich, and Holdren 1973). Michelson wrote that sociologists left the physical environment behind in the dust, and he quotes the human ecologist Quinn to the effect that "human ecology as a branch of sociology always studies the relations of man to man, and never the direct relations of man to environment" (1976:7–32).

Duncan and Schnore (1959) build a model of social organization based upon ecology. They write that for the sociologist "the relevant environment is the social environment, which is conceived in terms of individual perceptions. One searches the literature in vain for more than superficial reference to the brute fact than men live in a physical environment and that they employ material technologies in adapting to it" (p. 134). Duncan and Schnore analyze human ecology in terms of population, organization, environment, and technology, or the POET model of human organization and ecology.

The model of ecology utilized in CPTED (Jeffery 1971, 1977) is based on the biological ecology model as found in the literature cited above. To repeat, it assumes a physical organism in interaction with a physical environment. The human brain acts as the organ utilized by individuals to sense, adapt to, and respond to the environment. The model is *environment → organism* (brain) *→ behavior.*

In summary, the sociological model of ecology based on studies of the spatial distribution of offenders, social disorganization, and social learning ignores the physical environment within which crimes occur. Crime prevention based upon the physical environment must be developed. CPTED and situational crime prevention are both based upon the physical environment.

A History of Crime Prevention

As was indicated above, criminology has ignored crime prevention in favor of the legal model of revenge and deterrence. The positive or scientific approach to behavior resulted in a social environmental approach to the explanation of criminal behavior without attention to the temporal and spatial aspect of crime. In recent years a few criminologists have turned to an examination of the physical environment and its impact on crime sites and the distribution of crime in space by borrowing from urban design and urban geography. This move has been reinforced by environmental psychology and environmental sociology, but environmental criminologists are divided as to the nature of human nature and the role of biology and psychology in criminology.

The concept of crime prevention appears in the eighteenth century in the work of Henry Fielding, who developed the modern concept of urban policing for London. His concept of the role of the police included the idea of crime prevention. The concept of the police as a crime prevention agency re-emerged in the United States in 1971 with the establishment of the National Crime Prevention Institute at the University of Louisville, Kentucky (National Crime Prevention Institute 1986).

Crime Prevention through Environmental Design

In 1971 Jeffery published *Crime Prevention Through Environmental Design,* which was an early attempt from academic criminology to argue for a crime prevention model of crime control. CPTED rejected revenge, just retribution, deterrence, punishment, and the use of the police/courts/ prison system to control crime. The term *prevention* is used here to mean "to come before" as the term is found in its Latin roots.

The CPTED model was based on experimental psychology as found in modern learning theory. Jeffery's concept derived from his experience with a rehabilitation project in Washington, D.C. There, participating juvenile delinquents were paid money to attend classes and to take examinations, with the ultimate goal of developing those behaviors needed for a high school degree and for long-term employment. The behavioral model applied stated that the environment in which the delinquents lived controlled their behavior by furnishing pleasure and pain, or reinforcement and punishment as used by experimental psychologists.

Jeffery admits the project was a total failure, but from this experience he knew that the psychological model was the correct one. First, he realized he had not controlled the environment where crimes occurred, but only the environment where the delinquents attended school. Second, when criminals are sent to prisons there is no change in the environment that produced the criminal behavior and the environment to which they return upon release.

Jeffery's CPTED model took seriously the lessons of psychology and learning theory in that it emphasized pleasure and pain and the physical environment to which the individual responded. This was a stimulus-response (S-R) model of behavior, or an *environment → behavior* model without the mind or brain intervening between the environment and the response. S-R psychology has been criticized for ignoring the physical structure of the organism.

The major idea behind CPTED is that, by removing the reinforcement from criminal acts, criminal behavior will not occur since nonreinforced behavior will not take place. In his 1971 book Jeffery mentioned the biological basis of behavior and the role of the brain in behavior (pp. 171–72), but then dropped the concept from further discussion. He emphasized material rewards as opposed to social rewards, and the use of the physical environment to control behavior. Major behavioral disorders, including crime, would be brought under control by behavioral engineering, and in anticipation of his work from 1971 on, he even mentioned psychopharmacological studies of behavior. Since the 1971 book contained no detailed recipes for crime prevention and was published by a then relatively unknown publisher, it was widely ignored.

Jeffery's 1977 edition totally revised the theoretical model for CPTED. It revised the role of the physical organism in behavior by including statements about human genetics and brain functioning from modern biology and psychobiology. The mentalism of sociology and environmental psychology, and the empty organism approach of experimental psychology, were replaced by the *environment → organism (*brain) → *behavior* model of modern psychology.

This model of behavior is developed in detail in Jeffery's 1990 book, which discusses genetics and the brain sciences in some detail. This material will not be repeated to any great extent here except to refer to crime prevention techniques growing out of neurology and neurochemistry as applied to individual offenders and to violent personal crimes.

The major theoretical construct of CPTED is that the response of the individual organism to the physical environment is a product of the brain; the brain in turn is a product of genetics and the environment. The environment never influences behavior directly, but *only through the brain.* Any model of crime prevention must include *both* the brain and the physical environment.

It may be time to drop the term *Crime Prevention Through Environmental Design* in referring to the Jeffery model, as the term has been applied to many different models of crime prevention, including Newman's model, and recently Crowe (1991) published a book entitled *Crime Prevention Through Environmental Design*. The term *crime prevention* may be more accurate and more descriptive of the concepts included in the 1971 and 1977 Sage publications.

Urbanization and Urban Decay

It has been observed repeatedly that crime is very much related to the growth of urban areas and to the social change that urban change produces (Jeffery 1990). The urban crisis has brought about crowding, poor housing, homelessness, drug use, traffic congestion, overcrowded educational facilities, and many other social and political problems. Urban infrastructure, that is, bridges, highways, sewers, transportation facilities, and the like, are all in a state of decay. Ecologists and futurists such as Paul Ehrlich (1974) and Alvin Toffler (1970, 1980) have pointed to the impact of population growth and technological change on every aspect of our lives. Ehrlich places emphasis on the pollution of our planet, the air and water, the loss of an adequate food supply, and the exhaustion of our natural resources, especially the fossil fuels as a source of energy.

Criminologists cannot afford to discuss crime and its foundations without a deep awareness of the impact of urbanization on human behavior. Not only does the urban environment shape and control human behavior, but it changes the very structure of the brain through pollution of air, water, and food. As will be discussed at the end of this chapter, pollution and contamination have a great deal to do with violence, drug addiction, and other behaviors that are major issues for the criminal justice system.

The Death and Life of Great American Cities

Probably the earliest discussions of urban decay and its relationship to crime came as a result of Jane Jacobs' seminal work, *The Death and Life of Great American Cities*, which she published in 1961. Living in Greenwich Village, Jacobs experienced an urban environment in which drastically different social environments could be found within only a few city blocks of one another. This she attributed to the mix of land uses, consistent building setbacks, and short block lengths, among other characteristics, resulting in 24-hour-a-day activity and "eyes on the street." According to Jeffery, "Jane Jacobs really started a lot of us thinking along these lines, and looking at land use and how people relate to the land, how people interact with their environment as basic to crime prevention" (from the "Crime Prevention Through Environmental Design" video produced by the Office of the Florida Attorney General, Tallahassee, Florida 1988). Jeffery's work, discussed above, was among several theoretical and practical applications that followed the book's publication.

Newman and Defensible Space

In 1972, Newman published *Defensible Space,* based on his work in St. Louis and New York City, much of which was funded by the U.S. Department of Justice and its various entities. Subtitled *Crime Prevention through Urban Design* (Newman 1972) or, alternatively, *Architectural Design for Crime Prevention* (Newman 1973b) the approach stated as its goal, "to release the latent sense of territoriality and community among inhabitants so as to allow these traits to be translated into inhabitants' assumption of responsibility for preserving a safe and well-maintained living environment" (Newman 1976:4). If achieved, this approach would result in increased policing of residential neighborhoods by the residents themselves, and therefore would reduce opportunities for crime.

While Newman discusses three constructs for crime prevention, which he terms *corrective prevention, punitive prevention,* and *mechanical prevention* (1973a), his work focuses on those physical design ingredients that contribute to a secure environment. In other words, Newman's work has as its foundation the disciplines of physical planning and architectural design; less emphasis is placed on criminology and the other behavioral sciences. Defensible space, more than any other crime prevention program, is an operationalization of the themes espoused by Jane Jacobs.

Based on his earlier studies, Newman identifies four elements of defensible space: territoriality, surveillance, image, and safe zones. Territoriality is construed as a proprietary interest in one's property. Newman suggests that public housing residents, especially children, have a poorly developed sense of privacy and little respect for territory. Physical design of public, semiprivate, and private space not only improves resident feelings of territoriality, but this in turn deters criminal activity by creating spaces that are defensible. Surveillance is the ability of the residents to observe what is going on within their territory. This means environmental design that permits surveillance of lobbies, elevators, streets, parking lots, and the like.

Newman's concepts came to be the core of most environmental design planning related to crime prevention, including a series of demonstration programs funded by the U.S. Department of Justice, Law Enforcement Assistance Administration (LEAA) during the 1970s. The Westinghouse Electric Corporation completed a school demonstration in Broward County, Florida, a commercial demonstration in Portland, Oregon, and a residential/mixed use project in Hartford, Connecticut. Although these were defined as "crime prevention through environmental design" programs, they were not based on Jeffery's work by that title, but instead applied Newman's defensible space concept.

In Chicago, design and construction of the South Loop New Town Environmental Security Project, a mixed-income residential development, employed a broader orientation of Newman's philosophies developed by Richard Gardiner (1978). Gardiner's approach, environmental security, focused on neighborhood decay, and evaluated the impact that conflicts between existing and proposed land uses, development, and traffic and transportation, have on neighborhood decline.

Elimination of LEAA and other program cuts in 1979 forced the abandonment of all these projects without evaluation.

A series of British studies have revealed the inadequacies of Newman's concepts. Mawby (1977) found little or no support in Britain for defensible space, and Mayhew (1979) concluded that defensible space was not a workable approach to crime prevention. Mayhew et al. (1979) also found that surveillance was not as effective as Newman had suggested. Surveillance by employees, such as custodians, park attendants, shop assistants, and bus conductors, was somewhat effective though the primary role of such employees was not surveillance but other tasks (see also Clarke 1983). Tayler, Gottfredson, and Brower (1980) concluded that empirical tests did not support the ideas behind defensible space, and they noted, as had Mayhew, that Newman placed emphasis on social control and social surveillance that did not show any impact on deterring offenders. Also, in his later work Newman placed great emphasis on such social factors as number of children in the project, income, fear of crime, and other nonphysical variables.

The physical environment is processed as attitudes, images, and fear of crime by individuals, and attitudes in turn produce behavior (Taylor and Gottfredson 1986). This is consistent with the mentalistic interpretation of behavior found in sociology, criminology, and urban planning.

A test in Atlanta, Georgia, of the physical design model as put forth by Jeffery and the Brantinghams, and the social control model of Newman (Greenberg and Rohe 1984) found considerable support for the Jeffery/Brantingham model but not for the Newman model. In spite of the lack of empirical support, defensible space continues to be followed as a basic guide to crime prevention.

For example, in 1987 the Florida Legislature passed the Safe Neighborhoods Act. Under the act, local communities apply for planning grants, which are then used to develop a Safe Neighborhoods Improvement Plan. Administrators of each Improvement Plan must provide background information and an evaluation of the district, including data on crime, land use, housing and zoning, traffic and transportation, and demographics. This data is analyzed to determine any relationships between the physical environment and crime .

Once relationships have been determined, the district outlines a comprehensive strategy to reduce crime and improve the quality of environment in the district. While the language of the act suggests that crime prevention through environmental design, defensible space, or environmental security measures may be employed as part of the physical, social, and political strategies for improvement, training and technical assistance on CPTED focus on Newman's defensible space approach.

Research on CPTED has been very limited. Jeffery and several graduate students have worked on convenience store robberies (Hunter 1988; Hunter 1990; Hunter and Jeffery 1991). They found that stores with two clerks, gas pumps in front, and no single-family dwellings nearby had low robbery rates. In line with this research, the city of Gainesville, Florida, (Gainesville Police Department 1988) adopted a series of city ordinances that require specific cash handling procedures, minimum window obstructions, visible sales areas, high lighting levels, and two clerks in the store between 8:00 P.M. and 4:00 A.M. CPTED has been a very successful means of controlling convenience store robberies; Gainesville has reduced its convenience store robberies by 87 percent. However, such measures as having two clerks in the store have been vigorously opposed by convenience store owners and operators.

In recent years we (Jeffery and Zahm) have been conducting several other research projects with several graduate students, including Kenneth Clontz and Mark Hogue, on drug use in a public housing project, crime in a middle-class residential area of Tallahassee near a drug distribution area, and violent crimes on the Florida State University campus. These projects are in process and will be discussed briefly at the end of this chapter.

Opportunity Theory and Routine Activities

A theoretical model developed primarily by economists or by sociologists using an economic model has emerged in recent years under such titles as an "opportunity model," or a "routine activities model" for crime control. Such discussions have been related to crime prevention without there being any clear explanation of whether these models are related to other discussions of crime prevention as found in CPTED, defensible space, or environmental security.

Classical criminology holds these diverse approaches together — the idea that humankind is dominated by a rational choice of pleasure over pain. This model is found in Beccaria and Bentham as discussed above. The rational man model has been an accepted model of human behavior for hundreds of years without any basis in any of the sciences of behavior.

Gary Becker (1968) stated his rational choice economic model, the first in modern economics, in a paper entitled "Crime and Punishment: An Economic Approach." Here, he argued for the classical position that crime could be understood in terms of pleasure and pain, or as economists use the terms, as *utility* and *cost*. All behavior is rational, and seeks gain and the avoidance of cost. Criminal behavior is that behavior that maximizes gain over cost at a particular point in time. In Becker's words, "a person commits an offense if the expected utility to him exceeds the utility he could get by using his time and other resources at other activities. Some persons become 'criminals,' therefore, not because their basic motivation differs from that of other persons, but because their benefits and costs differ" (1968:176).

Becker's paper was followed by a large number of publications from economists on the value of viewing criminal behavior from the point of view of formal economic theory. The rational pleasure/pain model was developed by Phillips and Votey (1981), Adreano and Siegfried (1980), Witte, (1980), and Rottenberg (1973). These discussions all concluded that behavior is rational, and therefore the answer to the crime problem comes from the deterrence model, as found in more prisons, and punishment.

The National Academy of Sciences Commission on Rehabilitation (Martin, Sechrest, and Redner 1981) reviewed these economic models and came to the conclusion that it might make more sense to design treatment programs and to improve job training and job opportunities rather than to use more punishment to deter crimes.

Cook (1986), an economist, refers to this tradition as "opportunity theory," which he defines as the interaction of victims and offenders in relation to targets. Targets that are attractive because of a high payoff and little risk are perceived by potential offenders as "opportunities." A supply and demand for offenses governs the crime rate, according to the classical theory of the marketplace. Cook notes that the economic view of behavior is one of choice based on anticipated consequences of gain and cost. He cites Clarke and the rational choice model, and Felson and Cohen and the routine activities model, so he, in effect, joins the rational choice model, the routine activities model, and the opportunity model into one perspective. He does not refer to Newman or to Jeffery except as examples of environmental design strategies that differ from his model and that are problematic (p.15 n.5).

Felson and his associates (Cohen and Felson 1979; Cohen, Felson, and Land 1980; Felson 1983; Felson 1987) have developed a model of criminal behavior that they have labeled "routine activities." (In a personal communication Felson indicated he does not regard the work of Cook as closely related to his, nor does he find the work of Cohen and Land in agreement with his own position. He also indicates his work is closely based on CPTED though there are no references to CPTED in any of the articles cited in this paper. Just how routine activities are related to CPTED and the physical environment is still to be worked out so far as we are concerned.)

Felson and his associates look at the interaction of targets, potential offenders, and control agents as producing the crime event. This can be viewed as an "interactionist perspective," not to be confused with the interactionist perspective found in social psychology. "Routine activities" refers to what individuals do in the course of a day in terms of going to work, being at home, going shopping, and so forth. They chronicle a change in routine activities, for example, in where people shop or in when women leave the home to work during the day, that create opportunities for criminal activity. A growth in the number of automobiles, televisions, stereo sets, or video recorders affects crime rates because of the availability of more attractive targets. Such items are attractive because they are portable, easily stolen, and easily sold or traded for drugs.

Theories of routine activities, opportunities, and rational choice share a common assumption that behavior is a rational means to maximize gain and minimize cost (pleasure and pain). This model of behavior is not to be found in modern psychology or biology, and it will discussed in more detail in a later section of this chapter.

The Rational Choice Model

The rational choice model has been put forth by Clarke and Cornish in recent years. In 1983 Clarke (1983) published an article in which he outlined the situational approach as developed by Mayhew, Clarke, and others at the Home Office in London. Clarke reviewed situational crime prevention as found in British studies of vandalism, the role of telephone boxes in criminal activity, steering column locks, double-decker buses, and crime in the London underground, and he observed that situational crime prevention focused on surveillance, target hardening, and environmental management. He then observed that the individual offender must be a part of the model.

Clarke rejected the sociological and psychological approaches of positivism that looked at dispositional factors, and in place of such theories he moved to a rational choice model. He argued that a rational choice model would be able to explain why individuals behave as criminals in some situations and not in others. A rational choice model looks at "the wide range of factors that influence an offender's decision, including his assessments of the risks, rewards, and morality of the act in question" (Clarke 1983:232).

One of the major tasks of rational choice theory is to show that displacement is not as widespread a phenomenon as some critics have claimed (Clarke 1983; Cornish and Clarke 1987; Clarke and Mayhew 1988, Mayhew, Clarke, and Elliott 1989). Two major studies, one on motorcycle thefts in Germany following the introduction of laws requiring helmets, and the other examining the suicide rate in England following the introduction of natural gas, revealed that no displacement to other means of transportation or to other means of suicide occurred.

At the heart of rational choice is an analysis of the thought or cognitive means by which individuals process information from the environment. Rational choice theory focuses on the individual offender's perception of the opportunity structure of each environment and his decision to maximize gain and minimize loss from the environment. Clarke does discuss limited rationality as an aspect of the decision process.

Clarke has in this way recognized the inadequacies of a total environmental model as found in modern sociological environmentalism. He then moved to an *environment → organism (mind) → behavior* model in which the organism receives and processes information from the environment. The behavior that results from such cognitive activities derives from an individual's choice to respond or not to respond to the environment, and is based on the total gain versus loss (or pleasure versus pain) resulting from such behavior in such an environment. Situational crime prevention based on empiricism and science now includes a rational choice model based on classical ideas about human nature.

The rational choice model emphasizes the cognitive processes of evaluation, thought, and decision making as they occur at the individual level. Cornish and Clarke do not locate such cognitive activities however. Rationality is either a quality of the mind, in which case it is mentalistic psychology, or rationality is a product of brain function, in which case it is a part of the brain sciences. The prefrontal lobes are especially critical for rational behavior and the control of the emotional centers of the brain. The "black box" problem in psychology as found in mentalistic and behavioral psychology, can be resolved with the *environment - brain - behavior* model.

Social control theory as put forth by Hirschi, and routine activities theory as put forth by Felson, Cohen, and Land, have been incorporated into the rational choice model. Felson (1986; see also Cohen and Land 1987) wrote that rational choice is involved in the routine activities of potential criminals in interaction with potential targets and potential guardians, since altered possibilities for gain or loss occur under changing circumstances. Felson also noted that social control theory is compatible with both the rational choice and routine activities models of criminal behavior.

The rational choice model rejects positivism and is based on the free will and choice model of the classical school of Bentham and Beccaria, as well as the economic model of rational man as developed by economists. This model also fits the routine activities model of Felson and others, as well as the control model put forth in sociology by Hirschi. It should be noted that the rational choice model denies the theories from sociology and psychology with the exception of Hirschi's theory because, like Hirschi's theory, it reintroduces into twentieth-century criminology the philosophical ideas of the classical school.

Hirschi (1986: 106 ff) maintained that science and positivism as found in sociology argued against the rational choice model since positivism was based on the determinism of biology and the environment. Humankind is free to make choices that maximize pleasure and avoid pain, an assumption shared by the rational choice model and the social control model. Hirschi assumes a rational voluntaristic theory of behavior, and he also assumes all individuals have the same propensity to commit crimes. Individuals commit crimes when there is an absence of social control measures in society. To quote Hirschi, "there is no hope for reconciliation of rational choice theory and those theories derived directly from sociological positivism. . . . Rational choice theory and social control theory share an image of man, an image rather different from the image of sociological positivism" (1986:113).

The position put forth by Hirschi is basic to his view of human nature and criminal behavior. In an article with Gottfredson, (Gottfredson and Hirschi 1986), Hirschi states that social control theory accepts "the idea that the criminal propensity is lodged in a great bulk of the population. Whether advanced by economists (the rational choice theory) or by sociologists (social control theory), these explanations of crime share the view that crime occurs naturally in the absence of restraint. . . . The person committing criminal acts is thus a person free to follow the impulse of the moment" (1986:231).

The rational choice model also reintroduces deterrence as the basis for criminal justice. Gottfredson and Hirschi (1987) state that the classical school was justified in using the concept of deterrence. They also note that the positive school was not justified in dismissing the concept of deterrence, since deterrence is compatible with free will and with determinism. "In short, the classical school is . . . compatible with the idea of determinism" (p. 14).

Positivists argue that free will and determinism are incompatible because free will suggests a lack of scientific determinism as found in science. Hirschi, on the other hand, argues that classical theory is deterministic because free will determines and influences the decision process. By making such an argument Hirschi shifts determinism from physical causes such as the brain or the environment to the mind and choice based upon free will. (It should be noted that Clarke and Cornish [1985: 127] argue that they are not committed to a position on the free will-determinism debate.)

The rational choice model, like the social control model and the routine activities model, is based on the classical position of deterrence of crime through punishment. If one adds the element of punishment to the choice confronting the potential criminal, the individual must add the element of fear and potential punishment to one's calculus of pain and pleasure from the criminal act. Thus, these theories are deterrence theories in the tradition of the classical school.

The rational choice model is a mentalistic model based on the *environment → organism (mind) → behavior* model of behavior. The concept of choice is a mentalistic concept based on mental activities of the mind. Choice is neither empirical nor observable, and the investigator can only know when an individual has made a choice when he behaves in a given way. From the observed behavior the investigator inputs a cause (such as rational choice or social control) of the behavior within the individual. This is one reason why the rational choice model has not accepted positivism and science.

Carrol and Weaver (Cornish and Clarke 1986: 19 ff) attempt to address the issue of how one studies internal mentalistic events in their study of shoplifters' perceptions of opportunities. They did this through a study of shoplifters' thoughts, which they obtained by asking shoplifters to verbalize their experience as they walked through a department store. This is a form of the psychological interview, in which verbal behavior is used to study internal thought processes. What is actually studied, however, is not internal thought processes but verbal *behavior*. Verbal behavior is under the control of the brain, the same as other so-called thought processes. It is a physical and not a mentalistic process.

Taylor and Gottfredson (1986), in an article reviewing the work of Newman and Clarke, reaffirm the fact that potential offenders act upon the basis of cognitive maps, fear of crime, and rationality, all aspects of mentalistic psychology.

Bioenvironmentalism and Criminal Behavior

As has been argued above, the mentalistic model of behavior dominates most crime prevention theories. The rational choice model assumes a mind that has the capability of making decisions. Within biology and psychology this model has been replaced by the bioenvironmental model, in which a brain replaces mental processes. At this point in the chapter we will develop an argument for using the modern brain sciences as an important part of crime prevention efforts. An interdisciplinary approach to crime prevention is needed, including urban geography, urban planning, criminology, and the brain sciences (Jeffery 1990).

Information from the environment is taken into the individual organism through the sensory system and then to the brain. Within the brain, sensory information is processed and stored by biochemical means. The sensory/motor systems then send biochemical information to the muscles and glands, which produce behavior. Behavior is controlled by the brain, not the environment. Environmental input produces behavior only through the brain.

The brain is the most complex organ in the human body, involving millions of neurons as well as neurotransmitter systems. The brain is a complex information-processing system. However, information is processed in such a way so that several different brain centers communicate with each other. The sensory input goes to the sensory cortex, which in turn interacts with several motor systems including the premotor area and the supplementary motor area that allows for thought and planning. Information is then processed in the prefrontal lobes, which control future planning based on knowledge of the consequences of behavior. To quote a neuropsychologist:

> Memories of lengthy behavior consequences are apparently stored in the prefrontal cortex and connected to motivation by way of the orbitofrontal area. The prefrontal cortex and language areas are two parts of the brain that set us apart from lower animals more than any other brain differences. Because of the prefrontal area, humans can imagine future possibilities and plan ahead further than any other species. (Graham 1990:91)

Learning and memory occur in the brain. Environmental experiences actually change the structure of the brain, and this is why we are able to plan and to make decisions based on past environmental experiences.

The motivation for behavior occurs when experiences and information concerning the environment enter the limbic system of the brain, which in turn controls basic drives such as sex, hunger, thirst, violence, and survival. The prefrontal lobes of the brain control the manner in which the individual responds to the stimulation from the limbic system. If the

TABLE 14.1

Crime Prevention Model	Researchers	Basis	General Theories/Assumptions
Crime Prevention Through Environmental Design (CPTED)	Jeffery	Experimental psychology, learning theory, science, biology, urban planning	• Stimulus-Response model of behavior (1971) • Environment-Brain-Behavior (1977) • Bioenvironmentalism • Response of the individual organism to the physical environmenta is a product of the brain • Prevention, not deterrence
Defensible Space	Newman (LEAA, HUD)	Architecture, urban planning, physical design	• Territoriality, surveillance, image and safe zones • Physical design reinforces resident responsibility, resulting in resident policing and social control
Situational Crime Prevention	Clarke, Mayhew (Home Office, London)	Environmental opportunities, physical features	• Combination of CPTED and Defensible Space
Opportunity Model, Routine Activities Theory	Cohen, Felson, Land, Becker, Cook	Classical criminology, economics	• Criminal behavior maximizes gain over cost • Routine activities establish an interaction of targets, offenders, control agents • Deterrence model
Rational Choice Model	Clarke, Cornish	Classical criminology, economics	• Mentalistic model analyzes thought processes of offender, who makes a choice to commit crime based on gain/loss • Deterrence model
Social Control Theory	Hirschi, Gottfredson	Classical criminology	• No individual differences in motivation • Lack of social restraints • Deterrence model

prefrontal lobes are unable to control the neural activities from the limbic system, we have antisocial behavior in the form of rape, assault, murder, robbery, and burglary. Individuals who are violent have defective prefrontal lobes and neurotransmitter systems. We can never predict the response of an individual to an environmental stimulus without knowing how the stimulus affects the brain.

For nonviolent crimes, for which rational choice theory is better designed, the planning and decision process is the same except that it involves behavior of a nonviolent type. The behavior involved in a robbery or burglary or auto theft is processed by the sensory and motor centers of the brain, and the decision to commit the crime involves the neural activities of these areas. *Choice* and *rationality* are regarded in neurology as functions of the pre-frontal lobes of the brain. Behavior is a product of both emotional and rational processes within the brain. No behavior is solely the product of rationality.

The brain is involved in both violent and nonviolent offenses. The motivation and planning of criminal offenses involves brain activity regardless of the type of crime. It should be remembered that theft is related to basic biological drives. When one steals money one can trade the money for food, sex, medical care, or shelter. This is why Pavlov had an unconditioned stimulus (food) and an unconditioned response (salivation) as a basic foundation for his theory of learning.

The basic motivation for human behavior comes from the brain and the limbic system. Motivation is built into the biological structure of the human organism. This is in great contrast to the theories of social control, rational choice, and routine activities, which assume constant motivation for all individuals. As was pointed out above, such models conclude that motivation is not a variable to be considered in explaining criminal behavior.

On the other hand, the bioenvironmental model assumes that each individual differs in terms of needs and motivation. No two individuals are alike, due to genetic differences, brain differences, and differences in learning experiences. These individual differences must be built into our model of human behavior when we discuss crime prevention models.

The bioenvironmental theory places motivation in the pleasure and pain centers of the brain that are located primarily in the limbic system. Pain and pleasure control behavior, as was noted at the beginning of this chapter. What the economist refers to as cost and benefit, and the criminologist refers to as rational choice, are the activities of the pleasure and pain centers controlling behavior. Rationality and choice refer to the selection by the cortex of which behaviors will be pleasurable and which painful. Thus, bioenvironmental criminology ties into experimental psychology and the theory of reinforcement put forth by operant condition-ers.

Crime Prevention and Personal Crimes

Crime prevention programs have typically been designed for property offenses and not personal offenses. Jeffery (1990) has argued that per-sonal crimes involving friends or relatives cannot be prevented to any great extent by environmental design measures. Acquaintance rape that occurs in a car or an apartment cannot be prevented by putting extra locks on the door or better lighting in the parking lot. A redesign of public housing projects will not eliminate child abuse or domestic violence. Changes to the physical environment will not affect most murders, which occur between friends or acquaintances. Clarke (personal letter) has noted that environmental measures have been taken in the area of personal crimes, such as controlling murder by controlling gun ownership, separat-ing soccer fans in England to prevent fights, and protecting bus drivers with plastic shields. Such examples are fine but they do not address spouse or child abuse in the family, rapes or assaults involving acquain-tances, or murders that occur in the kitchen when the wife stabs the husband. Measures that address the biopsychological conditions of poten-tially violent individuals are also legitimate crime prevention measures.

Trasler (Heal and Laycock 1986) argues that situational crime preven-tion cannot be used for most personal crimes, and in that respect we are in agreement. Heal and Laycock (1986) stated that the Clarke-Cornish argu-ment ignores the measurement of motivation when it regards rape, wife beating, and homicide as rational choice decisions.

The model of crime prevention presented within a bioenvironmental theory of behavior would establish crime prevention programs at the indi-vidual level as well as at the environmental level. Individuals from an early age would be tested for brain damage, nutritional defects, heavy metal contamination, and other neurological problems. Treatments would include changes in nutrition that would affect on the chemistry of the brain. For example, people low in serotonin have a high incidence of violent behavior. Serotonin is a product of tryptophan, which is a dietary amino acid.

Crime prevention also would involve removing or reducing those envi-ronmental pollutants that ultimately affect the brain. Lead pollution is higher now than ever, and individuals with high lead concentrations in the brain often have malfunctioning brain patterns and behavioral patterns. More attention must be paid to the role of the individual in crime preven-tion.

Drugs, Alcohol, and Criminal Behavior

It is estimated that between 60 and 80% of all crimes involve drugs and alcohol. Addictions are a neurological process since the brain is responding through the neurotransmitter system to biochemicals we call drugs. Drugs act on the norepinephrine, dopamine, and serotonin levels of the brain. Low dopamine levels are related to cocaine addiction because cocaine acts as a substitute for dopamine in the brain. Dopamine feeds directly into the pleasure centers of the brain; therefore the use of cocaine is reinforced by its impact on these pleasure centers. It should also be noted that 90% of those trying cocaine do not become addicted because their brains have adequate levels of dopamine and therefore do not require the stimulation furnished by cocaine. In other words, the prevention and cure of addictions is a medical problem involving the biochemical structure of the brain.

A major problem in relating crime prevention to drug addiction is the assumption made by many criminologists that addicts commit crimes in order to purchase drugs. Cromwell, Olson, and Avary (1991) discovered that addicts take drugs before burglaries in order to alter the brain in such a way as to facilitate the commission of the crime. They found that drugs changed brain functioning and therefore also perceptions of risk and gain in the environment. The whole decision process was changed by the taking of drugs before the burglary. Cromwell and his colleagues concluded that "a rational, hierarchical, sequential decision-making process could not adequately explain a substantial amount of the variance in burglary" (p. 94). They also concluded that a reduction in the demand for drugs must be an integral part of any crime prevention project.

We have had a project in Albany, Georgia, for the past several years dealing with environmental design and cocaine addiction in a public housing complex. The major focus of this work has been the individual crime sites, not collective data, and the location of the crime site in respect to the physical environment. Such factors as the physical structure of the crime site, the type of building involved, the presence of shrubbery, the location of lighting, the pattern of residential traffic in the area, the pattern of vehicular traffic in the area, the presence of vacant lots, the presence of business areas adjacent to the residential areas, the presence of drug use and distribution in the area, and other such variables were analyzed and mapped. In all cases the relationship of the physical environment to the crime site was established, and remedial measures were or will be recommended.

The project also involved tenant's associations, social services, and youth groups in support of the physical design changes. Attempts to identify and address nutritional and behavioral problems, both in neighborhood children and in local cocaine addicts, were limited by available funding and by the Housing Authority.

Both environmental design changes and increased police activities in the project produced no reduction in drug use. Rather, the drug trade was displaced to other parts of the project, such as from the front to the side of an apartment, or from one section to another section of the neighborhood.

Other similar studies have reported a total displacement of drug dealers due to police or other prevention activities. We can conclude from our experience that it will never be possible to reduce drug addiction via situational crime prevention. Although, as Clarke points out (personal letter), drunkenness has been controlled by licencing measures and drinking bans, we can also design the drugs out of the addict. That does not mean that CPTED has no role in dealing with the drug/crime problem, only that the effort must include both the *individual* and the *environment*. Criminal behavior is a product of both, and both must be of concern to those developing crime prevention models.

Conclusions

The theoretical structure of crime prevention is divided into two camps based on the theory of human nature used by the theorists. Crime prevention through environmental design is based on an interdisciplinary model of human behavior involving biology and psychology. It involves a *brain x environment* model of behavior. Opportunity theory and rational choice theory are based upon a mentalistic model of human behavior involving *mind x environment* interaction.

Crime prevention theories and efforts must make use of new knowledge of human behavior. The crime prevention literature has often ignored the offender in favor of the environment, as seen in the 1971 book by Jeffery and the 1972 book by Newman. The work of Cornish and Clarke has been aimed at bringing the offender back into the picture, but on the basis of a classical model of human behavior.

Crime prevention must be integrated with current research on the career criminal (Blumstein et al. 1985; Blumstein et al 1986; Blumstein et al. 1988; Farrington, Ohlin, and Wilson 1986) wherein biological, psychological, and social factors have been integrated in a longitudinal research design. Crime prevention must also be integrated with current studies of the biological aspects of criminal behavior (Mednick and Volavka 1980; Mednick, Moffit, and Stack 1987, Wolfgang and Weiner 1982; Fishbein 1990; Jeffery 1990).

The approach contained in CPTED is crime prevention based upon scientific knowledge as found in the modern brain sciences, urban planning, urban geography, and criminology. It is designed to prevent crimes before they occur. The rational choice/social control models are oriented toward a deterrence theory of crime based upon punishment. Felson denies that his routine activities model is based upon deterrence, but the exact position he takes on prevention must be spelled out in clearer detail. As Bennett stated in the Cornish and Clarke book:

> The view of the criminal as a calculating individual who will weigh up the costs and rewards of crime has been used to justify deterrent and retributive policies on crime. It is possible that a similar shift in perspective in relation to addiction could see a move further away from "medicalization" toward greater use of the police and courts as a compatible control response in dealing with addiction. (1986:99)

This statement argues that we must control crime by using a criminal justice system based on arrests, convictions, and imprisonment. It rejects the medical treatment model advocated in this paper. CPTED is based on a rejection of the criminal justice system as a crime-control measure in favor of scientific efforts to control human behavior before it occurs.

The rational control/social control/routine activities approach perpetuates the classical ideas of deterrence and punishment as crime-control measures. CPTED is an extension of the positive school with biology, psychology, and urban planning playing major roles in crime prevention policy and projects. To be effective crime prevention theory must be translated into public policy. The ancient conflict between legalistic and scientific criminology is behind arguments concerning the theoretical structure of crime prevention programs (Jeffery, Myers, and Wollan 1991). At this point in history public policy concerning crime control is dominated by the legalistic view rather than the scientific view, and if we hope to control crime we must move to a better scientific approach to crime prevention.

References

Adreano, R., & Siegfried, J. 1980. *Economics of crime.* New York, NY: Halstead Press.

Altman, I. 1975. *The environment and social behavior.* Monterey, CA: Brooks/Cole.

Baldwin, J. 1979. Ecological and area studies in Great Britain and the United States. In N. Morris & M. Tonry (Eds.), *Crime and justice: An annual review of research* (Vol. 1). Chicago: University of Chicago Press.

Baldwin, J., & Bottoms, A.E. 1976. *The urban criminal.* London, England: Tavistock.

Becker, G.S. 1968, April. Crime and punishment: An economic approach. *Journal of Political Economy* 76(2):169–217.

Blumstein, A., Farrington, D.P., & Moitra, S. 1985. Delinquent careers: Innocents, desisters and persisters. In M. Tonry & N. Morris (Eds.), *Crime and justice: An annual review of research* (Vol. 6). Chicago: University of Chicago Press.

Blumstein, A., Cohen, J., Roth, J., & Visher C. 1986. *Criminal careers and career criminals*. Washington DC: National Academy Press.

Blumstein, A., Cohen, J., & Farrington, D.P. 1988. Criminal career research: Its value for criminology. *Criminology* 26:1–36.

Boulding, K.E. 1978. *Ecodynamics: A new theory of societal evolution*. Beverley Hills, CA: Sage.

Brantingham, P.J., & Brantingham, P.L. 1981. *Environmental criminology*. Beverley Hills, CA: Sage.

———. 1984. *Patterns in crime*. New York: Macmillan.

Byrne, J., & Sampson, R. 1986. *The social ecology of crime*. New York: Springer-Verlag.

Catton, W.R., & Dunlap, R.E. 1978. Environmental sociology: A new paradigm. *The American Sociologist* 13:41–49.

Clarke, R.V. 1983. Situational crime prevention: Its theoretical basis and practical scope. In M. Tonry & N. Morris (Eds.), *Crime and justice: An annual review of research* (Vol. 4). Chicago: University of Chicago Press.

Clarke, R.V., & Cornish, D. 1985. Modeling offender's decisions: A framework for research and policy. In M. Tonry & N. Morris (Eds.), *Crime and justice: An annual review of research* (Vol. 6). Chicago: University of Chicago Press.

Clarke, R.V.G., & Mayhew, P. 1980. *Designing out crime*. London: Her Majesty's Stationery Office.

Clarke, R.V., & Mayhew, P. 1988. The British gas suicide story and its criminological implications. In M. Tonry & N. Morris (Eds.), *Crime and justice: An annual review of research* (Vol. 10). Chicago: University of Chicago Press.

Cohen, L.E., & Felson, M., 1979. Social change and crime rate trends: A routine activities approach. *American Sociological Review* 44:588–608.

Cohen, L.E., Felson, M. & Land, K.C. 1980. Property crime rates in the United States: A macro-dynamic analysis. *American Journal of Sociology* 86:90–118.

Cohen, L.E., & Land, K.C. 1987. Sociological positivism and the explanation of criminality. In M.R. Gottfredson & T. Hirschi (Eds.), *Positive criminology*. Newburg Park, CA: Sage.

Cook, P.J. 1986. The demand and supply of criminal opportunities. In M. Tonry & N. Morris (Eds.), *Crime and justice: An annual review of research* (Vol. 7). Chicago: University of Chicago Press.

Cornish, D.B., & Clarke, R.V. 1986. *The reasoning criminal*. New York: Springer-Verlag.

———. 1987. Understanding crime displacement: An application of rational choice theory. *Criminology* 25:933–47.

Cromwell, P., Olson, J.N., & Avary, D.W. 1991. *Breaking and entering*. Newbury Park, CA: Sage.

Crowe, T.D. 1991. *Crime prevention through environmental design*. Boston, MA: Butterworth-Heinemann.

Downs, R.M., & Stea, D. 1973. *Image and environment*. Chicago: Aldine.

Duncan, O.D., & Schnore, L. 1959. Cultural, behavioral, and ecological perspectives in the study of social organization. *American Journal of Sociology* 65:132–46.

Dunlap, R.E. 1980. Paradigmatic changes in social science. *American Behavioral Scientist* 24:15–47.

Dunlap, R.E., & Catton, W.R. 1979. Environmental sociology. *Annual Review of Sociology* 5:243–73.

Ehrlich, P.R. 1974. *The end of affluence.* New York: Ballantine Books.

Esser, A.H. 1971. *Behavior and environment.* New York: Plenum.

Farrington, D.E., Ohlin, L., & Wilson, J.Q. 1986. *Understanding and controlling crime.* New York: Springer-Verlag.

Felson, M. 1983. Ecology of crime. In S.H. Kadish (Ed.), *Encyclopedia of crime and justice.* New York: Free Press.

———. 1986. Linking criminal choices, routine activities, informal control, and criminal outcomes. In D.B. Cornish & R.V. Clarke (Eds.), *The reasoning criminal.* New York: Springer-Verlag.

———. 1987. Routine activities and crime prevention in the developing metropolis. *Criminology* 25:911–31.

Fishbein, D. 1990. Biological perspectives in criminology. *Criminology* 28: 27-72.

Gainesville Police Department. 1988. *Gainesville convenience store robberies: An intervention strategy by the City of Gainesville, Florida.* Gainesville, FL: Gainesville City Commission.

Gardiner, Richard A. 1978. *Design for safe neighborhoods.* Washington, DC: U.S. Department of Justice.

Georges-Abeyie, D., & Harries, K. 1980. *Crime: A spatial perspective.* New York: Columbia University Press.

Gottfredson, M., & Hirschi, T. 1986. The true value of lambda would appear to be zero: An essay on career criminals, criminal careers, selective incapacitation, cohort studies, and related topics. *Criminology* 24:213–34.

———. 1987. *Positive criminology.* Newbury Park, CA: Sage.

Graham, R.B. 1990. *Physiological psychology.* Belmont, CA: Wadsworth.

Greenberg, S., & Rohe, M.W. 1984. Neighborhood design and crime. *Journal of the American Planning Association* 50:48–61.

Heal, K., & Laycock, G. (Eds.). 1986. *Situational crime prevention.* London, England: Home Office Research and Planning Unit.

Hirschi, T. 1986. On the compatibility of rational choice and social control theories of crime. In D.E. Cornish & R.V. Clarke (Eds.), *The reasoning criminal.* New York: Springer-Verlag.

Hunter, R.D. 1990, December. Convenience store robberies in Tallahassee, FL. *Journal of Security Administration.*

———. 1988. *The effects of environment factors upon convenience store robberies in Florida.* Tallahassee, FL: Office of the Attorney General.

Hunter, R.D., & Jeffery, C.R. 1991, March. Preventing convenience store robbery through environmental design. *Security Journal.*

Ittelson, W.H., Proshansky, H.M., Rivlin, L.E., & Winkel, G.H. 1974. *An introduction to environmental psychology.* New York: Holt, Rinehart, and Winston.

Jacobs, J. 1961. *The death and life of great American cities.* New York: Vintage Books.

Jeffery, C.R. 1971, 1977. *Crime prevention through environmental design.* Beverly Hills, CA: Sage.

Jeffery, C.R. 1990. *Criminology: An interdisciplinary approach.* New York: Prentice Hall.

Jeffery, C.R., Myers, L.B., & Wollan, L.A. 1991. Crime, justice, and their systems: Resolving the tension. *The Criminologist* 16(4):1–6.

Jenkins, P. 1984. *Crime and justice.* Monterey, CA: Brooks/Cole.

Jones, D.A. 1986. *History of Criminology.* Westport, CT: Greenwood Press.

Kalat, J.W. 1992. *Biological psychology.* Belmont, CA: Wadsworth.

Kimble, D.P. 1992. *Biological psychology.* Fort Worth, TX: Harcourt Brace Jovanovich.

Mannheim, H. 1970. *Pioneers in criminology.* Montclair, NJ: Patterson-Smith.

Martin, S.E., Sechrest, L.B., & Redner, R. 1981. *New directions in the rehabilitation of criminal offenders.* Washington, DC: National Academy Press.

Mawby, R.I. 1977. Defensible space: A theoretical and empirical appraisal. *Urban Studies* 14:169–79.

Mayhew, P. 1979. Defensible space: The current status of a crime prevention theory. *Howard Journal* 17:150–59.

Mayhew, P., Clarke, R.V., Burrows, J.N., Hough, J.M., & Winchester, S.W. 1979. *Crime in public view.* (Home Office Research Study No. 49). London, England: Her Majesty's Stationery Office.

Mayhew, P., Clarke, R.V., & Elliott, D. 1989. Motorcycle theft, helmet legislation, & displacement. *Howard Journal* 28(1):1–8.

Mednick, S.A., & Volavka, J. 1980. Biology and crime. In N. Morris & M. Tonry (Eds.), *Crime and justice: An annual review of research* (Vol. 2). Chicago: University of Chicago Press.

Mednick, S.A., Moffitt, T. & Stack, S.A. 1987. *The causes of crime: New biological approaches.* Cambridge: Cambridge University Press.

Michelson, W.H. 1976. *Man and his urban environment.* Reading, MA: Addison-Wesley.

Morris, T. 1957. *The criminal area.* London, England: Routledge and Kegan Paul.

National Crime Prevention Institute. 1986. *Understanding crime prevention.* Boston, MA: Butterworth.

National League of Cities. 1977, December. A special report: Crime prevention through environmental design. *Nation's Cities.*

Newman, O. 1972. *Defensible space.* New York: Macmillan.

———. 1973a. *A design guide for improving residential security.* Washington, DC: U.S. Department of Housing and Urban Development.

———. 1973b. *Architectural design for crime prevention.* Washington, DC: U.S. Department of Justice.

———. 1976. *Design guidelines for creating defensible space.* Washington, DC: U.S. Department of Justice.

Odum, E.P. 1975. *Ecology: The link between the natural and social sciences.* New York: Holt, Rinehart, and Winston.

Philips, L., & Votey, H.L. 1981. *Economics of crime control,* Beverly Hills, CA: Sage.

Piliavin, I., Gartner, R., Thorton, C., & Matsueda, R. 1986. Crime, deterrence, and rational choice. *American Sociological Review* 51:101–19.

Radzinowicz, L. 1962. *In search of criminology.* Cambridge, MA: Harvard University Press.

Radzinowicz, R. 1966. *Ideology and crime.* New York: Columbia University Press.

Rennie, Y. 1978. *The search for criminal man.* Lexington, MA: Lexington Books.

Rottenberg, S. 1973. *The economics of crime and punishment.* Washington, DC: American Enterprise Institute for Public Policy Research.

Shevsky, E., & Bell, W. 1955. *Social area analysis.* Stanford, CA: Stanford University Press.

Stokols, D. 1977. *Perspectives on environment and behavior.* New York: Plenum.

Taylor, R.B., & Gottfredson, S. 1986. Environmental design and crime prevention: An examination of community dynamics. In A.J. Reiss & M. Tonry (Eds.), *Communities and crime* (Vol. 8), Crime and Justice Series. Chicago: University of Chicago Press.

Tayler, R., Gottfredson, S.D., & Brower, S. 1980. The defensibility of defensible space: A critical review and synthetic framework for future research. In T. Hirschi & M. Gottfredson (Eds.), *Understanding crime.* Beverley Hills, CA: Sage.

Tien, James M. 1976. *Elements of CPTED.* Arlington, VA: Westinghouse Electric Corporation.

Toffler, A. 1970. *Future shock.* New York: Bantam Books.

―――. 1980. *The third wave.* New York: Bantam Books.

Witte, A.D. 1980. Estimating the economic model of crime and individual data. *Quarterly Journal of Economics* 94:57–84.

Wolfgang, M., & Weiner, N.A. (Eds.). 1982. *Criminal violence.* Beverly Hills, CA: Sage.

15

Theories of Action in Criminology: Learning Theory and Rational Choice Approaches

Derek Cornish

Recently, in a lively and disputacious article, Akers (1990) drew attention to similarities between rational choice and social learning approaches to criminal behavior. But while acknowledging some payoffs from the former, such as the encouragement of empirical studies of criminal decision making, he found it had little to offer in the way of a sustained theoretical or conceptual contribution. Instead, he proposed not only that the rational choice approach could readily be translated into social learning terminology but "that the primary concepts and valid postulates of deterrence and rational choice are subsumable under general social learning or behavioral principles" as special cases (Akers 1990:655). Rehearsing in some detail his own 25 years of work in developing social learning theory, he concluded that the adoption by some criminologists of the rational choice approach was largely the product of academic ignorance akin, as he ruefully put it, to the reinvention of the wheel.

Robust critiques are to be welcomed, and Akers raises many questions of considerable importance for criminological theory. But too many hares are started for this chapter. Accordingly, the present discussion will make no defense of the rational choice perspective in general: its heuristic value is incontrovertible. As Herrnstein (1990:356) points out, "it comes close to serving as the fundamental principle of the behavioral sciences. No other well articulated theory of behavior commands so large a following in so wide a range of disciplines."

Instead, this discussion will confine itself to three substantive issues raised by Akers' critique:

1. the need for adequate microlevel theories of human action in criminology;
2. the relevant (i.e., metatheoretical) requirements of such theories;
3. the competing claims and areas of convenience of existing candidates.

The Role of Action Theories

The Need for Common Frameworks

Because the various social science disciplines are concerned with different aspects of human behavior, the explanatory theories that they develop often seem at odds with one another. This is partly because they are trying to explain different phenomena; because they study different aspects of the same phenomena; because they use different variables or variable clusters; because they operationalize concepts in different ways; because they are trying to explain phenomena at different levels of explanation; because they are dealing with processes extending over different time scales; and, last, because their conceptualization of the way action is determined at the level of individual behavior—what is variously called the micro, microsociological, or social psychological level—is different.

For all these reasons, it is often hard to communicate between disciplines, to compare accounts, or to evaluate the adequacy of different approaches. Despite these problems, however, there is some sense of common endeavor. And there is persistent discussion, both within and across the social sciences—particularly neighboring ones, such as economics, sociology, and psychology—of the need to pool theoretical and conceptual resources. This sense of frustrated kinship leads from time to time to calls to develop shared frameworks of understanding—a "common language of concepts and definition . . . a single conceptual scheme" (Trasler 1964:425); an "anticipatory theory" (Yinger 1965); a "common theoretical vocabulary" (Pearson and Weiner 1985); a "general theory" or "general processes" (Tittle 1985); a "general orientation" or "metatheory" (Wagner 1984; Meier 1989).

The idea of a common language, although appealing, will not take us far unless there is agreement over what it should describe. Since the primary function of the social sciences is to explain human action or behavior, it might be thought that a useful way of operationalizing the idea of a shared framework would be to encourage convergence upon a common theory of human action. Each of the social sciences, after all—

including those that work mainly at the macro level of explanation (Alexander et al. 1987) — depends, implicitly or explicitly, upon some theory of human action when trying to explain behavior. And, as Collins (1987:195) comments: "It is at the micro level that the dynamics of any theory must be located. The structures never do anything; it is only persons in real situations who act. It is on the micro level that we must show the energizing processes. . . . "

If agreement could be reached, one single theory of human action at the microlevel might then provide the basis for a common framework, language, and perspective in relation to human behavior both within and between disciplines.

Disciplinary and Interdisciplinary Action Theories

Within particular disciplines, however, action theories are characteristically developed and tailored to meet more circumscribed theoretical and practical preoccupations. These relate to the fields' objectives, to the historical context of disciplinary development and to pressures to be applicable in particular areas of policy and practice. Thus, the criminal law has its rational, autonomous individual (Norrie 1986); psychology, its behavioral and other models (Chapman and Jones 1980); economics, its rational maximizer of utilities; sociology, its various theories of social action or value-rationality (cf. Parsons 1959; Merton, in Sztompka 1986; Etzioni 1988). Useful though these models and associated theories of human action may be in the context of disciplinary preoccupations and interests, they often selectively direct attention to particular aspects of action at the expense of others — to certain "behavioral images" (Glaser 1956). In consequence, their most notable feature is often their apparent incommensurability; and it becomes hard to discern the outlines of any potentially unifying action theory that might underlie, or be consistent with them.

In a multidisciplinary field such as criminology, these problems are further compounded, and theoretical disputes may often relate as much to incompatibilities between assumptive frameworks as to conflicts over empirical data. Criminologists differ, for instance, in their views about the real nature of human nature, the merits of a voluntarist or deterministic stance, the saliency of cognitive variables, the importance of current situational factors, the role of early experiences, the part played by learning processes, and, in consequence, the relative importance of rewards, punishments, facilitators, and constraints.

It is at the microlevel, and especially in relation to the explanation of criminality, that the theories of action being employed should in principle be most readily identifiable, and it is at this level of individual human action-in-context that they are most obviously required. But in practice neither the underlying models of human action informing theoretical orientations to phenomena, nor their core assumptions, are usually properly spelled out, and it is difficult to assess where and why incompatibilities between theoretical accounts occur. Thus, while criminology is offered the choice of well-articulated and vigorously supported action theories borrowed from other disciplines (Akers 1990), criminological accounts typically ignore them. Instead, theories of criminal involvement that incorporate poorly articulated and fragmentary theories of human action compete to dominate the field. While the resulting polarization of views is often presented as beneficial (Hirschi 1979), inadequate assumptive frameworks, tenaciously defended, can also create a powerful barrier to progress.

A Metatheory for Theories of Action

Given the difficulties outlined above, a fruitful starting point might be to establish what an adequate theory of human action might look like. For, when people talk of the need for integration and common frameworks, it appears that what they may in fact be appealing for is for some agreement about the parameters within which discussions of human action should take place. In contrast to any specific theory of human action, a metatheory tries to provide just such a set of guidelines about the terms in which human action may usefully be discussed, and the form that action theories should take.

These specifications may not be exhaustive, and others may wish to add to or subtract from the list. The roles of norms, values, beliefs, personality traits, and, indeed, a range of other cognitive concepts are not explicitly considered here since any influence on action that they have can be more usefully expressed as products of an individual's history of transactions with the environment, and of rewards and punishments received. Nor are the influences of biological factors included. In the absence of clear evidence of their differential implication in criminal as opposed to noncriminal behavior they add little to a general theory of action at this time—except to provide a sketch of what might be the biological substrate of adaptive behavior—and because, as in the case of hypothesized cognitive variables, their use tends to obscure the role of situational influences on behavior, and impedes their investigation. Authors of action theories constructed for particular theoretical purposes may well want to make additional assumptions relating to personological, cognitive, or biological mechanisms presumed to underlie action. But tails should not wag dogs, and action theories used for criminological purposes should not be constrained by hypothesized psychological or biological mechanisms. The dangers of conflating processes and mechanisms at different levels of explanation will become clearer later. Lastly, some of the assumptions listed below counsel one to avoid making specific assumptions in certain areas, either because this would be unduly restrictive in the light of present knowledge, or, in the case of the freewill-determinism assumption, because the use of alternative conceptualizations is largely dictated by the task for which the theory of action is being used.

It will be clear that the items on the list are highly derivative and widely cited: Sutherland (1956) suggested the importance of learning, interaction, and communication; Zuriff (1985:257) comments that "[w]ithin the behaviorist tradition, the central role of behavior is the adaptation of the organism to its environment"; and Sheley's (1983) suggested four elements necessary to describe a criminal act — motivation, freedom from social constraints, skill, and opportunity — can all be subsumed under the more general metatheoretical axioms below as can the similar set discussed by Pearson and Weiner (1985). But whatever the eventual lineup of conceptual criteria, the purpose of the metatheory is to supply the minimum requirements — the necessary and sufficient conditions — to which a theory of human action should conform.

The specifications laid down by any such metatheory might include the following requirements:

- that a heuristic approach to the freewill-determinism issue should be adopted;
- that no particular assumptions be made about the essential nature of human nature, since such qualities and responses cannot be viewed apart from conditions prevailing at different times and places;
- that actions be therefore viewed as the outcome of person-situation interactions, or interactional sequences taking place over time;
- that *situation* be taken to include settings and their physical objects as well as other people, and that all these be regarded as having enabling or constraining effects on action;
- that rewards and punishments be recognized as important features of situations, past and present;
- that consideration also be given to an individual's history of transactions with the environment (the influence of learning), and any effects these might have upon his or her present evaluation of rewards and costs;
- that some way of explicitly acknowledging the adaptive quality or functionality of most action be found, whether in terms of "maximizing," "satisficing," matching, "meliorating," or of some other

principle that balances benefits against costs (including "effort") as a basis for choosing between or responding to environmental contingencies; and

- that some way be found of explaining apparent errors of action or poorly adapted responses when they occur.

The most important superordinate function of all the above specifications is to support presumptions about the explicability, or intelligibility, of behavior — to support the view that, as Boudon (1987: 64) comments: "The actions of the social actors are always in principle understandable, provided we are sufficiently informed about their situation." While the strength and scope of this assumption are open to debate, its purpose is to reduce recourse to explanations of criminal behavior in terms of special traits, propensities, or deficits — at least until other avenues of explanation have been properly investigated. For example, however carefully such accounts are framed, the use of concepts such as time discounting (Wilson and Herrnstein 1985) and low self-control (Gottfredson and Hirschi 1990) to explain juvenile offending tends to divert attention from past circumstances and present contexts that might sustain individual behavioral strategies. Criminal behavior should in principle be viewed and explained in the same terms as any other behavior. That this criminological rule of thumb should still need emphasizing, recent arguments to the contrary (Akers 1990), suggests that criminologists may always have to take special steps to protect themselves against the tendency to explain blameworthy behavior in terms of psychological deficits, viewed apart from individual learning histories and current situational contexts.

The purpose behind the above list of metatheoretical specifications is to provide some initial and tentative guidelines as to how a properly articulated theory of human action might be constructed. As such, it provides a list of ingredients rather than a recipe or a blueprint, and the assumptions made are simply those thought most likely to generate the sort of action theory that can best address issues of current interest. Moreover, although the terms may specify the necessary criteria closely enough to identify partially articulated action theories masquerading as more comprehensive models, it is also clear that room is left for more than one candidate theory to qualify. For even if it were the case that only these ingredients could make a cake, rather different kinds of cakes may be baked by altering the relative contributions of the ingredients that have to be used.

As mentioned at the beginning of this chapter, the resulting prescription might be employed in several ways. First, it might give greater recognition of the importance of adequate action theories in criminological accounts. Second, it would enable the scopes, strengths, and weaknesses of the best-articulated contenders to be explored more thoroughly. Third, it would enable examples of inadequate ones, such as those embedded in some current theories of criminality, to be more easily identified and criticized. Last, looking beyond theories of criminality — since it is equally if not more important from a crime-control perspective to explain events as well as actions (Clarke and Cornish 1985) — it would also be helpful for criminology if the candidate action theories could be used to explain the histories and current dispositions of all the elements involved in the criminal event. In other words, it should also provide a way of looking at how things happen.

Some Candidates for the Role of Action Theory

At least three incarnations of metatheory are currently available to criminology and have already declared themselves candidates for adoption. The first two are based upon behavioral learning theory: radical behaviorism, which has long been proposed as an appropriate action theory for psychology (Skinner 1953, 1985) and sociology (Homans 1961, 1969; Burgess and Bushell 1969; Kunkel and Nagasawa 1973); and the more recent social learning approach (Rotter 1954; Bandura 1986). The third action theory candidate is the rational choice perspective, the origins of which lie in utilitarian philosophy, economic theory, and psychological studies of decision making (see Clarke and Cornish 1985, for an overview). Since each candidate claims equivalent scope as a general theory of human action and since the substitutability of each for the others has often been discussed (cf. Homans 1969; Elster 1986; Coleman 1987; Hogarth and Reder 1987; Earl 1988; Akers 1990), it is their usage within, and actual utility to, criminology — rather than their potential as action theories in general — that will be examined here.

Action Theories in Criminology — 1. Learning Theory Approaches

Behavioral learning theories — even the most recent (Bandura 1983, 1986) — represent the most sophisticated flowering of the determinist, positivist tradition within psychology. These theories of action (or, as they are usually termed, *behavior*) have not, on the whole, found their way into criminology in the form of general orientations across the board. Instead, their initial use has tended to be for specific purposes, and their influence confined to certain areas of the field.

Radical Behaviorism

Radical behavioral approaches have fed into criminology by way of a number of largely unrelated initiatives on the part of both sociologists and psychologists. Jeffery (1965) — a student of Sutherland — and Burgess and Akers (1966) originally set the agenda by attempting the translation of Sutherland's differential association theory into the apparently more rigorous noncognitive language of radical behaviorism. In this way it was hoped that the sociological account of the learning processes involved in becoming delinquent would benefit from the models and mechanisms of learning offered by behavioral psychology. Psychologists, on the other hand, have been more concerned with the behavioral assessment and treatment of delinquents (cf. Nietzel 1979; Hollin 1990, for reviews) than with causal explanation and prevention, and the present-oriented focus of behavior modification has tended to discourage behavioral accounts of involvement in offending over a longer time scale.

The use of behavioral principles in the analysis of crime commission is even rarer. There is, of course, Jeffery's (1971, 1977, 1990) seminal behavioral conceptualization of, and work on, crime prevention through environmental design. But apart from Scarr's (1973) research on burglary (which contains a mixture of behavioral and rational choice principles) and, more recently, studies of the discriminative stimuli used by burglars (Nee and Taylor 1988: Taylor and Nee 1988), behavioral accounts of cues and interactional processes have been remarkably few, considering the natural affinity between behavioral assessment techniques and crime-event analysis. In fact, Jeffery is one of the only criminologists to have used a (biological) version of learning theory as an organizing principle across the fields of explanation, treatment, and situational control — and the earliest to see the folly of restricting behavioral accounts to explications of differential association.

Social Learning Theory

In retrospect, the project of translating a highly cognitive symbolic interactionist theory such as differential association into radical behavioral terms was always bound to be a controversial one. Mead (1934), no enemy of behaviorism, had already identified where future problems might lie with such an enterprise, while Glaser (1956), after dismissing Skinnerian operant conditioning as a suitable action theory, pressed the claims of his own role theory interpretation of differential association, "differential identification theory." Many commentators therefore opposed Burgess and Akers' (1966) radical behaviorist interpretation. Some, like Jeffery

(1965, 1977) and Adams (1973), viewed differential association theory as failing to exploit the full potential of radical behaviorism as a general action theory for criminology. Others, such as Taylor, Walton, and Young (1973) and Halbasch (1979), criticizing the behavioral account both for its lack of attention to cognitive variables and for ignoring the essential nature of differential association theory, saw the exercise as irrelevant or damaging. There were, in any case, more suitable alliances: if fidelity to differential association had been the object, Rotter's (1954) social learning theory, with its ample room for cognitive variables, would have provided a much more sympathetic partner than radical behaviorism with its longstanding hostility to mentalistic "causes" (Skinner 1985).

Like radical behaviorism, social learning theory was first introduced into academic criminology not as a general action theory but as a way of supplying differential association theory with a more adequate explication of its hypothesized learning processes and mechanisms. With such a marriage in mind, Akers had by 1973 rejected radical behaviorism and turned to Bandura's version of social learning theory, which offered specifically social forms of learning, such as imitation (or "modeling"), and which paid explicit attention to the role of cognitive and symbolic processes in mediating behavior. The new account was to remain tethered closely to differential association theory and to the study of deviance causation.

The Deadly Embrace of Differential Association

Both social learning theory and radical behaviorism have suffered from their association with differential association theory, preoccupied as it is with the social aspects of delinquent behavior in relation both to its mode of acquisition and to the motives and reinforcements it recognizes. Thus, while the power of the radical behaviorist account lies precisely in its ability to analyze current situational influences on conduct, it was first used to underpin a theory of criminality that is uninterested in, and finds difficulty incorporating, immediate situational influences such as opportunities into its explanations (Kornhauser 1978; Sutherland and Cressey 1978; Matsueda 1988).

Social learning theory has paid an even greater price. First, its more cognitive reinterpretation of differential association has failed to escape the negative connotations of earlier behavioristic formulations. Roshier (1989:29), for example, is probably not unrepresentative of the views of many sociologists when he comments: "The more open . . . [the relationship between self and social environment] to cognitive, interactive and voluntaristic elements, the more misleading seems the whole vocabulary of learning theory as a means of describing it."

Second, it has compromised its status as a theory of action. Confusion abounds as the result of the equation, or conflation, of social learning theory with differential association. Commentators such as Hirschi and Gottfredson (1980) have at times found it hard to distinguish between the two: and Matsueda (1988:295), for example, talks of the "abstract principles of differential association or social learning theory" as if they were identical. This near-exclusive use of social learning theory in the service of a particular sociological theory of criminality may be the primary reason for the former's neglect and rejection as a general theory of action.

Differential association, in contrast, can and is often discussed with only passing reference to social learning theory (Matsueda 1982, 1988; Tittle, Burke, and Jackson 1986). Although allusion to particular mechanisms of learning may add some "scientific" plausibility to the product, it stands or falls as a social-psychological account of the sources and content of particular learning experiences. This point is only underlined by Sutherland's own attitude to the learning mechanisms involved in offending: "The process of learning criminal and anticriminal behavior patterns involves all the mechanisms that are involved in any other learning" (Sutherland and Cressey 1978: 92n). Rather than a confession of ignorance or of neglect to be remedied later, this should be seen as a strategic indifference to the precise nature of the psychological processes involved.

Just as psychological theorizing need not confine itself within the constraints imposed by current physiological understanding, so the criminologist is at liberty to take for granted the existence of the psychological (or, indeed, physiological) mechanisms necessary for humans to learn and act (cf. Lee 1988:162–63). (Indeed, the usual reason for drawing attention to them would be as a preliminary to making distinctions between offenders and others.) But if this indifference to precise psychological mechanisms has been a useful protection against positivism and reductionism, it has also prevented criminology from appreciating the contribution that well-articulated theories of action can make, and that behavioral learning theories exemplify. The failure to appreciate the distinctively different foci, objectives, and areas of convenience of differential association and of behavioral learning theory has been mutually damaging. Without a doubt, the preoccupations of differential association (and its corresponding inadequacies as a general theory of crime) have at times been underplayed, so that (for example) social learning theory could preserve its credentials as a theory of action linked to a historically important criminological theory. Indeed, instead of being exploited to challenge the scope and comprehensiveness of Sutherland's account (claimed by Cressey (1952:43) to be "a general theory of crime causation"), radical behaviorism and social learning theory have been largely reduced to the role of explaining how the limited range of phenomena on which Sutherland concentrated might have achieved its effects.

Status of the Behavioral Learning Theories as Action Theories

Both learning theory accounts are quite consistent per se with the metatheoretical specifications outlined earlier, and capable of handling accounts that focus on constraining factors and lack of constraints, on the importance of punishment and coercion as well as reward, on the roles of nonsocial reinforcers and nonsocial mediators, and on situational factors, including physical environmental ones: the work of Jeffery (1977), operating within a radical behaviorist tradition, clearly exemplifies these points. Moreover, while criticized for its noncognitive stance, radical behaviorism is still quite capable of mounting a strong, rigorous, and internally self-consistent defense of its parsimonious axioms (Zuriff 1985; Modgil and Modgil 1987; Skinner 1987; Catania and Harnad 1988). In a similar way, social learning theory is capable of being developed as an integrating framework across the range of criminological phenomena (Pearson and Weiner 1985). It is only the edicts of differential association and the self-denying ordinances of social learning theorists working within this sociological tradition that have prevented the latter from following the example of radical behaviorists.

It is not as if social learning theorists were themselves not intermittently aware of the integrating role that could be played by their perspective (Akers 1973; Akers et al. 1979; Akers 1985; and especially, Akers 1990). But attention has largely been confined to the use of social learning theory as a way of organizing existing theory and research, and of constructing persuasive and detailed accounts of the process of becoming involved in deviant behavior. Leaving aside the clinical applications of social learning theory by psychologists, the preoccupation with explaining criminality has limited the impact of this perspective on crime-prevention policy. Outside these areas only programmatic statements and the staking of prior conceptual claims have so far occurred (Akers 1990). The reasons why the merits of the social learning approach as an action theory have not been sufficiently appreciated relate to failures in two areas, theoretical and practical: its lack of clarity about its role in criminological explanation (a confusion akin to Ryle's [1949] categorical mistake), and its present failure to extend the scope of crime control (its practical utility). It is these problems that have accounted for the failure of social learning theory to be viewed as "an integrating orientation for the sociology of deviance" (Akers 1973:294).

Action Theories in Criminology — 2. The Rational Choice Approach

The Use of Rational Choice Concepts in Criminology

The language of choice has always played an important part in criminological theory, both in its reflection of the commonsense notions of autonomy that are enshrined in everyday language, and, more formally, in the discourse of the classical tradition in criminology (Roshier 1989). In more recent times, rational choice concepts have found their way into criminology by a number of routes: the application of economic theory to criminological issues (See Clarke and Cornish [1985], for a brief review; and White [1991], for a recent example in relation to bankruptcy); the investigation of the efficacy of legal sanctions (Gibbs 1975, 1986); the renewed interest in the assumptions of classical criminology, and their relationship to those of modern social control theory (Roshier 1989; Gottfredson and Hirschi 1990); and, last, the "rational choice perspective," initially introduced as a way of conceptualizing the problems and prospects of situational crime prevention (Clarke and Cornish 1985; Cornish and Clarke 1986).

All these efforts subscribe to a broadly similar voluntaristic, utilitarian action theory in which crime and criminal behavior are viewed as the outcomes of choices. These, in turn, are influenced by a rational consideration of the efforts, rewards, and costs involved in alternative courses of action. There are, however, differences of emphasis and purpose that reflect the particular preoccupations of those working within this broad tradition.

It was mentioned earlier that the conflation of social learning theory with differential association has hindered its ability to offer a general theory of action. Similar tendencies exist in relation to the use of rational choice as an action theory. The nature of its relationship to social control theory (Hirschi 1986; Gottfredson and Hirschi 1990) will be discussed later. But there is also a more general tendency to confuse the role of the rational choice perspective in criminology with its usage in economics.

Economists, for example, routinely employ normative models of rational decision making when modeling and predicting macroeconomic behavior, work with financial utilities or those to which money values can readily be assigned, and pay little attention to the sources and development of motives and preferences. Although deterrence research at the aggregate level has made good use of such procedures and assumptions, they may be of more limited usefulness in relation to microlevel research in criminology (Cornish 1978; Clarke and Cornish 1985). Here, where questions about the nature, origin, and development of preferences, motives (both instrumental and expressive), and behaviors are important issues, a descriptive rather than a prescriptive use of decision-making concepts may be more fruitful. It is neither necessary nor always helpful to use the concept of rational choice as an optimum standard of cognitive efficiency against which the actual decisions of offenders are to be measured.

Again, the rational choice perspective does not need to make restrictive pronouncements about the nature of criminal motivation: it need not suggest that the motives for offending are primarily financial or instrumental. Instead, what it offers, like any other theory of action, is a heuristic device for structuring criminological debate — a way, for example, of exploring the antecedents of criminal involvement and criminal events in terms of criminal decision-making processes, actual and reconstructed, that makes better sense of existing phenomena, encourages new ways of looking at offending, and increases the potential for successful crime control.

Situational Crime Prevention and Rational Choice

Although this less restrictive version of the rational choice perspective has also been used in recent studies of deterrence (Paternoster 1989) and criminal motivation (Agnew 1990), it was primarily developed to assist thinking about situational crime prevention measures, a collection of techniques concerned with the identification, analysis, and modification of situational opportunities (Clarke 1992). Situational measures have, of course, a long history in criminology (Gibbons 1971; Mayhew et al. 1976; Jeffery 1977; Clarke 1992), and their practical utility, if not their theoretical interest, has been widely recognized (Roshier 1989; Gottfredson and Hirschi 1990). Indeed, Sutherland and Cressey (1978:79) suggested that such "mechanistic," "situational," or dynamic explanations "probably could be a more efficient type of explanation of criminal behavior" — although they do not elaborate on this judgment.

A theoretical barrier to their wider acceptance, however, has been the fear that crime thus blocked would only be displaced in various ways — shifting the offender's attention to other times, places, targets, methods, or even other types of crimes (Reppetto 1976). A decision-making perspective utilizing rational choice assumptions was therefore developed in order to provide a framework within which to discuss this issue. It was thought that the closer attention to offenders' motives and other factors influencing their choices that this approach offered might enable the likelihood of displacement to be more fully assessed. Moreover, the everyday language of choice was thought to provide a natural way of gathering data from human subjects, while its means-ends formulation has seemed particularly appropriate to the study of crime commission. The rational choice perspective that was developed functions as a policy-oriented microlevel action theory to guide thinking about criminal decision making in relation to crime commission (see also Cusson [1985] for a similar approach), and criminal involvement.

Specifying the Rational Choice Approach in Criminology

The assumptions (see below) of the rational choice approach closely mirror the above concerns, and its decision-making aspects are intended to draw particular attention to the interactional processes involved in offending. Accordingly, while consistent with the metatheoretical specifications of action theories outlined earlier, it implements them in ways consistent with its own particular objectives. The rational choice approach makes the following assumptions about human action (Cornish and Clarke 1986):

- the rationality—albeit, bounded—of human (including criminal) action;
- its interactional, transactional, and adaptive nature;
- the need to study offenders' perceptions, decision-making activities, and choices as indicators of these interactional processes, and products;
- the need for a crime-specific approach, stressing the distinctive nature of different person-situation criminal interactions;
- the need for separate accounts of event and involvement processes to reflect differences in variables, decision sequences, and time scales involved.

The most important of these assumptions is the first: the presumption of rationality. The rest simply elaborate this presumption in ways that enable it to be applied in practice to criminological issues. As mentioned earlier, it was argued (Clarke and Cornish 1985) that the criterion of rationality employed should neither be unrealistically stringent, nor one which suggested the existence of a priori distinctions between the thinking processes of offenders and nonoffenders. The concept of "bounded" rationality (e.g., Simon 1990) was seen to fulfill these requirements.

But however "bounded," the presumption of rationality serves a larger purpose. The influence of what has been termed the *medico-psychological model* in criminology (Clarke and Cornish 1983) and, more generally, the failure sufficiently to locate criminal behavior within its interactional context, has given the discipline its characteristic preoccupation with criminality, conceived as a stable property of the individual. Add to this the moral climate within which criminological debates take place and it can be appreciated that constant pressures toward the pathologization of criminal motives and behavior are an inescapable factor in the field — a pervasive tendency to discount what Nettler (1961) termed, "the healthfulness of bad actors."

All the action theories previously discussed can point to features that might be expected to counteract these impulses. Radical behaviorism, with its noncognitive orientation and commitment to behavioral analysis, might be expected to be especially resistant to the construction of pathological accounts. But, in practice, this is not the case. Radical behaviorists are just as capable as others of constructing post hoc accounts of behavior that on other grounds the writer may have already identified as pathological (cf., for example, Wilson and Herrnstein's [1985] discussion of delinquents' time discounting, and Herrnstein's [1990:364] discussion of addiction as a "pathology of distributed choice").

Neither radical behaviorism nor social learning theory can offer more than a commitment to the thorough analysis of contingencies as a way to counteract such tendencies. And in the case of social learning theory, a belief in the causal significance of cognitive variables, such as self-efficacy (Bandura 1977), can provide further temptations to pathologize offending, especially where employed to construct post hoc explanations of behavior. (Ironically, the major application of social learning concepts outside criminology [Rotter 1954; Bandura 1989] is within the clinical setting, where the emphasis upon improving "self-efficacy" may be justified as the only practicable intervention.) The rational choice approach, in contrast, employs an explicit presumption of rationality as a safeguard against premature pathologization. In so doing it provides a necessary articulation of good criminological practice (cf. Cressey 1954).

Current Applications of the Rational Choice Approach

Work to date has been in two directions: first, to explore the theoretical implications and analytical utility of the perspective for looking at crime-control issues (Cornish and Clarke 1986; Cornish in preparation); and second, to use the perspective as a means of investigating particular crimes (e.g., Clarke and Harris, in press a and b). In both cases, most effort has been put into developing the situational crime prevention aspects of the rational choice perspective. This has been achieved by developing a decision-making approach to the understanding of target selection and crime-commission methods, with a view to developing situational measures that will increase the effort and risks, and reduce the payoffs, of committing particular crimes in particular situations, while minimizing the chances of its displacement.

As an action theory, the rational choice approach has, by and large, been used to tackle crime-commission issues. This has suggested to some commentators (e.g. Hirschi 1986; Gottfredson and Hirschi 1988, 1990) that the distinction between "event" (or "crime") and "involvement" (or "propensity," or "criminality") explanations, to which this apparent division of labor conveniently points, may also serve as a way of defining the reach and limitations of the rational choice approach. This suggestion does not, however, bear close examination. As in the case of differential association and behavioral learning theories, it perpetuates the confusion between criminological theories that explain behaviors or events, and action theories that provide explanatory frameworks. Since action theories are tools, they have the potential to inform all criminological theorizing and associated crime-control policies — deterrent, rehabilitative, preventive, and situational.

Moreover, although the rational choice approach provides a theory of human action, it is misleading to see the offender, or his or her perceptions, as always the central focus of concern to those who employ it. Where, for example, it is being used in order to develop situational measures, it is the event — the interaction sequence and its criminal outcome — which is the unit of interest. Under these circumstances the offender is but one element in the crime-generation system, and his or her role is confined largely to that of providing a window on the event in question. As Haferkamp (1987:182) points out:

> When studying meaningful action, the investigator commonly identifies the actor as the unit of analysis. This is also the case when we consider social definitions of situations. This focus on persons can be abandoned when we analyze the relation between behavior in situations and its antecedent causes. At this point we concentrate on the interaction in situations; this interaction is the unit of analysis. At this level we can also locate the dynamics and organization of behavior that may be above and beyond actors' awareness.

Although the rational choice approach has so far been used primarily to explore decision making in relation to the commission of particular crimes, it has also addressed the issues of initial involvement, continuation in, and desistance from particular crimes (Clarke and Cornish 1985; Cornish and Clarke 1986). It is true that the "present-oriented" perspective of rational choice might seem to pay less attention to the longer-term chains of "learning" processes through which individuals acquire the motives and abilities (or freedom from constraints) necessary to commit crimes. But, in fact, its particular orientation to the proximal circumstances surrounding the decision to offend provides, as will be shown later, a valuable corrective to traditional treatments of criminal involvement that tend to focus on distal causes of criminal behavior at the expense of the contemporary factors that initiate and maintain it.

For the problem with traditional criminality theories is the danger that they run of writing out the effects of immediate circumstances, instead of recognizing their ever-present potential for influencing the moment-to-moment direction of human action. The dangers are threefold: first, the temptation to view environmental events as having their primary causal impact only in the early life history of the individual (Gottfredson and Hirschi 1990); second, the danger of sketching out processes that, despite their poor record of predicting, acquire an exaggerated air of inevitability, finality, and closure (Lofland 1969); and third, the failure — which is often a corollary of the others — to give adequate attention to the current constellation of motives, habits, and settings that make up the contemporary life of the individual. The preoccupation with explanations in terms of distal "causes" not only diverts attention from proximal ones amenable to specific crime-control measures, but also directs attention to variables over which criminal justice has very little control.

In sum, use of crime-specific decision-sequences to structure inquiry about crime commission is a potentially helpful way of identifying likely cues guiding (or discriminative stimuli governing) the process of crime commission, and especially target selection. In all these efforts, there has been a wide streak of pragmatism. And although the rational choice approach may already have proven useful to crime control, consideration of its wider potential as a theory of action will rely not only on its continuing fruitfulness as a way of handling discussions of criminal means and situational controls, but also on its ability to extend its analysis further into the more immediate circumstances of initial involvement, continuation, desistance — and, perhaps, into the experience of offending itself (Katz 1988).

Further Applications of Action Theories in Criminology

What's in a Name?

The action theories that have been discussed are often linked to the theoretical accounts with which they have been most closely associated. Thus, the learning theory approaches have often been taken to exemplify the positivist tradition within criminology (Taylor, Walton, and Young 1973), while a line of descent for the rational choice approach has been traced from classical and neo-classical criminology (cf. Roshier 1989; Gottfredson and Hirschi 1990), and from the utilitarian action theory of economics (Holton and Turner 1986). But the distinctions between the positivist and classical traditions have become increasingly hard to maintain. Modern theories of criminality such as social control theory, for example, are difficult to locate conclusively within one tradition or the other (cf., for example, Roshier 1989; Empey and Stafford 1991), and there seems no good reason either for perpetuating these distinctions or, what is worse, using them as a basis for selecting a particular theory of action.

Indeed, in many ways the whole classical-positivism dispute in criminology has been jurisprudential rather than strictly criminological, turning largely on the issue of the boundary conditions for ascribing criminal responsibility. In such a debate, current theories of action have no particular allegiances, since all of those discussed above converge upon a more complex view of the interaction between person and environment: a reciprocal determinism, in the case of learning theories (Bandura 1984; Zuriff 1985); and a "bounded" and "situated" rationality, in the case of rational choice (cf., Clarke and Cornish 1985).

There are, in fact, striking parallels between the rational choice and learning theory approaches to action. The long and rigorous research programs of radical behaviorism, economics, and cognitive psychology show evidence of an undeniable convergence of concepts, methodology, interests, and results, and have attracted attempts to provide a synthesis of views (Cross 1983; Rachlin 1988; Herrnstein 1990). Attempts have also been made to develop behaviorism as a more abstract conceptual framework within which rival learning theories can be integrated (Zuriff 1985) and, more generally, to translate its terminology into the language of means-ends analysis (Lee 1988). Although the social learning theory approach has not been a major party to these proceedings, a similar case has been made for linking it with the rational choice tradition (Akers 1990). As Wilson and Herrnstein (1985:43) remark:

> These assumptions are commonplace in philosophy and social science. Philosophers speak of hedonism or utilitarianism, economists of value or utility, and psychologists of reinforcement or rewards. We will use the language of psychology, but it should not be hard to translate our terminology into that of other disciplines.

Perhaps this is so, although general resemblances do not necessarily imply conceptual identity. But whatever the similarities among the action theories, they have in practice not been used interchangeably. In part, this reflects their use within those areas of criminology in which contributory disciplines consider themselves to have a special interest. There are, for example, important technical tasks — the development of behavior modification and social skills programs (Hollin 1990) — which may well benefit from a close attention to the mechanisms of learning. In part, it relates to their use within the context of particular criminological theories. But it also reflects real, although sometimes subtle, differences of emphasis that arise from the very languages of action that they employ.

In the following two sections the implications of some of these similarities and differences will be discussed in relation to two important criminological issues: the question of theoretical integration; and the ways in which the portrayal of interaction is dealt with.

Integrating Theories

Integrating criminality theories. A major purpose of this chapter has been to suggest that theories of action can provide frameworks for criminological discourse. The explicit use of action theories as ways of integrating criminological accounts offers one such means of achieving this goal. In fact, however, action theories have tended to remain largely implicit within theories of criminality, and are rarely used in this way. Moreover, since the difficulties of integrating different accounts of the acquisition of criminal behavior are often attributed to allegedly deep-seated and irreconcilable differences in their respective basic assumptions (Hirschi 1979; Elliott 1985; Liska, Krohn, and Messner 1989), this might seem to limit the likely contribution to integration that any action theory might be able to make.

Although there may well be something in this argument, it seems somewhat premature to assume the existence or necessity of such basic incompabilities between accounts, given the sketchy and incomplete nature of existing criminality theories, which offer more in the nature of "sensitizing concepts" (Blalock 1970) — such as the role of social controls, or the role of social learning — than fully fledged explanations. Whether out of a desire to preserve links with earlier traditions within sociology or criminology, from considerations of parsimony and theoretical elegance, or as a by-product of the polarization entailed by the competitive head-to-head testing of their empirical consequences, one theory of criminality can often seem almost perversely silent in relation to variables and processes considered salient by another.

One way of explaining this theoretical asymmetry is to view the development of partial theories of criminality as a consequence of the application of poorly articulated, truncated, or partially applied theories of action. Thus, to the extent that social learning theory versions of differential association have failed fully to address the importance of constraints, punishments, nonsocial modes of learning and nonsocial reinforcements on behavior, they may be regarded as having failed to explore all the implications of the social learning action theory with which they are working. Similarly, the failure of social control theory to allow that the same poor parental child-rearing practices (Patterson 1980; Patterson et al. 1989) that it frequently cites as responsible for the failure to learn self-control (Hirschi and Gottfredson 1980; Gottfredson and Hirschi 1990) might also be responsible for the concurrent development of deviant emotional and motivational responses, argues an undue selectivity on the part of some social control theorists over the varieties of developmental experiences that they are prepared to recognize. This, again, may be attributed to some inadequacy in the action theory with which they work. No doubt the conflation of social learning theory with differential association must bear some of the blame for Hirschi and Gottfredson's reluctance to engage with the full implications of a social learning theory of action (Conger 1976, 1980) — of which Patterson's research, ironically, is such a leading example.

Perhaps the biggest stumbling block to theoretical integration has been the apparent disagreements over the nature of human nature. Michalowski (1977:37), for example, comments, "criminological thought hinges upon critical philosophical distinctions regarding the nature of man, and it is this level of thought which determines subsequent orientations to the study of crime."

Whether such distinctions are strictly necessary, rather than ideologically attractive, is another matter, however. None of the action theories discussed in the present chapter have found it necessary to make specific assumptions. Both Cohen (1966:60) and Gould (1977:257) criticize the view, implicit in social control theory, that the motives behind deviance are closer to our animal or unsocialized nature than are conforming impulses. This, both suggest, is part of a traditional tendency to ascribe bad behaviors to our animal past, and good ones to "mental transcendence of our biological limitations" (Gould 1977:260–61). Even if it were the case that people always maximized their utilities, self-interest is not necessarily to be equated with some notion of primordial selfishness. Moreover, it would still be something of a non sequitur to suggest that criminal behavior was always or only a product of such "natural" or "unlearned" motivation. Similar objections have, of course, been leveled at theories that may assume the naturally social nature of human nature (Wrong 1961). Since in both cases the assumptions seem more driven by preference, theoretical convenience and inadequately specified action theories than by basic metaphysical requirements, they should not be allowed, without stronger arguments, to stifle efforts at integration.

If, in contrast, existing explanations of criminality are viewed as merely fragments of a larger picture (Tittle 1985) then, given agreement over the action theory to be employed, integration at the microsociological level among involvement theories becomes essentially the task of reconciling and integrating accounts — a task achievable by establishing the specific conditions under which the accounts of different aspects of criminal involvement hold good.

Integrating crime and criminality. Even though the contribution of situational inducements and opportunities to involvement in offending has long been recognized (Briar and Piliavin 1965; Gibbons 1971), attempts to integrate situational factors into accounts of criminal involvement are still unusual. Minor (1977), for example, while recognizing their importance, explicitly excluded consideration of situational inducements in his attempted integration of social control and deterrence theories. It seems likely that it was the locating of situational variables within a rational choice perspective that provided the impetus for integrating accounts across explanations of criminality and crime. The first attempts were to forge links between the social control theory explanation of criminality and situational accounts of the occurrence of crimes, and these have tended to use a rational choice framework for the purpose (Felson 1986; Hirschi 1986; Gottfredson and Hirschi 1990). It is worth emphasizing, however, that situational accounts have no especial affinity with any particular theory of criminality. Since preparing a situational analysis does not require the making of presumptions about how an offender came to be motivated (although degree, type, and stability of motivation are factors that need to be taken into account when preparing situational measures), any explanation of criminality — whether in terms of special motivation or lack of constraints — may be, in principle, compatible. And any theory of action should, in principle, be able to act as a framework for any such attempts at integration.

As for the degree of integration that projects to link criminality and crime in fact provide, this itself may be more illusory than real. The time scales of the two types of account, and the relative degrees of detail in which their respective processes are described, are, after all, quite different, and may reflect distinctive purposes. Thus, while detailed accounts of interaction may be essential for changing the behavior of individuals or environments in ways that prevent crimes, those describing the construction of criminality may serve a different function — that, perhaps, of painting the broader contours of involvement in order to guide prevention policies.

Whatever the reasons, the ex post facto implacability of the rakes' progress portrayed by many traditional criminological theories fits poorly with the sheer contingent nature of human action — restoring to "contingent" its commonsense connotations of chance and accident — during the preliminaries to the criminal event. This lack of attention to the contemporary context of action leaves a gap between criminality and crime that excludes and neglects a host of important issues: the role of free will and choice in behavior, contemporary sources of motivation and constraints, situational inducements, and so on. It seems to this author that event and involvement perspectives can only be meaningfully integrated when, by way of life-style accounts, the offender's current needs, wants, and opportunities are properly located and addressed.

In summary, although its value as a pedagogical exercise should not be discounted, there has to be a clear rationale for integration; it is useful only if it suggests new possibilities, new ways of explaining phenomena, and, preferably, better methods of crime control.

The Portrayal of Life-styles

Of all the metatheoretical criteria for action theories, that of being sufficiently interactional deserves especial emphasis. The need to view action in terms of transactions with the environment has been widely, if intermittently discussed, under the general rubric of interactionism in sociology, psychology, and criminology (Ferri 1913; Lewin 1935; Yinger 1965; Cohen 1966, 1985; Ekehammar 1974; Magnusson and Allen 1983; Epstein and O'Brien 1985). To some it has often seemed a rather pointless exhortation. As Lemert (quoted by Taylor et al. 1973:159) commented: "Interaction is not a theory or explanation at all. It does little more than set down a condition of inquiry...." To others, such as Cohen (1966: 45), however, this condition is crucial to the whole criminological enterprise: "In short, what these theories add is a conception of the act itself as a tentative, groping feeling-out process, never fully determined by the past alone but always capable of changing its course in response to changes in the current scene."

The apparent failure of traditional crime-control solutions, such as rehabilitative and preventive programs, together with concern about the increase in offenses involving violence (Felson and Steadman 1983; Campbell and Gibbs 1986), have led to a revival of interest in studying the person-situation transactions facilitating criminal events (Gibbons 1971; Mayhew et al. 1976; Jeffery 1971, 1977). As we have seen, work in this "local interactional field" (Cohen 1985) has primarily been exploited for information relevant to the goal of disrupting the process of crime commission—hence the focus upon investigating the dimensions of target attractiveness. But a truly interactional perspective also has implications for the study of the immediate precursors of criminal involvement and, in particular, the somewhat more stable and longer-term interactional processes typically referred to as offender "life-styles."

In addition to the objective, mentioned in the previous section, of furthering theoretical integration by filling the gap between accounts of criminality and crime, there are a number of practical reasons for developing this interest in life-styles further. First, there is the need for situational crime prevention measures accurately to identify the motives behind particular forms of crime as a means of devising the most appropriate intervention (Levy-Leboyer 1988; Sloan-Howitt and Kelling 1990; Clarke and Harris in press a). Second, there are the obvious interactions between life-styles, routine activities, "awareness space" (Brantingham and Brantingham 1984), and opportunities, which make some forms of crime more or less easily available or attractive to certain groups of potential offenders: these again have implications for situational measures (see, for example, the use of the concept of "choice structuring properties" to explore these aspects of offending (Cornish and Clarke 1987, 1989). Third, there is the need to understand in more detail prevailing forms of crime and the links between them that give rise both to theoretical disputes over specialism-generalism issues in offending and to practical issues such as those of temporary crime waves and shifting fashions in offending (Tremblay 1986).

Lastly, in more general terms, there is a need to understand more about connections between crime and particular sorts of life-styles both in the short run (Gibbs and Shelly 1982; Shover and Honaker 1992), and over longer periods (Cusson and Pinsonneault 1986; Shover 1985; Shover and Thompson 1992), so that issues of involvement and desistance can be explored in more detail. For it is a mistake to see this emphasis upon proximal variables as irrelevant to involvement issues. As Katz (1988) has pointed out, there is something unsatisfactory both about our knowledge of crime and about our knowledge of offenders' motivations, a gap in our understanding of the person-in-situation. The use of the rational choice action theory as a way of exploring the contribution of life-style to criminal involvement starts where traditional theories leave off—in the continuous present.

Horses for Courses: Choosing a Theory of Action

Just as the contributions of social learning theory are at present more apparent in relation to the development of theories of criminality and to their integration, so is the value of the rational choice approach currently more noticeable in relation to the treatment of situational variables. Situational influences have often been treated as matters of chance ("aleatory processes," as Kornhauser [1978] put it) in traditional criminological accounts, and little systematic theoretical attention given to their independent histories outside of the offender's perceptions.

This gap began to be filled by the change of perspective that directed attention to criminal events rather than criminality. Viewing the offender as only one element in the interactional account (Felson 1986) meant that other situational aspects could be explored in their own right, and a crime-generation system that was truly interactional could be envisaged. Rationales could be developed for the presence of victims and targets, (Cohen and Felson 1979; Garofalo 1987); aspects salient to probability of victimization could be studied, either via offenders' perceptions or by target and victim surveys; and a sophisticated range of new situational control options could be explored and developed (Clarke 1992).

As well as playing a part in the project of developing policy-relevant accounts of crime commission, the rational choice perspective is also being used as a way of integrating accounts of criminality and crime. This latter objective may also be furthered by way of the framework that the rational choice perspective offers for investigating life-styles. Indeed, the current division of labor, whether or not sustainable in the longer-term, suggests a certain crucial difference of emphasis between social learning and rational choice theories of action — the one, more concerned with tracing the origins of current states-of-affairs, the other, more concerned with the detailed exploration of their emergent properties and causal implications. Zeckhauser (1987) makes a similar point when he discusses the comparative advantages of rational choice and behavioral approaches to economics.

The contribution of radical behaviorism is more difficult to judge; for although it has had little direct influence upon integration efforts, it offers a simple, but powerful heuristic for analyzing action. This has had — and continues to have — a profound influence upon rehabilitative strategies, either directly or by way of its influence upon later behavioral interventions. Its major contribution has at the same time been its greatest handicap: the noncognitive, instrumental model of action that, in psychology at least, has been long since supplanted by more complex cognitive and computational models. Unlike social learning theory, its refusal to acknowledge the relevance of cognitive variables has been responsible for its concentration upon the immediate situational determinants of action — and this emphasis makes it something of a rival to rational choice analyses of crime commission and crime events.

Whatever its potential, however, no single action theory can on present evidence lay claim either to universal utility or universal application. The lack of an outright winner in the action theory stakes has led to efforts at integration at the level of action theories themselves. Recent integrative frameworks (e.g., Pearson and Weiner 1985), trading on perceived similarities among the different action theories, have borrowed widely from across the social sciences—sociology, psychology, economics—so that concepts from social learning theory rub shoulders with those from radical behaviorism and rational choice. In such circumstances, however, the difficulties of integrating criminological theories (cf. Hirschi 1979) are compounded by the largely unanalyzed problems of integrating different theories of action.

It may be, then, that neither the adoption of one action theory at the expense of all the others, nor the blending of action theory concepts, is at present the most effective way to use these heuristic tools. For although, according to the argument pursued in this chapter, all of them meet a similar range of general metatheoretical specifications, the way these criteria have been implemented has been determined by the purpose(s) for which the theories have been constructed. Given our imperfect knowledge of the most fruitful way to view human action, a better strategy for the time being may be to let all flourish and continue vigorously to apply each one as a conceptual framework to as many criminological issues as possible. Since the metatheoretical assumptions upon which they all rest are relatively similar, and equally inaccessible to falsification, their relative fruitfulness would be judged by their contributions to theoretical development and integration, enhanced understanding of criminality, crime and criminal life-styles, and their practical payoffs in the way of successful crime control.

Conclusion: The Languages of Action

If a way of conceptualizing human action at the microlevel is a prerequisite for criminological discourse, then the development of metatheoretically adequate action theories becomes an essential part of the criminological enterprise. Where the role of action theories is ignored, accounts of crime and criminality run the risk of becoming at once simplistic and overambitious. This, at any rate, has been the theme of the present chapter. As a multidisciplinary activity, however, criminology has either ignored the need for action theories, or borrowed them without much thought from other areas. This is not necessarily a bad strategy. As Zuriff (1985:222) comments: "A heuristically fertile theoretical concept is open in the sense that its meaning develops as it is applied to new domains." Such action theories can often assist theoretical analysis by drawing attention to currently neglected features of criminal behavior.

On the other hand, theories of action offer the insidious dangers characteristic of all uses of models, analogies, and metaphors in the sciences (Nagel 1961). Outside the controlled environment of the experimental laboratory where terms are properly defined, the use of the technical language of the learning theories, for example, requires a degree of extrapolation that makes its application to real life behaviors almost purely analogical. Borrowing action theories may also pose other problems. Disciplines, after all, tend to generate the action theories they need to tackle the theoretical and practical challenges with which they are faced. Away from their own fields of proper application, there is no guarantee that the action theories that have been developed will perform similar functions of linguistic and conceptual renewal for a new host. This argues for caution before theories of action are imported, together with the conceptual baggage that they carry from their former home, into criminology.

However, the danger of failing to inform criminological theorizing with an adequate action theory is, perhaps, greater than the most uncritical borrowing of well-articulated perspectives from other fields. On this ground alone, all the action theories under discussion have some claim for consideration as adequate candidates for further development within criminology. If to this writer, the rational choice approach appears to strike most resonances, it is not for its superiority in any particular respect, but for its utility over a range of areas and issues:

- its explicit espousal of the presumption of rationality;
- its usefulness for conceptualizing and investigating the local interactional field;
- its use of everyday language, with its sense of choices, options, and rationality, however constrained;
- its use of concepts common to all the contributory disciplines, but avoidance of their restrictive assumptions;
- its avoidance of the need constantly to update its action theory as knowledge or intellectual fashions change;
- its eschewal of recourse to hypothetical psychological or biological mechanisms underlying action, in favor of maintaining a generality of conceptualization appropriate to the microsociological level of explanation at which it operates.

Although these features are not decisive advantages, they make the rational choice approach particularly suited to serve as an action theory in criminology.

References

Adams, Reed. 1973. Differential association and learning theory revisited. *Social Problems* 20:458–70.

Agnew, Robert. 1990. The origins of delinquent events: An examination of offender accounts. *Journal of Research in Crime and Delinquency* 27:267–94.

Akers, Ronald L. 1973. *Deviant behavior: A social learning approach.* Belmont, CA.: Wadsworth.

——. 1985. *Deviant behavior: A social learning approach* (3d ed.). Belmont, CA.: Wadsworth.

——. 1990. Rational choice, deterrence, and social learning theory in criminology: The path not taken. *Journal of Criminal Law and Criminology* 81:653–76.

Akers, Ronald L., Krohn, Marvin D., Lanza-Kaduce, Lonn, & Radosevich, Marcia. 1979. Social learning and deviant behavior: A specific test of a general theory. *American Sociological Review* 44:636–55.

Alexander, Jeffrey C., Giesen, Bernhard, Münch, Richard, & Smelser, Neil J. (Eds.). 1987. *The micro-macro link.* Berkeley: University of California Press.

Bandura, Albert. 1977. Self-efficacy: Toward a unifying theory of behavioral change. *Psychological Review* 84:191–215.

——. 1983. Temporal dynamics and decomposition of reciprocal determinism: A reply to Phillips and Orton. *Psychological Review* 90:166–70.

——. 1984. Representing personal determinants in causal structures. *Psychological Review* 91:508–11.

——. 1986. *The social foundations of thought and action.* Englewood Cliffs, NJ: Prentice-Hall.

——. 1989. Perceived self-efficacy in the exercise of personal agency. *The Psychologist* 2(10):411–24.

Blalock, Hubert M., Jr. 1970. *An introduction to social research.* Englewood Cliffs, NJ: Prentice-Hall.

Boudon, Raymond. 1987. The individualistic tradition in sociology. In Jeffrey C. Alexander, Bernhard Giesen, Richard Münch, & Neil J. Smelser (Eds.), *The micro-macro link.* Berkeley: University of California Press.

Brantingham, Paul, & Brantingham, Patricia. 1984. *Patterns in crime.* New York: Macmillan.

Briar, S., & Piliavin, I. 1965. Delinquency, situational inducements, and commitments to conformity. *Social Problems* 13:35–45.

Burgess, Robert L., & Akers, Ronald L. 1966. A differential-reinforcement theory of criminal behavior. *Social Problems* 14:128–47.

Burgess, Robert L., & Bushell, Don Jr. (Eds.). 1969. *Behavioral sociology: The experimental analysis of social process.* New York: Columbia University Press.

Campbell, Anne, & Gibbs, John J. (Eds.). 1986. *Violent transactions.* Oxford: Blackwell.

Catania, A. Charles, & Harnad, Stevan (Eds.). 1988. *The selection of behavior: The operant behaviorism of B.F. Skinner: Comments and consequences.* Cambridge: Cambridge University Press.

Chapman, Antony J., & Jones, Dylan M. (Eds.). 1980. *Models of man.* Leicester, U.K.: British Psychological Society.

Clarke, Ronald V. (Ed.). 1992. *Situational crime prevention: Successful case studies.* Albany, NY: Harrow and Heston.

Clarke, Ronald V., & Cornish, Derek B. (Eds.). 1983. *Crime control in Britain.* Albany, NY: State University of New York Press.

Clarke, Ronald V., & Cornish, Derek B. 1985. Modeling offenders' decisions: A framework for research and policy. In M. Tonry & N. Morris (Eds.), *Crime and justice: An annual review of research* (Vol. 6). Chicago: University of Chicago Press.

Clarke, R.V. & Harris, P.M. In press, a. A rational choice perspective on the targets of automobile theft. *Criminal Behaviour and Mental Health.*

————. In press, b. Autotheft and its prevention. In M. Tonry (Ed.), *Crime and justice: A review of research* (Vol. 16). Chicago: University of Chicago Press.

Cohen, Albert. 1966. *Deviance and control*. Englewood Cliffs, NJ: Prentice-Hall.

————. 1985. The assumption that crime is a product of environments: Sociological approaches. In Robert F. Meier (Ed.), *Theoretical methods in criminology*. Beverly Hills, CA: Sage.

Cohen, Lawrence E., & Felson, Marcus. 1979. Social change and crime rate trends: A routine activity approach. *American Sociological Review* 44:588–608.

Coleman, James S. 1987. Microfoundations and macrobehavior. In Jeffrey C. Alexander, Bernhard Giesen, Richard Münch, & Neil J. Smelser (Eds.), *The micro-macro link*. Berkeley: University of California Press.

Collins, Randall. 1987. Interaction ritual chains, power and property: The micro-macro connection as an empirically based theoretical problem. In Jeffrey C. Alexander, Bernhard Giesen, Richard Münch, & Neil J. Smelser (Eds.), *The micro-macro link*. Berkeley: University of California Press.

Conger, Rand. 1976. Social control and social learning models of behavior: A synthesis. *Criminology* 14:17–40.

————. 1980. Juvenile delinquency: Behavior restraint or behavior facilitation? In Travis Hirschi & Michael Gottfredson (Eds.), *Understanding crime: Current theory and research*. Beverly Hills, CA: Sage.

Cornish, Derek B. 1978. *Gambling: A review of the literature and its implications for policy and research* (Home Office Research Studies No. 42). London: H.M.S.O.

————. In preparation. *Crime and rationality*.

Cornish, Derek B., & Clarke, Ronald V. (Eds.). 1986. *The reasoning criminal: Rational choice perspectives on offending*. New York: Springer-Verlag.

Cornish, Derek B., & Clarke, Ronald V. 1987. Understanding crime displacement: An application of rational choice theory. *Criminology* 25:901–16.

————. 1989. Crime specialisation, crime displacement and rational choice theory. In H. Wegener, F. Losel, & J. Haisch (Eds.), *Criminal behavior and the justice system: Psychological perspectives*. New York: Springer-Verlag.

Cressey, Donald R. 1952. Application and verification of the differential association theory. *Journal of Criminal Law, Criminology, and Police Science* 43:43–52.

————. 1954. The differential association theory and compulsive crimes. *Journal of Criminal Law, Criminology, and Police Science* 45:29–40.

Cross, John G. 1983. *A theory of adaptive economic behavior*. Cambridge: Cambridge University Press.

Cusson, Maurice. 1985. L'analyse stratégique et quelques développements récents en criminologie. *Criminologie* 19:53–72.

Cusson, Maurice, & Pinsonneault, Pierre. 1986. The decision to give up crime. In Derek B. Cornish & Ronald V. Clarke (Eds.), *The reasoning criminal: Rational choice perspectives on offending*. New York: Springer-Verlag.

Earl, Peter E. (Ed.). 1988. *Psychological economics: Development, tensions, prospects*. Boston: Kluwer.

Ekehammar, B. 1974. Interactionism in personality from a historical perspective. *Psychological Bulletin* 81:1026–48.

Elliott, Delbert S. 1985. The assumption that theories can be combined with increased explanatory power: Theoretical integrations. In Robert F. Meier (Ed.), *Theoretical methods in criminology*. Beverly Hills, CA: Sage.

Elster, Jon (Ed.). 1986. *Rational choice*. Oxford: Blackwell.

Empey, LaMar T., & Stafford, Mark C. 1991. *American delinquency: Its meaning and construction.* Belmont, CA: Wadsworth.

Epstein, S., & O'Brien, E.J. 1985. The person-situation debate in historical and current perspective. *Psychological Bulletin* 98(3):513–37.

Etzioni, Amitai. 1988. *The moral dimension: Toward a new economics.* New York: Free Press.

Felson, Marcus. 1986. Linking criminal choices, routine activities, informal control, and criminal outcomes. In Derek B. Cornish & Ronald V. Clarke (Eds.), *The reasoning criminal: Rational choice perspectives on offending.* New York: Springer-Verlag.

Felson, Richard B., & Steadman, Henry J. 1983. Situational factors in disputes leading to criminal violence. *Criminology* 21:59–74.

Ferri, Enrico. 1913. *The positive school of criminology: Three lectures.* Chicago: Charles H. Kerr & Co.

Garofalo, James. 1987. Reassessing the lifestyle model of criminal victimization. In Michael Gottfredson & Travis Hirschi (Eds.), *Positive criminology.* Beverly Hills, CA: Sage.

Gibbons, Don C. 1971. Observations on the study of crime causation. *American Journal of Sociology* 77:262–77.

Gibbs, Jack P. 1975. *Crime, punishment, and deterrence.* New York: Elsevier.

———. 1986. Deterrence theory and research. In Gary B. Melton (Ed.), *The law as a behavioral instrument: Nebraska symposium on motivation.* Lincoln, NE: University of Nebraska Press.

Gibbs, J.J., & Shelly, P.L. 1982. Life in the fast lane: A retrospective view by commercial thieves. *Journal of Research in Crime and Delinquency* 19:299–330.

Glaser, Daniel. 1956. Criminality theories and behavioral images. *American Journal of Sociology* 61:433–44.

Gottfredson, Michael R., & Hirschi, Travis. 1988. A propensity-event theory of crime. In Freda Adler & William Laufer (Eds.), *Advances in criminological theory* (Vol. 1). New Brunswick, NJ: Transaction Publishers.

———. 1990. *A general theory of crime.* Stanford, CA: Stanford University Press.

Gould, Stephen Jay. 1977. *Ever since Darwin: Reflections in natural history.* New York: W.W. Norton.

Haferkamp, Hans. 1987. Complexity and behavior structure, planned associations and creation of structure. In Jeffrey C. Alexander, Bernhard Giesen, Richard Münch, & Neil J. Smelser (Eds.), *The micro-macro link.* Berkeley: University of California Press.

Halbasch, Keith. 1979. Differential reinforcement theory examined. *Criminology* 17(2):217–29.

Herrnstein, Richard J. 1990. Rational choice theory: Necessary but not sufficient. *American Psychologist* 45:356–67.

Hirschi, Travis. 1979. Separate and unequal is better. *Journal of Research in Crime and Delinquency* 16:34–38.

———. 1986. On the compatibility of rational choice and social control theories of crime. In Derek B. Cornish & Ronald V. Clarke (Eds.), *The reasoning criminal: Rational choice perspectives on offending.* New York: Springer-Verlag.

Hirschi, Travis, & Gottfredson, Michael. 1980. Introduction: The Sutherland tradition in criminology. In Travis Hirschi & Michael Gottfredson (Eds.), *Understanding crime: Current theory and research.* Beverly Hills, CA: Sage.

Hogarth, Robin M., & Reder, Melvin W. (Eds.). 1987. *Rational choice: The contrast between economics and psychology.* Chicago: University of Chicago Press.

Hollin, Clive R. 1990. *Cognitive-behavioural interventions with young offenders.* Oxford: Pergamon.

Holton, Robert J., & Turner, Bryan S. 1986. *Talcott Parsons on economy and society.* London: Routledge and Kegan Paul.

Homans, George. 1961. *Social behavior: Its elementary forms.* New York: Harcourt, Brace and World.

———. 1969. The sociological relevance of behaviorism. In Robert L. Burgess & Don Bushell, Jr. (Eds.), *Behavioral sociology: The experimental analysis of social process.* New York: Columbia University Press.

Jeffery, C. Ray. 1965. Criminal Behavior and Learning Theory. *Journal of Criminal Law, Criminology, and Police Science* 56:294–300.

———. 1971. *Crime prevention through environmental design.* Beverly Hills, CA: Sage.

———. 1977. *Crime prevention through environmental design* (2d ed.). Beverly Hills, CA: Sage.

———. 1990. *Criminology: An interdisciplinary approach.* Englewood Cliffs, NJ: Prentice-Hall.

Katz, Jack. 1988. *Seductions of crime: Moral and sensual attractions of doing evil.* New York: Basic Books.

Kornhauser, Ruth R. 1978. *Social sources of delinquency: An appraisal of analytic models.* Chicago: University of Chicago Press.

Kunkel, John H., & Nagasawa, Richard H. 1973. A behavioral model of man: Propositions and implications. *American Sociological Review* 38:530–43.

Lee, Vicki L. 1988. *Beyond behaviorism.* Hillsdale, NJ: Erlbaum.

Levy-Leboyer, C. 1988. Success and failure in applying psychology. *American Psychologist* 43:779–85.

Lewin, Kurt. 1935. *A dynamic theory of personality.* New York: McGraw-Hill.

Liska, Allen E., Krohn, Marvin D., & Messner, Steven F. 1989. Strategies and requisites for theoretical integration in the study of crime and deviance. In Steven F. Messner, Marvin D. Krohn, & Allen E. Liska (Eds.), *Theoretical integration in the study of deviance and crime: Problems and prospects.* Albany, NY: State University of New York Press.

Lofland, John. 1969. *Deviance and identity.* Englewood Cliffs, NJ: Prentice-Hall.

Magnusson, D., & Allen, V.L. (Eds.). 1983. *Human development: An interactional perspective.* New York: Academic Press.

Matsueda, Ross L. 1982. Testing control theory and differential association: A causal modeling approach. *American Sociological Review* 47:489–504.

———. 1988. The current status of differential association theory. *Crime and Delinquency* 34:277–306.

Mayhew, P., Clarke, R.V.G., Sturman, A., & Hough, M. 1976. *Crime as opportunity* (Home Office Research Study No. 34). London: H.M.S.O.

Mead, George Herbert. 1977. *George Herbert Mead on social psychology: Selected papers.* Anselm Strauss (Ed.). Chicago: University of Chicago Press.

Meier, Robert F. 1989. Deviance and differentiation. In Steven F. Messner, Marvin D. Krohn, & Allen E. Liska (Eds.), *Theoretical integration in the study of deviance and crime: Problems and prospects.* Albany, NY: State University of New York Press.

Michalowski, Raymond J. 1977. Perspective and paradigm: Structuring criminological thought. In Robert F. Meier (Ed.), *Theory in criminology: Contemporary views*. Beverly Hills, CA: Sage.

Minor, W.W. 1977. A deterrence-control theory of crime. In Robert F. Meier (Ed.), *Theory in criminology: Contemporary views*. Beverly Hills, CA: Sage.

Modgil, Sohan, & Modgil, Celia (Eds.). 1987. *B.F. Skinner: Consensus and controversy*. London: Falmer Press.

Nagel, E. 1961. *The structure of science*. London: Routledge and Kegan Paul.

Nee, C., & Taylor, M. 1988. Residential burglary in the republic of Ireland: A situational perspective." *The Howard Journal of Criminal Justice* 27:105–16.

Nettler, Gwynn. 1961. Good men, bad men, and the perception of reality. *Sociometry* 24:279–94.

Nietzel, Michael T. 1979. *Crime and its modification: A social learning perspective*. New York: Pergamon.

Norrie, Alan. 1986. Practical reasoning and criminal responsibility: A jurisprudential approach. In Derek B. Cornish & Ronald V. Clarke (Eds.), *The reasoning criminal: Rational choice perspectives on offending*. New York: Springer-Verlag.

Parsons, Talcott. 1959. An approach to psychological theory in terms of the theory of action. In Sigmund Koch (Ed.), *Psychology: A study of a science* (Vol. 3). New York: McGraw-Hill.

Paternoster, Raymond. 1989. Decisions to participate in and desist from four types of common delinquency: Deterrence and the rational choice perspective. *Law and Society Review* 23:7–40.

Patterson, Gerald R. 1980. Children who steal. In Travis Hirschi & Michael Gottfredson (Ed.), *Understanding crime: Current theory and research*. Beverly Hills, CA: Sage.

Patterson, Gerald R., DeBaryshe, Barbara D., & Ramsey, Elizabeth. 1989. A developmental perspective on antisocial behavior. *American Psychologist* 44:329–35.

Pearson, Frank S., & Weiner, Neil Alan. 1985. Toward an integration of criminological theories. *Journal of Criminal Law and Criminology* 76:116–50.

Pervin, L.A. 1985. Personality: Current controversies, issues, and directions. *Annual Review of Psychology* 36:83–114.

Rachlin, Howard. 1989. *Judgment, decision, and choice: A cognitive/behavioral synthesis*. New York: W.H. Freeman and Co.

Reppetto, Thomas A. 1976. Crime prevention and the displacement phenomenon. *Crime and Delinquency* 22:166–77.

Roshier, Bob. 1989. *Controlling crime: The classical perspective in criminology*. Milton Keynes, U.K.: Open University Press.

Rotter, Julian B. 1954. *Social learning and clinical psychology*. New York: Prentice-Hall.

Ryle, G. 1949. *The concept of mind*. London: Hutchinson.

Scarr, Harry A. 1973. *Patterns of burglary*. Washington, DC: Government Printing Office.

Sheley, J.F. 1983. Critical elements of criminal behavior explanations. *Sociological Quarterly* 24:509–25.

Shover, Neal. 1985. *Aging criminals*. Beverly Hills, CA: Sage.

Shover, Neal, & Thompson, Carol Y. 1992. Age, differential expectations, and crime desistance. *Criminology* 30:89–104.

Shover, Neal, & Honaker, David. 1992. The socially bounded decision making of persistent property offenders. *The Howard Journal of Criminal Justice* 31(4):276–293.

Simon, H.A. 1990. Invariants of human behavior. *Annual Review of Psychology* 41:1–19.

Skinner, B.F. 1953. *Science and human behavior.* New York: Free Press.

———. 1985. Cognitive science and behaviourism. *British Journal of Psychology* 76:291–301.

———. 1987. Whatever happened to psychology as the science of behavior? *American Psychologist* 42:780–86.

Sloan-Howitt, M., & Kelling, G. 1990. Subway graffiti in New York City: 'getting up' versus 'meaning it and cleaning it.'" *Security Journal* 1:131–36.

Sutherland, Edwin H. 1956. Development of a theory. In Albert Cohen, Alfred Lindesmith, & Karl Schuessler (Eds.), *The Sutherland papers.* Bloomington, IN: Indiana University Press.

Sutherland, Edwin H., & Cressey, Donald R. 1978. *Criminology.* New York: Lippincott.

Sztompka, Piotr. 1986. *Robert R. Merton: An intellectual profile.* London: Macmillan.

Taylor, I., Walton, P., & Young, J. 1973. *The new criminology: For a social theory of deviance.* London: Routledge and Kegan Paul.

Taylor, M., & Nee, C. 1988. The role of cues in simulated residential burglary: A preliminary investigation. *British Journal of Criminology* 28:396–401.

Tittle, Charles R. 1985. The assumption that general theories are not possible. In Robert F. Meier (Ed.), *Theoretical Methods in Criminology.* Beverly Hills, CA: Sage.

Tittle, Charles R., Burke, Mary Jean, & Jackson, Elton F. 1986. Modeling Sutherland's theory of differential association: Toward an empirical clarification. *Social Forces* 65:405–32.

Trasler, Gordon. 1964. Strategic problems in the study of criminal behaviour. *British Journal of Criminology* 4:422–42.

Tremblay, Pierre. 1986. Designing crime. *British Journal of Criminology* 26:234–53.

Wagner, David G. 1984. *The growth of sociological theories.* Beverly Hills, CA: Sage.

White, Michelle. 1991. Economic versus sociological approaches to legal research: The case of bankruptcy. *Law and Society Review* 25:685–709.

Wilson, James Q., & Herrnstein, Richard J. 1985. *Crime and human nature.* New York: Simon and Schuster.

Wrong, D. 1961. The oversocialized conception of man in modern sociology. *American Sociological Review* 26:183–98.

Yinger, J. Milton. 1965. *Toward a field theory of behavior: Personality and social structure.* New York: McGraw-Hill.

Zeckhauser, Richard. 1987. Comments: Behavioral versus rational economics: What you see is what you conquer. In Robin M. Hogarth & Melvin W. Reder (Eds.), *Rational choice: The contrast between economics and psychology.* Chicago: University of Chicago Press.

Zuriff, G.E. 1985. *Behaviorism: A conceptual reconstruction.* New York: Columbia University Press.

Contributors

PATRICIA BRANTINGHAM is a professor of criminology at Simon Fraser University (SFU) in British Columbia. A mathematician and urban planner by training, she has been involved in the design of low-crime communities and in the training of crime prevention officers for the Royal Canadian Mounted Police. From 1985 to 1988 she was director of program evaluation for the Department of Justice, Canada. More recently she was a member of the British Columbia Provincial Government's Task Force on Public Order. Her books include *Patterns in Crime* and *Environmental Criminology.*

PAUL BRANTINGHAM is a professor of criminology at Simon Fraser University. A lawyer and criminologist by training, he has been involved in environmental criminology and crime prevention for more than twenty years. From 1985 through 1987 he was director of special reviews for the Public Service Commission of Canada. Among his current projects is an ongoing analysis of crime and the physical structure of Vancouver. His books include *Juvenile Justice Philosophy, Patterns in Crime,* and *Environmental Criminology.*

RONALD CLARKE is dean of the School of Criminal Justice, Rutgers, The State University of New Jersey. He was formerly director of the British government's criminological research department (the Home Office Research and Planning Unit) and has held faculty appointments in criminal justice at the State University of New York (SUNY) Albany and Temple University. His books include *Designing out Crime* (1980, with Pat Mayhew), *The Reasoning Criminal* (1986, with Derek Cornish), and *Suicide: Closing the Exits* (1989, with David Lester).

DEREK CORNISH teaches psychology, criminology, and research methods in the Department of Social Science and Administration, at the London School of Economics. Prior to this he worked in the Home Office Research and Planning Unit. He is carrying out research on penal treatment and writing a book, *Crime and Rationality,* which deals with the development of rational choice perspectives on offending. He is a Fellow of the British Psychological Society.

MAURICE CUSSON is a professor and the chairman of the School of Criminology of the University of Montreal. He is currently undertaking research on homicide at the International Center of Comparative Criminology. His publications include *Why Delinquency?* (1983), *Le Controle Social du Crime* (1983), and *Croissance et Décroissance du Crime* (1990).

EZZAT A. FATTAH is a professor at Simon Fraser University in Vancouver, Canada, and is the founder of the university's School of Criminology. Prior to joining SFU he taught for several years at the University of Montreal. He has published widely in the areas of criminology, penology, and victimology. His written and edited books include, among others: *Towards a Critical Victimology; Understanding Criminal Victimization; Crime and Victimization of the Elderly* (co-author); *The Plight of Crime Victims in Modern Society;* and *From Crime Policy to Victim Policy.*

MARCUS FELSON is a senior research associate at the Social Science Research Institute, and professor of sociology and adjunct professor of geography at the University of Southern California. From 1972 to 1984 he was on the faculty of the University of Illinois at Urbana-Champaign, and he has been visiting professor at Carnegie-Mellon University, Rutgers University, and the University of Stockholm. He is currently principal investigator of a research project, "Designing Crime-Free Environments." Professor Felson is author of more than fifty scientific articles.

RICHARD FELSON is professor of sociology at the State University of New York at Albany. He is a social psychologist with interests in situational factors in assault and sexual coercion, and determinants of self-appraisals. He is presently working on a book on interpersonal violence with James Tedeschi, using a social interactionist approach.

RICHARD HARDING is professor of law and director of the Crime Research Centre at the University of Western Australia. He is a former director of the Australian Institute of Criminology (1984–87). His books include *Police Killings in Australia* (1970) and *Firearms and Violence in Australian Life* (1981).

JAMES HENNESSY is a professor and chair of the Division of Psychological and Educational Services in the Graduate School of Education at

Fordham University, Lincoln Center, New York, where he also directed the Ph.D. program in counseling psychology. He is an editor of *Current Psychology* and of *Comprehensive Mental Health Care* and a member of the editorial board of the *Journal of Offender Rehabilitation.*

Ross Homel is professor of justice administration at Griffith University, Brisbane, Queensland, Australia. Until 1992 he was an associate professor in the School of Behavioural Sciences at Macquarie University, Sydney. He has carried out extensive research on drinking and driving and alcohol-related violence, as well as on processes of police law enforcement and sentencing. He is the author of *Policing and Punishing the Drinking Driver: A Study of General and Specific Deterrence* (1988).

C. Ray Jeffery is a professor of criminal justice and criminology at Florida State University. He published *Crime Prevention Through Environmental Design* in 1970 and has engaged in research and writing in the area of crime prevention, including the biological aspects of crime prevention, since that time. He served as president of the American Society of Criminology (1977–78); as editor of *Criminology* (1969–74); as a Fulbright-Hayes scholar (1978–79); and as a George Beto Professor of Criminal Justice at Sam Houston State University (1983). He was the recipient of the Edwin H. Sutherland Award from the American Society of Criminology (1975).

Bruce D. Johnson is a principal investigator at National Development and Research Institutes (formerly Narcotic and Drug Research, Inc.). During his twenty five-year career in drug abuse research he has conducted eight major research projects for the National Institute of Drug Abuse and the National Institute of Justice, and has published extensively. Two of his books, *Taking Care of Business: The Economics of Crime by Heroin Abusers* (1985), and *Kids, Drugs, and Crime* (1988) rely upon ethnographic methods. His current research efforts include an ethnography of crack distributors, a survey of crack and other drug abusers, and an analysis of multiple indicators of drug abuse.

Pietro Marongiu is an associate professor of criminology and research coordinator at the Center of Forensic Psychiatry, Social Defense and Criminology at the University of Cagliari, Italy. He has been a visiting scholar at the School of Criminal Justice at the State University of New York at Albany (spring 1982) and visiting professor at the New York University Program in Italian Studies (spring 1988). He has been a regular visitor at the School of Criminal Justice at Rutgers. His books include

Teoria E Storia Del Banditismo Sociale in Sardegna (1980) and *Vengeance: The Fight Against Injustice* (1987, with Graeme Newman).

MANGAI NATARAJAN trained in criminology and criminal justice at Madras University, Michigan State, and Rutgers. She holds a postdoctoral fellowship from the Medical and Health Research Association of New York at the National Development and Research Institutes. Her current interests include comparative studies of crime and criminal justice systems, criminological and victimological theory, women in law enforcement, crime prevention, and drug abuse and crime.

NATHANIEL PALLONE is University Distinguished Professor, Psychology and Criminal Justice, at Rutgers, where he previously served as a dean and an academic vice president. A fellow of the American Psychological Association, the American Psychological Society, and the American College of Forensic Psychology, and a diplomate of the American Board of Professional Psychology, he is senior editor of *Current Psychology* and editor of the *Journal of Offender Rehabilitation.*

RAYMOND PATERNOSTER is a professor in the Institute of Criminology and Criminal Justice at the University of Maryland. His research interests include empirical tests of deterrence and rational choice theory and issues related to capital punishment.

HARRY SANABRIA is an anthropologist at the University of Pittsburgh. His research interests, ethnographic research, and publications include the production of coca in Bolivia and the social history of coca use and illegal cultivation in the Andes. He is preparing a book based upon his research. He also participated in ethnographic research on crack distribution and the life-styles of crack distributors in New York City during 1988–91.

SALLY SIMPSON is an assistant professor at the University of Maryland's Institute of Criminology and Criminal Justice. She is working on alternatives to formal justice models of corporate crime control. She has published articles on corporate crime etiology, courtship violence, patterns of female violent crime, and feminist theory.

MAX TAYLOR is professor of applied psychology at University College, Cork, Ireland. He has undertaken research in the areas of police behavior, political violence, and terrorism. Recent publications include *The Terrorists* (1988) and *The Fanatics: A Behavioural Approach to Political Violence* (1991).

GORDON TRASLER is a professor of psychology in the University of Southampton, England — a post that he has held since 1964. He was editor of the *British Journal of Criminology* from 1980 to 1985. He has published extensively in criminology and psychology, and was the recipient of the Sellin-Glueck Award of the American Society of Criminology in 1990.

PIERRE TREMBLAY is an associate professor at the University of Montreal's School of Criminology. Until June 1992, he was assistant professor in McGill's Sociology Department. His current interests include justice behavior, societal variations in punishment levels, and the analysis of the situational dynamics underlying specific crime patterns.

DIANE ZAHM is director of the Statistical Analysis Center at the Florida Department of Law Enforcement's Florida Criminal Justice Executive Institute. Dr. Zahm's other positions include assistant professor of community development at the University of Louisville, instructor for the National Crime Prevention Institute, and research and training specialist with the Crime Prevention Through Environmental Design Program at the Florida Attorney General's Office.

Author Index

Subject Index

Act. *See* Event

Action theory. *See* Theories of action

Action. *See* Event, Human action, Interactional perspective

"Activation vectors," 288n.26

Activity backcloth, 268–70, 277–788, 282. *See also* Backcloth, Routine activities, Structural backcloth

Activity space: patterns in, 270, 281; research topics on, 285

Addiction: as "pathology of distributed choice," 365. *See also* Cocaine addiction, Drug use

Adventurers: reasonable vs. unreasonable, 145–47. *See also* Search for stimulation

Age: as a choice structuring property of kidnapping, 186; and Crime, 30–31, 117–19, 240–41; and Desistance, 240; and Fatal violence, 134, 137; and Readiness to offend, 276; and Taste for risk, 136–37; and Victimization, 107, 240–41

Aggression, 103; angry vs. instrumental, 104; displaced, 121n.3. *See also* Violence

Akratic behavior, 305, 312

Alcohol: expenditures and criminal income, 204; intoxication and homicide, 128–29; intoxication and violence, 110–11; 149, 150–51n.2; use, 214. *See also* Alcohol-related road crashes, Drug use

Alcohol-related road crashes, 68–69; data on, 61 decisions re: risk of, 69–72; decrease in Australia, 60, 62, 77; effect of RBT on, 60, 62, 72, 76–77; responsibility for, 60

"Alibi tricks," 243

Armed robbery: precriminal situation in, 297–98; Quebec and U.S., 297–98. *See also* Robbery

Assault: offender-victim relationship, 138

Attempts: as offender adaptations, 303

Attention deficit disorder, 141

Australia: crime prevention measure used in, 59–81

Aversive inhibitory conditioning, 314, 316

Awareness spaces, 205, patterns in, 270

Backcloth: definition of, 287n.12. *See also* Activity backcloth, Structural backcloth

Bank sneaking, 299

Bar-related violence. *See* Violence: in bars

Behavior: presumption of intelligiblity of, 356; three models of, 326; Behavior: verbal, 339. *See also* Behavior analysis, Event, Person-situation interaction

Behavior analysis: cognitive factors in, 161; discriminative stimuli in, 160; focus on associated events, 160–61; focus on behavioral consequences, 160–61; free will in, 161; history of environmental events in, 166–67; individual focus of, 163; lack of special accounts in, 161–62; and Patholigization of behavior, 162; as a postivist approach, 161; and Rational choice perspective, 159–69, 175; and Rationality, 163–67; and Reinforcement, 160; and Rule governance,